Language and Social Issues

This engaging textbook provides a unique introduction to language and society by showing students how to tap into the linguistic resources of their communities. Assuming no prior experience of linguistics, it begins with chapters on introductory methods and ethics, creating a foundation for students to think of themselves as linguists. It then offers students the sociolinguistic tools they need to look both locally and globally at language and the social issues with which it interacts. The book is illustrated throughout with examples from ninety-eight distinct languages, enabling students to connect their local experiences with global ones, and each chapter ends with classroom- and community-focused exercises to help them discover the underlying rules that shape language use in their own lives. Students will gain a greater appreciation for, and understanding of, the linguistically diverse and culturally complex sociolinguistic issues around the world and how language interacts with multiple domains of society.

Mary-Caitlyn Valentinsson is a linguist and anthropologist of popular culture. Her research primarily focuses on the roles that authenticity and language ideologies play in our engagement with mass media.

Shiloh Drake is a linguist who has taught at several universities around the US. Her research explores how humans deal with words, word-bits, and word meanings.

Amy Fountain is Associate Professor of Practice at the Department of Linguistics, University of Arizona. She has over two decades of teaching and research experience, and is an expert in language revitalization, linguistics pedagogy, and sociolinguistics.

Language and Social Issues
An Investigator's Toolkit

Mary-Caitlyn Valentinsson
Shiloh Drake
Amy Fountain

Shaftesbury Road, Cambridge CB2 8EA, United Kingdom

One Liberty Plaza, 20th Floor, New York, NY 10006, USA

477 Williamstown Road, Port Melbourne, VIC 3207, Australia

314–321, 3rd Floor, Plot 3, Splendor Forum, Jasola District Centre, New Delhi – 110025, India

103 Penang Road, #05-06/07, Visioncrest Commercial, Singapore 238467

Cambridge University Press is part of Cambridge University Press & Assessment, a department of the University of Cambridge.

We share the University's mission to contribute to society through the pursuit of education, learning and research at the highest international levels of excellence.

www.cambridge.org
Information on this title: www.cambridge.org/highereducation/isbn/9781108837200

DOI: 10.1017/9781108938594

© Mary-Caitlyn Valentinsson, Shiloh Drake, and Amy Fountain 2026

This publication is in copyright. Subject to statutory exception and to the provisions of relevant collective licensing agreements, no reproduction of any part may take place without the written permission of Cambridge University Press & Assessment.

When citing this work, please include a reference to the DOI 10.1017/9781108938594

First published 2026

A catalogue record for this publication is available from the British Library

A Cataloging-in-Publication data record for this book is available from the Library of Congress

ISBN 978-1-108-83720-0 Hardback
ISBN 978-1-108-94043-6 Paperback

Cambridge University Press & Assessment has no responsibility for the persistence or accuracy of URLs for external or third-party internet websites referred to in this publication and does not guarantee that any content on such websites is, or will remain, accurate or appropriate.

For EU product safety concerns, contact us at Calle de José Abascal, 56, 1°, 28003 Madrid, Spain, or email eugpsr@cambridge.org

Contents

List of Figures	*page* xii
Reader Tips	xiv

1 A Linguist in the Community — 1
- 1.1 What Do You Mean "A Linguist"? — 1
- 1.2 Here Is an Anecdote to Get Us Started — 2
- 1.3 Wait. Isn't It Just "English"? — 3
- 1.4 This Is Important: Language Is Not Everything — 4
- 1.5 But Linguists Really Like Languages — 4
- 1.6 Languages Are Culturally Delineated Collections of Varieties — 5
- 1.7 Why Do I Think "English" Is a Thing, Then? — 6
- 1.8 So How Do We Go about Investigating All This? — 7
- 1.9 Microscope to Magnifying Glass … to Telescope? — 8
- 1.10 Great, Let's Have a Little Summary Then — 9
- 1.11 What Can I Do Next? — 10
- 1.12 An Overview of This Book — 10
- Linguist in the Community — 11
- Linguist in the Classroom — 12
- Glossary — 12
- Recommended Readings — 15

2 What Is Linguistics? — 16
- 2.1 What Is "Language"? — 18
- 2.2 Units of Contrast in Language: Phonetics and Phonology — 21
  - 2.2.1 Phonetics — 22
  - 2.2.2 Phonology — 25
    - 2.2.2.1 Fundamental Units of Contrast — 25
    - 2.2.2.2 Phonemic Inventories, Phonological Rules, and Phonotactics — 27
    - 2.2.2.3 Phonological Systems Can Change — 28
- 2.3 Words and Sentences: Morphology and Syntax — 30
  - 2.3.1 Morphology — 30

2.3.1.1 Finding Words	31
2.3.1.2 Words vs. Phrases vs. Sentences	33
2.3.2 Syntax	34
2.3.2.1 Putting Words in Order	34
2.3.2.2 Syntactic Variation	35
2.4 Meaning and Context: Semantics and Pragmatics	37
2.4.1 Semantics	37
2.4.1.1 Lexical Semantics	37
2.4.1.2 Compositional Semantics	39
2.4.2 Pragmatics	41
2.4.2.1 Speech Acts	41
2.4.2.2 The Cooperative Principle and Conversational Maxims	43
2.5 Conversation and Interaction: Conversation and Discourse Analysis	48
2.5.1 Conversation Analysis	48
2.5.2 Discourse Analysis	51
2.6 So What Is Linguistics?	53
Linguist in the Community	54
Linguist in the Classroom	55
Glossary	56
Recommended Readings	61
3 We Have a Starter Kit for You	**63**
3.1 Tools for Making Observations	63
3.2 Elicitation and Grammaticality Judgments	64
3.3 Interviews, Reading Passages, and Word Lists	66
3.4 Corpora and Collections	68
3.5 Participant Observation	70
3.6 Tools for Analyzing Your Observations	71
3.6.1 Phonetic Transcription Systems	71
3.6.1.1 For Spoken Languages	72
How to Learn the International Phonetic Alphabet	74
3.6.1.2 For Signed Languages	76
3.7 Multi-line Glossing Systems	78
3.8 Transcribing Conversations and Interviews	81
3.9 Corpus Analysis	85
Linguist in the Community	91
Linguist in the Classroom	92
Glossary	93
Recommended Readings	95

4 But We Want You to Make Us Some Promises — 96
- 4.1 Human "Subjects" Protections and Ethical Research Practices — 96
- 4.2 Key Principles of Human Subjects Protections or Ethics Programs — 96
  - 4.2.1 Key Practices for Protecting the People Whose Languages We Study — 99
  - 4.2.2 What about Collecting Data Online? — 100
  - 4.2.3 Some Basics of Community-Based Inquiry — 102
- 4.3 Some Basics of Research Integrity — 103
  - 4.3.1 It's Not Just Plagiarism, but Avoiding Plagiarism Is Important — 104
  - 4.3.2 Key Practices for Research Integrity — 104
  - 4.3.3 Referencing, Citation, and Intellectual Property — 105
    - 4.3.3.1 Using Appropriate Sources — 105
    - 4.3.3.2 Finding Your Sources — 106
    - 4.3.3.3 Referencing and Citation — 107
    - 4.3.3.4 Citing Dictionaries, Databases, and Corpora — 109
    - 4.3.3.5 Citing Writing Tools, Including AI Tools — 110
  - 4.3.4 Intellectual Property and Copyright — 110
- 4.4 Considerations for Responsibly Disseminating Your Research — 111
  - 4.4.1 The Contents of a Paper — 113
  - 4.4.2 Disciplinary Conventions — 115
  - 4.4.3 The Content of Your Writing — 116
- 4.5 Conclusion — 117
- Linguist in the Community — 117
- Linguist in the Classroom — 118
- Glossary — 119
- Recommended Readings — 120

5 Languages Fall in Love, Experience Fear — 121
- 5.1 Excuse Me? — 121
- 5.2 So Many Languages, So Little Time — 123
  - 5.2.1 Diglossia, Codeswitching, and Translanguaging — 123
  - 5.2.2 The Emergence of New Languages — 126
- 5.3 We Can All Coexist in Harmony — 129
  - 5.3.1 Multilingualism in the Maghreb — 130
  - 5.3.2 Multilingualism in the Vaupés — 132
- 5.4 Sometimes We Get Panicky — 133

5.4.1 English-Only Movements	134
5.4.2 Multiple Accents and Dialects	135
5.5 And Sometimes One Language Tries to Wipe Out Another Completely	136
Linguist in the Community	138
Linguist in the Classroom	139
Glossary	142
Recommended Readings	144

6 Linguists Meet Babies — 145

6.1 But Why Babies?	145
6.2 A Rough Timeline	147
6.2.1 The Very Beginning	149
6.2.2 First Words	152
6.2.3 Combining Meaningful Elements	154
6.2.4 Talking, Talking, Talking!	155
6.3 Language Socialization	156
6.3.1 … In US American Families	157
6.3.2 … Among the Kaluli of Papua New Guinea	160
6.3.3 … In Samoa	161
6.3.4 … Among Tzotzil Speakers in Southern Mexico	163
6.3.5 … In the Republic of the Marshall Islands	164
6.3.6 Some Takeaway Points	167
6.4 The Misconception of the "Word Gap"	167
6.5 Literacy Socialization	172
6.6 Conclusion	176
Linguist in the Community	177
Linguist in the Classroom	178
Glossary	178
Recommended Readings	180

7 Linguists Meet Computers — 181

7.1 Studying Humans' Computer-Mediated Language Use	188
7.2 Studying Language Technology	192
7.2.1 How Do NLP Systems Work?	193
7.2.2 Tokenization, Annotation, Labeling, Lemmatization, and Named-Entity Recognition	195
7.2.3 How Machines Do "Meaning": Vector Semantics and Word Embeddings	202
7.2.4 Types of Language Technology	204

	7.2.4.1 Group 1: Optical Character Recognition Systems, Image Processing	204
	7.2.4.2 Group 2: Spam Filters, Spell-Checkers, Search Engines	205
	7.2.4.3 Group 3: Sentiment Analyzers, Content Moderators, Machine-Reading Systems, Automatic Captioning (Speech-to-Text), Voice Synthesis (Text-to-Speech)	206
	7.2.4.4 Group 4: Predictive Text Generators, Chatbots, Digital Assistants, Machine Translators	207
7.2.5	Addressing AI and Language Technology Hype	207
7.2.6	Using Your Knowledge for Good	210
7.3	Computers, Meet Linguists!	212
Linguist in the Community		212
Linguist in the Classroom		213
Glossary		214
Recommended Readings		218

8 Languages Go to School — 220

8.1	Raciolinguistic Discrimination against Students	222
8.2	Language in School and the Illusion of "Standard" Language	224
8.3	A Case Study: Antiblack Racism in the US Classroom	226
8.4	A Case Study: Investigating Schools on the Warm Springs Reservation (Oregon, US)	228
8.5	A Brief: Chicano/Chicana English in the US Classroom	230
8.6	Raciolinguistic Discrimination against Teachers	230
8.7	In Teaching English as a Foreign/Second Language	232
8.8	But Schools Can Also Be Places Where Good Languaging Happens	235
	8.8.1 Schools as Engines for Linguogenesis	236
	8.8.2 Nicaraguan Sign Language	236
	8.8.3 Language Nests and Minority Language–Medium Schooling	237
	8.8.3.1 Te Reo Māori: Te Kōhanga Reo and Kura Kaupapa Māori	238
	8.8.3.2 Hawaiian: Pūnana Leo and Kula Kaiapuni	240
	8.8.3.3 Sámi: Giellabeassi, Kielâpiervâl, Ǩiõllpie'ss	242
8.9	Conclusion	244
Linguist in the Community		244
Linguist in the Classroom		245
Glossary		246
Recommended Readings		248

9 Languages Meet Genders and Sexualities Where They Are — 249
- 9.1 Grammatical Gender Bumps Up against Social Gender — 250
- 9.2 Languages and Genders — 254
  - 9.2.1 Gendered Expressions Differ across Communities — 255
  - 9.2.2 Gendered Linguistic Performances Also Differ — 258
    - 9.2.2.1 Is There a Phonetics of Gender? — 258
    - 9.2.2.2 Conversational Shitwork — 259
  - 9.2.3 We Teach Toddlers to Be Girls and Boys — 259
  - 9.2.4 Is Every Girl a Valley Girl? — 261
  - 9.2.5 "Muy Macha" in the Bay Area — 262
  - 9.2.6 Talking Like a Man? — 263
  - 9.2.7 Trans and Non-Binary Gendered Language — 266
- 9.3 Languages and Sexualities — 269
  - 9.3.1 Gay and Queer Sexualities — 269
  - 9.3.2 Straight Sexualities — 270
- 9.4 Us and Them? — 271
- 9.5 Conclusion — 272
- Linguist in the Community — 272
- Linguist in the Classroom — 273
- Glossary — 274
- Recommended Readings — 276

10 Languages Get a Job, Get Rich — 277
- 10.1 Language and Getting Hired — 277
- 10.2 Language at Work — 280
  - 10.2.1 Language and "Professionalism"? — 280
  - 10.2.2 More Languages, More Money? — 282
  - 10.2.3 Multilingualism at Work: Translation as a Profession — 284
- 10.3 Language and Socioeconomic Class — 286
  - 10.3.1 Grammar and Economics — 287
  - 10.3.2 Exploring Linguistic Correlates of Socioeconomic Class — 288
  - 10.3.3 Language and Consumption: You Are What You Eat — 291
- 10.4 Commodification of Language Itself — 296
- 10.5 Conclusion — 297
- Linguist In the Community — 298
- Linguist in the Classroom — 298
- Glossary — 299
- Recommended Readings — 300

11	**Languages Get Fired, Get Arrested, Go to Jail**	**302**
	11.1 Linguistic Discrimination Is Alive and Well	302
	11.2 Language and Housing Discrimination	304
	11.3 Language and the Legal System	306
	11.4 Trouble with Transcription	314
	11.5 Language and Employment	318
	11.6 Discrimination and Modality	322
	11.7 Conclusion	324
	Linguist in the Community	325
	Linguist in the Classroom	325
	Glossary	326
	Recommended Readings	327
12	**Languages Go to War, Languages Make Peace**	**329**
	12.1 Languages Go to War	329
	12.1.1 Languages and National Identity	331
	12.1.2 Languages as Targets of War	334
	12.1.3 Language as an Instrument of War: Propaganda	342
	12.2 Languages Make Peace	344
	12.2.1 A "Universal" Language of Peace? The Failed Experiment of Esperanto	344
	12.2.2 One Language for One World?	347
	12.2.3 Peaceful Coexistence: The Power of Linguistic Diversity	348
	12.2.4 Finding Peace after War: It's Not Too Late	349
	12.3 Conclusion	351
	Linguist in the Community	351
	Linguist in the Classroom	352
	Glossary	353
	Recommended Readings	354
	References	356
	Countries Index	389
	Languages Index	391
	Main Index	393

Figures

2.1	Map of northern cities chain shift.	page 29
3.1	ASL words for "interpreter," "bring-in," "take-to," and "hospital."	77
3.2	Screen cap from COCA.	86
3.3	Screen cap from COCA – Search.	87
3.4	Screen cap from COCA – Collocations.	88
3.5	Screen cap from Google Ngram Viewer "raccoon."	89
3.6	Screen cap from Google Ngram Viewer "pandemic."	90
4.1	Guidelines for using social media in linguistic research, adapted from Townsend and Wallace (2017).	101
6.1	Typical language acquisition timeline.	148
6.2	Map of Papua New Guinea (Google Maps).	160
6.3	Map of Samoa (Google Maps).	161
6.4	Location of Samoa in regional context (Google Maps).	162
6.5	Location of Zincantán, Chiapas, Mexico (Google Maps).	163
6.6	Map of the Republic of the Marshall Islands (Google Maps).	165
6.7	Location of the RMI in regional context (Google Maps).	165
6.8	Map of Shirley Brice Heath's research area (Heath 2012, p. 2).	174
7.1	"Who were the first humans to come to America" returns a top result describing current scholarship on the arrival of Homo sapiens to North America.	182
7.2	"Who were the first people to come to America" returns a top result describing current scholarship on the arrival of Europeans to North America.	183
7.3	"Careers for" autocompletion in a Google search.	183
7.4	USASCII chart by an unknown officer or employee of the United States Government.	194
7.5	A visualization of how often male and female pronouns appear in object and subject positions; retrieved from https://books.google.com/ngrams/, August 30, 2024.	199
7.6	Part of speech labeling; retrieved from https://corenlp.run, March 4, 2022.	201
7.7	Lemmatization; retrieved from https://corenlp.run, March 4, 2022.	201
7.8	Named-entity recognition; retrieved from https://corenlp.run, March 4, 2022.	202

7.9	Dependency parse; retrieved from https://corenlp.run, March 4, 2022.	202
10.1	House-brand coffee.	291
10.2	Starbucks-brand coffee.	292
12.1	The present-day boundaries descended from the thirteen original colonies of the US. (Attrib. Jengod, Wikimedia commons, CC BY-SA 3.0).	335
12.2	By USGS – 1970 USGS map., Public Domain, https://commons.wikimedia.org/w/index.php?curid=5824202.	336
12.3	"Hun or Home?," 1917–1919.	343
12.4	"Vote Leave, take back control."	343
12.5	Portrait of Zamenhof, by Universala Esperanto-Asocio.	346

Reader Tips

In this book, we will be introducing terms and concepts that you might be unfamiliar with. Each chapter includes a glossary, and any time we introduce a term or concept that we think you might need help with, we bold it in the text and put it in the glossary. You can scan through the glossary to find out what new terms and concepts you will be learning as you read the chapter.

Each chapter also has a list of selected references you can go to if you want to learn more, or find out where we got our information, and some exercises you can do in order to advance your understanding. We also provide some suggested classroom exercises for cases where this book is being used as a text in a class, as well as activities you could do outside of the classroom environment.

If this book is a textbook for a class you are taking, we encourage you to use it as follows:[1]

- Step 1: Scan the chapter you have been assigned to read, just noticing the section headings and bolded terms. Jot down some notes for yourself about what you think the chapter is going to be about and what questions you think it will answer.
- Step 2: Read the chapter in relatively small chunks – perhaps a paragraph or subsection at a time. After each chunk, see if any of the questions you jotted down in Step 1 got answered. Note any bolded terms from the section, and see if you can write a brief definition for each of them. You can use your own understanding and check the glossary – but try to write a definition in your own words. If you are not sure what the term means, highlight or circle it so that you can ask about it. Then put your notes away, and see if you can explain the main ideas to a friend, an imaginary listener, a pillow, or a pet. It doesn't really matter who (or what) you are explaining to. Rather, it is the act of explaining – not just reading – that actually works to help you learn.
- Step 3: When you are done reading the whole chapter, review your notes again. See which questions you had from Step 1 that were not answered

---

[1] These tips are adapted from McGuire 2015 and used here with gratitude.

by the chapter, and save those to ask about in class. Again, put your notes away and try to teach the main ideas of the chapter to someone (or something) else. Jot down anything that you are not sure about or are struggling with.

We have seen this method work well for students (both in our classes and in a lot of other venues too). It tends to be much more efficient and effective than the old "read-highlight-reread" strategy a lot of students use. If it works well for you with this book, you might consider trying it with your textbooks in other classes, too.

1 A Linguist in the Community

Language is at the heart of virtually all our day-to-day activities, but most people do not spend much time thinking about language itself. Rather than thinking about it, mostly we *use* language. We use it to communicate with others – and with ourselves – in order to organize our thoughts, accomplish our goals, negotiate our relationships, get ourselves into and out of trouble, and present ourselves to the world. When you start to study language, you change your relationship with it, and – if you find that relationship interesting – you become a **linguist** in the community.

1.1 What Do You Mean "A Linguist"?

A linguist is a scholar of language – someone who notices not only the **message** being conveyed by language, but also the **medium** in which the message is produced. As linguists, we develop and use tools that allow us to investigate relationships between the form of our language and the meanings we are trying to express. Many of these tools help us to understand how very small adjustments in the medium can have very large effects on the message. The tools of the linguist tend toward the metaphorical microscope rather than the telescope, but we will be using a variety of approaches, at a variety of scales, in our studies. Through linguistic analysis, we discover that both the medium of language and the messages we convey with it have rich and important effects. In this chapter, we will walk through some examples that you might not expect to be very interesting and complex – until you bring the linguist's toolkit to bear on them. You can expect that we will investigate language using a variety of tools that are designed to help us understand it on a number of different levels – from the tiniest details of pronunciation (language through the microscope), to the ways in which we build, use, and select individual words (language through the magnifying glass), to the ways we combine and use those words to make statements, ask questions, and give each other instructions (language through binoculars), to the ways in which we construct much larger linguistic objects like discussions, arguments, and literatures (do we also need a telescope?).

Before we go any further, we want to be sure we're clear about our terminology. When we use the term **language**, we include both **spoken** and **signed languages**. When we use verbs like "speak" or "pronounce," we refer to the act of producing language, and this can be oral production or gestural production. On the other end of the line, we will try to use modality-generic verbs like "understand" or "perceive," rather than "hear," unless we are literally referring to auditory perception in **spoken language**. We will use "see" to refer to visual perception in signed languages.

1.2 Here Is an Anecdote to Get Us Started

Let's assume that you are a speaker of **US English**. And let's assume further that you have a pet – a dog, a cat, a turtle, a snake – anyone, just not a human. Maybe you greeted your pet this morning with an utterance that we might write, using the conventions for spelling and punctuating written English that we learned in school, like (1):

(1)   "Hey, pumpkin. Do you need feeding?"

Let's start with the message. The intended message might be expressing an intent you have to feed your pet, and to do so in a way that also expresses affection toward them. But the medium maps onto this message in a complicated way.

You began your message with a word, "hey," that doesn't actually mean anything – at least not in the dictionary-definition sense of "mean." "Hey" is a word that exists solely to get someone's attention, or to start a **conversation**, or to get the **floor** – that is, to manage social interactions. You combined that attention-getter with another word, "pumpkin," that, in its dictionary-definition sense ("a large, orange, edible gourd"), seems completely unrelated to your communicative goals. You most likely selected this word for a different sense: some US English speakers can use the word "pumpkin" as a term of endearment – in this case, a literal "pet name." Other speakers might think that it is strange to associate affection with orange gourds, but it is part of your **linguistic repertoire**. You know that you use the term that way, but you probably did not think about it at all. And you might be perfectly willing to deploy that knowledge in an interaction with a conversational partner (what linguists would call an **interlocutor**) who you can be reasonably sure does not care which words you select, so long as your next act is to provide them with breakfast.

To think about all the ways in which that message is perfectly designed for *that* particular interactional context, imagine that instead of saying the sentence in (1) to your pet as you wake up in the morning to start your day, you said it to a stranger on public transit who looked like they might be hungry. The offer of a free meal might be sincere on your part, and even well-intentioned, but an offer expressed that way could generate significant trouble for you. You might be viewed as creepy and could be subject to investigation should the stranger feel threatened by your inappropriate approach. Your message will have very different consequences depending on the context, relationships, larger social norms, and even the legal and political spheres in which the interaction takes place. Most people negotiate these complex sets of cultural and social norms extremely skillfully, despite never being explicitly taught how to do so.

There are lots of cases where our negotiations might get messed up, though. When we move into a new **speech community** that has different norms than those we are used to, we can have trouble identifying the rules of use in our new community. When we are targets of stigma, prejudice, and discrimination, our language use may be policed by others, and we may suffer harm when they perceive it as wrong or inappropriate. When we experience a brain injury or other neurological difficulties that interfere with language perception or production, we may be treated as though we are not intelligent or are unable to understand things. In trying to understand how language works in our communities, the stakes can be quite high.

What about the medium? We have focused this tiny anecdote on a speaker of US English, which is a spoken language associated with the United States.

1.3 Wait. Isn't It Just "English"?

In our example, we have named the medium "US English." We could have just said "**English**," but we know that there are many, many different kinds of English spoken around the world. Some of them are so different from each other that speakers will have a hard time understanding each other. We live and work in the US, so we are most familiar with the ways in which English is used in the United States.

But even US English is spoken many different ways by many different people. If you live in the US, and maybe even if you do not, you may know that people who speak US English can use different words, different sentence patterns, and different pronunciations – often in a way that allows listeners to make pretty good (though far from perfectly accurate) guesses about the speaker's age, gender identity, ethnicity, place of origin, and so forth. A fifty-five-year-old white, straight, cisgender female from the Pacific Northwest will select different words, different **phrases**, different rhythms, and different pronunciation patterns than will a twenty-four-year-old African American, gay, cisgender man from Alabama. Both of these hypothetical people will also sound different from a thirteen-year-old Latinx child growing up in a small town in the Midwest. In spite of these differences, we would all very likely agree that we are speaking "the same" language.

What does it mean for us to use the "same" language in all these different ways? In addition to communicating messages, language is a tool we use to communicate what kind of person we are – in regard to our geographic, socioeconomic, and individual identities. The way we use language is a crucial part of our self-presentation in the world.

And if we have pets, children, parents, grandparents, romantic partners, close friends, bosses, clergy, and so on, we also modulate our language use to communicate effectively with each of those interlocutors. We all experience variable levels of effectiveness in doing this – sometimes including spectacular failures – and as we show throughout this book, the capacity for various sorts of miscommunication and troublemaking is baked into our linguistic systems right from the start.

1.4 This Is Important: Language Is Not Everything

Our language is certainly something we use in order to (try to) communicate, but it is important to distinguish the system we use from the goals we have when we use it. Think about communication as a function, which might consist of the transfer of information from at least one interlocutor to another with some acceptable level of fidelity (that is, you get most of the information I intended to send, and interpret it as I intended you to interpret it). A language is one system you could choose to use to accomplish that function. But you could just as easily choose other systems to fulfill your communicative needs, and sometimes language really is not the right one. We have certainly experienced situations in which what we wanted to communicate simply could not be put into words. This might be why all known human societies always also have art (including music, dance, visual arts, and many other such forms of communication). Our communication needs are perhaps too big for language alone to handle.

1.5 But Linguists Really Like Languages

Although language is not sufficient for all our communication needs, we can show that every language is infinitely expressive in the following ways:

1.6 Languages Are Culturally Delineated Varieties

- Don't have a word for something? You can just make one up! All languages give speakers resources to create brand new words, and many communities are just fine with borrowing words from other languages if they need one. There is no limit to the number of words a language can have.
- Want to say something that has never been said before? No problem! In fact, many of the sentences you say in a given day have never been said before in precisely the same way – and may not ever be again. That's fine, though; your interlocutor probably understood you just fine. Speakers of languages can create and interpret an infinite number of sentences, no particular experience required.

These are features that characterize every single human language, past and present, spoken and signed. But for now, let's go back to the idea that there is "a language" called "English" or "US English."

1.6 Languages Are Culturally Delineated Collections of Varieties

People who are using English and who grew up in the US will probably be identified as speaking "US English," and that will not be a controversial thing in most cases.[1] But it is odd, because, as we have already mentioned, two individuals from different parts of the US will likely sound different from one another. As linguists, we will refer to the different kinds of linguistic systems that communicate information about certain characteristics of speakers (e.g., gender, level of education, or regional affiliation) as linguistic **varieties**. The regional ones in particular tend to be referred to as **dialects**, or, to be clearer, **regional dialects**. You might also think of the term **accent** here – as in "I love to hear the Scottish accent" or "my professor has such a strong accent that I can barely understand them." Linguists have noticed that "accent" is generally used to highlight the pronunciation features of a particular **variety**, including things like rhythm, but we know that varieties differ also in word choices, sentence structures, and conversational norms – so we tend not to focus on "accent" as a separate idea. We even have a term, **idiolect**, to refer to a particular individual's relatively stable linguistic characteristics. And we

---

[1] "In most cases" is the key phrase. There are some cases that turn out to be problematic because of social and political factors. The varieties of English spoken in Puerto Rico, for example, are certainly "US English" – but some folks in the US will accuse them of being "foreign." That accusation is a product of politics and, in some cases, racism and/or ignorance.

note (and this is important) that every time anyone speaks, they are speaking in a linguistic variety that has features indicative of their regional affiliations, as well as other aspects of their personal identity. So every time you talk, and every time anyone else talks, they are speaking in a "dialect," and everyone has an "accent."

The linguistic resources we use in different communicative contexts (e.g., a church vs. a nightclub), or to negotiate different kinds of social relationships (e.g., talking to our grandparents vs. talking to children), are usually referred to as **registers** or **styles**. These differ from the terms "variety" or "dialect" in that they are tuned to each particular communicative event, not just to the speaker. That is, our language use reflects not only the characteristics of our self-presentation (like socioeconomic status, race, or age), but also the particulars of the given interaction. Thus, within our linguistic varieties we also deploy a wide variety of "styles" and "registers." We will accumulate more vocabulary along the way so that we can talk with even greater nuance about these resources, but for now, these concepts are sufficient.

1.7 Why Do I Think "English" Is a Thing, Then?

"Languages" typically get recognized as such because of social, political, or economic reasons – not really because of properties of their grammar or sound systems. You may have heard the quote "a language is a dialect with an army and a navy," attributed to Max Weinreich in a 1945 speech, which is illustrative of the distinction between the things that are considered "languages" and the things that are considered "dialects." We will defer to the political, social, and economic systems we are writing within when we say that there is "a language" called "English," and that "US English" is "a dialect of" that language. But as linguists, we should also notice that this is a fiction. There is no one single internally consistent thing we can point to in the world and call "English." Any named language is really just a collection of varieties and styles that are recognized within our speech community as such. As we try to understand language and social issues, we will learn about how powerful fictions like "English" can be. Even though there is no one single thing called "English" out in the world, there are very real, very concrete consequences of our belief that "English" exists and is distinct from other languages. In fact, people have died over this particular fiction, and there's no reason to think that this will change any time soon.

We will dive into this last point more in Chapters 11 and 12. But for now, let's go back to a simpler example from the beginning of this chapter – "Hey, pumpkin."

1.8 So How Do We Go about Investigating All This?

As linguists, we develop tools that allow us to investigate the various aspects of the messages we send using the medium of language. Many of these tools help us to understand how very small adjustments in the medium can have very large effects on the message. As we mentioned before, linguists' tools lean toward the microscope rather than the telescope, so we will often need to reach out for expertise beyond the confines of linguistics in order to really understand our object of study.

Here is an example of the microscope at work. If you speak US English and can use "pumpkin" as a term of endearment – say it with that meaning in mind. Then say it again, but this time say it to refer to the large orange gourd that we use as part of our Halloween tradition to carve jack-o-lanterns.

Something like this is likely to happen: As a term of endearment, we are very likely to say "pumpkin" as in (2), but when we are talking about the gourd, we are likely to say it as in (3):

(2) No "mp" sound at the end of the first syllable; instead, replace "mp" with an "ng" sound

(3) Keep the "m," maybe even pronounce the "p" (but that's optional)

You might be tempted to spell the endearing pronunciation in (2) sort of like this: "punkin." But as a linguist, you have much better tools to accurately reflect in writing the way the word is pronounced. We use a system called the **International Phonetic Alphabet** (IPA), which is managed by a professional organization called the International Phonetic Association (see www.internationalphoneticassociation.org/) to transcribe pronunciations when pronunciations matter (and they very often do). We usually enclose our **phonetic transcriptions** in brackets – square ones like [ ] for now, but other kinds later on. We will introduce you to the IPA in later chapters, but for now, you can rest safely in the knowledge that "p," "m," "k," and "n" are used to mean exactly the sounds you think they should mean. All the coolest action in the IPA, when we use it to transcribe pronunciations of "English,"[2] is in the vowels. And you can learn two new symbols right now – both of them spell a vowel that sounds something like "uh." The **caret** symbol, [ʌ], is used to write an "uh" sound that is stressed, like in the first syllable of "pumpkin." The **schwa** symbol, [ə], is used to

---

[2] Apologies to our readers for whom US English is not a first language, and especially to readers who are deaf. We think that you will be able to identify similar kinds of variation in your languages, in which a very small change in pronunciation or gesture can trigger a very big change in meaning and usage.

write an "uh" sound that is unstressed, like in the second syllable of "pumpkin," or in the last syllable of "sofa."[3]

With these tools, we can systematically show these small differences in pronunciation with the transcriptions in (2a) and (3a):

(2a) [pʌŋkən], where the [mp] sound is replaced by an **engma** [ŋ] representing the 'ng' sound

(3a) [pʌmpkən], where we keep the [mp] sounds in the first syllable and do not replace them

Without our microscope, we might not notice that there are two ways of pronouncing the word "pumpkin" in US English, each of which has a rather different meaning. If you were to walk up to a stranger on public transit and say "hey pumpkin," using the pronunciation in (3), the person would probably look around to see where the gourd is, but they might not feel as uncomfortable as they would if you used the pronunciation in (2).

Like all scientific instruments, the microscope that we use to investigate small details of pronunciation – the study of **phonetics** – can be pretty technical and difficult to learn to use effectively. In this toolkit, we will try to give you the starter set, enough that you will be able to capture and analyze some important patterns in languages that you observe. You will be well prepared to learn more, if you wish, from other resources (and maybe more advanced courses).

1.9 Microscope to Magnifying Glass ... to Telescope?

And what about the second sentence in (1), "do you need feeding"? The choice of the word "feed" is important. This might strike us as an appropriate question to ask someone like a child or a pet, but it would be an odd way to phrase things for a competent adult. If we ask our adult roommate "do you need feeding," and if we have a happy relationship with that person, it might be understood as a joke – perhaps the person has been working very hard, and has been unable to take the time to cook, and your remark is interpreted

---

[3] If you are not sure about the difference between [ʌ] and [ə], it might help to know that there used to be a furniture business in Northampton, England, called "Sofa King." Advertisements for the business included large "Sofa King" signs on public buses, and in a slogan about their prices being "Sofa King Low." The problem with this – and potentially the intended joke embedded in it – was that [ə] at the end of "sofa" was dangerously close to an [ʌ]. And if you stress that [ə] to [ʌ], you'll end up parsing the phrase "Sofa King" as though it has a word boundary between "So" and "fa King." The slogan was eventually banned as "likely to cause widespread offence" (see Parsons 2012).

as a statement of solidarity with them. This means our toolkit needs to be able to focus not just on small details of pronunciation, but also on small details of word choice and meaning – let's think of this as the magnifying glass level of inspection.

In addition to being able to say "do you need feeding?," some speakers of US English could say it this way:

(4)   "Do you need fed?"

Such speakers can probably also say sentences like the following, which we've borrowed from the Yale Grammatical Diversity Project's (https://ygdp.yale.edu/; see also Zanuttini et al. 2018) discussion of this construction.

(5)   That car *needs washed.*

(6)   That baby *wants fed.*

(7)   These puppies really *likes cuddled.*

The construction involves phrases – in this case, two verbs that combine to express a single complex event. The phrase "needs washed" means the same thing as "needs washing" or "needs to be washed." The same is the case with "wants fed" ("wants feeding" or "wants to be fed") and "likes cuddled" ("likes cuddling" or "likes to be cuddled"). It turns out that most speakers who can say things this way are from the Midwestern US (although this pattern may be shifting as you read this!). That means that this construction can be used by speakers as part of the expression of their affiliation with that region. Depending on their interlocutor's feelings about the Midwest, this could be used to bolster the speaker's solidarity with that person – or to express distance from them. Therefore, our toolkit needs to be able to zoom out to look at pieces of language larger than a single sound or a single word. We will need to be able to investigate behaviors at the level of sentence, and conversation, and **discourse**, and relationship, and speech community, and socio-political affiliation, and history, and...

Well, we may even need a telescope to take all of this in. It is hard to see where it all ends.

1.10   Great, Let's Have a Little Summary Then

Zooming back out to our point of view as a linguist in the community, we notice, think about, and study all of these things. What is the message, and what is it intended to accomplish? What does it actually accomplish, regardless of "intent," and why? What are the tools our language varieties give us that we can use to do all of these different things with language? How do those tools get used and misused? How do they change based on who we are and what community we are in?

And what are the characteristics of the medium – not just the pronunciation and rhythm of the speech or signing, but also the choice of words and construction of phrases? And, of course, larger chunks of conversation matter too. Patterns of conversational turn-taking, question and answer sequences, and interruption; discourses involving large passages of language (like the chapters in this book, speeches, and legal contracts); written language use – including both formal writing and the informal genres emerging from social media and texting, advertising, jargon, and academic language – all matter equally.

1.11 What Can I Do Next?

As the linguist in the community, you get to analyze and ask questions about all of it. If that sounds interesting to you, we think you will enjoy learning more. (And if it is not interesting yet, give us time!). So much of what we do every day is language – it occurs in social contexts, and how it works really matters. We are going to ask you to commit to doing this in a way that we think is least likely to hurt anybody and most likely to generate accurate and useful insights. We are going to have to deploy some safeguards so that we do not end up just confirming our preconceived beliefs (as well as biases, prejudices, and mistakes), and so that our findings can generate even more important questions to explore.

The good news is that there are far more questions than answers. You can tell you have found a really good question because when you try to answer it, your answer triggers even more questions. You can even make a career of this kind of thing if you want.

So let's dig in.

1.12 An Overview of This Book

The next two chapters will provide you with the basic skills for doing the type of language research that we have modeled in this chapter. Chapter 2 goes over some of the subdisciplines of linguistics, including the tools that can be used to look at language through these disciplinary lenses. In Chapter 3, you will learn how to use the tools in this toolkit. This will include learning more about the International Phonetic Alphabet, how to make similar **transcriptions** for signed languages and for entire conversations, how to provide detailed translations of words and sentences in other languages, and ways of collecting language data to analyze using audiovisual recording or social media.

Chapter 4 discusses how to be ethical and sensitive when you collect your data, including best practices for interacting with the people you are studying, how to protect their privacy, and how to avoid contaminating your data when you are one of the interlocutors. You will also learn other aspects of research integrity, including appropriate use of social media and referencing practices when it comes to others' intellectual property or language databases.

The rest of the book covers roughly one broad topic per chapter. We recommend starting with Chapters 1–4, in order. This set of chapters lays out the conceptual and practical tools in your "toolkit." The rest of the chapters you could approach in a more flexible order, depending on your goals. You might read each of these chapters in the order that we have presented them, or you might pick and choose the chapters you read based on your interests or your course syllabus. We have written Chapters 5–12 to be self-contained, so you don't have to know the information contained in (for example) Chapter 5 to have a good understanding of the content of Chapter 9. All you will need are the tools from your toolkit, as laid out in Chapters 1–4! You will also find exercises that you can complete individually (headed "Linguist in the Community") as well as ones you can complete in a classroom if that's where you are (headed "Linguist in the Classroom"). You will also find a glossary that contains definitions for the bolded terms in each chapter. The remaining chapters also provide a list of recommended readings you can do if you'd like to explore things further.

Ready? Check out the extra material below – or move on to Chapter 2!

Linguist in the Community

- First: Introspect on your own use of language. What language(s) do you speak? What varieties? Do the varieties you use most often ever get you in trouble, or praised? How similar or different are your home varieties from the ones that you find you need to use in school or at work?
- Next: Investigate your community. Go someplace where you can just observe people communicating. Do your very best to disregard the content of their conversations – it is important not to eavesdrop, but instead to just observe – in this case, paying attention to their linguistic varieties. Jot down some information about the location and setting of your observation: Your local coffee shop? The grocery store in your parents' neighborhood? A lecture hall at your university, just before class starts? A contentious social media post? Or perhaps a political debate at a

local town hall meeting? Listen for different languages and varieties, and just keep track of how many you hear or see while you are conducting your observation. Note that it can be hard to know what language is being spoken if you are not a speaker of that language (e.g., is that Mandarin or is it Cantonese?), but do the best you can. Also keep track of the number of distinct regional varieties you find (again, this can be tough, but do the best you can).

- Then: Reflect. How many languages or varieties did you notice? Why do you think you heard as many (or as few) languages/varieties as you did? Did you find any examples of speakers who changed their language or variety when they changed their interlocutor (i.e., talking to their friend vs. talking to a waiter)? Did you notice anyone struggling with a language issue? Did you get the impression that people were being successful in their communication, or did some of them have trouble? Imagine what it would have been like if you could not understand anyone's language. Could you still tell what the people's communicative goals were? Why or why not?

Linguist in the Classroom

- First: With your fellow students in class, jot down an estimate of the number of languages and varieties spoken by people in that class. Collect the estimates.
- Next: Have everyone in the class write down the languages/varieties they speak. Create a master list of languages and varieties in your classroom's linguistic repertoire.
- Then: Collect notes on any questions that came up in the process, or modify information that participants include in their language lists.
- As a class, or in small groups, discuss the lists and the questions. Were the estimates accurate – or were they way off? Why might that be? What do the questions and modifiers tell you about the problems of identifying "languages" and claiming to "speak" a language?

Glossary

accent A way of pronouncing a language that indicates affiliation with a social or geographic group. "Accent" differs from "dialect" in that accents are primarily patterns of pronunciation (including rhythm and intonation), while the term "dialect" refers to patterns of word choice and grammatical constructions, not just pronunciations.

caret The IPA symbol representing a stressed central vowel sound ʌ.

conversation A communicative exchange involving at least one attempt to send information to an interlocutor, and one attempt to receive that information.

dialect A linguistic variety. "Dialect" is sometimes used to focus our attention on patterns of pronunciation, word choice and grammatical constructions that are indicative of a person's geographic identity.

discourse Units of language bigger than the sentence. This can include multiple conversational turns, and/or more than one sentence.

English language A (very large and internally diverse) set of typically spoken[4] linguistic varieties that are socially, politically, economically, or historically categorized as a single "language," including the variety we are using to write this book.

engma The IPA symbol representing a velar nasal sound ŋ.

floor Control or command over a conversation or interaction. (Also called "conversational floor").

idiolect A linguistic variety unique to a specific individual.

interlocutor A participant in a conversation or interaction.

international phonetic alphabet (IPA) A transcription system that can be used to write the sounds used in any spoken human language, and that is governed by the professional society "The International Phonetic Association."[5]

language In the context of this book, "language" refers to a particular type of communication system of which US English, ASL, Navajo, Basque, and Mandarin are all examples, and which all known human communities use as their *primary* communication system.

linguist An investigator of language who carefully studies both the medium and the message.

linguistic repertoire The set of languages and language varieties that an individual or community knows and can use.

medium The mode through which a message is communicated.

message A meaning that one person wants to communicate to another.

phonetics The study of the physical and biological properties of the production and perception of a language.

---

[4] There is such a thing as "signed English," but that's typically used as an ancillary code. In the US, the dominant signed language is American Sign Language (ASL). In Britain, the dominant signed language is British Sign Language (BSL). Speakers of ASL, BSL, and other signed languages often learn English as a second language.

[5] Students who have full-time status can join the IPA (www.internationalphoneticassociation.org/content/membership).

phonetic transcription Any attempt to write using a phonetic alphabet so that you are writing down the *pronunciation* of words. This is distinct from the process of writing we do when we use spelled English, which is what you are reading now. [hiɹz haʊ dɪfɹənt ɪt kən bi].[6]

phrase Any unit of one or more words that function as a meaningful chunk within a sentence.

regional dialect A linguistic variety that shows the speaker's affiliation with a particular geographic region. For example, "US English" is a set of regional dialects that we would expect from a speaker of English who grew up in the US, and who doesn't mind the listener knowing where they are from.

register A linguistic strategy that is tuned to a kind of social situation. For example, a speaker might use a formal register of a language when they are giving a professional presentation, but a more casual register when they are talking on the phone with a family member. We will use this term synonymously with "speech style."

schwa The IPA symbol representing the unstressed central vowel sound ə.

signed language A language that primarily relies on the visual-gestural modality, and not much on the auditory-vocal modality.

speech community A group of people who share some set of norms and practices in their language use. We are all members of multiple speech communities, and speech communities can be small-scale (e.g., twins' special linguistic practices) or large-scale (e.g., US English speakers). The larger the speech community, the more internally diverse it will be.

speech style See register.

spoken language A language that primarily relies on the auditory-vocal modality, not so much the visual-gestural modality.

transcription A technical system for writing a language, designed to clearly identify some set of linguistic properties. Not the kind of writing we use in our day-to-day communication.

US English A set of varieties, including regional dialects, of spoken English that are characteristic of speakers who affiliate with (and perhaps live or study in) the United States.

variety A person or community's way of using a language. Every language includes speakers who use different varieties.

---

[6] "Here's how different it can be." See?

Recommended Readings

At the end of each chapter, we will provide a list of key readings that may help you deepen your understanding and appreciation of the topics we cover in a given chapter. While all the material we cite is available in the reference section at the end of this book, these Recommended Readings sections will give you a taste of the most useful material for a deeper dive into the topics you have just learned about. Happy reading!

Charity Hudley, A. H., & Mallinson, C. (2011). *Understanding English Language Variation in U.S. schools*. Teachers College Press.

Figueroa, M. (2024). Language development, linguistic input, and linguistic racism. *WIREs Cognitive Science, 15*(3), e1673. https://doi.org/10.1002/wcs.1673

Lippi-Green, Rosina (2012). *English with an Accent: Language, Ideology, and Discrimination in the United States* (2nd ed.). Routledge.

2 What Is Linguistics?

You are likely reading this textbook because you are in a class with "linguistics" somewhere in the title, or it is taught through a linguistics department, or it is taught by a linguist (or someone else generally concerned about language). You might be asking yourself the question that titles this chapter. Put very briefly, **linguistics** is a systematic, scientific study of language. This means that you will make observations, form hypotheses, and work with data that you collect – and it just happens to all be about language.

Language might not seem to be that complicated. We use it almost effortlessly every single day, we do not seem to have any difficulty learning language as a child (certainly with much less difficulty than we do when trying to learn other languages as adults!), and we may even think in words and sentences as we daydream. Since we're so good at using language from such a young age, why bother studying it at all?

Well, there is a lot that we do not know about language. Official counts of the number of different languages are inaccurate because there are **language communities** – groups of people who use the same language(s) – who haven't yet been counted, much less studied. Even very extensively studied languages – like English – change constantly in their use and in how different aspects of the language work together. There is even more that we do not know about how languages evolved over time, how languages influence each other, and even about the biology of language! You might instead think of language as being similar to games like go or chess that are advertised as easy to learn but difficult to master.

We can also reframe this way of thinking about language as a set of hypotheses and observations, to demonstrate how we can systematically study something:

Hypothesis 1: Language is not complicated.
Hypothesis 2: We use language all the time, so we know all there is to know about language.
Hypothesis 3: Languages remain the same over time.
Observation 1: Even though babies seem to learn language easily, it feels more difficult to learn a language as an adult in a language class.

Observation 2: Although people use language all the time, they also use language differently depending on who they're talking to.

Observation 3: Languages seem to influence each other and change over time (for example, languages borrow words from each other: the English word "zero" originally came from the Arabic word صفر "Sifr").

... and so on. Even from this small set of hypotheses and observations, we can generate some research questions:

Research Question 1: Are there parts of language that are easier to learn than others?

Research Question 2: Do people talk to their pets and children in the same way in different languages?

Research Question 3: What other parts of your language of interest have been affected or influenced by other languages?

Of course, there are many, *many* more questions you can ask – these are just some of the topics that make it so exciting to study linguistics. You might also realize, as you think more about these research questions, observations, and hypotheses, that there are many components of language that you could explore through these questions.[1] What do we mean when we ask whether people talk to pets and children in the same way? Are we talking about the **pitch** and **intonation** of their voice? Or about the specific words that they use? Or even whether language differs depending on the context that the person and pet/child are operating in?

Since linguists are aware that language is so multifaceted, we conventionally divide the systematic study of language into its subcomponents, which we can then observe and analyze in different ways. We will spend the rest of this chapter discussing the different subcomponents of language: **phonetics, phonology, morphology, syntax, semantics,** and **pragmatics**. Then we'll end by discussing how we analyze entire **conversations**. Of course, it is important to note that these distinctions are conventions – in other words, they are norms for how to divide up the study of language. In reality, all of the different subcomponents of language, from pronunciations[2] to words to sentences to conversations, all work together, mutually influencing one another, and often there is not a clear-cut boundary between what makes a particular linguistic element, for instance, a word vs. a sentence. Still,

---

[1] When you are writing a research paper for a class and the instructor tells you that your topic is too broad, this is usually along the lines of what they are talking about.

[2] Pronunciations of spoken languages are segments, pronunciations of signed languages are gestures; throughout this book we want to emphasize that languages come in at least those two modalities, with neither any more basic or primary than the other.

dividing the study of language up in this way is a useful starting point – by isolating how these different structural components operate separately, it is easier to see how the system works together as a whole.

It's common for linguistics textbooks to cover each of these topics a chapter or so at a time, and, similarly, for linguistics courses to spend several days on each of these topics. In this textbook, we've taken a different approach by offering within this one chapter a high-level overview of each of these components of language.[3] Our hope is that this method gives you just enough information about these structural components of language that as we delve into what this book is *really* about – the links between language and social issues – you will have a greater understanding of and appreciation for the linguistic complexity that underlies these connections. Whether your instructor takes a similar approach to your textbook authors or delves more deeply into these components of language, you can always refer back to this chapter for a general sense of what we are referring to when we discuss the links between social issues and segments, words, sentences, conversations, and so on.

First, though, let's back up and define language so that we are all on the same page.

2.1 What Is "Language"?

In the context of this book, "language" refers to a particular type of communication system that all known human communities use as their *primary* communication system in daily life: US English, American Sign Language, Navajo, Basque, and Mandarin are all examples of this type of communication system. Language is *specialized for transmitting and interpreting ideas* using units we will call **utterances**. You can think of an utterance as any communicative turn that uses some bit of your language, spoken or signed. An utterance might be a single word or it might be many connected sentences, but it will be a continuous unit. If you are interrupted by someone else, their utterance ends yours (assuming their interruption is successful), and you start a new one when you get the floor again. Linguistic utterances can be broken down into smaller pieces and built up into larger pieces; they can be used to talk about things that are concrete or abstract, about nothing at all, about things that are right in our communicative context, about things

---

[3] We also want you to know that while this chapter may seem extraordinarily long, it is (by far) the longest chapter in the book, and the rest of the chapters are not this long. Bear with us!

that are false, or things that are removed from us in time and space, or things that are imaginary. And the pieces and parts that make up utterances have very complicated relationships with each other; both the pieces and their relationships matter to the meaning of the whole utterance.

Almost as soon as we start to define "language," linguists are often asked whether or not language is unique to humans, or whether it's found in other species. The answer depends crucially on the things we've mentioned in the previous paragraph – all human languages do all those things. Not every communication system does. For example, not every communication system allows us to communicate about things that are false, or about things that happened in the past or could happen in the future. Further, not every communication system is built on small pieces that are combined with each other systematically to create larger meaningful elements. *Language* as defined here has so far only been conclusively demonstrated to exist in human communities: there is not any case in which a nonhuman animal *has been demonstrated* to use a communication system of this type as part of its natural communicative repertoire. For example, we know that dolphins have a highly complex and interesting communication system, but we don't (yet) know that it can be used to talk about imaginary things, or that it is built of meaningful bits whose relationships with each other play a part in the meaning of each utterance. These are the kinds of things we must be able to demonstrate in order to justify a claim that dolphins "have language."

There are also no successful cases of human researchers "teaching" nonhuman animals to use a system like language in the way that humans use it. This is not for want of effort (Gardner & Gardner 1969; Kellogg & Kellogg 1933; Patterson 1978; Pepperberg 1981; Savage-Rumbaugh 1986; Terrace 1979, and many, many more). To see what we mean, let's work through a quick example of a very famous nonhuman primate, the lowland gorilla Koko, who was raised and studied by Penny Patterson (Patterson 1978). People communicated with Koko using spoken English, along with a set of signs taken from American Sign Language.[4] Koko would respond in her own set of signs, which often differed from the human ones based on anatomical differences between gorilla and human anatomy and physiology, combined with other nonverbal communication (such as taking a caregivers' arm to ask for a tickle). If you do a quick search for online videos of Koko, you'll find

---

[4] This is important. Our best reading of the literature on Koko suggests that her caregivers were not fluent ASL signers and that they used spoken English a lot. Signs taken from ASL may have been used in the absence of ASL's grammar. There is no discussion in Patterson's work of true grammar acquisition, a fact that's discussed at length in Petitto and Seidenberg (1979).

many of them and you can see that the communication between Koko and the humans and other animals in her company is complex and nuanced. But you'll also see that her signing – that is, her linguistic expression – is often limited to one or two signs in each utterance, often repeated, and not (apparently) arranged in any kind of meaningful order or structure. That is, she seems to not use **morphology** or **syntax** in her productions. Her comprehension of the communications of others and her expressive abilities showed, at least in our opinions, great intelligence – but her communicative behavior was not particularly similar to humans' use of language. We suspect you'll note the same kinds of capabilities and limitations in the communicative behavior of other nonhuman animals who are trained to communicate using some kind of human language–based code. Does this mean that they could not, in principle, master something language-like? And why would we expect that a nonhuman could acquire human language when, to our knowledge, no human has successfully acquired the primary communication system of any other creature?

Some scholars conclude that this failure to show evidence of true language outside of *Homo sapiens sapiens* means that it is in principle impossible for anyone other than humans to do language. But this is not a settled question. Interested readers might refer to an inventory of features articulated by Charles Hockett (1960) that seem to distinguish human language from other systems of communication, like birdsong; to the ethnological work of Frans de Waal (2016); and to Irene Pepperberg's (2017) summary of what happened to nonhuman animal language research for detailed discussions of the intricacies and sociologies of these scientific debates.

On the other hand, to our knowledge there is not now, nor do we have reason to believe there ever has been, a community of *Homo sapiens sapiens* that truly lacks language.[5] And since we are immersed in language all the time, much of how it works is invisible to us – we take it for granted. So it is important to be aware of our biases when talking about language. Hearing people tend to associate language with languages that are spoken and may ignore signed languages, or assume that signed languages are not "real" languages at all (and they most definitely are). Literate people tend to assume that language is written, but only about half of the world's languages

---

[5] Evidence from early writing goes back about 7,000 years, and the languages being written then had all the same properties as modern human languages do. But of course most languages are never written down, and the deep history and evolution of language in humans is a subject of active scholarship. Most linguists agree that we can reconstruct language history at least 10,000–15,000 years pretty accurately – but *Homo sapiens* have existed for more like 200,000 years, and we don't know for certain whether they had language from the beginning or got it somewhere along the way.

currently have writing systems. Speakers of majority languages like English may refer to minority languages as "primitive," "rudimentary," or as having other untrue negative characteristics. As we continue to discuss language and linguistics, we are working under the assumption that all naturally occurring human languages are created equal, capable of expressing similar concepts and ideas regardless of modality (i.e., spoken vs. signed), how long they have been around, number of speakers, whether they have a writing system, and so on. As you continue reading this book, you might find that this can be a very contentious idea.

Now that we have a definition of what language is, let's talk about the different subcomponents of language according to linguistics. We will start with the smallest unit of language, segments, and work our way up through larger units of language (words, sentences, and meaning) to end up at full conversations.

2.2 Units of Contrast in Language: Phonetics and Phonology

Charles Hockett (1960) is widely credited with describing a property that is fundamental to language, but not to all systems of communication: duality of patterning. Duality of patterning occurs when a communication system's smallest units are not themselves meaningful, but they create meaning in combination.

Think about a language that you use regularly, and see if you can identify the very smallest units that the language is built of. If you are an English speaker, you might start with a very common word – maybe "cat." And you might identify that the word is built of three units: a [k] sound (which you spell with the letter "c"), an [æ] sound (which you spell with the letter "a"), and a [t] sound (which you spell with the letter "t").

Those sounds do not have individual meanings associated with them – but you can use them in different orders to make things that do have meaning including "cat" [kæt] (a furry quadruped probably of the genus *Felis*, etc.), "tack" [tæk] (something you can stick into a wall, or something you can do in a sailboat, etc.), and "act" [ækt] (something you do in a play, or forms part of a play, etc.).

If you use a signed language like ASL, you might start with a word for "cat" that's produced with one hand at about jaw level, and consists of moving the first two fingers in a pinching motion while moving the hand slightly outward, ending in something like an "OK" sign. And you might identify that the word is constructed of three units – the handshape, the location, and the movement. The handshape by itself could be used in signs for other meanings, as could the location and the movement – but when they are combined correctly, you get a meaning.

The units we have identified – those that don't have meaning of their own but can create meaning in context, like individual speech sounds for spoken languages and components of gesture for signed languages – can be referred to collectively as **segments**. In both cases, there are sounds and gestures you can make that aren't used in your language at all and some sounds and gestures you can make that aren't used in any human language. Linguists try to identify the inventory of *possible* segments and study their use and combination, and the subdisciplines that focus on these are called "phonetics" and "phonology."

2.2.1 Phonetics

Phonetics is the study of the physical properties of the fundamental units of language – the segments. In spoken languages, the segments are speech sounds. Just like any other type of sound, speech sounds are waves that are generated by rhythmically compressing air molecules, and then we interpret the fluctuations of air against our eardrums and bones of the inner ear as meaningful sounds. We can measure many different aspects of speech, including our overall vocal pitch or **frequency** (how high or low our voice is) and **amplitude** (how loud our voice is), vibrational frequencies at points along our vocal apparatus called **formants**, how air flows out of our mouth and nose as we speak, and more. With these measurements, we can compare different characteristics of speech within an individual, within social groups or language communities, or across languages.

In signed languages, the fundamental units are not as discrete as are the sounds of spoken languages. They involve much larger articulators – the hands, the arms, and even the face and body can be involved in the production of signs – and because signed languages are produced in the visual modality, individual elements are often produced simultaneously – for example, a handshape is done with a particular movement and body orientation in order to form a word. Even the position of the hands in space can shift within an utterance, and often does – signed language utterances tend to end with a slightly lower hand position than they started with (Brentari 2019). The study of the phonetics of signed languages is often divided into the study of the motor and neurological capacities required to produce and combine signs and the study of the visual and cognitive skills required to process signed languages. In the remainder of this section, our discussion is limited to the study of the phonetics of spoken languages. Our decision to focus on spoken languages is an artifact of our own training – unfortunately, the discipline of linguistics has been slow to focus our collective attention on

2.2 Units of Contrast in Language

the study of signed phonetics, so your authors' training is not sufficient to provide you with a careful discussion of these topics here.[6]

Very broadly, we can classify the study of phonetics of spoken languages into two subfields: **articulatory phonetics** and **acoustic phonetics**. Articulatory phonetics for spoken languages is concerned mainly with how speech sounds are created and shaped through constrictions of our **vocal tract**, while acoustic phonetics is concerned with measuring the fluctuations present within the speech signal. In the rest of this section, we'll start by discussing articulatory phonetics and then acoustic phonetics. Many of the topics in later chapters are concerned with how people sound when they speak – in fact, one of your first judgments about another person may be whether they sound like you do or not. These judgments are based on our ability to distinguish between minute details in language, like the slight difference between the "t" sounds that begin words in English (produced with the tongue tip in contact with the roof of your mouth just behind your upper teeth) and Castilian Spanish (produced with the tongue tip in contact with the back of the upper teeth, as described in Martínez-Celdrán et al. 2003).

If you think about it, we humans are made of a rather long tube with different openings and closures, and this very long tube performs a lot of different functions – most of which we will not be discussing in this book. Part of this very long tube, from your lungs to your nose and mouth, is crucial for spoken language, though! In essence, this part of the tube contains a noise-maker and a series of malleable sound-shaping devices, or a **source** and several **filters**. Air from our lungs forces our **vocal folds**, which you may also know as your "vocal cords," to open and shut rapidly, which creates a buzzing sound and is the source of our speech.

Find a mirror and take a good look at your face.[7] When we think about spoken language, most people probably think about using their mouths in various configurations to generate speech, but this is only part of the whole picture. We express air through our lungs, through our vocal folds, and then interfere with the resulting sound waves to make different sounds that we

---

[6] We encourage any readers who participate in Deaf communities to join us and work to better understand the fundamental structures and functions of signed languages on their own terms. Our discipline needs you!

[7] Much of our vocal tract cannot be seen from the outside, but our mouth is one exception. There are many videos and simulations today that you can use to see what your interior vocal tract looks like (you might search the internet for something like "vocal tract model").
We would like to caution you against the types of experiments performed by the late Peter Ladefoged to examine his vocal tract, among which included attempts to cast his own vocal tract in plaster while hanging upside down (Maddieson 2007).

can recognize as speech. Let your mouth hang open and make the sound "ah." Your tongue should be lying flat behind your lower teeth, and if we had a light and a long camera, we would be able to see that there is very little obstruction between your vocal folds and the end of your mouth. This is the speech sound that you might hear in the word "father," or that a baby might include in their first words for "bottle," "mom," or "dad" ("baba," "mama," "dada"). By itself, this sound doesn't mean much – we need to combine it with additional sounds for that.

Make the sound "ah" again, but this time open and close your mouth as you make the sound. You should be hearing something like "amamama" or "abababa" as your lips (and maybe your teeth) come together to obstruct the air coming out of your mouth. You have just made another type of speech sound! Now we have enough to associate some meaning with the sounds you are making: you might call your mom "Mama" or your dad "Baba" even as an adult. You have just articulated two types of sounds: a **vowel** and an **obstruent** (which you can think of as a consonant for now). In Chapter 3, we talk about the International Phonetic Alphabet, a system for annotating the different types of vowels and consonants according to where in the vocal tract the airflow is restricted (called the **place of articulation**) and how the airflow is restricted (called the **manner of articulation**), along with a few other criteria for vowels.

Let's return to our vocal exercises. This time make the same vowel, first at your normal speaking pitch, then at a higher pitch. This is one feature of language that we can measure in acoustic phonetics: the frequency of our voice. This is useful in many areas of research; for example, speech that has a wide variation in pitch seems to hold infants' attention better than the less variable speech that we use with other adults (Fernald & Kuhl 1987), and differences in pitch can be used to index gender identities and sexual orientations across languages (Camp 2009; Munson 2007; Suire et al. 2020). Some languages also use pitch differences as one of the cues to meaning differences in words: Vietnamese has seven different **tones**, so depending on whether you say "ma" with a high pitch, a low pitch, a rising pitch (similar to a question in English), or a falling pitch, it could mean "ghost," "louse," "cheek," or "but" (Kirby 2011).

Now let's change our vowel again. Start out again saying "ah," then "ay" (as in "face"), "ee" (as in "fleece"), "ooh" (as in "goose"), and finally "oh" (as in "goat"). You have just said five different vowels, potentially all in the same breath, just by lifting and lowering your jaw and tongue and, for the last two sounds, rounding your lips. If you didn't notice this, try again – this is why the mirror is handy! We can talk about vowels being rounded or unrounded; high, mid, or low; and back, central, or front as our manner of articulation.

Think of these as the most basic vowels in your variety of English; we don't use the exact same configuration of our vocal tract every time we use one of these vowels, and we also accept quite a bit of variation when we listen to others with a different accent than our own.

At this point, we hope that you are wondering how we can measure these minute differences in speech sounds, and whether we can use methods more precise than just looking at ourselves (and others) in mirrors – and the answer is a resounding YES. We have the technology available to measure the amplitude, frequency, and **harmonics** of speech, as well as being able to visualize where the tongue touches the roof of our mouth and upper teeth using **electropalatography**. One piece of software that gets heavy use in phonetics research is called Praat (www.fon.hum.uva.nl/praat/),[8] which takes recordings as input and creates visual graphs called **spectrograms** and **waveforms**. Using these two visualizations and calculations that are built into Praat, we can quantify and characterize how speakers make their speech sounds, and also observe the variation that occurs within these different parameters that we might be interested in.

You may also be curious about how we go from studying the physical properties of speech sounds to how they pattern in language. For that, we can zoom out to the field of phonology, which studies exactly that.

2.2.2 Phonology

Phonology is the study of the patterns of **contrast** among segments within different languages, and also the study of speakers' mental representations of these contrasting segments. If you study the phonology of spoken languages, you might be particularly curious about how common a given sound pattern is across the world's languages, or which patterns simply do not exist in languages that we have found so far. You might take this a step further and investigate what the qualities of an acceptable sound pattern are for a single person, social group, or group of language users. You may also create hypotheses on the sound changes in language that lead to some of the variation that we see in contemporary speakers.

2.2.2.1 Fundamental Units of Contrast

Let us give you an example from spoken English. Most English speakers don't realize that they have (at least) two different kinds of "l" sounds – one that is produced with the tongue tip right behind the front teeth and the sides of the tongue low. You'll likely make this kind of "l" sound in the word "light," and

---
[8] Praat is free to use and download, so you can explore it yourself if you're curious!

we will use the character [l] to write that sound phonetically. The other "l" is found in words like "dull," where you produce the "l" with the tongue tip low, and the tongue body bunched in the back. Linguists sometimes call this "dark 'l'," and we use the character [ɫ] to write it. These are definitely distinct segments – but in English, the difference between them is not contrastive: it will never change the meaning of a word.

Try it out – see if you can say "light" with [ɫ] and "dull" with [l]. It will probably feel strange, and it might sound funny, but the words will be recognizable and you won't be misunderstood as having tried to say something different. You might not even hear a difference at all.

But if you speak a language that contrasts those segments, you will almost certainly know the difference. Albanian is an example of such a language, and the description of learning about this difference provided by an English speaker, Erica Lush (2015), working with an Albanian speaker named Leticia Lucaj, tells us more about what we mean by contrast. Lush writes:

> Albanian, unlike English, has two distinct lateral approximant phonemes. As a native speaker of English, which only has one phonemic /l/, I had a lot of trouble hearing the difference between the Albanian "hard" and "soft" [l]'s. To Leticia, however, they were quite distinct, and she explained that in Albanian speech it is very clear which one they pronounce.

Lush goes on to provide the following pair of Albanian words that are distinguished only by the kind of "l" they have:

(1)   [diˈəl] "sun"

(2)   [diˈəɫ] "Sunday"

The notion of contrast is fundamental to signed language study as well. How different do two handshapes have to be, for example, in order to change the word in which they are included? In American Sign Language, the difference between the sign for "apple" and that for "onion" is only the position of the sign: For "apple," the signer uses a closed hand, with the knuckle of the index finger against the cheek, and the signer rotates the hand back and forth. The sign for "onion" is the same – except that the knuckle is higher, closer to the forehead. This tells us that those two sign locations – cheek vs. forehead – are contrastive in ASL (see entries in Lapiak 1996). It is possible that there are other signed languages in which that difference in location does not matter to word meanings – it might be used for different emphasis, or the two locations might correspond to regional dialects of the same language, or they might just not matter at all. The differences needed in order for two signs to count as different words, rather than different pronunciations of the same word, are the differences that phonologists study – they are the contrasts.

2.2.2.2 Phonemic Inventories, Phonological Rules, and Phonotactics

The inventory of contrastive segments, or **phonemic inventory**, that we have in our first language(s) and the **phonological rules** that go along with them affect how we speak in other languages too, which leads to "having an accent." For example, you may notice that a French speaker might use /s/ or /z/ in "think" or "that,"[9] which is because the sound inventory of French does not contain the first sounds in either of those words. This means they have to use the "next best" sound – /s/ is the same as the first sound in "think" except in one dimension: its place of articulation (and even then, its place of articulation is very close as well). When we speak a language that we didn't grow up speaking, we have a new set of sounds and rules that we need to square with the ones we already know, and we may do that very differently from how someone who knows the language as their first language would. We do our best to approximate sounds that we do not have in our phonological inventory, and as listeners, we can also train ourselves to be better at comprehending different accents (Sheppard et al. 2017).

Our knowledge of how segments combine into patterns means that in our first language, we know what makes a "good" word and what makes a not-so-great word – this knowledge is referred to as the **phonotactics** or phonotactic constraints of our language that influence which segments are allowed to appear next to each other. For instance, "zbink" would not be very likely to be a word in English, but "spink" could be a word in English. Although you may not be able to explain exactly why "zbink" is very unlikely to be an English word and "spink" is a plausible word, you *just know*. It just so happens that the phonotactic constraints in English are such that you cannot have a voiced stop following a voiced fricative at the beginning of a word (or syllable).

Phonotactic constraints aren't universal by any means: just because a sequence of segments is unacceptable in one language doesn't mean that it's unacceptable in every language. In Vietnamese, "Nguyen" (roughly [ŋwiən] or [ŋwiəŋ]) is a common surname that can be difficult for English speakers to pronounce without practice. Part of the reason is because Vietnamese allows the segment [ŋ] at the beginnings *and* ends of syllables, while English only allows it at the ends (like "ring").

---

[9] If they are a speaker from France, that is – but if they speak varieties of Canadian French, they are more likely to instead substitute a /t/ or /d/ in the same situations (Brannan 2011)! You might listen carefully to interviews conducted in English with Canadian French and European French speakers to see if you notice this difference yourself.

2.2.2.3 Phonological Systems Can Change

Something we have mentioned repeatedly is that language seems to follow patterns. Phonology is no different! The phonemic structures of languages also change over time in systematic ways, and these changes can occur throughout a whole language, or only in certain regions that a language is spoken in (or only among a particular social class, and so on). One example of a region-restricted shift is known as the **Northern Cities Chain Shift**, which typically occurs in white American English speakers in the upper Midwest, near the Great Lakes region and the Canadian border, as seen in Figure 2.1 (Labov et al. 2006).[10]

You can think of a chain shift as being similar to a chain reaction: one segment in a system moves, and this triggers additional changes. The vowels of English are the segments that are moving around in the Northern Cities Chain Shift, so it's helpful to think again about vowel sounds. In this case, one of the vowels "moved" – it changed its pronunciation a bit – and this left an opening into which another vowel could shift, and so on and so on. The first vowel change in this shift was the vowel that is at the beginning of the word "apple." That sound, which for non-shifted US English speakers is articulated low and front, started to get pronounced higher and diphthongized – sort of like the vowel in the exclamation "yeah!". Try it out and see if you can reproduce this shift – on a word like "apple" as "eah-pple," or "cat" as "cyeaht"!

Once the "apple" vowel moved, people started pronouncing the "ah" vowel in words like "father" or "Chicago" – which is usually pronounced with the tongue low but further back, as the old version of "apple" or "cat." So if you are not someone whose speech is affected by this shift, when you're listening to someone whose accent has undergone the Northern Cities Chain Shift, you might hear words like "Chicago" pronounced with the first segment in "apple" rather than the first vowel segment in "father" – or, speaking to a phonologist or phonetician, they might describe the vowel as being **fronted**. If you are in a speech community that has undergone the shift, and you talk to someone from a different community, they might point out to you that your words sound different from theirs – and you might think that they say "Chicago" in a way that shows they are clearly not from Chicago!

After these first two shifts happened (or "hyeahppened"), other changes ensued, and they're pretty complicated. Some "uh" sounds, like the one in "bus," come out like the old "ah" sound from "boss," and the like

---

[10] Image from Angr, CC BY-SA 3.0, via Wikimedia Commons, http://creativecommons.org/licenses/by-sa/3.0/.

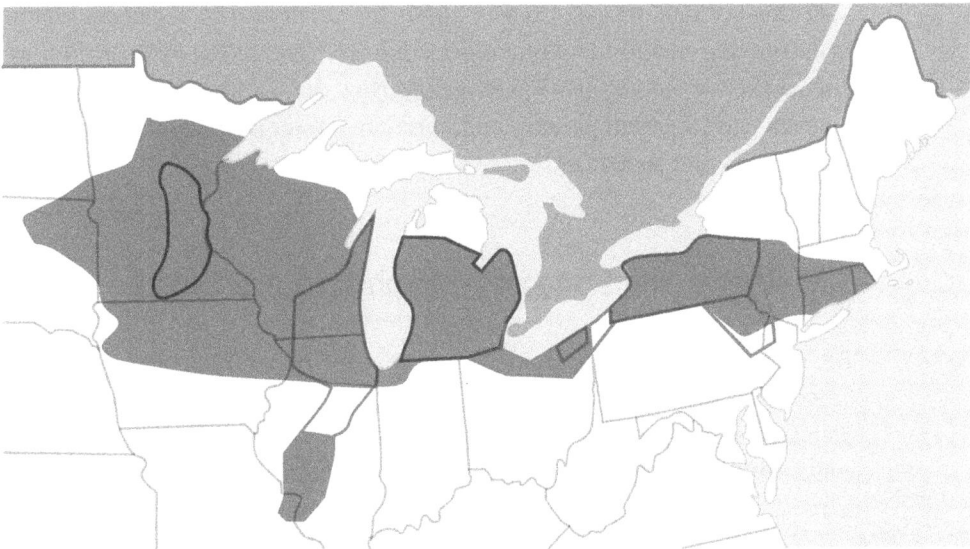

Figure 2.1 Map of northern cities chain shift.

(Siegel & Labov 2006). The Northern Cities Chain Shift is especially exciting for linguists because it is a shift in progress. We rarely get to see language changes in progress because most language change occurs so slowly. However, since we can observe differences in the pronunciation of vowels based on speakers' age, where younger speakers are shifting their vowels and older speakers aren't, *and* that not all of the younger speakers' vowels are where we would expect them to be if they had shifted completely, we can tell that this is a change that is still occurring (Labov et al. 2006; McCarthy 2011).

If this example seems daunting, don't worry; you can revisit this section when we mention shifted vowels in Chapter 9. Chain shifts are complex, and we aren't telling the whole story here since we have simplified some of the details. However, we hope that what you take away from the Northern Cities Chain Shift is that when phonology changes, it changes incrementally, systematically, and predictably. We can predict how the vowel segments will shift based on what we know about phonological rules of the language we're investigating, and in some very rare cases, we can observe the shift – and any effects that it has on language users – as it progresses.

Chain shifts are just one of the aspects of language that we can examine under phonological theory and principles. Phonological rules are also useful for explaining some of the variation we hear in people's accents, and when we incorporate the aspects of social class, gender, race, and more, we can do a more accurate job of describing a language's full segment system and how it is represented in the minds of language users.

In this section, we have talked about the properties of segments within language, the smallest building blocks that we have. In the next section, we discuss the next largest parts of language. Now that we know how to describe segments and segment patterns appropriately for our language, we can create some words and sentences.

2.3 Words and Sentences: Morphology and Syntax

The contrastive segments of a language give us the building blocks to use in order to create elements that have meaning, but they don't mean anything by themselves. In this section we zoom out one step to look at how we take those contrastive segments and arrange them into the basic meaningful units of language – morphemes, words, phrases, and sentences.

2.3.1 Morphology

Morphology is the study of the structural properties of words. If phonetics and phonology are microscope-level phenomena, you can think of morphemes and words as the magnifying glass-level phenomena. They're still pretty small pieces, but a little easier to make sense of. Most people are pretty comfortable identifying words in their languages, so we suspect you are too. However, you may have noticed that there are some words that you can break apart into multiple pieces, like *sunfish* or *zookeepers*, and others that you can't, like *sun*, *fish*, *zoo*, and *keep*. The parts of words that you can't break apart are known as **morphemes**. A morpheme is the smallest unit of meaning or grammatical function in a language – so there is one morpheme in each of the words "zoo" and "keep," but *four* morphemes in the word *zookeepers* – *zoo* and *keep* are each words by themselves, but at the end of *zookeepers* we have an "-er" suffix that means something like "one who does whatever the rest of the word says"[11] and an "-s" suffix that means there are more than one of a thing. Morphemes can be described as **free** or **bound**: free morphemes can stand by themselves as individual words (like *cat*, *zoo*, and *keep*), while bound morphemes need to be attached to another morpheme (like the past tense "-ed" in *walked*). Morphemes might also be described as **derivational** or **inflectional**, which roughly correspond to morphemes that

---

[11] In fancy grammatical terms the "-er" on "zookeeper" is called an "agentive" suffix, because it turns whatever it attaches to, which is usually a verb, into a person who does that thing – the "agent" of the action. If this jargon makes you feel happy, you might already be a linguist! But if it makes you anxious, don't worry. You don't have to care about the jargon to understand the point.

change the meaning of a word (like the "un-" in *unwrap*, or the "-er" in *zookeeper*) and morphemes that have some kind of grammatical function (like the "-s" in *snakes* and *zookeepers*).

2.3.1.1 Finding Words

Linguists who study morphology are curious about how morphemes can be combined in to words, which morphemes are productive (or used most frequently), whether there are universal or crosslinguistic tendencies in how words are structured, and, believe it or not, what constitutes a word. "But it's obvious what a word is!" you might say. "It's whatever we put spaces between!" Well, yes and no. If you counted each piece of text surrounded by spaces in this paragraph, you would come up with one answer. But what about contractions, like *it's*? *It's* is a shortened form of *it is*. Are *it's* and *it is* composed of one word or two? They both have the same amount and type of information, but one has a space in the middle and the other does not. What about idioms, like *kick the bucket* or *let the cat out of the bag*? If you are not literally talking about kicking over a bucket or releasing a cat from a bag, you are using a lot of words to express the concepts *to die* and *to tell a secret*, respectively. That is a lot of words to express one unit of meaning! So are these idioms composed of one morpheme or multiple morphemes? One word or multiple words? Idioms have some constraints that other phrases don't have, too: We can make phrases passive to eliminate the subject, like *The text was studied* instead of *I studied the text*, but you do not get exactly the same meaning if you say *The bucket was kicked* as opposed to *They kicked the bucket*. Instead, when you use the passive, you get the literal meaning of a bucket being kicked. This suggests that if you say *They kicked the bucket* and mean *died*, the whole unit might be considered just one morpheme (Harley & Noyer 1999; Harley & Stone 2013).

That being said, we can also follow general phonological rules to determine whether an utterance is a word or a phrase (or more!). English, for example, allows one primary stress per **phonological word**, which is the loudest "beat" in a word. As we discussed in the previous section, there are also sequences of segments that are not allowed to occur next to each other in a single word, but may very well occur across word boundaries. When you listen to speech, you might hear "morphologyandsyntax" as one unit, but this unit has two equally strong stresses: *morPHOlogyandSYNtax*. We can say that "morphologyandsyntax" consists of two **phonological words**, three morphemes, and three words as we usually think of them.

Similarly, in American Sign Language we see cases of signed elements that aren't words by themselves but that can be added to other elements to create more complex expressions. For example, there is a morpheme in ASL that can be translated into English as "wrecked," and that is created by moving a sign toward and then against the opposite arm (Schembri 2003). The "wrecked" morpheme can be used with a handshape indicating a moving car, and depending on the trajectory of the movement at the time the hand makes contact with the opposite arm, the sign can be understood as referring to a front-end collision, a side-collision or a rear-end collision. In some ways, the "wrecked" morpheme works like a suffix, in that it appears at the end of the sign sequence. How much information is wrapped up in a unit that an ASL speaker would identify as one *word* is not always straightforward, but it is clear that the morphological system in ASL is able to use modality-specific advantages to convey very rich meanings in a single element.

To further complicate our understanding of what exactly a word is, languages are diverse in the way that words are formed: some languages, like English and Vietnamese, average a little more than one morpheme per word, while other languages like Turkish, Navajo, and Quechua average many morphemes per word. The Diné Bizaad (Navajo) word *áhodidiniishtłóóh* means something like "I'm overcoming nervous tension/anxiety" (McDonough 2016), and the Turkish word *evleriden* means something like "from their house." Languages can also be categorized by how easily different morphemes can be distinguished from each other. In languages like Finnish, you can easily separate out individual morphemes: the sentence below means something like "In Finland, you wind up in a sauna," and each of the morphemes can easily be separated from each other.

(3)   Suome -ssa   joutu -u   sauna –an
       Finland -in   get -3rd sg.   sauna -in[12]   (Laitinen 2006)

However, in a language like Russian, individual pieces of meaning are more difficult to tease apart. The words below all have to do with chairs, combined with **case markers** that describe the grammatical relationship of a word or morpheme to the entire sentence.

(4)   stol   -ov   stol   -y   stol   -a
       chair   -of.the.plural   chair   -nom[13].plural   chair   -of.the.singular
       "of the chairs"   "the chairs"   "of the chair"   (Comrie 1988)

As you can see, you can readily separate out the morpheme meaning "chair" from the rest of the word, but you can't do the same for separating

---

[12] The technical terms for the morphemes that we have translated as "in" in this sentence are called the inessive and illative case markers (and case markers identify a word or morpheme's grammatical relationship to the sentence), but – as always – you don't need to know this to understand what morphology is!

[13] "Nom" stands for "nominative case," which is used to identify the subject of the sentence.

something meaning "plural" from the morpheme meaning "of the," or "nominative case."

2.3.1.2 Words vs. Phrases vs. Sentences

It is also important to remember that languages exist along a continuum with the number of morphemes per word and our ability to excise pieces of meaning from each other. Languages that are completely **isolating** with morphemes and words at a one-to-one ratio do not exist: English is one of the languages that is considered more isolating, but we are still able to add more morphemes to individual words (like *cat -s, walk -ing, baby -sit -ing*). There are also words in English that give it more **fusional** characteristics, where it is difficult to separate individual pieces of meaning from each other (as in *geese* or the plural form of many herd animals, like *sheep* or *deer*).

On the other end of the continuum are **synthetic** languages, which have higher morpheme-to-word ratios. Synthetic languages can be further subdivided into fusional languages, where it is difficult to tease apart meaning components from one another, and **agglutinative** languages, where components of meaning are easier to separate. Turkish and Finnish are examples of agglutinative languages, while Spanish and Ukranian are examples of fusional languages.

This flexibility that languages have in how words can be defined means that we need to be especially clear on what we as linguists define as a "word" when we talk about **lexical variation** in sociolinguistic research. A lexicon is a kind of mental list or set of all the words and word-like elements that a person knows, sort of like your mental dictionary. When research is done on English, words and morphemes are easy to conflate: To use a well-loved example, the morphemes that mean "the generic term for a sweet, carbonated, nonalcoholic beverage" are the words *soda, pop,* and *Coke* (in some varieties of American English). All three of these are words, and all three of them are morphemes. However, we can also focus on bound morphemes that must be attached to another morpheme, like *-ity* and *-ness*: Säily (2011) found that men and women use those two suffixes to form new words at different rates in British English, even though their function is largely the same. All this is to say that we need to be precise and recall our potential bias toward English (or other languages that we speak!) when we describe studies that are looking at lexical variation as opposed to morphological variation.

As we build up enough words, we can combine them into sentences. Much like the other fields that we have looked at so far, language users seem to follow patterns and rules to combine words into sentences. These patterns seem to be determined by the language that we speak as well as external factors, and syntacticians study different portions of the things that go into making a sentence.

2.3.2 Syntax

With syntax, we zoom out in our scope even farther to take in full phrases and sentences: syntax is the study of the structure of sentences and how words are allowed to be combined into sentences and phrases. For example, you know that the sentence *The turtle basked happily on the rock* is a well-formed sentence in English, while **Turtle basked happily on rock* is not. (We use an asterisk preceding a sentence to mark it as ungrammatical.) In Russian, though, determiners like *a* and *the* are not used, so the Russian equivalent to *Turtle basked happily on rock* would be a well-formed sentence.

Syntacticians study the similarities and differences of sentence construction across languages and form theories about how sentences work in general. You can think of these studies as being documentary in nature, where a native speaker of an **un- or under-documented language** is interviewed about how to express different shades of meaning and whether sentences that the linguist comes up with are feasible. Other studies focus on how we process sentences by tracking our eye movements, reading speed, error detection speed, and more: these studies tell us what's happening "under the hood" in our minds as we read, hear, and interpret sentences. For example, early studies of sentence processing examined sentences like *The horse raced past the barn fell*,[14] where you may need multiple read-throughs (or a rephrasing) to grasp that the sentence is grammatical (Ferreira et al. 2001; Fodor & Inoue 2000). Why are these sentences so difficult to interpret, and how do we believe the linguistic mechanisms in our mind construct and repair meanings?

2.3.2.1 Putting Words in Order

Regardless of the language, sentences need a set of minimal components to get their meaning across. In English, we typically need a subject and a verb, in that order: *The cat eats*. We can continue adding additional components, which depend on what the verb allows: *The cat eats quickly, the cat eats her breakfast, the cat eats fourteen tiny pieces of kibble hungrily*, and so on. In theory, there is no limit to what we can add on to a sentence – the only limit is our memory! However, you can see that English is relatively strict

---

[14] This, and sentences like it, is known as a "garden path sentence" – the first part of the sentence seems to be leading you to an anticipated meaning (the horse ran quickly past a barn), but then it takes an odd turn (... fell?). You might rephrase this sentence as "The horse *who was* raced past the barn fell" to get the intended meaning.

about the order in which each element is allowed to appear. *Breakfast the eats cat her* instead of *The cat eats her breakfast* is not grammatical in English, and if you test other combinations of subjects, verbs, and objects, you will notice that the vast majority of combinations will require you to put each element in the order subject, verb, object. We can abbreviate this as SVO when we talk about **constituent order**, one of the potential places of commonality in constructing sentences. SVO is the second most common ordering of these components; the most common word order that has been attested in the world's languages is SOV (as in *The cat her breakfast eats*), and every other possible ordering of subject, verb, and object can be found in at least one of the world's languages (Dryer & Haspelmath 2013).

Constituent order is a potential problem for syntacticians because in practice, we are all born with roughly the same linguistic capabilities regardless of location, culture, or language. Infants born in the English-dominant United States but adopted at an early age by a Russian family will acquire Russian just as easily as they would have acquired English if they had stayed in the US. This suggests that all humans start out with the same aptitude for language and something about our exposure to languages outside the womb causes us to adhere to the proper word order rules (for example) of our language. Are we all born with the same underlying assumption that all languages have a particular word order? Does something in our linguistic environment cause us to rearrange elements of a sentence? It's not clear! How exactly this happens and how much of our linguistic mechanisms are innate are both questions that are currently debated in the field[15] and are questions that are outside the scope of this book.

2.3.2.2 Syntactic Variation

Theories of syntax often emphasize the need to describe the linguistic knowledge of the "ideal speaker-listener, in a completely homogeneous speech-community" (Chomsky 1965, p. 3) and so do not always provide useful tools for describing and understanding syntactic variation within a community of speakers. However, some scholars are working to test and revise theories to account for syntactic variation. Researchers argue that, in fact, the existing theories of syntax can account for the variability we see from person to person (Adger 2016; Adger & Smith 2010; Conrod 2020). One proposal is that essentially, different meaning components line up with their syntactic components in different ways, so meanings of sentences are

---

[15] And they are certainly important questions to scholars interested in human cognition, evolution, ethology, and the like, and they may shed light on processes of human cognition, evolution, language and communication disorders, and other allied disciplines.

interpreted differently – but in a finite number of ways. For instance, you probably learned in your English courses that *they was* is ungrammatical and should be *they were*. However, there are dialects of English where *they was* is completely grammatical, from African American English (Green 2002, p. 38) to a variety of Scottish English (Adger & Smith 2010). Similarly, you may have learned to use a generic *he* pronoun in sentences like "Everyone loves his mother," but there is quite a bit of work showing that we do not actually perceive these *he*s to be gender neutral (Conrod 2020); instead, we can use the pronoun *they*, which does not have any gendered associations in English.

One thing that's important to remember when talking about syntax is that we can talk about structure independently from meaning. The sentence *Colorless green ideas sleep furiously* is a well-loved example because it is structurally well-formed but does not have a clear meaning. Ideas aren't colorful and they cannot sleep, something cannot be both colorless and green, and what does it look like to sleep furiously? Similarly, we can intuit something about the meaning of a sentence or phrase without fully knowing what words mean by using the context in which the words appear. Take the first stanza of Lewis Carroll's (1871) "Jabberwocky":

> 'Twas brillig, and the slithy toves
> Did gyre and gimble in the wabe:
> All mimsy were the borogoves,
> And the mome raths outgrabe.

Although you may not know many of the words, you know the **parts of speech** of each word based on its position in the sentence and the other words around it. "Slithy" is an adjective that comes between an article and a noun; "borogoves" is a noun since it comes after an article and before a conjunction, and it must be plural because it comes in a sentence with the verb "were" rather than "was." We don't know everything about what a "mome rath" is, but we know that it's a noun and we can have one mome rath or many mome raths.[16] In the next section, we discuss the way that we create meaning in language – what happens when we go from Jabberwocky nonsense to the words around us. It turns out that as long as we have function words in the mix, we can figure out a lot about what the content words mean.

---

[16] You might also wonder whether "mome rath" is a compound word like "washing machine," or if "mome" is an adjective that could describe other nouns in Jabberwockish. Can you have a mome Jabberwocky?

2.4 Meaning and Context: Semantics and Pragmatics

2.4.1 Semantics

When we think of the "meaning" of words, we usually think of their dictionary definition. Perhaps we conjure a mental image of the thing or action the word describes. But the study of meaning in linguistics is much more complex (and exciting!) than this. Semantics is the subdiscipline of linguistics that specifically focuses on this issue. **Lexical semantics** – the study of the meanings of words – and **compositional semantics** – the study of the meanings of phrases and sentences – are two key components of this area of linguistics. But first, let's get a better idea of what linguists mean by "meaning."

2.4.1.1 Lexical Semantics

Linguists typically distinguish between **sense** meaning and **reference** meaning. The "sense" of a word, sentence, or phrase is its mental representation in the mind of a language user, while the "reference" is the thing (if there is one) in the world that is picked out or identified by the expression. The word "dog" in English, and "chien" in French, and "łééchąą'í" in Diné Bizaad (Navajo) share the same reference – anyone who fits the definition of "dog" in one of those languages will probably fit the definition in any of them. But they may have different senses across these languages, and also for different speakers of the same language.

To our knowledge, in both English and French, "dog" or "chien" might create a mental representation for speakers of those languages of a cuddly, possibly playful, and probably loyal companion – sort of diminutive, one whom some speakers might think of as a kind of surrogate baby. Speakers of Diné Bizaad may share some or all of these senses for "dog," but they will also have senses that are built into the word itself. Let's look at how that word, łééchąą'í, is built.[17]

(5) łééchąą'í
 łéé-chąą-í
 horse-poop-one.who
 "dog (one who follows horses around for their poop, or one who is a kind of a horse- poop)"

---

[17] This information comes from Fountain's training in Diné Bizaad classes at the University of Arizona. Any errors are her own. The element łéé is a combining form that's used for words for different kinds of horses, the element chąą' is a root morpheme meaning excrement, and the -í takes a word and turns it into an agentive form – sort of like the -er suffix in English "writer" or "teacher."

This word has built-in knowledge that goes beyond its referent "dog." It evokes some characteristic behaviors of dogs (they do enjoy rolling in and tasting horse manure), and it also fits into a cultural pattern of affectionate teasing and joking (we are told that one favorite teasing name for small children is *chąą mą'íí*, literally "coyote-poop"). These evocative qualities of the word are part of its sense – but not really part of its reference. That is, a łééchąą'í who for some odd reason doesn't enjoy horses – or has never met one – is still a proper referent for the word łééchąą'í.

So "sense," as opposed to "reference," includes meanings you might think of as connotative or emotive and also meanings that are built into the word but don't necessarily play a part in determining its reference. English has words like this too: a "mailman" is built of morphemes "mail" and "man," and this generates a "sense" that centers around maleness for many English speakers, so we change the expression to "mail person" or "mail carrier" – same reference, different sense.[18]

You may already know some of the key terms and concepts that lexical semantics begins with. In addition to understanding the sense and reference of words, we can explore how words relate to each other within a language. Languages seem to be extremely tolerant of word relationships that seem to be built to generate confusion – for example, **homophony**. Homophony exists when there are two or more words in a language that have the same pronunciation as each other. In spoken English, "ewe" and "you" are homophonous, even though they mean completely different things. You are unlikely to confuse the two, because they're likely to appear in different contexts, and of course if you see them in writing you'll definitely not be confused. But languages also allow homophony between words and morphemes that might be confused with each other – for example, English has three homophonous -s suffixes, all of which are found in the following example sentence:

(6)   Mom's cat chases dogs.

The plural and possessive -s cause no end of trouble to English writers, who often write the wrong one. Even in spoken form, these two can mess us up.

You may also be familiar with these named relationships among words: **synonymy** (when two or more different words mean the same thing, like

---

[18] Recall from the previous section that a word that is masculine, such as "he" or "mailman," and is also meant to be generic and refer to people of all genders, is not actually comprehended as being gender-neutral – hence the change from the masculine-affixed "mailman" to "mail carrier," which has no reference to the gender of the person carrying your mail. We discuss generic masculine pronouns and implications of their use a little more in Chapter 9.

2.4 Meaning and Context: Semantics and Pragmatics

"six" and "a half dozen"), **antonymy** (when words have opposite meanings, like "large" and "small"), **hyponymy** (when a word names a subcategory of another word, like "apple" is of "fruit"), and **hypernymy** (when a word names a larger category to which another word belongs, like "fruit" is of "apple"). These terms and concepts become most interesting when they seem to not work as expected. For example, if "six" and "a half dozen" are really synonyms, why would a speaker ever choose to say "a half dozen"? If "large" and "small" are antonyms and "small" and "little" are synonyms, why don't we think of "little" as an antonym of "large"? And what's the opposite of "jaguar"? The questions one can ask are endless.

2.4.1.2 Compositional Semantics

Linguists and nonlinguists are often very interested in word-level meanings – lexical semantics – but we also understand that meaning in language arises not just from the meanings of words but also from their combination. Consider the following expression of English, found on a sign in a US parking area, with arrows indicating the direction drivers should go in order to access a particular park. The sign said "Temporary Dog Park." At least one clever user of social media took a photograph of the sign and captioned their photo like this: "They're called werewolves."

That joke capitalizes on the role of grouping in generating linguistic meaning – compositional semantics. The grouping intended (we think) by the sign makers was [temporary [dog park]], that is, a dog park that's been set up temporarily. But the grouping [[temporary dog] park] is also grammatically possible in English, and it would result in a reference to a park that was intended for use by "temporary dogs."

Compositional semantics can even be important within single words, when the words are made up of more than one morpheme. A very famous example of this from English is the word "unlockable." English speakers on seeing or hearing that word are likely to immediately recognize that it's built of three morphemes: un-, lock, and -able. They are also very likely to immediately understand the meaning of the word. We ask you to take a moment, before reading further, to do the same. What does that word mean? In what scenario would you use it? When you have that idea firmly in mind, read on.

The word "unlockable" can refer to at least two situations, depending on how the morphemes are grouped. The meaning you first came up with will likely be one of these two. It's possible that you organized the morphemes like this: [[unlock] able] – meaning "able to be unlocked." But it's also possible that you organized the morphemes like this: [un [lockable]] – meaning "not able to be locked." If you're referring to the lock on the exterior door of your home or apartment, that first meaning would be good news and the second meaning would be terrible news. Our experience is that most people get one meaning or the other in mind when they first come across the word – and don't realize that there's another possibility until it's pointed out to them.

Compositional semantics also considers meanings that span multiple utterances. For example, if a person says something like "Gracie is a dog," there are meanings baked into that utterance such as "Gracie is a mammal" (because "dog" is a hyponym, or subcategory of, "mammal") and "a dog exists" (because "is" asserts existence). The fact is that if the sentence "Gracie is a dog" is true, it must also be the case that a dog exists, and that Gracie is a mammal. The relationship between our first sentence and these facts that follow is called **entailment**, and we often explore meaning in language by asking about the entailments of an expression.

Thinking about entailments can lead to interesting questions. For example, does the statement "Gracie is a dog" entail the statement "Gracie is a quadruped," and if so does it also entail that "Gracie has four legs"? On first pass, you might think so, since "dog" as a category is a hyponym, or type of, quadruped, and "quadruped" means "four-legged." But what if Gracie has had a leg amputated? Is she still a quadruped? Why do you think so, or not, and what might that tell you about what these different statements really mean?

There are a variety of relationships among statements that are important to understanding compositional meaning. Consider this question, which could be asked by an attorney of a witness in a trial:

(7)   Attorney: "Did you stop stealing cars?"
        Witness (who was never a car thief): "..."

Embedded in the question is a statement that the witness must have stolen cars in the past. The question puts the witness in an awkward quandary: If they answer "yes," the good news is that they can claim they are not currently committing crimes ... but they are also tacitly admitting that they used to be doing just that. But if they answer "no," they seem to be admitting to being a car thief right now. The only way they can respond to the question in a way that doesn't incriminate them is by sidestepping it, or opting out of the conversational structure, to say something like "Wait, I've never stolen any cars."

These kinds of embedded statements are called **presuppositions**. Presuppositions can be used by speakers in a variety of ways, and understanding what an utterance presupposes tells us more about what that utterance really means. Lots of question and answer pairs revolve around presuppositions, and we imagine you will find lots of cases in which presupposition failures cause very interesting conversations indeed.

There are many other aspects of meaning in language that you will learn about if you dive more deeply into the study of semantics. Importantly, you'll develop an excellent response to anyone who complains about your careful analysis of language by saying, "Oh, that's just semantics!". Yes, it is semantics, and semantics is linguistic meaning, and it's nothing to scoff at.

But semantic meanings – those thoroughly embedded into morphemes, words, and sentences – are only part of how people use language to create meanings. Language doesn't exist in a vacuum – we need to extend our understanding beyond these baked-in meanings in order to really study how language works. In fact, it's time to back away from our microscopes and magnifying glasses to start looking at the bigger picture.

2.4.2 Pragmatics

Meaning goes far beyond the references, senses, and compositional meanings of morphemes, words, and sentences. Meaning is also shaped by context. The subfield of linguistics that studies the role of context in shaping meaning is called **pragmatics**. **Context** means the who, what, when, where, and why of an instance of language use. While the discipline of pragmatics typically focuses on the immediate context of an utterance, we also talk of context when we want to refer to the broader social, cultural, historical, and political environment in which language use happens – and linguists know that all of these factors can shape the meaning of an utterance. For now, we'll keep our focus on the immediate environment of a specific instance of language use, and we'll consider an example to better understand this. We'll focus on two main approaches (and their very old original citations) in this section – if you know the basics of these, you'll have a good framework you can add to with newer scholarship.

2.4.2.1 Speech Acts

Say a sign goes up on a building in your neighborhood: "Teddy's Tea Shop: Coming Soon!" As a lover of a good cup of tea, you are excited about this new development! In fact, you just cannot wait for the tea shop to open. You announce loudly to everyone on the street, "I now pronounce Teddy's Tea Shop open for business!"

You are probably able to see right away that something is off here. It isn't that the utterance was ungrammatical, or that the meanings of the words you used were unclear or inaccurate. Rather, you used a **speech act** – a **performative** – without satisfying the proper **felicity conditions**. We will go over these concepts one by one to reveal what was off about the example above.

Speech acts are, quite simply, actions that are accomplished through language (Austin 1975). We use language to accomplish actions such as greeting ("Hello there!"), requesting ("Could you close the window?"), describing ("It's raining so much!"), evaluating ("This rain is awful"), and so on. Because humans are so creative and flexible with language, linguists often see cases where an utterance that looks like one kind of speech act actually takes the form of another – but of course, these require context to understand. The interrogative "Could you close the window?" might very well be answered with an answer of "yes" or "no." But when your friend utters this question after seeing the rain clouds come in, you are likely to interpret it as a command or a directive to just go close the window, not a question about your abilities. This is the difference between **direct speech acts** – when the form of the utterance matches up with the intended effect – and **indirect speech acts** – when the form of the utterance is different from the effect.

A special category of direct speech acts – relevant to our Teddy's Tea Shop example above – are performatives. Performatives occur when the action mentioned in the utterance is accomplished by the saying of the utterance itself. Cases like our "I now pronounce this place open for business" *accomplish* the act of "making a declaration" simply by the saying of it. Or, saying "I promise to pay you back for lunch" accomplishes the very act of *promising* by the saying of it. Like all aspects of language, there are rules that constrain how we use these kinds of utterances. These are the felicity conditions: all of the things that have to be true in order for your performative utterance to work.

And now we can return to consider why the above example feels so off: it is due to the fact that you are not the business owner, and thus have no standing to declare Teddy's Tea Shop open for business. In other words, the felicity conditions for that performative speech act were not met. Similarly, a performative utterance like "I now pronounce you married" requires several felicity conditions to be met in order for the utterance to accomplish the work of changing two people from a not-married state to a married state. The person uttering those words must be authorized to perform marriages; it must be uttered in the presence of the two people who wish to become married (and are not already, and are permitted to be married to each other); sometimes it has to be uttered in a specific place (like a place of worship or a courthouse). If any of those felicity conditions fail to be met, uttering the sentence "I now pronounce you married" does *not* accomplish the act of getting two people married.

But what if it was not actually your intent to open the business with your declaration "I now pronounce Teddy's Tea Shop open for business"? Perhaps you said it to make your friend laugh – both of you wishing the appropriate felicity conditions were in place to pull off this performative speech act, but understanding that the context in which it was uttered was not amenable to this. Linguists have ways to capture *this* kind of meaning-in-context as well!

2.4.2.2 The Cooperative Principle and Conversational Maxims

Let's start with the notion of the **cooperative principle** (Grice 1975). The cooperative principle is the idea that a mutual understanding of meaning is achieved by speakers working together. This does *not* mean that we agree all the time, or get along with each other perfectly, or that everyone is always polite. Instead, it means that meaning in context emerges from a process of mutual effort (conscious or unconscious), and that speakers rely on the hearer's understanding of meaning just as much as they consider their own intention. If this sounds vague, don't worry – we can break the cooperative principle into four underlying **conversational maxims**.

First, we have the **maxim of quality**. Quite simply, this maxim means that speakers cooperate by being truthful, and we try – and assume others are similarly trying – to avoid saying things they know to be false. Of course, this doesn't mean that people never lie! If your roommate is sipping her beverage from Teddy's Tea Shop and utters, "Yum, this tea is delicious!", you probably do not fret about whether or not it is actually nice-tasting. You assume she is abiding by the maxim of quality. But we know that people do not *always* abide by the maxim of quality. We can **violate** maxims by failing to observe them, with the hope that our interlocutors do not notice we are doing so. Your roommate might be violating the maxim of quality if she reports her tea is delicious when it in fact tastes bad, perhaps to avoid offending you or hurting the feelings of the tea shop proprietors. We can also **flout** maxims by failing to observe them in obvious, purposeful ways. If you and your roommate were both enjoying a delicious cup of tea, perhaps even downing the tea ravenously in a few gulps, finishing much more quickly than you'd anticipated before sharing a satisfied sigh, and then you both uttered, "Ugh, this tea is horrible!", it would probably be understood by both of you to be an instance of flouting the maxim of quantity as a form of sarcastic humor.

The second conversational maxim is the **maxim of quantity**. This one means: give the right amount of information, not too much and not too little. What counts as "too much" or "not enough" information will, of course, depend on the sociolinguistic context. In the United States, where the authors of this book live, an appropriate response to the question "How are you?" usually requires a response along the lines of "Fine, thanks!". Even though this response gives very little information, it is in fact just the right amount for our culture. Consider what a more technically informative response might look like: "My day has been wonderful – I woke up five minutes before my alarm went off in an excellent mood. Then I listened to the radio while I took a shower, and my favorite song came on! Now I'm on my way to Teddy's Tea Shop where I think I'll order a lovely Earl Grey tea." If you answered the "How are you?" question with all of that information in the US, you would probably be considered to be flouting the maxim of quantity.

Next, we have the **maxim of relevance**, which really just means what it says on the tin: be relevant! Just like the maxim of quantity, what counts as "relevant" to a given utterance is highly dependent on context. If someone asks you the way to Teddy's Tea Shop, for instance, and you respond with "It's not open yet," this might be interpreted as a flouting of the maxim of relevance. After all, instead of providing them with directions – the most directly relevant way to respond to their question – you've told them something about the availability of the shop. At the same time, it is also easy to see how information about the tea shop being closed would be relevant to someone asking for directions – you might intuit that they would be disappointed to get all the way over there and find it shuttered.

Finally, we have the **maxim of manner**. This maxim is often summarized as "be brief, clear, and unambiguous." But that itself can get confusing! Shouldn't "be brief" fall under the umbrella of the maxim of quantity? One way to look at it is this: the maxim of quantity refers to the amount of *information* given, and the maxim of manner refers to the amount (and type) of linguistic units used to convey that information. The "clear and unambiguous part" also has to do with the linguistic units that the message is delivered in: do not use situationally inappropriate jargon, do not use vague words, and keep your utterances orderly. If your server at Teddy's Tea Shop greeted you at your table by listing every single type of tea they have ever tried, using technical agricultural jargon to explain how each tea was grown and processed, you could probably claim they were violating the maxim of manner.

Instead of thinking about maxims as "rules" that speakers are obligated to follow, think of them instead as underlying principles that we expect to be true, most of the time. When you look at them this way, you can see how violations and floutings of these maxims are not really "breaking the rules" but are actually doing meaningful communicative work! We have already covered how flouting and violating maxims can lead to inferences – such as when you and your friend both purposefully say your tea is gross, when in fact it is delicious, as a form of humor. Speakers can also **opt out** of uttering anything that could be evaluated using this framework of conversational maxims – such as when a defendant in a trial refuses to utter something that would incriminate them. Of course, this, too, might lead a listener to infer

2.4 Meaning and Context: Semantics and Pragmatics

something about the defendant's guilt. But, technically speaking, they haven't uttered anything that could be evaluated based on the maxims of quality, quantity, relevance, or manner. The inferences that we generate based on whether conversational maxims are followed, violated, flouted, or opted-out-of are referred to in pragmatics as **implicatures**. In essence, implicatures are the indirect meanings we understand based on someone not following the norms of conversation as one would usually expect.

Now, we can return again to the example of uttering the phrase "I now pronounce Teddy's Tea Shop open for business!". If you uttered this to a group of your friends, it would probably be clear to everyone involved that the appropriate felicity conditions were not in place to carry out this performative speech act. Most likely, everyone knew you were flouting the maxim of quantity – saying something untrue about the world – on purpose. Thus, your speech act generated the implicature that you hoped to be able to enjoy a nice cup of tea there soon and perhaps make your friends laugh!

Another way that linguists have approached the study of language in context is through the linguistic study of politeness (Brown & Levison 1987). Brown and Levinson argued that forms of politeness are rooted in a desire to preserve and protect the public self-image all adult interlocutors have in conversation – what they refer to as **face** – and managing our face and those of our interlocutors is sometimes called **facework**. Our face, or public self-image, has both a *positive* and a *negative* component to it. **Positive face** refers to the general desire for one's public self-image to be accepted and liked, whereas **negative face** refers to the desire for one's public self-image to be free from imposition or responsibility to others. We can construct a grid to help envision the kinds of considerations involved in facework (Table 2.1):

Linguistic acts that threaten either our positive face or our negative face are referred to, cleverly, as **face-threatening acts** (often abbreviated as FTAs). Politeness strategies are the linguistic actions we take to mitigate the force or effect of FTAs. To better understand this, let's dig into some examples of FTAs.

Table 2.1 Types of facework

	Positive face	Negative face
Self	i.e., work to be included, close, engaged	i.e., work to be independent, private, autonomous
Other	i.e., work to include others, keep them close, engage them	i.e., work to respect others' independence, privacy, autonomy

FTAs operate on at least two dimensions: they can threaten either the speaker or the hearer, and they can threaten either a person's positive face or negative face. While there are significant cross-cultural differences in the specific attributes of a positive or negative public self-image (for example, in some communities and contexts being "ambitious" will be understood as a positive trait, but in others it may be understood as a negative one), and also on the specific behaviors that are understood as FTAs, and also on the specific politeness strategies that are appropriate to use to moderate them – we think that the logic of FTAs and linguistic facework is a reasonable way to understand linguistic politeness across communities. In the examples here, we focus on how these things work in communities with which we're familiar.

Since positive face has to do with a person's positive self-image, FTAs that threaten positive face often have to do with personal criticism, negative opinions, disagreements, expressions of taboo topics, and the like. Thus, an FTA to a *hearer's* positive face would be any speech act in which the speaker threatens their public self-image – maybe the speaker criticizes the hearer's new hairstyle, or a speaker tells a hearer that their taste in music is silly. Frequent interruption could also be considered a threat to positive face, as it might demonstrate that the speaker does not care for the hearer's contributions. Meanwhile, FTAs that threaten a *speaker's* positive face include all those speech acts in which the speaker essentially has to own up to their own mistakes or highlight a negative quality of themselves. If you are very late to meet a friend, and you open your greeting to them with an apology, that's a way to manage a threat to your positive face.

What do we do to minimize threats to the positive face of ourselves and others? Linguistic strategies that protect, support, or maintain either the speaker or hearer's positive self-image are referred to as **positive politeness strategies**. These include techniques that largely center around highlighting solidarity and friendliness – so they include linguistic behavior such as giving compliments, using nicknames or in-group slang (if the cultural context you are speaking in values informality over formality), and establishing common ground or shared qualities between interlocutors.

Negative face, as you now know, has to do with an individual's personal freedom – from responsibility, from imposition, from control, and so on. Thus, negative FTAs often include speech acts like demands, warnings, or even expressions of strong emotions like envy or hatred. A negative FTA toward the hearer, then, could be a speech act that obligates the hearer to do something. For instance, if you ask a friend to lend you their favorite novel, that creates a double imposition on them: not just that they are pressured to agree to your request, but also, by lending their property out, that their ability to do what they wish with that book is restricted. Negative FTAs toward speakers tend to involve cases in which the speaker threatens their own face in order to maintain the hearer's face – in other words, restricting their own personal face-maintaining on behalf of their interactional partner's face. For instance, when you pretend to not notice your coworkers' mistakes on a report – perhaps just quietly taking care of the issues yourself – you restrict your own freedom from imposition, threatening your negative face, while at the same time maintaining your coworkers' positive face.

Negative face threats can be avoided, or at least mitigated, by a range of **negative politeness strategies**, most of which center around showing deference. If you are speaking in a culture that values formality and social distance in interactions, using honorifics and titles might accomplish this, as it avoids imposing too much familiarity on your interlocutor. Hedges are another common negative politeness strategy – rather than expressing a negative face threat outright, you might try to tone down the force of it through formulations such as "That wasn't the dish for me *personally*, but *I suppose* I can see why others might like it." Indirectness is another common negative politeness strategy. Imagine you arrive in your linguistics classroom and quickly realize you left your notebook at home. You know that demanding or directly requesting a spare sheet of paper from a colleague would be a threat to their negative face, so perhaps you mitigate this FTA by stating, "Oh dear, it looks like I left my notebook at home!" Your expectation here is that your classmates will step in to protect your positive face by offering you a sheet of note paper – without you having directly asked for it!

All that said, there are some situations that call for us to dispense with these politeness strategies and just plainly and directly state what is on our mind. This kind of linguistic strategy is referred to as **bald on-record utterance**, and you might hear such formulations in cases where urgency or efficiency is of the essence. While "Get out of the way!" would be an extreme negative face threat when shouted to someone standing in front of you at the grocery store, this bald-on record utterance is utterly appropriate when a doctor is rushing to care for an injured person. In short, the way face threats are mitigated (or not), and the type of politeness strategies used to do this, depend on *context* – and that's what pragmatics is all about!

A linguist needs to understand the contributions of speaker intent and immediate context to language even when we're looking at utterances one by one. But most of the time when we talk, we're talking with someone else. The last two areas we'll discuss in this chapter, conversation and discourse analysis, focus on linguistic exchanges between multiple speakers or signers.

2.5 Conversation and Interaction: Conversation and Discourse Analysis

We are continuing to widen our lens to include language behavior that involves more people and more time. The previous subfields of linguistics we have covered help us understand the underlying principles of language structure and use. But to fully understand how language shapes social issues, we are still missing one important component of linguistic study: how conversation and interaction work. This aspect of language in social context is approached most often through the disciplines of **conversation analysis** and **discourse analysis**. While at first glance they may sound very similar – and indeed, both do share an interest in language in interaction – they are built from rather different intellectual and scholarly histories. What is important for us here is not so much how they differ, but what frameworks and strategies they can add to our toolkit.

2.5.1 Conversation Analysis

At a basic level, **conversation** happens when any two or more humans engage in social interaction together through talk. When conversation analysts (Sacks et al. 1978) study language, they typically draw from data sets of audio and/or video-recorded conversations between pairs or groups of people. They might gather such data from call centers, from recording family dinner time conversations, or from video-taping checkout counters at stores. There are also conversation analysts who study speech in more formal or controlled settings, but by and large, this discipline has a strong focus on everyday, naturalistic speech contexts. Just like a phonetician or a morphologist might seek to uncover the systematic, underlying structures of segments or words in a language as it is actually used by the speakers, conversation analysts want to understand the structures and patterns that occur in natural, everyday conversation.

One of the most basic observations about conversation is that speakers tend to take turns. One interlocutor speaks for a bit, and then another, and then another, and so on. Of course, anyone who has participated in a conversation can tell you that the order of conversational turn-taking is rarely so rigid as this. But empirical observation of everyday conversation has shown that patterned structures do occur. We avoid calling them "rules" because the norms for **turn-taking** vary interpersonally, situationally, and cross-culturally. While you may feel comfortable interrupting your friend's story about their day, for instance, you probably would be much more careful about interrupting a speech your boss was making at a formal work dinner.

Similarly, some communities and cultures are comfortable with a high degree of **overlap** and **interruption** in their conversations. In your community, it may be normal for two people to speak at the same time. In others, it might be considered unspeakably rude. Turn-taking norms are fundamentally about determining the **sequence of speakers**; in other words, the expectations about which participant speaks when, and for how long. These are issues, in other words, of who controls the **conversational floor**.

We do not usually worry about overtly naming who is to speak when in a given interaction. This kind of **speaker selection** tends to occur in more formal situations. One example can be seen in formal legal discourse, such as when the United States Speaker of the House says something like "The Speaker recognizes the representative from Arizona." This performative speech act accomplishes the task of formally establishing who is allowed the conversational floor – if someone other than the representative from Arizona begins to speak, it is considered a major violation of the rules. Less formally, you have probably been in classrooms where you are expected to raise your hand and wait for the instructor to call on you by name before you are given the floor. But in everyday conversation with our friends or family, we typically do not rely on such formalized conventions for organizing turn sequences in conversation. You might allocate a turn to one of your interlocutors by naming them ("What do you think, Stanley?"), gazing at them, or gesturing at them. All of these speaker-selection strategies are referred to as **other-selection**, meaning that someone other than the next speaker has allocated the upcoming turn to them. It is also common for interlocutors to **self-select** as the speaker of the next turn. This can happen in formal situations, such as a US congressional representative uttering "Madam Speaker, I ask for consent to address the House," and informal situations, like when you hear your friend nearing the end of a story they are telling, and you jump in to say "Oh! Something similar happened to me..."

Conversation analysts also observe sequencing in what interlocutors say. Across many different cultures, conversation analysts have observed sequences called **adjacency pairs** – this is a unit of conversation in which two speakers make one utterance each in an ordered fashion. Think about your typical greeting on an American college campus. If you see a friend walk by on their way to class, you might wave and say "Hey, Kim!" Kim, in turn, might reply "What's up?" as you both keep walking. Adjacency pairs, like greetings, have two parts – a first pair part and a second pair part. In this example, your first-pair part of a greeting has been met with another greeting from Kim. When our conversational partners complete adjacency pairs in the way that we expect, we call that a **preferred** response. Note here that "preferred" doesn't mean "the response we like the best" – it just means what the usual or typical conversational norms of that community expect to come next. In the example of greeting Kim, we can also easily imagine what a **dispreferred** response might be. Although Kim's second pair part of "What's up?" is formulated like a question, those familiar with the conversational conventions of American college students will know that in this context, no response to that question is required. Indeed, if you began to tell Kim in great detail what is up with you, she may be confused or annoyed, thinking, "I'm obviously trying to get to class here! Why is my friend telling me their whole life story and clearly flouting the maxims of quantity and manner?"[19] The difference between preferred and dispreferred responses can be seen in other types of adjacency pairs, too. When one speaker uses their turn to make a request, the preferred response is acceptance – for instance, when you call your parents to ask to be picked up from the airport (request), you expect them to say, "Of course, dear! We'll be there when the flight lands" (acceptance). You probably are less prepared to have the request you put forward in the first part of this adjacency pair rejected – but it might happen, if they say, for instance, "Sorry sweetheart, we are both working today." Hopefully they try to mitigate the dispreferred response by offering to send you money for a taxi.

Despite the underlying sequentiality of conversation, we sometimes make mistakes in our interactions. But even when conversation analysts examine "mistakes," they have been able to find evidence of order and patterns. The various strategies that conversational participants use to correct an error are referred to as **repair sequences**. Just like speaker selection, repair can be **self-initiated** as well as **other-initiated**. Self-initiated repair is, as you might expect, when the speaker corrects their own mistake. This happens often when we stumble over our words, mispronounce something, or make some sort of slip of the tongue. Often, we catch ourselves mid-mistake and correct it right away, like if you started to call your new colleague "Elizabeth," but halfway through remember they are called "Emily." Other times, we may get a bit further into our utterance before we initiate the self-repair, such as: "When Elizabeth sent me this report, she said – Oh, I'm sorry, I meant when *Emily* sent me the report."

When we are not able to catch our own mistakes, or do not realize we have made them, our interlocutors might initiate a repair sequence. This is called other-initiated repair. If someone has ever corrected a speech error, pronunciation mishap, or slip of the tongue that you have made, you have experienced other-initiated repair. Other-initiated repair sequences also offer us another place to look at preferred and dispreferred segments. If your

---

[19] If this is how Kim reacts to your dispreferred response to "What's up?," she is probably a linguistics major.

interlocutor initiates a repair of your speech – like when you get your new colleague's name wrong – the preferred response is most likely a combination of acknowledgment and correction. It might look something like this:

(8) a: "When Elizabeth sent me this report, she said –"
     b: "Elizabeth? Did you mean Emily?"
     a: "Oh, that's right! Sorry. When Emily sent me the report..."

Dispreferred responses in this case might look like ignoring the correction or getting rude. Either way, we can see a pattern here: first, a mistake is made, then, a repair is initiated (either by the speaker themselves or their interlocutor), and finally, a correction is uttered.

Conversation analysis is an incredibly useful set of tools for investigating the patterns and systematicity in everyday conversation. Here, we have reviewed just a few of the organizational principles underlying conversation. This is crucial to a linguist's work because it helps us to understand how our linguistic moves are organized in interactions with others – a context that is arguably fundamental to language as a system of communication. Language shapes interaction and communication in all areas of life – even beyond everyday talk. So, let's turn now to talk about discourse analysis, an approach that looks to even larger units of language.

2.5.2 Discourse Analysis

While conversation refers specifically to social interaction through language use, discourse is often taken to mean something slightly broader. In fact, some scholars distinguish between "discourse" with a small d, and "Discourse" with a capital letter D (Gee 2014). Lowercase-d discourse is usually used to refer to an umbrella term for all sorts of processes of language use, including both spoken/signed and written modalities, in terms of both production and reception. As you can see, it is a broader term than conversation, capturing both the kind of everyday conversation than conversation analysts typically study[20] as well as other forms of language use. Meanwhile, capital-D Discourse tends to refer to general ways of using language, as well as ways of "behaving, interacting, thinking, [and] valuing that are characteristic of specific discourse communities" (Kramsch & Widdowson 1998, p. 127). In many ways, discourse analysis can seem quite similar to conversation analysis and pragmatics. And there is indeed a good deal of overlap between these three areas of linguistic research, particularly in the way that discourse analysts collect data (often quite like conversation

---

[20] To be clear, Conversation analysts do not *only* study everyday conversation, but this kind of language use is the prototypical focus for that field.

analysts) and in the analytical tools they use (drawing from pragmatics as well as conversation analysis). The way that discourse analysis can focus simultaneously on lowercase-d "discourse" and capital-D "Discourse" is part of what makes this field unique – studying both at the same time helps us better understand the relationship between language use and social issues.

Take the notion of the "speaker," for instance, which was central in our overview of conversation analysis. The terms "speaker" and "hearer" are examples of what discourse analysts may call **participant roles** – the relationships that interlocutors have with respect to one another's behavior within a given speech event. "Speaker" and "hearer" both seem at face value to be relatively straightforward. The "speaker" is the one who talks, and the "hearer" is the one who listens. Scholars like Erving Goffman,[21] however, have shown that it is in fact *not* quite so simple. He distinguished between three different ways we can conceptualize the "source" of an utterance (Goffman 1981):

(9)   a. The **animator**: the person who physically produces the speech sounds and/or signs
        b. The **author**: the individual responsible for the content of the utterance produced by the animator
        c. The **principal**: the entity whose viewpoint or belief is being represented by the utterance

Now, of course, these three roles can overlap in the same interlocutor – this is usually the case in everyday conversation. But in political discourse, for example, the person delivering (i.e., animating) a speech may not have composed (i.e., authored) it, and it may be designed to represent the viewpoint of the entire political party (the principal!) rather than their own beliefs. This insight can help us understand both big-picture capital-D Discourses as well as lowercase-d discourse: a discourse analyst might note different rhetorical strategies at work when these production formats all overlap in the same speaker vs. when they diverge (lowercase-d discourse observation) as well as how the content of what a speaker says maintains, defies, or otherwise contributes to broader cultural expectations (capital-D Discourse observation).

Discourse analysts also consider how, through language use and interaction, speakers and hearers position themselves as social actors. This sort of positioning work is referred to as **stance-taking**. In some cases, it is obvious when a speaker is taking a stance about something: we can see it in straightforward statements such as "I like chocolate!" or "I did not enjoy that film." In other cases, stance can be trickier to investigate, as speakers and hearers can use many different aspects of language structure and

---

[21] Goffman is perhaps more properly considered a sociologist, but his ideas have been so influential in discourse analysis that we often claim him as one of our own.

conversational patterns to indicate their alignment with or against a topic, an idea, a comment, another speaker/hearer, and so on. If you move to a new region and start picking up the pronunciation and slang words of your new community, this may be taken as an indication of your positive stance toward this community. On the other hand, if community members want to demonstrate their lack of alignment with a newcomer, they may increase or even exaggerate the unique features of their dialect to mark themselves as different. Or, these linguistic choices could mean something completely different – context is always central to the work of a discourse analyst, and in both of these cases we would need to use information about the surrounding social structures and power dynamics of the community members and speakers in order to justify these claims.

As you read in a previous section, the meaning(s) of words and phrases comes in part from within the system of language itself, and in part from implicatures and entailments generated by the context in which phrases are uttered. But a discourse analyst is attuned to yet another level of meaning – **social meaning**, or the nonlinguistic associations and links that come to exist between certain linguistic forms and social or cultural categories. Take the word "y'all," for instance. Its semantic meaning is something akin to "second person plural pronoun" – that is the linguistic "meaning" for this word that is stored in the mental dictionary of a native speaker. But for American English speakers, it has another layer of meaning as well – it is culturally associated with speakers from Southern regions of the US. When an American English speaker hears someone use this word, they may assume that speaker is trying to signal their regional identity through their speech. Discourse analysts call this property **indexicality**. A linguistic feature, like the pronunciation of a vowel, a pronoun, or a slang term, is said to **index** a cultural category, social identity, or some other nonlinguistic meaning like a particular stance or style. "Y'all" indexes (among other things) Southern American identity and a casual, friendly speech style. Understanding how these social meanings emerge through language use is another way that discourse analysts link lowercase-d discourse with capital-D Discourse. This is what makes discourse analysis so important – it allows us to clearly see the link between individual linguistic features, conversational moves, or rhetorical strategies and fit them into a broader social context.

2.6 So What Is Linguistics?

Linguistics is a field of study in which researchers try to understand human language as it is – in our minds, in our cultures and societies, and in our daily lives. The linguist's toolkit includes methods and techniques that help us to better describe, understand, and explain our languages and our language behavior. We describe ourselves as *scientists of language* because we try to carefully observe language behavior, document the atoms, molecules, elements, and interactions of languages, and in doing so better understand how this system of communication is built and how people use it.

Linguistics is not the only discipline that brings scientific methods and principles to bear on the study of language, but we are one such discipline – our sister disciplines include anthropology, psychology, sociology, communication, speech and hearing sciences, and others. What distinguishes linguistics from those fields might be our value for studying all varieties and forms of language and languages while focusing our attention carefully on the smallest details of linguistic patterns and structures in as wide a variety of language communities as we can, in as broad a set of contexts as we're able to.

If you're ready to try being a linguist in your community, read on. Our next chapter outlines some of the key tools in our toolkit. Let's get to work!

Linguist in the Community

- Perceptual dialectology: While most linguists focus on what people actually say and how they use language in their everyday lives, the subfield of sociolinguistics called "perceptual dialectology" studies what we *think* about how other people talk. You can examine your own perceptions about language by printing out a few blank maps of your country and asking your friends, family, and neighbors to label it for you: Where do they speak the "best"? Where do they sound the "worst"? Is there a particular style of speaking associated with a given region – maybe a specific pronunciation or a special set of words? Is speech in one area considered more "rude," and in another more "polite"? As a linguist, you know that there is no one single "best" way of speaking, but how people perceive the varieties around them can reveal a great deal! As you look over the observations people have made about speech varieties in different regions, consider what elements of language they are noticing: Are they describing syntactic differences? Pragmatic differences?
- Test how language works in context: One strategy for uncovering how conversational maxims work in everyday life is to test them by violating them. See what happens in a conversation with a friend or family

member when you obviously flout a maxim – maybe you flout the maxim of quality by remarking on what a lovely day it is when it's raining outside. Or maybe you flout the maxim of quantity by responding simply "Food" when your roommate asks "What's for dinner?" Be careful not to be rude here – but observe the reactions of your interlocutors. If you can, follow up with them later in an informal interview. What assumptions, expectations, or inferences did they draw in these instances of maxim flouting? What can this tell us about language use in context?

Linguist in the Classroom

- Hypotheses and observations: This book covers the intersections between linguistics and issues related to society and culture. You can prime yourself for the other material in this book by starting to generate your own hypotheses about the relationship between language and social issues. Individually, or with your classmates, discuss what predictions you have about possible connections between language and social issues. (You can follow the model laid out in the first section of this chapter – aim for about three predictions.) Then, in small groups, examine your hypotheses. What evidence for or against these hypotheses might you and your classmates have observed in your everyday life? Save your predictions in a place that you can go back to – you can see whether any of your hypotheses were borne out in the rest of this book!
- Compare your dialect with someone else's: YouTube is a great repository of videos and recordings of different dialects. Now that you know the basic units of linguistic structure, you can compare your variety to others' speech in general terms. Head to YouTube and search for a video of a speaker of a dialect other than your own. (Search terms like "dialect challenge," or "English dialect of [region]" will give you great results.) Or, if someone in your family or household speaks a different dialect from you, ask them to speak to you for a few minutes. After listening to this dialect for several minutes, see if you can describe, in general, where you notice differences: Is your phonology different from theirs? Do they use different words to describe everyday items than you do? Or maybe the video describes different conversational norms. Try to explain, in broad terms, which area of linguistics would most likely study the difference you observed.

Glossary

acoustic phonetics A subtype of phonetics that primarily looks at the physical properties of soundwaves in speech.

adjacency pairs A unit of conversation in which two speakers make one utterance each in an ordered fashion.

agglutinative A type of language that uses multiple morphemes per word, where morphemes are easily separated from each other.

amplitude The loudness of a sound.

animator The person who physically produces the speech sounds and/or signs.

antonymy A relationship between words whose meanings are taken to be opposites of each other. "Big" and "small" in English are "antonyms" of one another.

articulatory phonetics A subtype of phonetics that primarily looks at how different parts of the vocal tract work together to produce speech.

author The individual responsible for the content of the utterance produced by the animator.

bald on-record utterance An utterance made with no effort to mitigate face threats.

bound (morpheme) A morphological unit that cannot stand alone as a word and must be attached to another morpheme, as its semantic meaning cannot stand alone.

case marker A morpheme that indicates a word's grammatical relationship to other words in an utterance.

compositional semantics The study of the meanings of phrases and sentences.

constituent order The arrangement of the subject, verb, and direct object within a typical sentence in a given language.

context The circumstances of a speech event, including who speaks, what is said, when it is uttered, where is it uttered, and why is it uttered.

contrast Any difference in pronunciation (spoken or signed) that can change the meaning of a word. Systems of contrast differ in different languages, and this is one reason why learning a second language can be so challenging.

conversation A communicative exchange involving at least one attempt to send information to an interlocutor, and one attempt to receive that information.

conversation analysis A linguistic field of study that focuses on the structure and patterns of everyday spoken interactions.

conversational floor Control over a given conversation, including topic, direction, and speakers.

conversational maxims The assumptions typically made about utterances that underlie the cooperative principle.

cooperative principle As articulated by H. P. Grice, the overall assumption that in interaction, people will work together to design contributions that are suited to conversational goals.

derivational (morpheme) A morpheme that changes the meaning of the main word, like the *un-* in *unhappy*.

direct speech act A pragmatic achievement in which the form of the utterance matches up with the intended effect.

discourse analysis A linguistic field of study that studies how the patterns and structures of language used in context shapes social interaction and reflects broader sociocultural values.

dispreferred (response) An unexpected or atypical response in an adjacency pair or other conversational turn.

electropalatography A tool that can be used to measure the placement of the tongue in relationship to the teeth and roof of the mouth, using an artificial hard palate with embedded electrodes.

entailment A relationship between statements such that if the first statement is true, the following statement(s) must also be true.

face An individual's public self-image or self-presentation.

face-threatening act (FTA) Linguistic acts that threaten positive or negative face needs of the speaker or hearer.

facework The interactional and conversational strategies used by speakers and listeners to construct and maintain the face of themselves and others.

felicity conditions Conditions of context that must be satisfied in order for a performative utterance to have the desired effect.

filter In a source-filter model, the portion that shapes soundwaves into something that sounds like language.

flout (a maxim) Failing to observe a conversational maxim in an obvious, purposeful way.

formant A concentration of sound energy around a particular frequency.

free (morpheme) A morphological unit that can stand alone as a word and carries semantic meaning independently.

frequency The number of cycles or vibrations a soundwave goes through in a set period of time. In linguistics, we measure this in hertz (Hz).

fronted A speech segment produced further forward in the mouth than we canonically expect: a fronted /ɛ/ sound like in US English /dɛk/ "deck" might sound more like /dɪk/, which is a process that happens in New Zealand English.

fusional A type of language that uses multiple morphemes per word, but distinctions between individual meaning components are difficult to find.

harmonics Individual simple periodic waves that can make up a more complex sound, like speech.

homophony A relationship between two words that are completely different in meaning but have the same pronunciation – for example, "you" and "ewe" in our American English dialects sound exactly alike, but they are not remotely related to each other.

hypernymy A relationship between words such that one counts as a super-category of the other, for example "fruit" is a hypernym of "apple" in English.

hyponymy A relationship between words such that one counts as a subcategory of the other, for example "apple" is a hyponym of "fruit."

implicature An indirect meaning generated by a speech act. *Conversational* implicatures arise when expectations about conversational maxims are broken; *conventional* implicatures are generated by the semantics of words like "however," "but," "yet," and so on.

index A conventionalized link between a particular linguistic form and a social category or feature that it "points to."

indexicality The property by which a particular linguistic form "points to" some social category or feature.

indirect speech act A pragmatic achievement in which the form of the utterance does not match up with the intended effect, leading to different kinds of inferences.

inflectional (morpheme) A morpheme that is necessary for the word given its position and role in a sentence, like the -ed in *walked*.

interruption Typically, when an instance of conversational overlap leads to one speaker taking control of the conversational floor.

intonation The variation in pitch while speaking, especially when this variation is not used to convey differences in meaning.

isolating A morphological system with a relatively low morpheme-to-word ratio.

language community A group of people who use a particular language.

lexical semantics The study of the meanings of words.

lexical variation Patterns of variation in words and morphemes.

linguistics The scientific study of language.

manner of articulation How airflow is restricted during oral speech.

maxim of manner The conversational expectation to be brief, clear, and unambiguous.

maxim of quality The conversational expectation to be as truthful as possible.

maxim of quantity The conversational expectation to give the correct amount of information.

maxim of relevance The conversational expectation to make one's utterances relate to ongoing conversation.

morpheme The smallest meaningful unit of language.

morphology The subfield of linguistics focusing on the structure of words.

negative face The general desire for one's public self-image to be free from imposition or responsibility to others.

negative politeness strategy Linguistic actions taken to avoid creating imposition on someone or implicating them in some responsibility.

Northern Cities Chain Shift A set of sound changes occurring in the English spoken around the Great Lakes region of the Northern/Northeastern United States.

obstruent A type of speech sound formed by obstructing or highly restricting airflow.

opt out (of a speech act) Not producing speech that could be evaluated within the framework of conversational maxims.

other-initiated (repair) When one party in a conversation corrects an error or issue in the speech of another.

other-selection When someone other than the next speaker has allocated the upcoming turn to them.

overlap When two or more speakers produce utterances at the same time.

participant roles The relationships that interlocutors have with respect to one another's behavior within a given speech event.

parts of speech Groups or types of words that play similar roles within the structure of a sentence.

performative A type of utterance in which the action mentioned in the utterance is accomplished by the saying of the utterance itself.

phonemic inventory The complete catalogue of segments that are contrastive in a language.

phonetics The study of the physical and biological properties of the production and perception of a language.

phonological rule Systematic ways of describing how a segment is treated with respect to other segments around it.

phonological word A prosodic unit that can be preceded and followed by a pause.

phonology The subfield of linguistics focusing on the patterning and mental representation of speech segments.

phonotactics Linguistic constraints that dictate which segments are allowed to appear next to each other within a given language.

pitch The perceived frequency of a sound.

place of articulation The place in the vocal tract where the airflow is restricted in the production of a speech segment.

positive face The general desire for one's public self-image to be accepted and liked.

positive politeness strategy Linguistic actions taken to preserve and to emphasize acceptance of and like of an interlocutor.

pragmatics The subfield of linguistics that studies the role of context in shaping meaning.

preferred (response) The expected or typical response within a conversational adjacency pair.

presupposition An implicit assumption or background information about the world contained in a linguistic choice (e.g., a word or phrase).

principal The entity whose viewpoint or belief is being represented by an utterance.

reference The truth-value of the meaning of a word, or the actual instantiation(s) of that meaning outside of the language user's mind.

repair sequences Strategies that conversational participants use to correct errors or clarify misunderstandings in their or their interlocutor's language use.

segment An individual unit of a language. In spoken languages, segments are the consonants and vowels, while in signed languages they are created using handshapes, positions, direction, orientation, and nonmanual elements.

self-initiated (repair) When a speaker corrects an error they made in their speech themselves.

self-selection When a conversational participant selects themselves as the next speaker.

semantics The subdiscipline of linguistics that focuses on understanding how meaning is created in language.

sense The mental representation of a word in the mind of a language user.

synonymy A relationship between words that seem to mean the same thing as each other, for example English "six" and "a half dozen."

sequence of speakers The order in which participants in a conversation make their contributions.

social meaning Nonlinguistic associations and links that come to exist between certain linguistic forms and social or cultural categories.

source In a source-filter model, the places where sounds are generated, such as at the glottis or some point along the length of the vocal tract.

speaker selection The norms, expectations, and processes by which the next speaker in a conversational event is chosen.

spectrogram A visual representation of sound that encodes information about frequency.

speech act An action that is accomplished in and through language.

stance-taking Social and cultural positioning accomplished through linguistic strategies.

syntax The subfield of linguistics focusing on the structure of sentences.

synthetic (language) A morphological system with a higher morpheme to word ratio.

tone The use of pitch in a language to distinguish or inflect words.

turn-taking The back and forth alternation between two or more speakers during a conversational event.

un- or under-documented language A language that has not been described or recorded in a way that might allow scholars or future generations of speakers to know much about it if they did not have access to fluent or first-language speakers or signers. A *well-documented* language might be documented in things like dictionaries and grammar descriptions, audio and video examples, and the like.

utterance Any communicative turn that uses some bit of language, spoken or signed.

violate (a maxim) Failing to observe a conversational maxim with the expectation that our interlocutors do not notice us doing so.

vocal folds Two pieces of tissue, formed of muscle, ligaments, and mucus membranes, that are attached at the front and back of your larynx (or voicebox) and vibrate against each other to convert the air from your lungs to sound.

vocal tract The physiological space in human bodies where sounds are produced and filtered.

vowel A type of speech segment formed by leaving airflow relatively unrestricted.

waveform A visual representation of a sound that encodes information about amplitude.

Recommended Readings

If the material in this chapter struck your fancy, you might want to do a little more reading on the topics we've presented. As always, you'll find complete reference citations for all the material we've used at the end of this book, but if you'd like to get an idea of the works we would probably send you to first if you should ask us for more information on the basics of linguistics, here's a mini-list of references that we think you might especially benefit from. All of these works ought to be available to you without cost through any good scholarly library. If you don't have access to one already, you could ask any local college or university about community access.

Austin, J. L. (1975). *How to Do Things with Words* (Vol. 88). Oxford University Press.
Brentari, D. (2019). *Sign Language Phonology*. Cambridge University Press.
Conrod, K. (2020). Pronouns and gender in language. In K. Hall & R. Barrett (Eds.), *The Oxford Handbook of Language and Sexuality* (online ed.). Oxford University Press. https://doi.org/10.1093/oxfordhb/9780190212926.013.63
de Waal, F. (2016). *Are We Smart Enough to Know How Smart Animals Are?* WW Norton and Company.
Green, L. J. (2002). *African American English: A Linguistic Introduction*. Cambridge University Press.
Grice, H. P. (1975). Logic and conversation. In P. Cole & J. L. Morgan (Eds.), *Speech Acts* (pp. 41–58). Brill.
Hockett, C. F. (1960). The origin of speech. *Scientific American, 203*(3), 88–96. https://doi.org/10/ftqv2r

McCarthy, C. (2011). The northern cities shift in Chicago. *Journal of English Linguistics, 39*(2), 166–187. https://doi.org/10/bffxdz

Pepperberg, I. M. (2017). Animal language studies: What happened? *Psychonomic Bulletin & Review, 24*(1), 181–185. https://doi.org/10.3758/s13423-016-1101-y

Savage-Rumbaugh, E. S. (1986). *Ape Language: From Conditioned Response to Symbol*. Columbia University Press.

3 We Have a Starter Kit for You

This chapter lays out the tools in your "starter kit" for observing language and social issues. In the following sections, we will explain some of the tools that linguists use to collect data about language, and then we will explain some of the strategies that linguists use to analyze the data they have collected. Really understanding language in your community requires careful observation, faithful reporting, and systematic analysis. We humans are very quick to perceive things as we expect them to be, rather than as they are – and the tools in this chapter will help you to gather your observations, and analyze any patterns you find there, in a way that helps you guard against the biases we all have. You will very likely be surprised at what you find when you use them!

Please be sure to consult and abide by the ethical obligations of the researcher, as we outline in Chapter 4, and as is required in your own community, as you make your observations. While your casual impressions are very valuable in identifying the kinds of questions you'll want to investigate, once you move into actual research it's very important to take this process seriously and to be careful that you are not causing harm by your work.

3.1 Tools for Making Observations

Linguists begin their work by systematically collecting data. Linguistic data can be collected almost any time or place humans are using language – so the possibilities are nearly limitless! Depending on the sort of linguistic form or pattern one wants to investigate, different tools for systematically making observations will be appropriate. Some of these tools allow you to use your language microscope (as we described in Chapter 1) to focus on tiny details of language. Others ask you to use your language telescope to see how a piece of language fits within a larger system. In this section, we outline a few of the most common tools that linguists use for this purpose. Keep in mind that some linguistic studies might use more than one of these tools at a time, and also that there are many more tools for making observations than just these! The ones we will describe to you here are, in our opinion, some of the most useful for making observations about the relationship between language and social issues.

3.2 Elicitation and Grammaticality Judgments

Linguists often use the term "**elicitation**" to refer to a structured process of question-asking. This kind of question-asking usually involves finding out how another person uses their language, rather than just observing their language behavior or asking them to reflect on it. Some kinds of elicitation are meant to discover segments and words and others to investigate phrases, sentences, or even some aspects of conversation (that is, elicitation can be used as a tool for studying most of the aspects of language described in Chapter 2).

Elicitation of segments, words, and basic phrases is one way a linguist might approach early study of an unfamiliar language. To begin identifying words, the linguist might prepare a set of concepts to ask about, using a frame like "How would you say X in your language?". The concepts might be planned by the linguist based on some set of topics they want to learn about, or they might be based on a more or less standardized set of "core vocabulary" concepts that are found in most human languages. Core vocabulary elicitation is often done by means of an instrument called the **Swadesh List**. The Swadesh List is a set of conceptual items that are argued to exist in every human language, independent of culture. It includes certain personal pronouns (I, you, we), some demonstratives (this, that), as well as common nouns (dog, mouth, sun), verbs (walk, give, say), and adjectives (hot, cold). By using a set of common concepts to compare across languages, linguists can understand how different languages are related or may have changed over time. These sorts of concepts are fairly small components of language, but they aren't the tiniest possible building blocks – so we might think of elicitations and grammaticality judgments as a magnifying-glass level of zoom into specific linguistic details.

At the microscopic level, the linguist might look at the words they've elicited and see whether they are finding patterns of segments within the words – in terms of segment inventories, rhythmic patterns or the like. Imagine, for example, you were eliciting words from a spoken language, and you found that there were two words: *taba*, meaning "hand," and *taaba*, with that first *a* sound really lengthened, meaning "dog." You might take note that the language you're investigating seems to have a contrast between a short *a* and a lengthened *a*, and this might be something you'll want to

3.2 Elicitation and Grammaticality Judgments

keep track of going forward. Even in a familiar language, if you begin with elicitation of individual words that are, perhaps, unique to a group's distinct way of using language, you might find segmental or rhythmic patterns that you'll want to pay attention to and describe. For example, in eliciting words for traditional treats from a friend whose linguistic heritage is Vietnamese, you might find words like *phở* that have been borrowed into English in a way that messes with the segments, rhythms or melodies.

We may also use elicitation to discover different kinds of grammatical patterns that we think the person might have in their language – perhaps a language that we also speak. In these cases, the linguist might prepare examples of the pattern and ask the person whether they find those examples **grammatical** or **acceptable**. In this case, we're using a task called a "grammaticality judgment." It is absolutely key for you to understand that, in linguistics, calling something "grammatical" means simply that the utterance could be made and understood by a native speaker of that language. It doesn't necessarily have anything to do with people's perceptions of "correctness" or "properness" of language use, like whether or not you should end your sentence with a preposition or split an infinitive. If native speakers can and do say it (regardless of whether it is considered "correct," or "proper"), it can be deemed grammatical in a linguistic sense.

For example, we might be interested in whether or not you can use a grammatical pattern called "double modals." In some varieties of US English, a person can use more than one modal verb (elements like "might," "may," "could," "can," etc.) in a single sentence (Coats 2024). A linguist interested in double-modal varieties could prepare a list of sentences like in (1a–d):

(1a)   I might go to the market today.

(1b)   I could go to the market today.

(1c)   I might could go to the market today.

(1d)   I could might go to the market today.

Then the linguist would say these sentences one at a time, with the respondent saying whether or not the sentence sounded OK. In that elicitation session, the responses might pattern as in (2a–d), where ✓ indicates that the speaker things the sentence sounds right, but * indicates that the sentence isn't acceptable:

(2a)   ✓ I might go to the market today.

(2b)   ✓ I could go to the market today.

(2c)   ✓ I might could go to the market today.

(2d)   * I could might go to the market today.

The linguist can then ask follow-up questions about when the speaker might use the sentence in (2c) and provide the speaker with different scenarios and ask how they would say things to fit those different scenarios. For example, if (2c) is acceptable, we could ask whether they would use it if they were 100 percent certain of their plans, or if they would use a different form in that case. The linguist may be successful in generating other example sentences that we hadn't thought of but that shed light on when and why the double-modal construction is used by our speaker.

3.3 Interviews, Reading Passages, and Word Lists

Elicitation and grammaticality judgments are useful tools for answering some kinds of questions about how people use language. But they have significant limitations, too. They shine a light on the particular linguistic features that the researcher is interested in, thus drawing a speaker's attention to that feature in a way that might affect the speaker's behavior. Labov (1981, p. 30) notes a set of problems that have already, perhaps, come to your attention as you consider those methods. Researchers studying language change and variation in a community are faced with "the *observer's paradox*: Our aim is to observe how speakers talk when they are not being observed" (emphasis in the original).

We of course must not ever surreptitiously or sneakily record for study the language behavior of others in our community even though it may seem that this would be the easiest way out of the observer's paradox. Instead, we rely on systematic strategies that reduce or control the effects of observation on language behavior while maintaining respect for other people's right to decline to be studied.[1]

A particular set of strategies that have come to be called the **sociolinguistic interview** (Labov 1966) and that help to control for the effects of the observer's paradox might be useful. A linguist in the community could draw from some or all of these components – depending on how important it is to their research question that they are collecting "natural" or unselfconscious language examples.[2] The full sociolinguistic interview, as it has been used by Labov and scholars that follow in this tradition in the US, consists of five parts, or modules, often conducted in the order listed in Table 3.1. Note that this system is developed and used in a community to explore *variation* and *change* in language behavior for a language that is both spoken and written,

---

[1] See our discussion of the ethical conduct of research in Chapter 4.
[2] There's nothing "unnatural" about being self-conscious, of course. Linguists are interested in all the ways we use language, including those that indicate awkwardness.

Table 3.1 The sociolinguistic interview

Module	Method	Level of self-awareness about language
Personal narrative	Request a personal story about a situation about which the participant may have a strong emotional investment	Lowest
Interview	Ask structured interview questions that engage the participant in a conversation	Low
Reading	Provide a paragraph that the participant can read aloud	Medium
Word list	Use fill-in-the-blank style or a written list to elicit words with the linguistic features of interest	High
Minimal pairs	Ask the speaker to produce word pairs that are very similar to each other, but only vary in one feature of interest	Highest

among participants who are literate. We think that a researcher could relatively readily adapt these modules for other modalities and language situations, however.

The principle behind these different modules is that the closer attention the speaker must pay to the words they are uttering, the more likely they are to be actively aware of *how* they are uttering those words. For instance, in the minimal pair and word list modules, speakers are deeply focused on specific, individual words. This means that they will most likely be taking extra care to pronounce them "as written," and this in turn means that linguists can microscopically analyze individual sounds that might be of interest. In the personal narrative module, however, the speaker is talking extemporaneously about a topic they have an emotional investment in – here, they are likely to be less focused on how they pronounce each and every little word, so linguists often expect to see more variability in this kind of speech.

Some of these methods may make more sense to you than others, and we haven't provided you here with enough information to really build out a plan for any particular piece of the sociolinguistic interview. A great approach, should you be interested in using this technique, would be to find a scholarly article that reports a study that uses it – such as Alicia Wassink's study of Seattle English, which uses word lists and reading passages (Wassink 2015), or Norma Mendoza-Denton's work with Latina youth in California, which relies on extensive sociolinguistic interviews (Mendoza-Denton 2008). Then, modify the specifics (the topic of the personal story, interview questions, reading selection, etc.) to elicit the language pattern you want to study. The specific linguistic feature you seek to investigate may also shape your choice of recording equipment. **Sociophoneticians** – linguists who study the relationship between phonetics and social patterns – often use high-quality audio recorders in order to capture the fine-grained detail needed to conduct phonetic analysis on sounds. Sociolinguists focusing on words or sentence structures may not need such high-powered recording devices and often rely on the built-in recording app on their phones or computers. You might look into the work of scholars such as Fridland and Kendall (2022), Villarreal et al. (2020), Farringon et al. (2021), or Coto-Solano (2022) as examples. In short, the tools you use to collect linguistic data should suit the type of research you are doing. You'll be able to see more examples of this approach to data collection – as well as the others we'll cover in this chapter – throughout the book, so don't worry if you don't fully grasp these nuances just yet, or if your instructor hasn't yet covered these topics. With that in mind, let's continue.

3.4 Corpora and Collections

In the age of the internet and social media, there is a tremendous amount of language behavior that is available for analysis online, and there are a wide variety of techniques we might use to access it. A **corpus** is a bunch of data, groups of examples, or sets of data points, all collected together and organized in a way that allows researchers to use it to answer questions, and there are lots of corpora that a linguist in the community can access in order to learn more about how we are using language.

Corpora[3] used by linguists can contain lots of examples of text, and/or lots of examples of audio or video resources, that a researcher can search through, analyze quantitatively, or describe qualitatively. We'd encourage you to take a look at some of the freely available language corpora that you have access to – if you are reading this book as part of a class, your institution's library will be able to help, and you can also find these corpora by running an internet search on the terms "linguistics research corpus." We will mention a couple of important US English corpora here, which are freely available at least within North America[4] and the UK.

---

[3] It's OK if you want to use the regular plural form "corpuses." We use "corpora" here because it seems fancier. Both plural forms are perfectly fine!

[4] We currently find COCA at this URL: www.english-corpora.org/, a resource created and maintained by Mark Davies. This resource provides a central location and consistent interface for web users. Users who want to download corpora or conduct many searches are asked to create a free account on the site, and there are appeals to donate to site maintenance. But the materials there are genuinely open and free for use.

The Corpus of Contemporary American English (Davies 2008–), or COCA, is a text-based corpus of US English, containing more than a billion words collected beginning in 1990 and drawn from a variety of books, magazines, newspapers, academic texts, web pages, subtitle tracks, and spoken sources. Linguists can use COCA to look for different words and ways of speaking, see how often they appear, and find out more about where and when different variations might have occurred.

COCA is an example of a traditional linguistic corpus in three ways: First, the words in the corpus have each been labeled (by an automatic labeling system, or **parser**) for their part of speech (i.e., noun, verb, adjective, etc.), and second, it provides a display called a **concordance**. When you search COCA, you'll get a concordance view that shows examples of the search term with some number of words preceding and following the search term. The third way in which COCA is an example of a traditional linguistic corpus is that it is a collection of material that is biased toward and focused on written genres of language, and it is presented in text only.

A simpler view of a very big corpus is provided by the Google Ngram Viewer[5] (Michel et al. 2011). In this case, Google extracted text from those millions of books you find in Google Books and created a fast, flexible, and easy search tool that can be used to do some basic linguistic analysis. We'll discuss this one, with examples, in the corpus analysis section below.

While traditional corpora like COCA aim to be big, not all corpora need to have billions of words, and they also don't have to be text-based. Research that looks at the public speech of a political figure (e.g., Holliday et al. 2020) or the tweets of a single celebrity (e.g., Valentinsson 2018) is likely based on a smaller corpus of language data coming from just that one source. Corpora built for signed language communities such as the Philly Signs project (https://pennds.org/phillysigns) are much more video rich and are likely to be relatively small in size, but big in scholarly promise. Corpora that focus on particular spoken varieties like the University of Oregon's Corpus of Regional African American Language (CORAAL, https://oraal.uoregon.edu/coraal) are also likely to include more multimedia material and provide important resources for scholars. These smaller corpora are no less valuable than the big ones – it all depends on what sort of question the researcher is asking about language use and social issues.

In fields like **conversation analysis**, these groupings of linguistic examples are often referred to as **collections**. Rather than pulling together big sets of data that researchers can then search through for particular words

---

[5] The Ngram Viewer is provided as a Google tool at this URL: https://books.google.com/ngrams.

or features, collections of the conversation analytic sort tend to be more narrowly focused on the specific feature the linguist wants to study. In a sense, they are a bit like corpora-within-corpora. A team of researchers using conversational analysis might, for instance, have a big corpus of phone calls made to a tech support hotline. This corpus would include speech from many different callers and technicians, talking about lots of different topics within the realm of "tech support." But if the research team is specifically interested in how greeting and closing sequences are done on these hotlines, they would compile every single instance of an opening or closing sequence in the entire corpus. This collection would then serve as the basis of their analysis. Depending on whether you use a multimillion-word corpora to study patterns in specific words or a collection of recordings of conversations in order to explore turn-taking routines, you can adjust your level of "zoom" into different details of language as your analysis requires.

3.5 Participant Observation

Sometimes, linguists are interested in questions about language that go beyond whether a speaker varies in their pronunciation of a certain word, or whether a certain syntactic strategy is acceptable in their dialect. They might instead be interested in how language is used in everyday life – the types of greetings we use with people of different social standings, how certain rhetorical strategies are used by politicians, or the way advertisers frame their products using language. While in some cases it may be possible to study these elements of language by building a corpus or a collection of such cases, linguists and other scholars of language also know that sometimes you need to really see what's going on out in the real world. Although these methods do require you to get into the fine-grained details of everyday life (consistent with a "zoomed in" approach), the goal is to see language use as part of a broader social system – so these sorts of tools work like telescopes to see a big, complex system as it works altogether.

Participant observation is a research method developed by anthropologists starting in the late nineteenth century (Dewalt et al. 1998). At its core, this method involves "hanging out and doing stuff" with one's research participants. Do not be fooled by the simplicity of this statement – good quality participant observation can involve years of living in the field with your research participants and putting aside everything you take to be obvious, natural, or common sense to do as they do day in and day out. The ultimate goal of participant observation is to understand the habits, beliefs, and behaviors of a group (such as linguistic practices!) within the context of that group and on their terms. This is why extensive **fieldwork** – living with and amongst your research participants – often goes hand in hand with participant observation. When conducting participant observation, scholars often make sure to write detailed **fieldnotes** each and every day. These fieldnotes serve as a record of everything they noticed, felt, thought, and saw. Through these observations, researchers start to notice the unstated cultural beliefs that underlie patterns of language use. For instance, research on dialectal variation in Mandarin Chinese had long established **rhotacization** as a regional marker of the Mandarin spoken in Beijing. Zhang's (2008) study – involving years of fieldwork and participant observation amongst business workers in Beijing – illustrated that there were cultural assumptions attached to this variable that went far beyond a simple regional marker. Residents of Beijing varied in their use of rhotacization based on whether they were male or female, whether they were employed at state-run businesses or global enterprises, and how they oriented to the idea of upward class mobility. These sorts of findings would simply not have been possible by only recording a word list elicitation from various Beijing residents – it required an in-depth understanding of the cultural context of this linguistic pattern. This is what participant observation allows us to uncover.

3.6 Tools for Analyzing Your Observations

Once you have made your observations, you will need to process them to facilitate the kind of systematic analysis that is required of us, and to share your analysis and your findings with others. In this section, we focus on ways to convert language observations for analysis and presentation in writing – for example, in a class research paper or a contribution to the scholarly literature. Depending on these and other considerations, it might be appropriate to find an analytical tool that works more like a microscope and allows you to really zoom in on language, or you might be better served by tools that zoom out and let you see the broader picture. If you are working in multimedia, you will certainly have a richer set of tools you can employ, but we think these will also give you an excellent basis for the development of your observations for presentation in media beyond writing.

3.6.1 Phonetic Transcription Systems

Phonetic transcription is a tool that is best used when you are in microscope mode as a linguist. That is, if your data are small units – sounds, words, phrases, sentences, individual utterances – and your goal is to microscopically analyze the details of language, you might find phonetic transcription to be useful. Learning phonetic transcription can be challenging, but it's also fun. And once you have this skill, you can use it in a wide variety of contexts.

3.6.1.1 For Spoken Languages

> **You'll need:** audio or video recordings of language, and a way to write non-Latin alphabetic characters. In the olden days, you might have transcribed by hand, but it's now likely that you're transcribing on a computer – and for that you will need access to tools that allow you to easily access and embed special characters in your writing. We recommend the tools that are maintained by the International Phonetic Association, but you will undoubtedly find lots of great technology by searching for "IPA Font," "IPA Keyboard" and/or "Interactive IPA Chart."

As language researchers, we're often in a situation where we need to represent the details of spoken or signed language in writing. But writing is a funny thing in that the kind of writing we are familiar with is almost never an accurate representation of the actual sounds or gestures used in language. Before you get particularly outraged with the weirdnesses of English spelling,[6] please rest assured that even more regular spelling systems like the ones used for Spanish just aren't careful enough to capture the details a linguist needs to pay attention to.

Here's an important example from spoken English. When we pronounce the word "ask," our pronunciation can differ to show something about our social identity. There are several variants, but let's consider the variants in (3):

(3)   "ask" [æsk] or [æks]

Just to be clear, we will use double quotes like this, "ask," when we are using the spelled English word. We will use square brackets like this, [æsk], when we're using a writing system whose intent is to accurately represent the actual sounds the speaker said. You may also see slashes, like this, /æsk/, when linguists are representing the underlying pronunciation of sounds. Both slashes and brackets can be used when doing phonetic transcription. In this book, we will use a specific phonetic transcription system called the International Phonetic Alphabet,[7] abbreviated IPA.

---

[6] ... for example, how the "ough" in *dough*, *rough*, *cough*, and *through* are all pronounced completely differently.

[7] We specifically use the International Phonetic Alphabet that is managed by the International Phonetic Association (www.internationalphoneticassociation.org/). You may find many variations on this system in your work; although the IPA aspires to be an international

Instead, what we see in (3) is a change in the order of the consonant sounds in "ask." Some speakers say the sequence [sk], but others say it [ks]. Linguists have a name for processes in variant pronunciations of a word that differ only in the order of sounds: metathesis. English-speaking children sometimes show metathesis in their pronunciations of "spaghetti" as "pasgetti." Metathesis is a natural, normal kind of language variation.

In the practical writing system of English, both pronunciations in (3) would map to the same spelled word, "ask." When (nonlinguist) writers want to indicate the difference between the two pronunciations in (3), they often use an informal system of "nonstandard" spelling, as in (4):

(4)   "ask" vs. "ax"

This works fine for getting the point across to a reader about how the pronunciations sound. But it causes us to miss a really important property of the variability – that the two pronunciations are really just two different orders of the "k" and "s" sound: they are a metathetic pair. Representations like (4) will – intentionally or not – make it seem like the "ax" speakers are pronouncing the word in a way that's more different from the "ask" speakers than it really is. That can be bad news for speakers of less prestigious variants because it can fuel people's (incorrect) stereotypes that such speakers are "lazy" or "wrong" in their pronunciation.

Of course there's nothing "wrong" or "lazy" about either ordering, and both have been available pronunciations for this word since at least the Middle English period (that's the era usually exemplified by Chaucer, about AD 1100–1600 or so, per the Oxford English Dictionary (Oxford University Press 2021).

So far, we have seen that we need phonetic transcription so that we can accurately reflect the systematicity in spoken language pronunciation. Next, we will see that we need it in order to accurately reflect the sounds themselves. We will stick with "ask," but now we will focus on the vowel that we have transcribed: [æ].

It turns out that English speakers say that vowel in a bunch of different ways depending on their regional dialect, social and cultural identification, and the like. A team of linguists at the University of Pennsylvania (Labov et al. 2006) focus much of their research on regional variation in White English[8] on just this vowel.

---

standard, it turns out that when humans use writing systems, we tend to use them in variable ways.
[8] This is an atlas of regional varieties of North American English in which Black and Latinx speakers were eliminated systematically from the participant pool – a fact that is discussed explicitly in the book's methods chapter. Participants were selected based on living in the

See if you can find a variety of **tokens** of "ask" from friends, family, celebrities, etc., and see if you can hear any differences in that vowel. You might hear some or all of these (you can use the site www.international phoneticassociation.org/ or any interactive IPA chart – honestly, just google "Interactive IPA Chart" and you'll find a lot of them) to hear and/or see the pronunciations of these vowels:

(5)   "ask"
         a.   [æsk],
         b.   [ask],
         c.   [ɑsk],
         d.   [ɛsk],
         e.   [ɛəsk][9]

This is not an exhaustive list, and if you're like us, you might not even be able to hear clearly the differences between each of these different vowel sounds, but we can likely tell the difference between the [æ] ("cat," "tap"), [ɑ] ("father," "top"), and [ɛ] ("bed," "step"). According to Labov et al. (2006), we're likely to hear pronunciations (d) and (e) from blue collar white speakers in the northern cities of the US and pronunciations (a) and (b) elsewhere in North America. We might hear pronunciation (c) in (potentially inaccurate or fake) "British" accents, or, delightfully, among younger speakers from the US West Coast (particularly California).

We might even observe speakers changing the vowel depending on who they're speaking to, where they are, or what they're talking about. These changes may be systematic – and if they are, we want to be able to accurately report them.

Did you observe the different pronunciations of "ask"? Did you find any variability? What do you think that variability means? Consider also that in example (5), we used the [sk] variant of "ask." We think that pronunciations (5a–e) can all be found in that word. Does the [ks] variant also come with all the different vowels listed in (5a–e)? How would you be able to find out? These are the beginning steps that linguists take to analyzing data that is phonetically transcribed.

How to Learn the International Phonetic Alphabet Learning the IPA well is a lifelong process, but getting started with it is not hard. Do not be afraid to

---

     same location for a long time (having many people in an area with the same last name meant inclusion) and based on being white.

[9]   [ɛə] is a diphthong, one vowel that shifts its quality as you pronounce it. This pronunciation is most likely to be found in the US among blue-collar white people in the cities of the inland north (Chicago is a prime example).

explore, make mistakes, share your ideas with others, and take pride in your progress!

The IPA is a Latin-alphabet-derived system developed by (mostly European and North American) linguists, and like all writing systems it is a dynamic social contract among users. That means that it can grow and change, and inevitably individuals will vary in how they use it.

The International Phonetic Alphabet is governed by the International Phonetic Association (www.internationalphoneticassociation.org), who maintain the alphabet as part of their work documenting and understanding the sounds of spoken languages. As a student, you can join the IPA if you would like – and you can utilize the resources provided by the IPA to take a deeper dive into this system, whether or not you join!

If you're taking an introductory linguistics class (and there are both credit and open online classes you can take to do this), chances are you'll learn some or all of the IPA. So, that's one strategy you might use to learn how to use it. But if you're not, or if you just want to self-study, there are two strategies that you can use to learn the IPA on your own. As you do this, please remind yourself often of these two caveats:

Caveat 1: Because the goal of the IPA is to transcribe spoken language, and because there is a lot of variability in how any individual, let alone any group of individuals, pronounces things, there is always going to be more than one "correct" transcription of a word.

Caveat 2: The IPA is just a language related technology. It does not capture all of the important aspects of the sounds of spoken language (for example, it does not capture intonation, or relative duration of sounds, or many other factors), so it is imperfect. And it is a human invention, so different humans use it in different ways.

Strategy 1: [fajnd pæsədʒəz əv fəmɪljeɹ tɛksts ðæt aɹ ɹɪʔn ɪn ði ajpijej ænd pɹæktəs ɹidɪŋ ðɛm]. Find passages of familiar text that are written in the IPA, and practice reading them. We have transcribed several in (6–10) for you to get started with.

(6) [ɑl fəɹ wən ænd wən fəɹ ɑl]

(7) [hɛlow maj nem ɪz inigow mɑntojə ju kɪld mai fɑðɹ pɹɛpeɹ tu daj]

(8) [tajm muvz sloʊli bʊt pæsɪz kwɪkli]

(9) [ɪt wəz ðə bɛst əv tajmz ɪt wəz ðə wəɹst əv tajmz]

(10) [ju kən tun ə pijænoʊ bət ju kænt tun ə fɪʃ]

Strategy 2: Find a dictionary that uses IPA as its guide to pronunciation. Make yourself a list of words to transcribe, and use your interactive IPA charts and best guesses to try to transcribe them. Then use the dictionary to give yourself feedback on your work.

At the time of writing, we know of at least two dictionaries of English that use this system: the Oxford English Dictionary and the web-based dictionary aggregator Dictionary.com. The latter uses a non-IPA "sound-spelling" system by default, but offers a "show IPA" button that you can use to test yourself.

But remember, the dictionary pronunciations are not the only possible correct pronunciations of words – dictionaries select representative pronunciations (from North American and/or British English) to use. The representative pronunciations are typically taken from **prestige varieties** (that is, varieties associated with economic and political power). For North America, the typical choice would be a pronunciation associated with older, middle- or upper-class white people who don't have linguistic features that would be interpreted by a listener as strongly regional. For the UK, the typical choice might be a pronunciation that is generically codified as "received pronunciation" or RP. This means that if your transcription deviates from the dictionary's, you're not necessarily wrong!

3.6.1.2 For Signed Languages

> **You'll need:** video recordings or photographs of language, and a way to create, manage and embed image and/or media files into the resource you're creating. We recommend working with any video or image editing software you're comfortable with (there are open access resources as well as software packages that your school may have licensed for use by students).

There is not yet a single, standard method used by linguists to transcribe signed languages such as ASL. There are many available systems, and it may be the case that in time one will emerge as more useful than others. There is also not a single, standard method used by speakers to read and write any signed language (at least, not that we're aware of). That is, signed languages are so far exclusively signed, not written. The Deaf community in the US, at least, has been engaged in discussion about whether or not it's even a good idea to try to write ASL, and in this way ASL is similar to most languages on earth. Writing is a minority technology – it's an innovation that is used by only a minority of languages and language speakers – and its introduction involves both advantages and disadvantages, communities' choices about writing vary, and the choice to not write is a reasonable one in many cases.

3.6 Tools for Analyzing Your Observations 77

Figure 3.1 ASL words for "interpreter," "bring-in," "take-to," and "hospital."

As a linguist in the community, though, we should be aware of, and interested in, signed as well as spoken languages around us. Scholars of signed languages often utilize embedded media (photos, videos, or gifs) as a way of presenting language examples. Figure 3.1 is from Lepic (2019):

In Figure 3.1, the author is presenting images of the signer rather than trying to "transcribe" the signs. Scholars interested in pronunciation in signed languages have developed various tools and proposals for transcribing signed languages (for example, Johnson & Liddell 2011), but to our knowledge none of these has yet solidified into a standard transcription system. The fact that images and video materials are relatively easy to include in electronic publications may be a factor that reduces the perceived need for transcriptions of signed languages in scholarly work.

While the means in which the smallest units of spoken and signed languages are represented in writing will differ, other aspects of presenting linguistic examples are very similar, as we'll see in the next section.

3.7 Multi-line Glossing Systems

> **You'll need:** transcribed and analyzed examples of words, phrases, sentences, and/or larger texts in a language that your reader might be unfamiliar with. You'll need to know at least the pronunciation of your examples, the word-internal structures of your examples (i.e., their morphology), and their translation into English or whatever language you are using to present your work to a reader. You'll likely need a way to type special phonetic characters (see Section 3.6.1.1 for IPA transcription), and you'll need patience and the willingness to find the best ways in your word processing system to do things like vertically align elements and perhaps automatically number examples.

Multi-line glossing is a tool that is probably best used by linguists in magnifying glass mode and when describing a language or linguistic variety that is likely to be unfamiliar to your readers. If the bits of language you're studying are at least one word at a time, and not too much longer than a few conversational turns or a short narrative, you might find a technique like this to be useful.

Let's look at Examples (11a–b), again from Lepic (2019). You'll see that for both utterances presented, there are three lines of material. The top line in this case is the video record of the articulation of the utterance, which is in American Sign Language. Below that, in all capital letters, is a sign-by-sign translation of the original utterance into written English words. Here the reader can tell that the signer has produced three distinct signs. In (11a), the first means "OK," the second means "interpreter," and the third means "bring-in." And below that, in double quotes, is a written English translation of the whole utterance:

(11) a. Source: https://youtu.be/uXdL5njDiBU?t = 1m48s
        OK, INTERPRETER BRING-IN
        "they agreed to get an interpreter"
      b. Source: https://youtu.be/PhVxvTsIsrw?t = 8m29s
        ASK, LAST NIGHT INTERPRETER WHICH AGENCY BRING-IN
        "I asked them, 'which agency assigned you the interpreter from last night?'"

Multi-line glossing systems like this one display different kinds of linguistic information in different lines of text and use vertical alignment between the lines to indicate to a reader which element in one line corresponds to the elements in other lines. It's as if we're "stacking" information for the reader in order to make it clear how the language of interest works.

Let's look at how this might work for a spoken language, using Examples (12) and (13), which we've drawn from our own study of the Tohono O'odham language.[10]

(12) go-gogs ʔo   g   ban   ha-huhuʔid
      pl-dog   is/was a/the coyote 3pl-chasing
      "A/the coyote is chasing some/the dogs"

(13) gogs ʔo   g   baː-ban   ha-huhuʔid
      dog   is/was a/the pl-coyote 3pl-chasing
      "A/the dog is/was chasing some/the coyotes"

Note that in these examples, we use the abbreviation "pl" for "plural," and "3" for "third person."

In these examples, the top line shows how we would transcribe each sentence phonetically, using the International Phonetic Alphabet. If you don't yet know that system, don't worry – we've chosen examples where you'll get almost the right pronunciation just by reading the first line as though you were reading spelled English – the only special bit of information to know is that the symbol "ʔ" stands for a sound called a "glottal stop." That's the sound that English speakers use to separate the syllables in "uh oh!"

The hyphens in this top line show where the words can be broken down into separate meaningful pieces (or *morphemes*). For example, the first word in (10) is pronounced [gogogs]. The first [go-] in that word is a prefix,[11] and it makes the word plural. The [gogs] is the root word and it means "dog."

You can identify the meanings of each of these elements just by looking at the second line. Directly underneath each meaningful element is a short translation or abbreviation that tells the reader what that element means, or what it does. This is how you can learn that in both (12) and (13), the word [ʔo] in Tohono O'odham can be translated as either "is" or "was." The word [g] can be translated as either "a" or "the." The word [ban] means "coyote," and the word [hahuhuʔid] has two meaningful pieces: a prefix [ha-] that means "third person plural," and a root [huhuʔid] that means "chasing." Note that we haven't indicated in our glossing that [ha-] is a third person plural marker that indicates plurality of the direct object of the verb (or that the closest English gloss of [ha-huhuʔid] by itself would be something like "chasing them"). Careful readers of the multiline glossing might be able to

---

[10] Tohono O'odham, formerly called "Papago," is an Indigenous language of the Southwestern US and Northern Mexico, currently spoken by around 10,000 people. We are grateful to our Tohono O'odham teachers for helping us to learn about these examples, and any errors are our own.
[11] Based on our analysis. There are competing analyses of O'odham plural formation that would make a different claim here.

infer this from comparison of the second and third lines, but the example would need to have further explanation from the linguist in order to make this part clear.

And the last line provides a brief English translation of each sentence, complete with some of the messiness that always happens in translation. Sentence (12) could mean any of the following things in English:

(14)   Possible English translations of (12) that can be inferred from the multi-line glossing.
   1. A coyote is chasing some dogs.
   2. The coyote is chasing some dogs.
   3. A coyote is chasing the dogs.
   4. The coyote was chasing the dogs.
   5. A coyote was chasing some dogs.
   6. The coyote was chasing some dogs.
   7. A coyote was chasing the dogs.
   8. The coyote was chasing the dogs.

The examples in (12) and (13) use three lines, but for different languages and/or different purposes, scholars can use more lines or fewer lines. We could imagine multi-line glossing of a variety of US English in a paper intended for English-speaking readers to use just two lines, as in (15):

(15)   a lot-ta guys would-n't-'ve done that
       a lot-of guys would-not-have done that

We've also seen multi-line glossing using four or more lines, where we want to show the pronunciation of the example as well as its practical spelling. For example, (16) is constructed using our non-native understanding of Diné Bizaad.[12] We've used the abbreviation NOM to mean "nominalizer" (a part of a word that is used to form nouns) and the abbreviation "indef" to mean "indefinite."

(16)   díí   łééchąą'íí   át'é
       díí   łéː-chãː?-iː   á-t?é
       that   young.horse-poop-NOM   indef-be
       that   dog   is
       "That is a dog"

The top line in (16) shows how the sentence would be written in Diné Bizaad. The next line down shows the pronunciation (using fancy IPA transcription) and includes hyphens to show how each word breaks down into separate meaningful bits. The next line down shows what each bit means, and then

---

[12] Also known as "Navajo." Again, we thank our teachers for helping us learn about the language, and we hope this example is correct. But if it's not, it's our fault.

the line below that shows how each word translates into English. Finally, the last line shows how the sentence could be translated as a whole.

The basis of multi-line transcription is that we use vertical alignment of elements to help a reader better understand the structures and meanings of the example. There are lots of ways to modify this system for different uses[13] – and the rubric for "good multiline glossing" is whether or not the result is clear to the reader. We did our best to do exactly that in these examples.

3.8 Transcribing Conversations and Interviews

> **You'll need:** video or audio recordings of your conversations or interviews, and a way to play them back slowly to allow yourself to write out what's being said in careful detail. Depending on how you decide to transcribe, you may also need the tools referred to in Section 3.6.1 for phonetic transcription (though conversation and interview texts are often presented in a practical orthography – phonetic transcription is not necessarily useful for these larger chunks of language). Transcription takes a long time, so you'll also need to have reasonable expectations about how much material you can transcribe and analyze for a given project (it's often much less than you expected).

Your observation and analysis might focus less on things like the details of pronunciation and more on things like how speakers formulate and negotiate thoughts, meanings, and positions in their language behavior – capturing relevant variation without going into every last detail, as a magnifying glass would do better than a microscope. There are techniques that have been developed in a variety of scholarly disciplines that you can draw upon for this kind of analysis.

These techniques generally begin with some sort of recording (audio or video) of the language behavior that the scholar is interested in. Note that recording other people's speech is always something that must be done with care and honesty – never secretly,[14] and never in a way that might

---

[13] One example of a system of conventions for multi-line glossing is the Leipzig Glossing Rules, which can be found here: www.eva.mpg.de/lingua/pdf/Glossing-Rules.pdf.

[14] You might worry that if people know you're recording their speech, they won't use language in their "normal" way. This perception of "observer's paradox" can cause us to think it might be worthwhile to record secretly. But rest assured, it's not – and scholars have developed a set of ethically sound techniques to help us better understand and account for these kinds of issues. See Section 3.3 for more on this topic.

reasonably be expected to cause harm to those you are recording. But recording is important because few of us are fast enough to write exactly what people say as they say it (though this is possible for those trained, e.g., in shorthand or as court reporters), and our memory is unreliable as it relates to exactly how people use language. We need to begin by documenting the actual behavior we want to analyze.

Once your data is audio and/or video recorded, you can begin transcribing your data.[15] Recall that for this kind of analysis, we aren't focused so much on the specific pronunciation of a word, but rather we want to get a sense of the unfolding of a whole conversation or interview, and what that might mean within a broader social context. The discipline of conversation analysis has developed a rigorous notation system to transcribe the fine-grained details of pauses, overlaps, interruptions, and all the other chaotic aspects of everyday conversation. The most commonly used transcription system within conversation analysis was developed by Gail Jefferson (2004) and is hence often referred to as Jeffersonian transcription. Because of its precision, scholars of sociolinguistics, linguistic anthropology, and discourse analysis often make use of this transcription system as well. Conversation analysts tend to be highly detailed and precise in their transcription, to the point of counting out and recording in the transcript the length of a conversational pause in milliseconds! If you are interested in how pauses and silence work to create social meaning in conversation, you probably want to do this too. But scholars of language have also adapted the general conventions of the Jeffersonian system to suit their needs at the level of "precision" that is appropriate for their research questions – because sometimes, the conversation analytic "microscope" that allows you to count the number of milliseconds in a pause gives far more detail than you really need to conduct a thorough analysis. Some researchers may even include stills from video recorded alongside audio data or illustrations of key scenes in the transcript. The work of Charles Goodwin (e.g., 2004) and Marjorie Harness Goodwin (e.g., 2006) offer especially good examples of this practice. But let's now turn to see how the Jeffersonian system can be adapted, or how researchers develop their own styles of transcribing interviews and conversations.

When a scholar is following the Jeffersonian system precisely, they need only mention that in a footnote or somewhere in the text of their research – we then know to go look up the Jeffersonian transcription conventions if we need a reminder of what they mean. When a scholar decides to forego some

---

[15] If you are working on a signed language, you may not be transcribing, but you may be instead creating screenshots or video snippets to present to the reader.

3.8 Transcribing Conversations and Interviews

of the precision of the Jeffersonian system to focus more clearly on certain aspects of the recorded speech, they may include a transcription guide or key as a footnote or addendum to their published research. In this way, we can adapt how we transcribe data in a way that makes the most sense for our research questions.

We can learn about this from the way one of your textbook authors (2018, p. 734) approached transcription of a media interview with pop star Lady Gaga and reporter James Montgomery (17).

(17) JM: James Montgomery, LG: Lady Gaga
   1. JM: s- so I'm interested in the idea of Gaga sort of y you know th- the cha-
   2.   The character I don't know if that's even I don't mean that in a derogatory
   3.   way but do you have to sort of get yourself in to a space to be Gaga
   4.   All the time or [has it has it sort of become like =
   5. LG: [no(.)   = do you have to get yourself
   6.   Into a space to be [yourself all the time?
   7. JM: [but well I I I don't really I mean but n the reason I ask

You can identify some techniques used in this transcription system that help the reader to understand phenomena like conversational overlap (or interruption) and ensure that the author can refer back to specific points in the interview.

Following the Jeffersonian system, Valentinsson's transcript:

- Uses line numbering
- Labels lines where a new interlocutor begins speaking with the initials of that interlocutor
- Uses alignment and square brackets "[" to indicate overlap
- Uses the equal sign " = " to indicate latching (when there is no discernable pause between the end of one turn and the start of another)
- Uses hyphens "-" to indicate cut-off speech and restarts
- Uses single periods inside a pair of parentheses "(.)" to indicate a short pause

Unlike full conversation analysis–style transcripts, however, Valentinsson has not precisely timed each pause, has not described paralinguistic features in double parentheticals (such as "((shakes head))"), or indicated volume or tone in any way. And all of that is OK – because those specifics were not central to her analysis. Since a guide to which features she used, and how, was presented in this article, we can easily imagine what this excerpt of speech would have sounded like and follow along with Valentinsson's analysis of the features her transcript highlights.

Let's look at another excerpt in (18), this time a passage from the work of anthropologist Barbra Meek (2010, p. 146) as a model.

(18) "Adele: The only, the only time we would uh maybe speak up was when they ask us questions, but often they would, the Elders would just come and tell stories and we'd listen... We don't disobey, ya know, somebody tell you you gotta do something, we do it, even /???/ everywhere. We say, kids, they have to learn how to be respectful to everything, you can't pull flowers (and) when somebody talk to you gotta listen. Ya hear? You listen to your grandma when she talks to you? (to three year-old child)... When you grow up that's how you got to teach your kids, you gonna have kids when you grow up?"

Meek's work with the Kaska community in Canada focused on community members' beliefs about the role of the community's language, and its future, as they work through the legacy of attempted genocide and continuing struggles for recognition of their human rights. This example illustrates a number of techniques that Meek has employed to accurately capture the speaker's intended meaning and variety of English using practical orthographic conventions. Take a moment and see if you can identify any of these techniques – and then review the list below to see how many you noticed.

Techniques in Meek's transcription:

- The quoted material being introduced with an identifier of the speaker ("Adele:")
- The use of ellipses ("...") to indicate pauses
- The inclusion of disfluency markers like "uh"
- The use of alternative or non-standard spellings (like "ya" for "you," "gonna" for "going to") to better match the speakers' actual variety
- The use of parentheses to add clarifying information when needed
- The inclusion of markers for incomprehensible or inaudible material ("/???/")

Like Valentinsson, Meek includes an appendix in her book that clearly explains her notational conventions, including citation of the scholars who developed it and whose work she is indebted to. This is common practice and very important for anyone who wants their reader to understand their examples.

In the examples above, we've focused on analysis of what was said, but you may also be interested in understanding and analyzing more about who said it, under what circumstances, and in what kind of physical, social, cultural, historical, or political context. The scholar will need to find ways to faithfully note and record all of the aspects of the scene that are of interest to them. We certainly know that all of these factors – and many more – go into the production and understanding of language and generate language variation and change. If you're interested in studying it, it's almost certainly valid to include in your records! But the possibilities are so varied and endless that we leave the specifics of how to do this as a problem for the researcher.

3.9 Corpus Analysis

You'll need: access to a corpus, and some understanding of the structure and architecture of the corpus you are using. Many open-source language corpora are available, and many proprietary corpora are likely available to students via your school's library. Each corpus probably has its own set of rules and instructions, and you'll want to be sure you read that information carefully. Some knowledge of mathematics and statistics can be helpful, but is not necessary for smaller scale projects.

There are many ways to approach corpus data, and as with the tools already discussed, the selection you make will be driven by the questions you would like to ask. Here are a few tools that might be of use, with much of this taken from McEnnery and Hardie (2012).

Corpus linguistics, because it typically focuses on large or very large sets of examples, probably has the closest connection of any of the tools we've discussed here to the world of computational linguistics and natural language processing. If you are the kind of scholar who is interested in the study of language and computer applications to language, corpus linguistics would be an excellent place to begin your exploration!

First, you will need to select a corpus. We provided some examples in Section 3.1 of some corpora that are freely available, at least in the US and UK.

For this example, let's use the COCA corpus (www.english-corpora.org/coca/). Remember that COCA is a large corpus of contemporary American language use, or language use for the last thirty years: at the time of this writing, the data in COCA only dates back to 1990, so if you wanted to look at the frequency of *-ize* in the year 2020 compared to in the year 1920, you would have to use a different corpus.[16] COCA also has many subsections that you can analyze separately if you were interested in a particular language genre: works of fiction usually use very different words from news reports, for example.

Next, you'll need a linguistic question to explore. Let's say that we have a hypothesis that raccoons get talked about more in books than

---

[16] One corpus that you could use is COHA, the Corpus of Historical American English (www.english-corpora.org/coha/). COHA contains 475 million words from the 1820s to 2010s, so you could potentially track a word's usage for nearly 200 years!

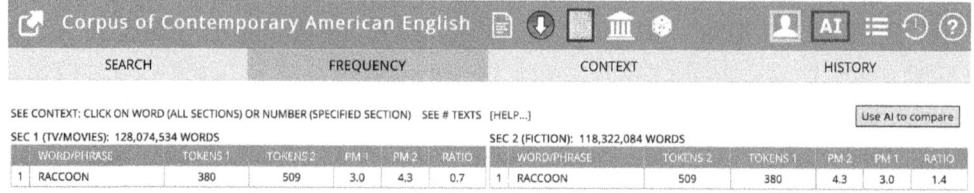

Figure 3.2 Screen cap from COCA.

in TV and movies, so any reference to a raccoon should occur more often in the fiction section of COCA. It is fairly straightforward to find frequency counts in COCA; you can use the search function much like you would your favorite search engine and use the options below the textbox to narrow your search to particular years or genres. Once we type in "raccoon" and select our relevant options, we see something like Figure 3.2:

On the left, we have results from the TV and movies section of COCA, while on the right, we have results from the fiction section. We can see that, indeed, our hypothesis is borne out: "raccoon" occurred 374 times in the TV/Movies corpus but 509 times in the Fiction corpus. However, the **raw frequency** count doesn't tell us much; generally, corpus studies looking at frequency are interested in how often a given word occurs per million words. We can look at the next two columns in our results, headed by PM 1 and PM 2: occurrences **per million** in section 1 (the TV/Movies corpus) and section 2 (the Fiction corpus). Looking at the number of occurrences per million words gives us a ratio for how often a word occurs and therefore a better idea overall of how common (or uncommon) a word is. A word that occurs 509 times in a 100,000-word corpus is much more frequent than a word that occurs 509 times in a 1,000,000,000-word corpus!

What if you want to know about more than how often a single word appears? Corpora become much more interesting when you're looking at more than just one word. Let's take our other example of how the use of *-ize* has changed over time. To search for every word that contains *-ize*, we have to use a **regular expression**. Regular expressions define the set of characters you want to find in a text. Believe it or not, you use a regular expression every time you search for something on a search engine! Here, we're going to use a more complex regular expression than we did before: *ize_v. In COCA, this means something like "find words that end in "ize" with any number of any letters in front of it, and only find words that have been flagged as

3.9 Corpus Analysis

	WORD/PHRASE	TOKENS 1	TOKENS 2	PM 1	PM 2	RATIO		WORD/PHRASE	TOKENS 2	TOKENS 1	PM 2	PM 1	RATIO
1	COMPUTERIZE	21	2	0.2	0.0	10.6	1	INCENTIVIZE	124	0	1.0	0.0	101.0
2	MORALIZE	21	3	0.2	0.0	7.1	2	DENUCLEARIZE	92	2	0.7	0.0	45.4
3	ECONOMIZE	41	7	0.3	0.1	5.9	3	WEAPONIZE	56	2	0.5	0.0	27.6
4	DECENTRALIZE	50	9	0.4	0.1	5.6	4	MONETIZE	95	4	0.8	0.0	23.4
5	LIBERALIZE	99	18	0.8	0.1	5.6	5	CHARLIZE	20	0	0.2	0.0	16.3
6	PROFESSIONALIZE	26	5	0.2	0.0	5.3	6	STRATEGIZE	74	11	0.6	0.1	6.6
7	INSTITUTIONALIZE	121	27	1.0	0.2	4.5	7	DECRIMINALIZE	39	6	0.3	0.0	6.4
8	INDUSTRIALIZE	31	7	0.3	0.1	4.5	8	DELEGITIMIZE	104	17	0.8	0.1	6.0
9	TANTALIZE	23	7	0.2	0.1	3.3	9	PRIORITIZE	401	69	3.3	0.6	5.7
10	DEMOCRATIZE	72	23	0.6	0.2	3.2	10	METASTASIZE	32	6	0.3	0.0	5.3

Figure 3.3 Screen cap from COCA – Search.

verbs.[17] The * in front of -ize is the part of the regular expression denoting "any number of any letters," while the _v following -ize is the part asking only for words that are tagged as verbs. Using our filtering options, we'll look at just words formed using -ize from 1990–1994 in the first section and from 2015–2019 in the second section. Here are our top ten results, as of January 2021 (Figure 3.3):

These results contain the same kinds of information as they did in our search for "raccoon" – information about each word's frequency in each section that we selected, occurrences per million, and frequency ratio – but there are more words listed. This is because we searched for every word fitting a particular criterion (that it was a verb ending with -ize) and not just a single word (like *raccoon*). You'll also note that some rows are shaded more darkly than others. Lighter-shaded rows contain words that occurred in the selected section less than five times as often as other words, and darker shaded rows contain words that occurred in the selected section more than five times as often.

This time, the "Tokens 1" and "Tokens 2" columns are more interesting than before: Tokens 1 refers to how many times the word appears in the first section, while Tokens 2 refers to how many times the word appears in the second section. We can see that while *computerize* is the top result for the 1990–1994 section, it only appears twice in the 2015–2019 section. *Incentivize* is the top result for the 2015–2019 section with 124 occurrences,

---

[17] You'll notice that the part of speech information isn't always 100 percent correct: the fifth word in the right-hand section of Figure 3.3 is "Charlize" and refers to the actress Charlize Theron rather than a verb written the same way.

but it doesn't appear at all in the 1990–1994 section. If we go all the way to the right to see the "Ratio" column, which is how the words are sorted by default, we can see that *computerize* occurs 10.9 times more frequently per million words in the 1990–1994 section than in the 2015–2019 section.

From this short exploration, you can see that corpora contain a great deal of data and potential insights as long as we know how to look for it. In addition to the questions we asked here, you might be interested in doing some basic statistics on your findings – for example, a **type/token ratio** tells us how often a particular word, construction, or utterance is used across a whole corpus or a subset of a corpus. We use token to refer to the total number of words we're looking at in a corpus (or subsection of corpus), while we use **type** to refer to the phenomenon we're searching for (like the -*ize* ending we just explored). You can use additional **significance testing** with the appropriate statistical tests to see whether there is a meaningful difference in frequency, for example, or if the difference is there but is too small to be significant.

We might also be interested in a word's **collocations**, or other words that commonly appear with it or near it, and we can also search for this in COCA. You can see our top ten results in Figure 3.4 when we search for collocations of "chair" in different written contexts, circa January 2021:

Once again, we have the same kind of frequency information that we saw in the previous two charts, but there's a small difference since we searched for a criteria other than "match 'raccoon'" or "find verbs ending in -*ize*." In these results, you can see words like "division," "engineering," and "program" in the academic texts section on the left. Division chairs, engineering chairs, and program chairs are typically people who are in charge of

#	SEC 1 (ACADEMIC): 119,790,456 WORDS						#	SEC 2 (FICTION): 118,322,084 WORDS					
	WORD/PHRASE	TOKENS 1	TOKENS 2	PM 1	PM 2	RATIO		WORD/PHRASE	TOKENS 2	TOKENS 1	PM 2	PM 1	RATIO
1	DIVISION	56	1	0.5	0.0	55.3	1	KITCHEN	293	3	2.5	0.0	98.9
2	ENGINEERING	53	1	0.4	0.0	52.4	2	WING	111	0	0.9	0.0	93.8
3	ABA	55	0	0.5	0.0	45.9	3	WAY	87	1	0.7	0.0	88.1
4	PROGRAM	46	1	0.4	0.0	45.4	4	FEET	220	3	1.9	0.0	74.2
5	EDUCATION	42	0	0.4	0.0	35.1	5	FOOT	72	1	0.6	0.0	72.9
6	RESEARCH	34	1	0.3	0.0	33.6	6	MOTHER	134	2	1.1	0.0	67.8
7	FACULTY	38	0	0.3	0.0	31.7	7	COMMAND	65	1	0.5	0.0	65.8
8	ASME	36	0	0.3	0.0	30.1	8	LEATHER	409	7	3.5	0.1	59.2
9	COMMISSION	30	1	0.3	0.0	29.6	9	CANVAS	58	1	0.5	0.0	58.7
10	ROLE	33	0	0.3	0.0	27.5	10	BEACH	67	0	0.6	0.0	56.6

Figure 3.4 Screen cap from COCA – Collocations.

divisions, engineering departments, and programs. In the fiction section on the right, we see words like "kitchen," "wing," and "beach," and kitchen chairs, wing chairs, and beach chairs are devices that we can sit on (rather than people who are in charge of kitchens, wings, and beaches). Therefore, this data tells us that the word *chair* gets used in different ways depending on its context: in academic texts, it's more likely to refer to the head of a department or committee, whereas in fiction, it's more likely to refer to the object that we sit on.

When we divide up COCA into sections, as we have been doing when we limit our searches to academic texts, fictional texts, books, TV and movies, and the years 1990–1994 or 2015–2019, we are using the **metadata** that further describes the language in the corpus. COCA has metadata that defines the year and type of text in various ways, and other corpora have metadata that might describe a speaker's age, gender, occupation, region of residence, and so on, which we can use to further inform our search. If we are interested in how language use varies across different social statuses, this type of metadata is incredibly important.

You can also use different tools to visualize your data. Google has a large corpus of books that have been digitized, published as early as 1800, and you can search for words and terms within them. This is called the Google Ngram Viewer (https://books.google.com/ngrams). As long as the word or phrase has appeared in a published, digitized work, the Ngram Viewer will plot the relative frequency of your search term over time. We searched for "raccoon" again to see how it has fared in books over the last 200 years (Figure 3.5):

You can see that the usage of "raccoon" has had quite a few peaks and valleys over time. If you wanted to, you could examine this further to see if there was anything that could have contributed to more raccoon talk in the late 1920s compared to the 1910s, since that's a particularly sharp rise of

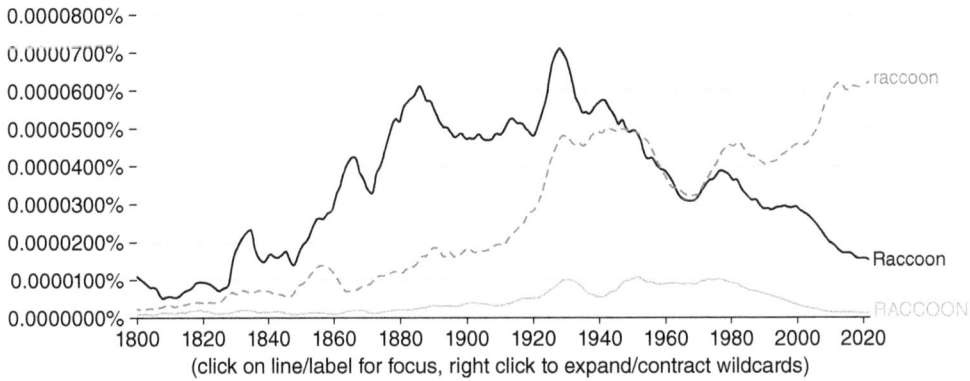

Figure 3.5 Screen cap from Google Ngram Viewer "raccoon."

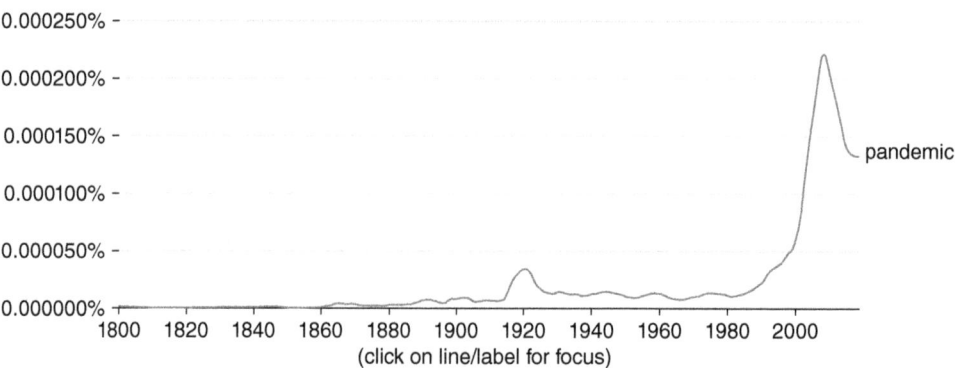

Figure 3.6 Screen cap from Google Ngram Viewer "pandemic."

published material with "raccoon" written in it. For another example, let's search "pandemic" (Figure 3.6):

Here, we see a much smoother graph with peaks roughly corresponding with the influenza pandemic of 1918 and the swine flu pandemic of 2009. Why do you think the 2009 peak is so much higher than the peak a hundred years earlier? Remember, whenever we do corpus research, we need to be aware of the composition of the corpus that we use – it could very well have something to do with the difference in the number of published books, newspapers, and magazines, for instance.

There are still more ways to analyze corpora. For example, you might be interested in how complex a piece of text is, and there are different ways to define "complex" based on what you're interested in. You can analyze the corpus' **lexical diversity**, or the number of unique words contained in the text, similar to the type/token ratio we discussed previously; you could also analyze the corpus' **lexical sophistication**, or the amount of low- and high-frequency words in the text. If you're doing this, you might be interested in whether a novelist's writing changes over time due to Alzheimer's disease (Garrard et al. 2005; van Velzen & Garrard 2008), or whether there is any difference between intermediate and advanced language learners' writing (Engber 1995; Laufer & Nation 1995), or whether interlocutors will change the types of words they use when they have to converse with someone in a noisy setting (Baese-Berk et al. 2021; Lee & Baese-Berk 2020).

If you're inclined toward programming, you can write a script[18] that will go through a corpus and match the criteria you specify, but there are also tools that others have made that can do similar things if you aren't inclined

---

[18] Your authors have seen (and used) scripts written for these purposes using languages like Python, R, and Matlab, for instance.

toward programming. We invite you to continue exploring the possible tools that you can create or use to analyze corpora, but we won't go into the details here. We have given you some starting points in our exercises at the end of the chapter.

As you keep reading through this textbook, we hope this chapter will serve you as a resource for different ways to observe your linguistic community, and perhaps also as inspiration for more of the questions you can ask. Keep in mind that these aren't all of the possible tools you could use, either! The tools and techniques that we have discussed in this chapter are used frequently in a lot of sociolinguistic research. Before you conduct any formal observations on your own, though, we encourage you to read Chapter 4 to learn a little more about your ethical obligations as a researcher.

Linguist in the Community

- IPA some names: Find the International Phonetic Alphabet's consonant and vowel charts at www.internationalphoneticassociation.org/content/full-ipa-chart. You can also look up "clickable" charts on the internet that play the sound associated with each symbol for more practice. Then, find 3–4 friends, family members, or community members: ask each one to pronounce their name clearly, while you attempt to write it in IPA. When you have tried an IPA transcription of each name, reflect on the process. In what ways is the IPA easy to use and figure out? Where does it pose problems? What sounds did you struggle to figure out how to represent? You can "check" your work by using online tools that pronounce IPA transcription for you (e.g., https://tophonetics.com/). At the time of writing, the machine voice does not sound very much like a human voice, so doing this process will help you to better understand all the aspects of pronunciation that the IPA does not capture.
- Transcribe a conversation: Ask a pair of family members or friends to let you record a short snippet of their conversation. If members of your community use a signed language, this would be a video recording; for a spoken language community, it could be audio only. Try to keep your recording truly short – no more than a minute or so of speech! Then, practice transcribing the recording in as much detail as possible, using the Jeffersonian transcription system (available at https://universitytranscriptions.co.uk/jefferson-transcription-system-a-guide-to-the-symbols/). Once your recording is fully transcribed, reflect on what you noticed about the process. How long did it take? What does this tell you about how much material you can collect and expect to analyze in a short

amount of time? Also reflect on what conversational features you noticed. Were there many overlaps or interruptions? Did the speakers use non-verbal cues that you struggled to accurately represent in the transcript? If you used an audio-only recording, did you lose information that turns out to be important?
- Participant observation: Practice observing language use in the world around you through participant observation. Find a public space where you can sit and observe people greeting each other frequently. Maybe this is through your work at a reception desk, or at your favorite cafe, or at a public park in your city. Sit for at least an hour, and take some handwritten fieldnotes about any greeting interactions you see. Note down the gestures people use to greet one another, the formulaic language they use, any particular words or phrases that are often used, and so on. Simultaneously, keep track (in a general, anonymous way) of what kinds of people use what sort of greeting language. Do men or women hug more upon greeting? Do older folks or younger people use politeness terms (like "please" and "thank you") when ordering at a coffee shop? Once you have about an hour's worth of observations written up, turn to reflection. Describe the patterns you noticed, and think about what these observations might reveal about greeting practices in your culture.

Linguist in the Classroom

- Elicitations: If your classroom has speakers of multiple languages in it, arrange yourselves into small groups, and elicit a common set of words in the non-English languages they know. (You can look up Swadesh lists of varying lengths to get started). Alternatively, work in pairs or small groups where each group is assigned a non-English language, and use web resources to find the equivalents in their language of a subset of English words on a Swadesh list. Then compare together: what similarities do you notice between the English words and the words in the other language?
- Organize the IPA: Create lists of all the IPA characters that represent the sounds they expect them to (for example, the Latin alphabet "p" and the IPA [p] seem like a straightforward match). Then make lists of IPA characters that are hard to remember because they do not make the sound expected (for example, the IPA [c] does not behave at all like the orthographic "c" in English). Finally, make a list of IPA characters that are not in the Latin alphabet and so may be hard to type as well as difficult to remember (for example, the IPA [ə]). Cocreate an "IPA cheat

sheet" that the class can share so that they can more easily find the characters they need, and also find online tools to help type the special characters.
- Play with Google Ngrams: Generate a question about an expression (a word, a short phrase, or an idiom) that you believe might have become dramatically more or less frequent in use over time. Use the Google Ngram Viewer described in this chapter, using that word or expression, to get a graphic representation of the frequency of use. Is it what you expected? Do the results raise questions for you? Then, go to the "about" page and find out the characteristics of the corpus you searched. Change to a different corpus and do the same search again. Is it the same or different? Why might it be? Use the "about" page to learn how to use wildcard searches, inflection searches, and other more advanced techniques to see if you can answer the questions that arose on the first simple search. Then do the same on any word or phrase of interest to you or your group, and report your results.
- Use COCA in the classroom: See if you can access COCA and replicate the searches you've seen in this chapter. Your results will likely differ from ours since this corpus is updated frequently. Once you are familiar with the interface, take some time to play – see if you can find a term of interest and generate a type or token frequency, per million.

Glossary

acceptable A word or phrase that a native speaker would use in their language (see also **grammatical**).

collection (conversation analysis) A set of data examples all illustrating the same conversational or discursive feature, within the context of a transcript.

collocation Sets of words that are found together or near each other often, like *salt and pepper* or *peanut butter and jelly*.

concordance A listing of the word or pattern that was searched for in a corpus.

corpus (pl. corpora) A collection of language examples (corpora can be collections of text and/or audio or video examples) organized to facilitate linguistic analysis and usually meant to be approximately representative of a language/speech community or genre (web pages, conversations, newspapers, etc.).

elicitation A structured process of asking questions in order to elicit information about a particular linguistic form or structure.

fieldnotes A detailed recording of observations, which may include the researcher's thoughts and feelings, collected during a period of field work.

fieldwork A data collection process involving spending time in and among the language community one is studying.

frequency (low or high) The number of times a word occurs in a corpus, or in all of the words you're exposed to. A word that doesn't occur very often is low-frequency, while a word that occurs very often is high-frequency.

grammatical A word or phrase that conforms to a native speaker's judgment about whether it can be used in their language (see also acceptable).

lexical diversity The number of unique words in a corpus.

lexical sophistication A relative measurement of high- and low-frequency words in a corpus.

metadata Additional information about entries in a corpus, which could include the source text, information about speakers'/writers' social variables, and so on.

observer's paradox The double bind faced by many linguists, that they seek to collect examples of natural language use, but their mere presence in a speech situation as a researcher makes the data somewhat "unnatural."

parser A computer program designed to process text in a corpus in a certain way – for example, guessing at morphological boundaries.

participant observation A data collection method in which the researcher engages in the same habits and activities of daily life as the group or community under study.

prestige variety The language variety that is associated with social power in a given community.

raw frequency The number of times a word occurs in a corpus which has not been converted to a standardized measurement, such as frequency per million words.

regular expression A string of characters that defines the pattern you want to look for in a text.

rhotacization A phonological process whereby certain sounds become more /ɹ/-like under certain conditions.

significance testing The use of statistical tests that determine whether an observed difference is based on chance or error.

sociolinguistic interview A method for eliciting a linguistic variable in a range of different speech styles.

sociophonetician A linguist who studies the ways in which social patterns correlate with speakers' use of different phonetic features.

Swadesh list A set of basic concepts and words that linguists can use to compare one language to another.

token An individual instance of a set or class of related forms.

type A set or class of related forms.

type/token ratio A ratio that describes how often a particular linguistic form (type) is used across a whole corpus or subset of a corpus (tokens).

Recommended Readings

Further reading on methodological and analytical tools in linguistics can get quite technical, but there is plenty of material out there for the enterprising student who wants to learn about the tools in our toolkit in greater detail. Don't forget that most of these materials are free or available through a college or university library.

Davies, M. (2008–). The Corpus of Contemporary American English (COCA) [Data set]. www.english-corpora.org/coca/

Farrington, C., & Kendall, T. (2021). The Corpus of Regional African American Language. https://doi.org/10.7264/1AD5-6T35

Farrington, C., King, S., & Kohn, M. (2021). Sources of variation in the speech of African Americans: Perspectives from sociophonetics. *Wiley Interdisciplinary Reviews: Cognitive Science, 12*(3), e1550. https://doi.org/10.1002/wcs.1550

Holliday, N., Bishop, J., and Kuo, G. (2020). Prosody and political style: The case of Barack Obama and the L+H* pitch accent. In N. Minematsu (Ed.), *Proceedings of the 10th International Conference on Speech Prosody* (pp. 670–674). Speech Prosody.

Jefferson, G. (2004). Glossary of transcript symbols with an introduction. In G. H. Lerner (Ed.), *Conversation Analysis* (pp. 13–31). John Benjamins Publishing Company.

Meek, B. A. (2010). *We Are Our Language*. University of Arizona Press.

4 But We Want You to Make Us Some Promises

4.1 Human "Subjects" Protections and Ethical Research Practices

Linguists want to find out how people in different language communities use and understand language. To do this, we need to observe people's language behavior – often, in order to really carefully observe, we need to find ways to record it. Then, as scholars we are obligated to write about our work in order to share it with others. It is very important that in doing these things we do not behave in ways that interfere with others, put others in harm's way, violate anyone's privacy, or misrepresent ourselves or our work. In this chapter we discuss some standards of practice that we ask you to agree to abide by any time you are acting as a linguist in the community.

If you are new to this kind of work, not everything here will be relevant to you right now. For example, our section on human subjects protections lays out steps that you might only need to take if you are writing a thesis or preparing a manuscript for publication. But whatever your level of participation in the study of language in the community, we want you to have the tools and knowledge to conduct your work in a way that helps you build and maintain strong scholarly habits. We think it's useful for everyone to know about these things, regardless of where they are in their scholarly career!

4.2 Key Principles of Human Subjects Protections or Ethics Programs

Best practices around respect for and protection of others in the context of linguistic and other social scientific inquiry are often codified by academic institutions and local, state, and federal governments in the form of **human subjects protections programs (HSPPs)**, or discipline-specific **ethics boards**. Depending on your institution or location, they may also be called institutional review boards (IRBs), ethics review boards, or research ethics boards (or something else along these lines). If you are using this text as a part of a class, you should check with your instructor to find out what kinds of programs your school has, and if they have one at all. If they do, you might consider reaching out to the people who run that program and enrolling in trainings that they offer, or doing other forms of research on the rules and standards that you'd be expected to follow in your context. Our chapter isn't a substitute for that process, but we will highlight some of the key principles that HSPPs and ethics boards work to support:[1]

- Respect for individuals: The first responsibility of a researcher is to ensure that their work is not harmful to others. To the extent that the research poses a risk to participants, the benefit to participants must outweigh the risk.
- Respect for individuals' autonomy: Participants must be able to withdraw their participation at any time, without harm or disadvantage. Participants must not be coerced into any aspect of participation.
- The necessity of **informed consent**: Participants must know what the possible risks and benefits of participation are before any observations are done or any data have been collected. They must also know whether and how their data will be anonymized, whether and how it might be shared, and who they can contact in case they wish to retroactively withdraw participation, report problems, or ask questions.

The rules and regulations around these issues have been codified under the rubric of **human subjects** protection, and this model comes out of concerns raised by unethical and sometimes genocidal use of science to harm populations physically, economically, and psychologically. Many of these occurred in the domains of biomedical research, where "subject" might be a reasonable way of thinking about research participants. In language work, we do not typically refer to those whose behavior we observe as our "subjects"; instead, we are more likely to refer to them as "**participants**" – if we do our work well, they will be active participants in helping us to better understand a community's linguistic practice. Also, if we do our work well, our participants will benefit from our work and will be interested and happy to work with other linguists in the future.

---

[1] These principles were codified in a document titled the Declaration of Helsinki, which was composed by the World Medical Association and first published in 1964 (World Medical Association General Assembly 1964). This document focuses on medical research, but its principles are fundamental to all forms of scientific investigation for which human beings are the focus.

You might be wondering why we are making a big deal of human subjects protections in a book about observing the ways in which people use language. It is pretty obvious that medical studies involving new drugs or investigating disease and the like could be risky to those who participate in them – but is using language dangerous?

It can be. People's language behavior can get them into trouble if they express unpopular beliefs or disclose secrets about themselves or others. The way we use language is so integral to our individual self-presentation that there are now **forensic linguists** to assist law enforcement in identifying individuals based on their distinctive use of language.[2] People may experience backlash or disapproval if their way of speaking is **stigmatized** or if they say something that discloses information that shouldn't be shared.

We mentioned human subjects protections programs and ethics boards at the start of this chapter, and this is a good time to refer to those at the institution where you are conducting your research. If you're working at a college or university and you expect that your work might be shared beyond something like a class assignment or project, it will be important to work with your instructor and your school to ensure that you take all required steps to have your project reviewed and assessed for compliance *before* you begin to gather your data. The process of requesting and receiving permission to conduct your research will likely be labor intensive, and it can take a significant amount of time – but it is crucial to both your and your school's work that you give it the attention and effort it deserves.

Furthermore, you should know that there might be local or national institutions that govern human subjects protections and research ethics, so if you are doing work outside of your own home community it will be very important to find out whether any such institutions exist and, if they do, to find out how to work with them to ensure that you don't violate any applicable laws, policies, or guidelines. For example, in North America, many American Indian / Native American / First Nations governments have their own human subjects protections programs, and these sometimes prohibit any recording or sharing of the community's language data by anyone who has not first gotten official permission. In our experience, non-Indigenous students and scholars in the US are sometimes quick to believe that they can take a trip to a Native American tribe or nation and just ask people about the language or record events at which the language is being used. For many

---

[2] You may know that "forensic linguistics" first came to the fore in the US in the so-called "Unabomber" case. Ted Kazinsky, who is currently imprisoned for a series of bombings, was identified in part by the turns of phrase he used in a written statement, known as his "manifesto" (see Davies 2017 for discussion).

communities, doing this is not just offensively intrusive, it is illegal. In the US, many of these communities are sovereign nations that have the right to determine who may and who may not use or disseminate their language.

4.2.1 Key Practices for Protecting the People Whose Languages We Study

So in this context, we think that the following are key practices that we all should agree to whenever we are studying language behavior:

1. Never record or report anyone else's language behavior without first asking for and receiving their permission to do so. Make sure that you ask permission in a way that allows the person to politely and gracefully decline.
2. Always anonymize participants when you share examples or clips from their language behavior, unless there's some very important reason not to (and in that case, be sure that when you do Step 1 you talk to them about the fact that they won't be anonymized).
3. Never use anyone's language behavior against them, and never frame anyone's language behavior as "wrong"; never mock it, and never use it to demonize them or any group that they are members of, even if you are looking at language behavior that you find damaging or immoral (for example, **hate speech**). Remember, a linguist's perspective asks "how *do* people use language," not "how *should* they."[3]
4. Always treat people's language with the utmost care and respect. If you take recordings of someone, back them up and keep them safe. Store them in a way that preserves participants' anonymity and privacy. Present them in a way that is not needlessly violent, exotic, or sensationalized.[4]
5. Never use people's language for purposes other than those for which you have their permission.

---

[3] This is tricky in cases where you are describing and analyzing language behavior that is harmful, such as the use of **racial slurs**, the practice of **disinformation**, and the like. Scholars are at least allowed, and may even be obligated, to make those who access our scholarship aware of the damage that can be caused by these linguistic practices. What we are saying here is that our scholarship must describe rather than accuse, and it must be conducted and presented in a way that acknowledges both our and our participants' autonomy, right to privacy, and the like. We suggest using existing scholarship on these topics by important authors such as Baugh (2018), Jones et al. (2019), Lanehart (2002), Rickford and King (2016), Tebaldi and Jereza (2024) and many others as models and guides.

[4] As an example, it was long the habit of some linguists to present example sentences for grammatical analysis that had violent or misogynistic themes – like using "John hit Mary" as a canonical example of a basic clause. The exact same grammatical information can be presented for a sentence like "Chris hugged Alex."

And, finally, if you are doing research in an institutional setting and/or with a community that has laws, policies, or regulations regarding human subjects protections or research ethics, scrupulously follow and abide by those laws, policies, or regulations.

This might be a good moment to talk about the related concepts of **anonymity, confidentiality,** and **privacy**. When we talk about anonymizing our observations, this refers to the removal from your work product of any personally identifiable information about the source of the observations. You might anonymize your data by, for example, assigning pseudonyms or referring to participants by assigning each a number. Anonymizing your data may also require redacting material that a reader could use to figure out who the participant was.

Confidentiality is the right of the participant to not have their identity or participation shared with others. Anonymizing our data is one thing researchers do in order to ensure our participants' right to confidentiality, but it is not the only thing. We also provide ways for participants to consent to participation without their participation being shared or publicly known. We retain records of participation in order to document our informed consent process, but we typically separate the records of consent from the actual data collections. Any connection between the pseudonyms or participant numbers used in our work is managed in a way that supports the confidentiality rights of participants.

Privacy is the right of the participant to not share information about themselves that they wish not to share and to control the disclosure of information they provide as part of their participation. Anonymization and confidentiality protocols support participants' right to privacy, but the privacy right extends to participants' ability to rescind consent to publish or share their data at all, and/or to determine whether any of the content they've shared with us should be removed from analysis and publication or further sharing by the researcher.

Unless there are compelling reasons not to, language researchers should strive to provide maximal anonymity, confidentiality, and privacy for our participants. If there is a reason that doing so would harm our ability to do our research, we must always carefully and openly secure informed consent from our participants. If our research goals conflict with the rights of others, the rights of others must always prevail.

4.2.2 What about Collecting Data Online?

There are many public or semi-public online spaces in which we can observe humans' language behavior. These range from media that are obviously intended for public consumption to those that are clearly intended for only

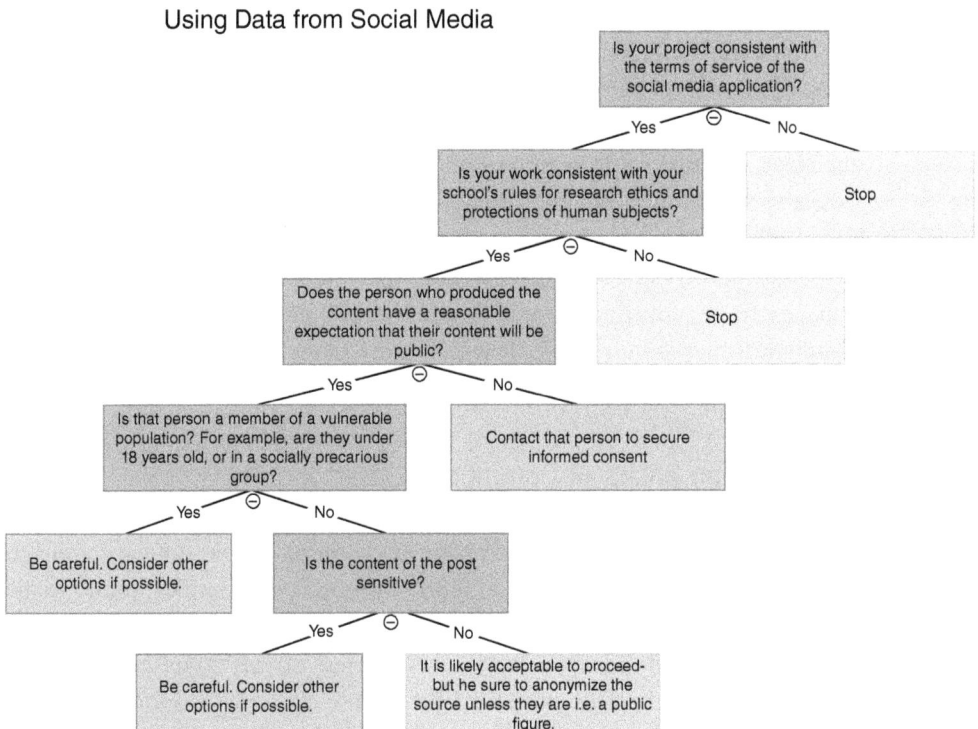

Figure 4.1 Guidelines for using social media in linguistic research, adapted from Townsend and Wallace (2017).

the poster's friends, family, or acquaintances. What are the rules for using language observations taken from social media, journalistic reports, and the like? And how do these media complicate notions of privacy and informed consent?

Townsend and Wallace (2017) provide us with a set of guidelines for consideration of research ethics for research using social media as data. The graphic in Figure 4.1 is adapted from their work.

Your first step in evaluation of data from social media or other online platforms is to check and ensure that your project does not violate the **terms of service** (TOS) agreements you and your participants agreed to when you accessed the application. TOS statements are typically publicly available – and searchable – so you can look for policies on privacy, copyright, and use of data.

If (and only if) your project is not ruled out by the application itself, make sure you have checked with any relevant school or community research offices so that you can ensure compliance with local policies and rules – just as you would for a project in which you collect data in a face-to-face modality.

If (and only if) your project can be done in a way that is consistent with the rules and policies that you are responsible for, your work can likely proceed. If the people whose data you are accessing have a reasonable expectation that their language behavior would be public, if they are not members of **vulnerable populations** (such as children),[5] and if the content you are collecting is not sensitive, your project can likely continue – with appropriate safeguards for anonymity, confidentiality, and privacy. But if your idea involves collecting data that might be sensitive in nature, has the capacity to get contributors into trouble, or is coming from children or any population that is vulnerable, it would more likely be wise to explore other options if you can.

4.2.3 Some Basics of Community-Based Inquiry

There is at least one fundamental difference between how many of us in the US, and perhaps in other places, have been taught to be scholars and the ways in which we might want to work with our communities. Many of us have been taught that the research questions, methods, and approaches to study should be decided on by the researcher, on the basis of their own interests and goals. This attitude likely arose in part through a broader approach to science where the notion of "objectivity" demanded that the researcher operate at a distance from the populations they were studying. In short, the belief was that researchers should avoid getting too "close to" or involved with the communities and populations they studied. However, we may want to consider that in some cases, the research questions, methods, and approaches should be determined by the needs, interests, and values of those who we think of as our participants. Collaborative, community-based work has a number of advantages over researcher-led scholarship in terms of its ability to focus on and apply to real problems and concerns that people have with regard to their language context and their community well-being. Community-led scholarship on the impact of community-based programs in heritage language reclamation for endangered language communities in North America, for example, shows that these programs can reduce a number of public health hazards, including rates of youth incarceration and suicides (Whalen et al. 2016). These are not topics that academic researchers had necessarily thought to pursue.

---

[5] There is not a single definition of a vulnerable population, but there are many subgroups that make up vulnerable populations. Groups that are commonly named as vulnerable populations by ethics boards include minors (children under 18), pregnant people and their fetuses, prisoners, and mentally disabled adults.

Community-based research is founded on the same kinds of values that underlay the protection of human subjects: respect for autonomy, informed consent, and concern to do no harm. In the world of language research, community-based work has come to the forefront in two primary domains: work with minoritized and endangered communities on language revitalization and reclamation (e.g., Rice 2011), and sociolinguistic work with minoritized communities on issues of language bias and discrimination (e.g., Baugh 2018; Wright 2019).

If you think you might be interested in community-based inquiry, we recommend that you start with communities of which you are a member. Doing work like this in a familiar community will benefit from your experiences, and you will be less likely to develop some of the bad habits that can come from overconfidence in your own understanding of the needs and desires of others. Reaching out to other communities of interest is also a great idea, and one that should be allowed to happen slowly and respectfully with the development of mutual understanding and trust being a primary objective. We encourage new scholars interested in community-based inquiry to find existing partnerships and collaborations to work with first before trying to forge a brand-new relationship with an unfamiliar community.

4.3 Some Basics of Research Integrity

Research integrity is based in the core value that researchers should tell the truth and should be frank and open about our work, including our positionality (who we are and what our role has been in the research), the contributions of others (those whose work we use to build our own scholarship, those who we work with, those who inspire our work), and our methods and data. Some key ideas in the domain of research integrity include:

- Ensuring that our referencing and citation practices are sufficient to make it clear to others what in our work is our own and what we have drawn from others; and for the latter, how the reader or viewer could locate those sources (that is, avoiding plagiarism);
- Ensuring that our work is properly credited, and that errors are attributed correctly, addressed responsibly, and not hidden or perpetuated;
- Ensuring that our data are reported accurately, and that (with appropriate protections for participants' privacy, confidentiality, and anonymity) they are appropriately archived and/or accessible.

4.3.1 It's Not Just Plagiarism, but Avoiding Plagiarism Is Important

Plagiarism is a form of research integrity violation that is often emphasized in school, where it is defined as some variation of "the action or practice of taking someone else's work, idea, etc., and passing it off as one's own; literary theft" (Oxford University Press 2021). Certainly any case in which you copy someone else's work and put your own name on it would count as plagiarism, but things can get complicated pretty quickly as you really try to put anti-plagiarism practices in place in your work. It might be more useful for us to think about plagiarism not as *theft*, but as *dishonesty*. In scholarly writing, we want our readers to be able to track down the history of our ideas so that they can engage with our work and with the work that influenced us. If we paraphrase an idea that we got from another scholar but fail to cite them, then our reader might be fooled into believing that the idea started with us and has no history to follow. That's harmful to the scholarly endeavor!

You may be aware that there is such a thing as "self-plagiarism," which is an idea that, on the "stealing someone else's ideas" definition, seems absurd. But on the "dishonesty about an idea's history" definition, it begins to make sense. If I've written a paper before in which I've made a particular claim or set out a particular idea, when I incorporate that information into my future paper, I need to cite my past one. If I fail to do that, my reader might be fooled into thinking that the idea has not been shared before, and they would not be able to find and access any previous discussion of it. Avoiding plagiarism is maybe best accomplished by working to be scrupulously honest about the history of your ideas, whether that history involves you or others or both.

4.3.2 Key Practices for Research Integrity

Violations of research integrity in the form of overt fraud or falsification, plagiarism, or misattribution of authorship are unfortunately not as rare as we all would prefer. The worst of these violations, of course, are those that are done with malicious intent. But all scholars are likely to be worried about inadvertently violating norms of research integrity – so we encourage you to develop good habits early on. These include:

- **Managing references as you read and from the beginning of your writing process.** Development of an annotated bibliography is a good way to do this – when you are planning your research, make a place where you will store your notes about everything that you read, and always get the complete reference citation in your notes right away.

Where relevant, include page numbers next to any paraphrased or quoted material. Consider using a reference manager application if you are able to integrate that into your workflow (especially if you're planning to do longer scholarly works, like theses or dissertations).
- **Never copying and pasting out of your sources.** Even if you quote someone, type the quote yourself[6] – this will cue you to add the correct reference citation as you go and help you to avoid leaving a quote or paraphrase in your work without the accompanying citation.
- **Always safely storing your data, in anonymized form, and citing it in a way that would allow other scholars to review your examples and replicate your findings.** Berez-Kroeker et al. (2018) provide a set of broad guiding principles for the storage, citation, and attribution of language examples. They advocate careful, anonymized, and secured storage of examples in a format that could be responsibly shared with other scholars for purposes of expanding on and/or replicating your work. As a student researcher, you might not be able to follow all of these guidelines all of the time, but you can work to ensure that you are managing your data and observations in the most responsible way you can.

4.3.3 Referencing, Citation, and Intellectual Property

Research integrity, as we have said already, centers around our frankness, openness, and honesty about our own work, and on acknowledging how that work benefits from others' work. It also serves to facilitate our readers' or audience's ability to find others' work that we used so that they can benefit from it directly as well. Referencing and citation practices support both of these purposes.

4.3.3.1 Using Appropriate Sources

In most scholarly contexts, we are expected to use and cite scholarly materials – and, in particular, materials that have undergone **peer review**, or have been thoroughly reviewed and assessed by other scholars in the field. We discuss this topic more fully in Section 4.3.3.2, but for now, we just want to note that it's important that the sources you use and refer to are appropriate for the purposes to which you are putting them in your work!

---

[6] Or, if you're concerned that you'll introduce typos by hand-typing the quote, make a habit of first typing your quotation marks, "", and then pasting into the space between them. However you manage this, make it very difficult for yourself to accidentally include an unmarked quotation in your work!

One important source that you probably use regularly (it is one of the top ten most commonly used websites on the planet according to Statista 2022) is Wikipedia. Wikipedia is written and edited mostly by volunteers, and while it's often an excellent starting place to learn more about a topic, it's not typically viewed as an acceptable scholarly source. One of the great practices of Wikipedia contributors, though, is the creation and maintenance of bibliographies for each entry. Using a Wikipedia article to get started on a review of sources for your topic is often a great way to begin!

4.3.3.2 Finding Your Sources

We have alluded to a "literature review" throughout this section, and it may seem simple and straightforward: read some papers, consolidate the ideas, and write them down to point out the gap in the literature you are trying to address with your research (and how your research fits into the rest of the literature). Sometimes it can get tricky, though, because there are a lot of people writing about language and culture, and when writing a paper, we want to make sure we are drawing accurate conclusions. How do you know when you have found a good source for your research?

One way to start is with a book, like this one, or other textbooks and popular science books. These books are secondary sources: they have collated and organized a lot of primary sources and pieces of research and are often great places to start when you have a broad idea that you want to learn more about. Books might have a "further reading" section or something similar where there is a list of titles and authors that you can read if you're interested in a topic, but they will also have a reference list. You can use the authors in the citations throughout the book to find the papers in the reference list, working in reverse of how you would cite something in your own research.

Another way to start is to use some search terms in a repository or database, like your library's search tool or in Google Scholar (https://scholar.google.com). You can start your search broadly and then narrow down from there. If you wanted to see some research that uses word frequency counts from the COCA corpus that we discussed in Chapter 3, you could begin by searching for "word frequency COCA" (without quotes). When we performed this search in mid 2021, there were about 40,000 results for scholarly articles that used these keywords, a lot of which discussed second language learning. If this is what you were looking for, great! If it was not, you might change your search terms until you find a set that gives you something closer to what you are looking for. Repositories and databases are powerful tools that can be used in many ways, so we encourage you to consult with a research librarian to get a better idea of how to best go about your search.

As you work through your literature search, be aware of the quality of the sources you are using. For example, peer-reviewed journal articles, presentations, and books are the "gold standard" of academic literature: they have been vetted and edited by not only the author, but also other researchers in the field for quality control purposes, and they are generally reputable sources of information. However, you should be a little skeptical if you are reading an article supposedly stating a universal truth about language published in an economics journal, or an analysis of language and culture in a business journal – in those cases, you will want to corroborate what you read in that article with others written in linguistics journals. You want to be sure that you are reading someone's work when they have expertise in the field, rather than the musings of someone without experience. We discuss of what this type of work looks like in Chapter 10.

You may also be interested in a topic that borders different fields, which can complicate these guidelines. For example, if you are interested in language and society, you will probably want to read not only articles written by linguists but also those written by anthropologists and sociologists. If you are interested in language development, you will want to read articles by linguists, psychologists, anthropologists, and so on. This is where your detective skills will come in handy, because then you can see common ideas and themes that crop up across fields – these are probably robust findings if many people are testing them in many ways and getting the same results. It can seem daunting, but do not let this discourage you!

4.3.3.3 Referencing and Citation

Referencing and citation practices can also differ across different academic and cultural contexts. Different communities of scholars develop different standards for how to provide their audiences with information about the sources that researchers have built their work on. If you are a student at a college or university, you have no doubt encountered two or more referencing "styles" – these are sets of rules and practices for presenting information about our scholarly sources and for typesetting and presenting our work in writing. In this text, we are using the referencing style of our publisher, and most standard referencing and citation styles are developed by organizations or corporations that are involved in the publication of research papers.

Referencing and citation styles of different disciplines themselves can provide us with information about the scholarly culture of that discipline. For example, styles used in mathematics and computer science tend to involve significant use of abbreviations and acronyms in referencing – to the extent that a reader who is not a participant in that community of practice may not be able to decode the full names of scholarly journals cited – while those used in literature and humanities tend to use fully spelled-out styles with more attention paid to typeface variations (e.g., obligatory use of italics for some parts of a citation) and other aspects of human-readability and beautification. Our purpose here is not to advocate for any particular referencing and citation style but instead just to overview the components that all styles share.

Referencing is the provision of complete bibliographic or source information for all materials that have been used by the author/researcher in developing and explaining the research product. A complete reference should provide the reader with enough information about the source that the reader could easily locate that source and use it for their own purposes. References might be provided as footnotes or endnotes in some styles, or as a separate page titled "References," or "Bibliography," or "Works Cited."

Citation is the inclusion of notes in the body of the work that connect particular statements, ideas, quotations, or paraphrases with the reference from which they came. For styles that use footnotes or endnotes for references, the citation is simply the index number of the note, which usually appears as a superscript.[7] For styles that use reference pages, citations might appear in parentheses in running text. A citation of the book you are currently reading might look like "(Valentinsson, Drake, and Fountain 2026)" or "(Valentinsson et al., 2026)." An adequate citation is one that unambiguously identifies the reference that was used as a basis for the passage in which the citation appears. Depending on the citation style you're using, there will also be particular rules about when you must or must not include the page number[8] of the material you're citing. In some styles, page numbers are required elements of quoted – but not paraphrased – material. Check with your research mentor to learn the rules you'll need to follow.

In most referencing styles, there must be a match such that every citation corresponds to exactly one reference, and every reference corresponds to at least one citation. It is not typical for referencing to include resources that the scholar used along the way but that aren't mentioned or alluded to in the text or body of the work in question, although some disciplines do use bibliographies that are intended to list all the works you've consulted during the preparation of your paper, whether or not they're cited in the text. If you're not sure which form you should use for a project, you should ask! In order to appropriately attribute source information about materials that you learned

---

[7] Like this!

[8] If there is one. Some web-native resources that are perfectly reasonable to cite, such as online databases or dictionaries, don't have page numbers. But most books and articles in the scholarly world are still formatted as if they'll be printed on actual paper, and so will have numbered pages.

from but do not quote, paraphrase, or otherwise cite in the text or body of your work, you can use explanatory footnotes, endnotes, or acknowledgments. Some works include a bibliography separate from the reference page that is intended to assist interested readers in finding out more about the topic.

To give you a sense of how different references can look in different styles, compare example references of John Baugh's 2018 book: (a), which is written in the style of the American Psychological Association's 7th edition, (b), which is written in the style of the Modern Languages Association's 9th edition, and (c), which is written in the style of the journal *Nature* (and which would appear as a footnote rather than as an entry in a references or bibliography page).

(a) Baugh, J. (2018). *Linguistics in pursuit of justice.* Cambridge University Press.
(b) Baugh, John. *Linguistics in Pursuit of Justice.* Cambridge University Press, 2018.
(c) Baugh, J. *Linguistics in Pursuit of Justice.* (Cambridge University Press, Cambridge, UK, 2018).

You may have noticed that referencing and citation practices tend to be very much oriented toward attribution of source material in written work. This is probably because they developed in the context of print publishing, during a time in which most or all source material used by scholars was also published or provided in print. One challenge for referencing and citation in the modern era is figuring out how to adapt our practices for work that we share in forms other than standard academic papers, and for resources that we use that are not originally from print. At the time of the writing of this chapter, most standard referencing styles have developed formulas for citation of websites and mainstream media types (film, television), for internet-based publications, and for social media (like social media posts), but not necessarily for other evolving forms of presentation. We think that the most important thing for scholars to focus on is not the specifics of a style but the function of referencing and citation: to ensure that our audience can find and access the sources that inspired our work, and to ensure that our audience can identify particular ideas within our work that came from someone else, and connect those back to the correct source. These practices are part of our work to ensure that we are frank, honest, and open in our scholarship.

4.3.3.4 Citing Dictionaries, Databases, and Corpora

If you investigate language using data collected by others – for example, using searchable databases such the Oxford English Dictionary

Online[9] or corpora such as the Google Ngram Viewer[10] or the Corpus of Contemporary American English[11] – you may have trouble finding stylesheets or other information about how exactly to cite and refer to these sources. At the time of writing, specific standards for doing so are not universally agreed upon, but the general principles will suffice: you want to cite and refer to these resources in ways that correctly attribute them to their creators (i.e., Davies 2008; Michel et al. 2011; Oxford University Press 2021, for example) and that would allow a reader to find the examples or entries that you used. The latter means that you should carefully document your search terms or queries and discuss them in a "methods" section. Some corpora, dictionaries, and databases are structured so that you can easily refer to each entry, but others are not – so use your best judgment, and always work to ensure that a reader could replicate your work if they wished to.

4.3.3.5 Citing Writing Tools, Including AI Tools

As we write this chapter, a variety of artificial intelligence (AI) tools[12] have emerged and are being used by scholars, students, artists, and others. These tools typically allow writers to enter "prompts," and then they produce text or images that respond to the prompts. We urge you to use the guiding principles of honesty, frankness, and openness if you use these tools – and that means clearly declaring which, if any, such tools you have used, and distinguishing clearly between your work and work that was generated by a machine.

4.3.4 Intellectual Property and Copyright

In the US, and in a variety of other national contexts, researchers may also need to negotiate rules, policies, and laws regarding intellectual property and copyright. Even if we are clear about referencing and citation of materials that we use, if we draw works into our own research that were authored or created by others, we also need to consider their rights as creators and our obligations as users. While the particulars of intellectual property and

---

[9] A proprietary database version of the Oxford English Dictionary, to which you may have access through your school's library or a personal account.
[10] A publicly accessible, searchable corpus of books digitized by Google, with information here: https://books.google.com/ngrams/info.
[11] An openly available scholarly corpus of US English, currently hosted here: www.english-corpora.org/coca/.
[12] At present, the most prominent of these are called "ChatGPT" and "Gemini," but we're confident that by the time you read this there will be many more such tools, and they will have many names.

copyright law differ in different jurisdictions, we think that ethical considerations go beyond these specifics and, with respect to language in particular, can be surprising to majority language communities. There are, in fact, considerations of intellectual property rights in the recording and use of language data of some communities of practice. As an example, we can turn to the US film adaptations of the "Twilight" series of books, written by Stephanie Meyers, and the films that followed.

The setting of the novels involves a Native American community, the Quileute Tribe, and the filmmakers chose to invoke some elements of Quileute language history and language. Where Meyers' books were not known for the accuracy or rigor of research around her fictional setting, the films specifically used snippets of (supposed) Quileute language and symbology (see Carpenter et al. 2010; Kowal 2006). This use was not pre-approved by the tribe, and the franchise's earnings from this expropriation did not benefit the tribe's language program. The Quileute community is not alone in the US in asserting that they have, and claim, intellectual property rights for their language – we have seen similar assertions from a number of Indigenous communities around the world. Whether or not courts or legal experts would agree with these claims, we believe that ethical research practices would involve respecting such claims, and only sharing language data from such communities with their expressed informed consent.

Other areas in which intellectual property and copyright considerations may be important include, but are not limited to, our use of video and audio clips, images, and graphic elements created by others. Our principles of honesty, frankness, and respect for others in our research methods and scholarly presentation should always guide our behavior in using or sharing works created by others.

4.4 Considerations for Responsibly Disseminating Your Research

After your data has been ethically collected and analyzed, you will find yourself in the position of needing to write about your findings. If you are just writing for a class, you'll not need to be worried about the legal and policy requirements beyond those provided by your instructor – though we still hope you abide by the guiding principles that underlay those requirements. While the technical specifications of your writing for a class may differ from what is expected of published scholarly work, it is still worthwhile to make your best effort to abide by the writing norms and standards of the discipline you are writing in, to the extent you can. But if you're writing for a broader audience – perhaps as an independent scholar, or as someone who aims to publish their work, we have some advice about how to approach that.

In this section, we will review two considerations for scholarly writing. First, we will discuss how the expectations of the structure of a scholarly paper in linguistics might differ from that of other fields, and some of the differences you might notice between writing styles across the various subfields of linguistics. Then, we will discuss some considerations for how to best represent your data, the participants in your research, and your claims.

We believe that it is important to recognize that there are many genres of academic writing, just as there are many genres of fiction, and that it is a good idea to familiarize yourself with the generic conventions of your field. This will help you not only to write a paper for your class more easily, but also to be able to have a good idea of how to find the information that you need in the scholarship that you are reading. Since linguistics is inherently interdisciplinary – we use language in just about every situation and circumstance, and many people are curious about how language works! – you will find that there is no one specific way to "write a linguistics paper," or even to "write a phonology paper" or "write a linguistic anthropology paper." There are some commonalities that we can look for, though.

Most linguists use the scientific method, and the scholarly writing they do reflects this. Scientific writing in linguistics typically includes an introduction, a background section, a methods section, a discussion of results, and a conclusion. This kind of sectioning can vary tremendously, depending on the subfield, the research question, or the approach. But you will probably see at least a few sections like these in most scholarly articles you read that are related to linguistics in some way. Why section academic writing in this way? The microscope / magnifying glass / telescope metaphor from Chapter 1 can help us understand.

Introductions in scholarly work operate primarily at the magnifying glass level: we zoom in narrowly enough to see what is interesting or unusual about a particular linguistic phenomenon, but not so narrowly that we cannot see elements of how it might relate to other phenomena. A background or literature review section will operate at a similar level, though perhaps zooming out just a bit more: Here, we want to see what research has already been conducted on this phenomenon, as scholars will also often write about topics that are related and relevant, though not quite the same. This helps us better understand what we already know about the problem, and any related issues. Methods and results / findings sections tend to operate on the microscope level: this is the very fine-grained, specific information you need to understand what was done to analyze a particular linguistic data set and what the scholars found using these methods. Finally, discussion and conclusion sections will zoom out a bit more. In the conclusion in particular, you may find the authors switching to a telescope view: this is the spot in scholarly writing when researchers often take the specifics of their findings and situate them within a broader body of work. At this stage they may even present new questions that their study generated rather than answered, setting the stage for even more research. Again, keep in mind that not all scholarly writing in linguistics (or any discipline, really) will have all of these components all of the time. These are simply the most commonly used sections of scholarly research papers, articles, and books. With that caveat, let's turn to exploring some of these sections in greater detail.

4.4.1 The Contents of a Paper

Although you may not write a title and abstract for a class paper, you will probably see them in articles that you read. The title is something you are accustomed to seeing in other types of writing: it tells you the basic topic of the paper or book. The abstract is a very, *very* brief overview of what the research question is, the methods used to collect the data, any other analyses that were performed, and a big-picture look at how the question fits into the literature as a whole. If you are writing a thesis or literature review, reading just the title and abstract of a paper can tell you whether it is related to your work and therefore worth spending time reading the whole paper carefully, or if the paper is not quite what you were looking for and can be set aside for now. You can also apply this knowledge as you write your own titles and abstracts since you know how important they are for other scholars looking for research findings.

Most papers begin with the claim that they are making or the question they are trying to answer, with a short review of the relevant literature that has led them to this claim or question. This is what we have referred to already as the introduction and background or literature review sections. Reviewing the related scholarship to your question is another way we can demonstrate our frankness and openness about our research: although it may be tempting to ignore a piece of research that pokes holes in your claim or a paper that seems to be asking (and answering) the same question that you have, it is still important to acknowledge it in some way and highlight how your work explores the question in a new light. Intentionally failing to mention work that you've read but that you find inconvenient to deal with is a form of academic dishonesty.

Methods sections focus on laying out the evidence that you have gathered to support your claim and how you went about getting that evidence. As we alluded to earlier in this chapter, one of the goals of doing research is to make it reproducible: that is, to say what you did and how you did it clearly enough that someone else can follow the same steps to collect the same kind of data and see if they come to the same conclusion. In some subfields, this will look like several sentences that have been glossed and had the important parts highlighted; in others, this will look like a series of transcribed conversations; and in others still, this will look like technical descriptions of software, coding procedures, and statistical analyses; it can even describe an experiment with participants, materials, procedures, and measures! Although these look very different, they all describe the same kind of information: how the reader could do another version of the same research.

Results sections describe specifically what you found by following the methods you describe. This information may include examples, counts, statistical results, and/or close analysis. In papers that distinguish results from discussion sections, which is common in many subdisciplines, the results section lays out the observed patterns in the data in as clear a way as possible. The discussion section then interprets or explains why the data are important and how they relate to the claim or question you started with.

Finally, papers usually conclude by going back to the big picture and where your research fits with everything else that you described in the first section of the paper. This section may be called a "discussion" or a "conclusion," or a paper may have both a discussion *and* a conclusion section, but they all cover roughly this type of information. In this portion of the paper, you describe the findings of your research and how it fits into the rest of the field. Does it support other claims that were made by other researchers, or does it contradict them? What are some reasons that your research turned out differently? Are there limitations to your study (perhaps you collected only one type of data when another type of data would also have been helpful to explain your results, for example)? Are there questions that are left unanswered by your research, or ones that have been raised by your results? Any given paper may or may not answer all of these questions, but they are things to keep in mind as you write your discussion.

While we have referred to the process of writing a paper in this section, it is important to remember that this can also help you figure out how to read a piece of research for the information you are looking for. Scholars may not read a paper all the way through from beginning to end because they are looking specifically and only for how some conversational conventions were annotated, example sentences, or which statistical tests were performed, all of which are in the methods section. They may also read the introduction and discussion to get an idea of the research question and claim that the paper is making and how the paper's author(s) see it fitting into the literature. We do not endorse skimming articles for *all* of your assigned readings, but when you are doing a review of the literature, it is useful to know that you can skim the methods section if you are not looking to do a similar experiment or use a similar observational method, for example.

4.4.2 Disciplinary Conventions

While we have been discussing the similarities of writing across linguistics, there are some conventions that are used depending on whether you are writing a sociolinguistics paper, a psycholinguistics paper, a linguistic anthropology paper, a syntax paper, or a computational linguistics paper, just to name a few examples. As you read more of the literature in a particular subdiscipline, you may notice that there are different ways of introducing the data that you have collected or the methods that you have used, or even in introducing researchers and their ideas and papers. The three of us authors are from slightly different subfields, so you might notice some of these tendencies throughout this textbook!

Some of these conventions may be more obvious than others. In disciplines where you perform statistical tests on your data, you will probably also include charts, graphs, and tables that summarize your data. In disciplines where you analyze portions of words, sentences, or conversations, you will likely have transcriptions of those parts of language that you are focusing on. These transcriptions will be in the format that is appropriate for the kind of data you're looking at: for instance, transcripts of conversations will include pauses and interruptions; syntax papers will have glossed sentences that may or may not also have morphemes delineated; phonology and phonetics papers will have glossed sentences that use the IPA rather than a Latinate orthography; in ethnographies, you will know a great deal about the community and participants, but you will not in psycholinguistic studies; and so on.

Some disciplinary writing conventions are more subtle. Some disciplines tend to have a more "literary" writing style, and some tend to have a more "scientific" style – but remember that these stylistic differences do *not* mean that one subdiscipline's research is more rigorous or valid or better than another's! You might notice that papers written in linguistic anthropology, syntax, and other subdisciplines may use more foregrounding to introduce their authors, like "In her foundational paper, animal communication scholar Artemis Cat (2021) argues...". On the other hand, papers written in psycholinguistics, computational linguistics, and other subdisciplines may not introduce authors at all, like "Animal communication is very complex (Cat, 2021)". As you gain more practice working in the various genres that are represented in science writing, we are confident that you will find more commonalities and differences – but you can use these as starting points.

4.4.3 The Content of Your Writing

Once you know *how* to write in linguistics, what should you say? Broadly speaking, it is a good idea to be as precise and specific as possible, particularly in describing your data and research participants. This norm is apparent in two rules of thumb formulated by linguists working at the intersections of sociolinguistics and other disciplines. While these rules are not always followed, we strongly encourage you to use them as guidelines when you write! Both rules require you to be highly specific in describing the languages you are studying and the communities who speak those languages.

The first guideline, the "Bender Rule" (Bender 2019), was born out of an effort to encourage computational linguists to write accurately about their data (Bender 2011; Bender & Friedman 2018). For many years, much of computational linguistics focused on data sets from English and other major world languages. However, the patterns of language structure studied by computational methods may not work equally well across all languages. Thus, the Bender Rule says: State which language your study is based on. For example, if your data set uses only English words, say that your findings are applicable to English, rather than language as a whole. When English is assumed as the default language, as it tends to be, it results in an implicit standard being set where English is a "normal" language and other languages are not. We know this is not the case!

The second guideline, which we have termed the "Lanehart Rule" after the sociolinguist Sonja Lanehart, is built on advocacy led by Black sociolinguists, including Sonja Lanehart, Nicole Holliday, and many others. This guideline is to explicitly state the parameters of the population you study. If your population is homogeneous in some way, especially if you intended to recruit a heterogeneous population, say so. This goes for populations that are racially homogenous (e.g., all white people), linguistically homogeneous (e.g., all American English speakers), or however else your population is homogenous. This is because we cannot attribute some trait to "all English speakers" or "all language users," for instance, if we only study white American English speakers. In all of our scientific work, we need to make sure that all of our variables are accounted for and described accurately so that we can be sure that we're drawing accurate conclusions.

Not all scientific writing uses these guidelines, but we believe it improves and clarifies our writing when we do. You can also think of it as doing something that is ethically sound: there is no reason to omit or obscure these details. Even if you think that using them (or not) is inconsequential, sometimes it makes a huge difference whether you are discussing data that came from a homogenous population of white American English speakers or a heterogeneous sample of American English speakers from many racial and cultural backgrounds, for example.

4.5 Conclusion

We have presented some best practices and resources in this chapter that will help you to conduct your work in ways that are helpful and constructive and to report on and share the findings of your research in ethical ways that meet the norms of linguistics as a scholarly community. Sometimes thinking about research ethics, human participant protections, and the like can feel overwhelming – almost to the point of discouragement. We hope that rather than feeling overwhelmed, you are feeling empowered. In carefully considering your research practices to ensure that your work is honest, compassionate, fair, and accessible, you can rest easy in the knowledge that you are doing your best to make our community of scholars better by your presence in it.

Linguist in the Community

- Explore the human subjects protection program(s) / research ethics board of your university (or a university near you). You can start by conducting an internet search for "[name of university]" plus the keywords IRB, HSPP, or research ethics board. Review the information on their website and consider the following questions together:
  - Who sits on the review committees? Are members primarily part of the university community? Are there other individuals who participate in reviewing research projects? Can you find any information about how one can become a member of the review committee?
  - What steps do researchers have to go through in order to receive approval for their projects?
  - What resources are available to research participants on this website?
- Find a book or paper on a linguistic topic that you'd like to read, and see how it matches up with the claims we've made in this chapter. What outline does it follow, and what sections does it use? Can you find something that looks like an introduction, a literature review, a methods section, results and/or discussion, and then conclusion? If it is structured differently than what we've described here, why do you think it was?
- Practice a peer review! Using a paper you are interested in, pretend that you have been asked to review that paper pre-publication. Look at the structure and content of the paper, and check for signs of compliance

with the rules of human subjects protections and research integrity. Check the referencing and citations and see if you agree that it is sufficient and appropriate. It's unlikely that even the best published paper is perfect – so we think you'll find at least one or two revisions that you would propose the author(s) consider for a revision!

Linguist in the Classroom

- In small groups, or with your entire class, discuss the ethics of collecting data from various online sources in the scenarios posited below. In each of these cases, consider: What would be the best way to obtain informed consent from all participants? Is this even possible/realistic? How would you go about protecting the confidentiality, privacy, and anonymity of participants?
    - Writing a script to download thousands of tweets in order to look for frequencies of a certain word or phrase.
    - Engaging in in-depth participant observation with a private Facebook group.
    - Tracking the language use and communicative decisions of a small group of friends across several different social media platforms.
- In small groups, decide on some search terms to use in your library's article database or on Google Scholar. Use these search terms to find sources that discuss the ideas that you're interested in. Do the sources you've found seem like good ones? Why or why not? Can you find more information about the people who wrote the sources? Are they a reputable source of information?
- Individually or in small groups, skim some published research articles in the discipline of linguistics (broadly understood) and compare their structure. You may want to set one small group or individual to focus on papers in phonology, another in syntax, another in sociolinguistics, and so on. Look for the typical elements of introduction, methods, results, and conclusion, but keep in mind that some disciplines may not follow this pattern. How do they section the paper and what subheadings do they use to refer to different sections of the article? What topics or issues do they cover in each section – do they have one that seems to be primarily dedicated to reviewing the literature, and others that seem to focus more on data? In a larger group, compare your findings. What are some common elements in how academic articles across subfields present their findings? What are the big differences? Did you notice authors applying the Bender Rule or the Lanehart Rule (whether or not they name the rule outright)?

Glossary

anonymity The state or condition of any personally identifiable information about research participants being removed from the data.

community-based research A research process that involves scientists, scholars, community members, and research participants equitably in the decision-making about and ownership of the research, with community members generally in the lead in terms of what is important to study and in what ways.

confidentiality The right of a participant in a research study to not have their identity or the fact of their participation shared with others.

disinformation False information that is deliberately shared in order to mislead or deceive.

ethics boards Governmental and/or academic institutions that codify regulations about best practices and ethics in scientific research, as they are generally known in the UK; see also **human subjects protection programs**.

forensic linguists The application of linguistic analysis and science to criminal investigation and legal or judicial decision-making.

hate speech Language use that weaponizes bias with violent intent.

human subjects A living individual from whom a scientist or other research investigator collects identifiable private information for the purposes of systematic research aimed at contributing to generalizable knowledge.

human subjects protections programs Governmental and/or academic institutions that codify regulations about best practices and ethics in scientific research, as they are generally known in North America; see also **ethics boards**.

informed consent The process of obtaining permission from a potential research participant to include them in a scientific study and collect data from them.

participants People who volunteer to take part in a scientific study after receiving informed consent.

peer review A process by which academic papers and books are often published, and which is a form of quality control that's used in scientific writing. Peer review happens when your paper is read by experts in the field in which you're writing (these are your peers) who then either confirm that it meets scholarly standards as-is or else discuss the revisions that would be required before the work should be published. Occasionally, peer review results in a decision that the work is so far away from the standards of the field that it cannot be published at all. Scholarly papers that are published in academic books and journals are almost always the result of successful revision after peer review.

plagiarism Incomplete or dishonest referencing and citation; can include "taking someone else's ideas and passing them off as your own," but can also include failure to cite your own ideas from previous work and other examples of incomplete or dishonest referencing.

privacy The right of a participant in a research study to elect to not share certain information about themselves, and to control the disclosure of any information they provide as part of their participation in the study.

racial slurs A disparaging or denigrating term or phrase specifically directed at members of minoritized racial groups.

stigmatized Socially marked as inappropriate, inadequate, or shameful.

terms of service (agreements) A set of legal agreements between service providers and users of that service.

vulnerable population A group who is in need of additional protections because they are not fully autonomous, may be in precarious social groups, or may otherwise be coerced by researchers.

Recommended Readings

Doing linguistics responsibly, and with care for all the human speakers involved, is a very important part of being a linguist. For more information on the material we covered in this topic, check out our recommended readings below. If you need help finding these resources or any of the other readings we cite in this chapter, reach out to your local college or university library.

Bender, E. M. (2019). The #BenderRule: On naming the languages we study and why it matters. *The Gradient.* https://thegradient.pub/the-benderrule-on-naming-the-languages-we-study-and-why-it-matters/

Berez-Kroeker, A. L., Andreassen, H. N., Gawne, L., Holton, G., Smythe Kung, S., Pulsifer, P., Collister, L. B., The Data Citation and Attribution in Linguistics Group, & The Linguistics Data Interest Group. (2018). The Austin Principles of data citation in linguistics. Version 1.0. *Linguistics Data Citation.* https://site.uit.no/linguisticsdatacitation/austinprinciples/

5 Languages Fall in Love, Experience Fear

5.1 Excuse Me?

Whether you know it or not, languages have profound effects on one another. For example, you might think about how many of the words you use in English have their origins in other languages. Some words came into English a long time ago, like the Latinate vocabulary English speakers use in domains like education, the law, and science. Others entered the English lexicon more recently, like borrowed words for delicious foods like phở, which comes to English via Vietnamese, and to Vietnamese from French. This chapter discusses some of the mechanisms through which languages change because their speakers come into contact with one another, the policies that are enacted in efforts to keep languages separate, and the various reactions from speakers with regard to the languages spoken in their community.

If we return to our microscope metaphor from Chapter 1, think of our focus here being at roughly binocular level. We are not focusing yet on small, intricate, and subtle details of language that would require our microscope; we also are not focusing on the global picture that requires our telescope. Instead, we will section out communities of language users to see how they use the languages at their disposal, and how that language use causes change over time. You will also get some ideas about how you can learn more about this by observing your own language use, and the use of others in your community.

Let's try a quick exercise using English. Consider the vocabulary in Table 5.1:

Table 5.1 English words for animals vs. English words for the meat from those animals

cow	beef
swine	pork
hen	poultry
deer	venison
sheep	mutton

The words on the left refer to the English words for animals that many human communities have kept as livestock for generations. The words on the right refer to the meat that comes from each.

Consult any good etymological dictionary – that is, a dictionary that includes not only definitions of words but also information about their history. (**Etymology** is the study of word origins and histories.) Look up the language of origin of each of the words for animals, and then for each of the words for the meat of the animals.

It turns out that English began as a variety of Western Germanic, so it is a cousin of modern German. The first speakers of "English" were actually speakers of Germanic varieties who had invaded the British Isles and were fighting the Celtic communities who had arrived much earlier. Most scholars place the origins of "English" as a linguistic, political, and social entity separate from the other Germanic languages at about AD 400–450.

Five hundred or so years later, the English-speaking population was facing invasion by another group, led by speakers of Norman, Breton, French, and Flemish. The so-called Norman Conquest culminated in the Battle of Hastings in 1066, and it's today called a "conquest" because the invading armies won. In the years following, the language of state, of education, and of wealthy elites shifted away from the Germanic English to Latinate French.

Modern-day English retains the effects of this social and political upheaval in our language. Consider how livestock production and food consumption work, especially with regard to consumption of meat. Meat eating has been historically the province of the wealthy, but animal husbandry has often been relegated to the poor. Do you see evidence of this kind of distribution of labor and benefit of labor in the etymology of the words for animals vs. the words for the meat of these animals in English? It's there.

There are many ways in which a linguist in the community can explore how Latinate vs. Germanic words shape how language is used, and also how community members *think* about language. Scholars have observed a persistent sense in many English-speaking communities that words that sound like they come from Latin also sound fancy, elite, or educated in a way that Germanic words do not. Based on the list of words you investigated in Table 5.1, do you think that this is so? How could you use your skills in observation to discover other patterns in people's language behavior that might answer this question? How might you use **corpus**-based tools to explore the distribution of Latinate vs. Germanic vocabulary in different spheres of use?

But this chapter is not about the history of English. We want to invite you to explore broadly the question of what happens when languages meet each other. We will look at how language communities react to situations in which they come into contact with one another in a variety of social, historical and political situations. Through this, we will see that reactions can range from falling in love to lashing out in fear and anger, and a lot of things in between.

5.2 So Many Languages, So Little Time

Let's be clear at the outset – language communities are, and have always been, in contact with each other, and humans are incredibly well-adapted to **multilingual** and **multidialectal** environments. There is no such thing as a "pure" or completely isolated language. Throughout the world, being multilingual and multidialectal is completely unremarkable – perhaps even more common than being **monolingual** or **monodialectal**. And communities that are isolated from one another geographically, economically, or socially are very likely to use multiple languages or varieties. Because language can occur either as a spoken/auditory code or as a signed/visual one, many communities have signed as well as spoken languages. Signed language speakers in many communities will (and often must, in order to participate fully in the social, economic, and political activities undertaken in a hearing community) be multilingual with one or more spoken languages. Communities that have high rates of hearing impairment among their population may well use a signed language as primary, such that community members without hearing impairment will (must) be multilingual with the signed language. As humans, our biology and our social nature mean we are very, very good at using languages of all kinds. And in our communities, we have different ways of organizing which languages are used when.

5.2.1 Diglossia, Codeswitching, and Translanguaging

Some multilingual communities may use one language at home and another in the workplace; or they may use multiple languages at home and others in the workplace; or any other conceivable combination. Linguists use the term **diglossia** to refer to situations in which one language is used for informal, everyday conversation, and another one used for more formal genres. In diglossic communities, neither language is "better" or "worse" than the other – it's just that each one is used in a different context. We can see this at work in the Alsatian region of France, near the border with Switzerland and Germany. Here, everyday life and casual conversations are conducted in the Alsatian language (although this is changing as the pressure to participate in the globalizing economy causes people to use their "home" varieties less and less – we discuss this topic more in Chapter 10). Meanwhile, newspaper writing, television broadcasts, and formal business are conducted in French

(Kloss 1968). Diglossia can also be used to describe a situation where two varieties of the same language occupy different contextual roles. In Myanmar, for instance, there is both a "literary" form of Burmese – used in literature, formal speech, and news reporting – and a "spoken" form, used in daily conversation and informal writing (Bradley 1977).

That said, there are also multilingual communities that do not keep each of their languages (or dialects!) separate from each other. If you eavesdrop on a conversation between two multilingual people who share more than one language, you may find that they **codeswitch**, or change between multiple languages, throughout their conversation (and sometimes even in the same sentence). We also use these terms to describe switching between two varieties of the same language, such as between two regional dialects.

One of the clearest findings of linguistic research on **codeswitching** is *not* "sloppy" language use, or "bad language," or evidence of having incompletely learned a language. Instead, codeswitching is quite the opposite: it's really only possible to codeswitch seamlessly and fluently if you speak the languages in question very, very well. This means that children in multilingual, codeswitching communities learn these rules very early on, and deploy them without having to think much about the how or why behind them. We talk about how children go about learning their languages more in Chapter 6.

Codeswitching is also rule-based and predictable (Lippi-Green 2012; Myers-Scotton 1993; Poplack 1980, 1988; and many more). We might find that speakers in a given multilingual community switch languages **intersententially** – that is, the language being used changes at sentence boundaries. We also see evidence of multilingual speakers switching languages **intrasententially**, or within the boundaries of a sentence. There are even examples of codeswitching within a single word! Take the word "janguear," which might also be spelled "janguiar." If you speak Spanish, and especially if you come from a community where Spanish–English codeswitching is common, you might have heard this word used in a way that's roughly equivalent to the English verb "to hang out." The word starts with something that looks and sounds like the English word "hang" (spelled differently to better reflect Spanish orthography), but it has word endings that indicate its use as a verb in Spanish (like the *-ar* in *caminar* "to walk").

This last example is also illustrative of a type of codeswitching you may be familiar with: **Spanglish**. This term is used as an umbrella term to identify a particular brand of codeswitching between English and Spanish in the US. While some people use the term "Spanglish" as a pejorative, the linguistic practice of producing connected speech in a way that blends vocabulary, grammar, intonation, rhythm, and wordplay from multiple source languages is an act of multilingual genius. Far from being "broken" versions of one or the other language – as these varieties are often accused of being by listeners for whom the blend feels threatening – they are rich, nuanced, and often quite beautiful communicative codes.

It should come as no surprise, then, that codeswitching can be an important identity marker (Price 2010; Toribio 2002). Still, studies of codeswitching in and of itself tend to focus primarily on the underlying rules governing switching as it occurs in a particular communicative moment. Recently, scholars of multilingualism have developed the concept of **translanguaging** as a new framework for understanding what happens when two (or more) languages get to know one another. While studies of codeswitching tend to focus on how two (or more) languages come to operate together, translanguaging looks at how speakers of multiple languages or varieties create new social and cultural meanings out of blending and hybridizing all of the varieties within their linguistic repertoire. In other words, it focuses not just on the structural rules governing codeswitching but allows us to look at how speakers might deliberately manipulate and play with their multiple varieties to shape their identities and reflect their understanding of their culture. One example of this comes from Jonathan Rosa's work (2016) on what he termed **Inverted Spanglish**. While studying Latinx high school students in Chicago, he observed these students using Anglicized pronunciations of Spanish vocabulary items to create new jokes, insults, and wordplay – kind of like speaking Spanish "through" English. Using a (mocking) English pronunciation to utter Spanish words might not be considered codeswitching in and of itself, but it does show how these young people blended linguistic resources they had from English with the resources they had from Spanish to make sense of their racial and ethnic identities in their school.

All of these effects of multilingual contact tend to be quite apparent, even to folks with no training in linguistics. But the ways in which languages in contact can mutually influence one another are innumerable. To readjust to the microscopic view for just a moment, consider two of the largest communities of Welsh speakers in the world: in Wales, and in the southern Argentinean province of Chubut. Many people are surprised to learn that there is a community of Welsh speakers in Argentina, but it's true! A small group of Welsh people sailed to Argentina in 1865 in an effort to protect their language and culture from the encroachment of English in Wales. Fast-forward over 150 years, we see two distinct varieties of Welsh shaped by contact with distinct languages. Research comparing the phonetic systems of Welsh–Spanish bilinguals in Argentina with Welsh–English bilinguals in the UK reveals that each language has had a distinct effect on the vowel system of Welsh (Bell 2018). All this goes to show that even if it's not immediately obvious, and even though the effects may be as subtle as the shift in a few vowels, languages in contact with one another will inevitably be shaped by one another.

5.2.2 The Emergence of New Languages

Sometimes when language communities come together and speakers engage in prolific codeswitching and translanguaging, we see the birth of truly **blended varieties**: languages that for all linguistic, political, and social purposes have their own individual identities – but that seem to draw large swaths of their machinery from two or more distinct languages. Examples of this include Maltese, which is spoken in the Republic of Malta, and Michif (Barkwell 2017; Gillon & Rosen 2018), a language spoken by the Métis people in communities throughout Saskatchewan and Manitoba in Canada and South Dakota in the United States.

Both of these language communities are marked by long periods of the native or indigenous population being exposed to European colonizers: French settlers in the case of Michif, and Sicilian and British settlers in the case of Maltese. Both groups of colonizers came into the community with their own language, and eventually both colonizers and locals learned enough of each others' language to get by and interact. Over time, not only were words from each language borrowed back and forth, but ways of structuring language were too. With enough contact between two languages, a new language emerges or an old language changes substantially.

When this happens, there may be a smaller, older "core" of the new language that contains basic nouns, adjectives, verbs, and grammatical structures, while a newer "shell" might contain more words and slightly different grammatical structures. In Maltese, this is nicely represented with a split between Arabic-like words and structures and Sicilian- or English-like words and structures. Basic sentence structures, pronouns, and many verb conjugations look like Arabic – the older "core" of Maltese – whereas newer vocabulary and word formation processes look more like Sicilian Italian or English. Basic color names (as defined typologically; Berlin & Kay 1969) like black, white, red, and green are very similar to their Arabic counterparts; on the other hand, words for colors like orange, purple, gray, and pink are similar to their Sicilian Italian counterparts (see Table 5.2). Similarly, older concepts like *dog* and *love* are similar to Arabic (*kelb* and *mħabba* in Maltese compared to *kelb* and *ħobb* in Arabic), while newer concepts like *computers* are similar to English (*kompjuters*).

In the case of Michif, the language of the Métis people of the Northern Plains, the blend takes some of its vocabulary and grammar from French, an Indo-European language, and some of its vocabulary and grammar from

Table 5.2 Color words in Maltese, Arabic, and Italian

	Maltese	Arabic	Italian
black	/iswɛd/	/aswad/	/nɛro/
white	/abjad/	/abjad/	/bjaŋko/
red	/aħmar/	/aħmar/	/ros:o/
green	/aħdar/	/axdar/	/verdi/
orange	/orandʒo/	/burtuqali/	/arantʃoni/
purple	/vjola/	/bənafsadʒi/	/vjola/
gray	/griz/	/rəmadi/	/gridʒo/
pink	/roza/	/warədi/	/roza/

Plains Cree, an Algonquian language indigenous to North America. According to Métis elder Lawrence Barkwell (2017, p. 1),

> Michif emerged in the 1700s as a mixed language which was regularly commented on in the fur trade journals as a distinct language of the Métis between about 1820 and 1840. Michif combines Plains Cree (y dialect or nēhiyawēwin) and old Métis French, a derivative of Canadien French that was spoken in New France and later in Lower Canada and was based on the amalgamation and standardization of various langues d'oïl dialects from northwestern France. Michif has some additional borrowing from English, Plains Ojibway (Nakawēmowin) and Nakoda.

The stage was set for the emergence of a mixed language by the development of trade networks including Indigenous peoples and European immigrants, especially from France. When people come into contact, some of them create families – and in this case, those families developed a way of speaking that became its own political, social, and linguistic entity: the Michif language.

In Michif, speakers can say sentences like (1) and (2) below (adapted from Gillon & Rosen 2018, p. 8). Although Michif has influences from a number of other languages, we focus here on a distinction between French-derived and Cree-derived elements. The Cree-derived words in these examples are underlined, and the French-derived words are not underlined. (Keep in mind that we are simplifying the word-by-word translation of the Cree words from that presented in the original, which is a highly technical grammatical analysis.)

(1) li   kofii   for   pi   <u>kamaachiishpakwak</u> <u>nimiyoihten</u>
     the   coffee strong and   it.tastes.bad   I.like.it
     "I like strong and bitter coffee"

(2) sae'nk lii   sheezh ver   <u>ndajaan</u>
     Five   the.plural   chair   green I.have
     "I have five green chairs"

In these examples, the Cree-derived vocabulary includes the words that mean "it tastes bad," "I like it," and "I have (them)." These words are verbs at heart, but they actually contain enough information to provide a complete sentence. These words are built of many meaningful pieces (roots with prefix-like and suffix-like parts), as is necessary for any Cree verb. They also appear at the end of the sentence, which is how the grammar works in Cree.

The French-derived vocabulary in these examples includes the nouns that mean "coffee" and "chair," the articles, the conjunction, and the adjectives like the words that mean "five," "strong," and "green." And the French-derived words aren't built up of lots of distinct meaningful parts. As in French, the articles come right before the noun or adjective-noun combination.

Michif blends words as well as phrase- and sentence-building rules from both of its source languages, and the language is a really clear example of how at home languages can get with each other under some circumstances. The Cree-derived and the French-derived elements of Michif are not the same as European French or neighboring Cree – it is all Michif, all the time.

If a linguist in the community wanted to dive more deeply into the social and cultural factors that drive language mixing, there are a lot of avenues that would be useful to explore. It is almost certain that you yourself, or someone in your own community, is multilingual or multidialectal in a way that includes a codeswitching ability. If you pay attention, and develop a responsible research protocol that would allow you to ethically record examples of codeswitching, you might notice patterns in the switches. Are there patterns of meaning that you find in speakers' choice of words, phrases, or expressions in one language compared to the other? Where do speakers switch? Is it always in the same place? Can you find any examples of switching within a word, like where a root might be from one language but a prefix or suffix from another? Document your findings and discuss them with peers or share them with your instructor. You may well develop insights about speakers' beliefs and values about the languages reflected in their patterns of use. You may also find evidence of creative genius in speakers' multilingual utterances! We will have some suggestions for reflection on these topics at the end of this chapter.

If you are fortunate enough to live in a place where mixed languages like Michif or Maltese are spoken, we encourage you to learn more about how those languages work, and how they may be used differently by different speakers. And if you speak, or know someone who speaks, any language that has the word "pidgin" or "creole" in the language name, you can be assured that their language probably originated as a mixed variety. By themselves, the terms **pidgin** and **creole** are technical terms that describe language varieties that arise in situations of intense multilingual contact. It's important to distinguish between the technical use of these terms in linguistics and the cases when these words are used in the names of languages themselves – it can get a bit confusing at times!

For linguists, a pidgin is a language that emerges when groups of people need to communicate with each other but do not share any languages in common. The classic example is when two groups who do not share a mutually intelligible language need to find a way to trade over an extended period of time. In this case, the groups in contact will develop a rather simplified code to make communication in that particular setting work. Pidgins are typically not used in other social contexts or spoken at home – they mostly serve as second languages, used in specific situations. However, with continued use and spread throughout a community, a pidgin may become a creole. Creoles emerge when a community using some kind of contact variety, like a pidgin, starts to teach that contact language to their children. In other words, the language gains native speakers and is used in a wide range of communicative contexts. When a pidgin becomes a creole, it develops a distinct grammar and becomes more structurally complex.

This is all a simplification, of course, but it is the rough story of pidgins and creoles. It is also important to remember that many speech communities have adopted the words "pidgin" and "creole" to name their complex, fully-formed languages: When you hear of a language like Hawaiian Pidgin, you need to know you are talking about a complete language, not a simplified linguistic variety used to bridge a communicative gap. Similarly, Haitian Creole is the name of a language with many generations of native speakers at this point. Keeping track of when the technical linguistic definition is in play and when the actual name of a language chosen by a speech community is being used can be tricky, but context clues can help you figure out what is meant whenever you hear those words. The words pidgin and creole have both also been used as pejoratives in the past, so we advise you to read more about them before deploying them in your own work. Exploring these kinds of linguistic varieties will teach you a great deal about how languages can share space in speakers' minds and in their social worlds!

5.3 We Can All Coexist in Harmony

Several languages might also exist together in one geographic or cultural area, with the people inhabiting the area speaking many of the languages represented, but there may not be very much exchange or blending between them like we saw in the Michif and Maltese examples in the previous section. One of these areas you are probably familiar with already is the European Union (EU), but we will also look at two additional areas: countries in northwestern Africa frequently referred to as *the Maghreb*, and the Vaupés region of Amazonian Colombia and Brazil.

The European Union is a group of twenty-seven European countries that are, to various extents, affiliated politically, legally, and economically. One of the EU's stated goals is to embrace multilingualism among its member states (European Union 2019). One of the ways that this is illustrated is by incorporating the **official languages** represented in each member state, which results in there being a whopping twenty-four official languages in the EU. Theoretically, you should be able to use any of these languages to contact government agencies and institutions in the EU! The governing body has also stated two additional sub-goals: every EU citizen being able to communicate in at least two languages in addition to their native language, and protecting minority languages in Europe, some of which include Basque, Catalan, Welsh, and Yiddish.

What distinguishes the multilingualism in the EU from the multilingualism resulting from colonization (such as in the Michif and Maltese examples) is that the EU itself does not formally or officially prioritize any of its official languages above another. Contrast this with places like the US, where colonizers have forced out speakers of the Indigenous languages and the speakers themselves by insisting upon important documents being written in English, among other things. (More on this is coming up at the end of the chapter.) If the US of old looked more like the EU today, we could imagine that in addition to English, you might be expected to also be able to communicate in Tohono O'odham and Diné (Navajo) if you lived in Arizona, or Arapaho and Cheyenne if you lived in Colorado. If you worked in a governmental agency, the citizens would expect to be able to contact you in their native language, whether that was a language commonly spoken today like English, Spanish, or Mandarin, or something else. We talk more about the state of language in the US in Section 5.4. But first, the Maghreb.

5.3.1 Multilingualism in the Maghreb

The Maghreb is a region encompassing five countries in Africa bordering the Mediterranean Sea: Algeria, Libya, Mauritania, Morocco, and Tunisia, along with the Western Sahara territory. Although it had been formally declared a political and economic union in the 1980s similar to the EU,[1] the people

---

[1] The official status of the union is dormant today and no longer functions in quite the same way as a political and economic body.

living in this area have traditionally been grouped together for thousands of years. People in this region typically speak the countries' official languages, French and Arabic, along with several others. Modern Standard Arabic (also called MSA or *fusha* /fʊs.ħa/), like in other Arabic-speaking countries, is used in official documents and in religious contexts, but is generally not used when speaking to other Arabic users from the same region. In addition to French and Arabic, many people also speak Tamazight (Berber), which was the language in the region prior to the Arab colonizers arriving sometime around the seventh century AD. This region is known especially for having varieties of Arabic and French that are distinct from those languages spoken elsewhere, and for codeswitching in ways that were not previously seen in other populations (Davies & Bentahila 2012).

In the Maghreb, the divide between using Arabic and French is contentious (Alalou 2006); recall that language use contributes to how a person views themselves, and also how the world views them. Proponents of French language use and education argue that French is important for aspects of society today, including media, technology, and as a window to communities outside Africa. However, proponents of Arabic language use point out that French is the language of the colonizers, and as such, Arabic should be embraced. This is made all the more difficult by the status of Tamazight being viewed as a culturally important language to some (but not all!) of its speakers, but not one that is viewed by the community or by outsiders as a language of international significance (Davies & Bentahila 2012).

This divide is further complicated by how Maghrebi varieties of Arabic are perceived in comparison to other Middle Eastern varieties (also called Mashreqi varieties), like the Egyptian and Lebanese Arabics frequently used in popular media. Even when being friendly, speakers of Mashreqi varieties of Arabic joke that they can't understand Maghrebi Arabic, and Maghrebi Arabic speakers may change their language to accommodate Mashreqi speakers (Hachimi 2013).

Despite this tension among the three languages, they coexist relatively harmoniously and each receives some support from the government, the community, or both. There are some fine-grained expectations about when to use each language: Modern Standard Arabic is typically used in governmental documents and signage, and French in particular is seen as the language used by elite, educated people (but also by colonizers, and is not native to the "true" identity of the population). Thanks to intentional use and activism, though, both Maghrebi Arabic and Tamazight are also seeing increases in the number of language users, which also points to the languages being perceived in a more positive light. Compare this situation to the examples we gave earlier of diglossia: language politics in the Maghreb illustrate that communities can also be tri- and multi-glossic, assigning different languages to a range of different social contexts beyond just a "formal" and "informal" register.

5.3.2 Multilingualism in the Vaupés

Now we move across the Atlantic Ocean to the Vaupés. The Vaupés is a region located near the Vaupés River in South America, running through northwestern Brazil and southeastern Colombia. This area is home to a large number of languages, and the inhabitants are known for speaking multiple languages (Grimes 1985; Silva 2020; Sorensen 1967; Stenzel 2005). However, each language in the Vaupés is typically associated with one smaller territory in the region, with women moving to their husband's region rather than staying in their family's region (Stenzel 2005). This is known as **virilocal** language use.

You might be wondering if this means that once a woman marries, she will stop using her original language. Fortunately, this is not the case! After marriage and moving to her husband's region, she still identifies as a user of her original language and will continue to use her language with her children and any other women from her language group who marry into her husband's group (Stenzel 2005). However, once the children become slightly older, they are expected to only use their father's language in public and maintain identities that are in line with their father's language. However, this cultural expectation does not always match up with people's everyday language use (Silva 2020) since people living in this area are indeed highly multilingual.

The way family structures work in the Vaupés region means that multilingualism is the inevitable and expected outcome due to **linguistic exogamy** (Sorensen 1967; Stenzel 2005). The practice of exogamy means that community members do not marry others within the same community and instead only marry outsiders. This is combined with the language practices of groups in the Vaupés region, where one language is usually associated with one group, resulting in many languages gradually being incorporated and intermingled despite only one language having "official," socially acceptable status. This means that a Wanano woman who marries a Desano man will speak both languages to her children, Desano throughout the community, and Wanano with other Wanano women. If one of her children (officially Desano, but who speaks both Wanano and Desano) marries a Yuruti man, it is possible that their children could speak Wanano, Desano, *and* Yuruti in this very simplified example. You can imagine extending this example to incorporate all of the complexity that you could encounter in human relationships, and you would have a large community of people who are all very happily multilingual and who, based on social norms, identify primarily with one linguistic group.

You might be able to think of more settings where multiple languages coexist harmoniously: each language gets used in some way, even though there might be one language that gets used more often than another under certain circumstances. You might also think of settings where this happens not on a national or international level, but on a smaller community level: maybe you live in a neighborhood with a lot of people who are multilingual, or you work somewhere where it's the unspoken (or spoken!) rule that you should be able to use multiple languages competently. You might also notice whether your language changes in these situations.

Recent study of the community of scientists who work at a remote base in Antarctica shows that when people who speak differently come together, their language reflects their close contact. Harrington and his colleagues (2019) found that after a single winter, the scientists' pronunciations of English vowels had changed so that they were more similar to each other than they were when they started. That is a speech community for whom close collaboration and mutual dependence is key to everyone's scientific success as well as their survival over a harsh Antarctic winter.

Unfortunately, not everything is quite so rosy. The unspoken societal rules governing how we act also affect how we speak and how we perceive other people's speech, whether positively or negatively. We alluded to this a little bit before, but let's discuss some of the discrimination that happens in multilingual communities in more depth now.

5.4 Sometimes We Get Panicky

In the US, where the authors are based, being monolingual is the presumed norm. Many of us are surprised when we encounter someone who can competently speak multiple languages, and on the occasion that we travel outside the country, we might be intrigued by the children who speak two (or more!) languages fluently. The reality in the US is that nearly 30 percent of American families use a language other than English at home (US Census Bureau 2018), and many others speak multiple dialects of English at home, at work, with their friends, and in other social settings. Unfortunately, the presumed norm of English monolingualism in the US (and of only speaking one variety of English) has frequently led to discrimination. In Chapter 11, we will dig more deeply into how **linguistic discrimination** shows up in the law and justice systems, but for now, we will explore one example that shows how discrimination can arise from language contact situations specifically.

5.4.1 English-Only Movements

In states like California and Arizona, political discourse surrounding immigration and racism against Latinx communities has led legislators to implement various efforts to control when and where Spanish is spoken. In the summer of 1998, voters in California passed a ballot measure, called Proposition 227, which made significant changes to how public education dealt with students classified as having **Limited English Proficiency**. Specifically, the measure meant that students who came into public schools were taught entirely in English. There were to be no special bilingual classes, and the time that schools were allowed to spend bringing these students up to speed in English was drastically cut – students were allowed only one year in special English instruction classes, regardless of actual need. While some exceptions were available to schools with large numbers of students from non-English speaking backgrounds, critics of this measure saw it as telling students to simply sink or swim, leaving students who might need more help learning English floundering. And, indeed, education researchers found that this law did not substantially improve English learning among California's students. Fortunately, Proposition 227 was repealed by California voters in 2016.

Although this proposition did not make specific reference to other linguistic communities, it was widely understood to be a racist reaction against the growing immigrant, and specifically Latinx, populations of California. By attempting to control what languages are used in public settings, lawmakers and public officials gave credence to a fear that other languages are "taking over" English in the US. We can see these fears operating on a national level in policies that support the "English-Only Movement," also called the "Official English Movement."

Surprising as it may be, English is *not* the official language of the United States. While many states have designated English as their official language (sometimes alongside indigenous languages, like in Alaska and Hawai'i), the federal government has no statute mandating English as the official language of the country. Scholars like Shirley Brice Heath (1981) have even argued that this was a purposeful decision – perhaps because implementing an official language on a federal level would limit people's ability to exercise their right to free speech as outlined in the Bill of Rights. On the other hand, the early United States government rejected proposals to publish official government documents in multiple languages (Baron 1990), so it's not the case that the early years of the United States were a multilingual paradise. In any case, English is clearly the ***de facto* language** of the United States government, even if this is not explicitly stated in any particular statute or law. But throughout US history, various politicians and advocacy groups have attempted to formalize this state of affairs, and such political moves were often tied to broadly xenophobic, racist, and anti-immigrant fears. During World War II, German-speaking communities that had lived in various parts of the northeastern US were encouraged to avoid using German in public. California's anti-bilingual education policies are closely related to fears of Spanish speakers "taking over" the state. Today, stories about folks harassing people speaking Spanish in public with demands to "speak English, because we're in America" frequently go viral. Not only has English never been the official language of the United States – it has never even been the *only* language of the country. When you encounter public discourse asserting that this should be the case, keep an eye out for the political rhetoric that goes along with it. Chances are people are expressing fear of other languages, and (more importantly) speakers of those other languages.

5.4.2 Multiple Accents and Dialects

Even when we are all speaking the same language, differences in **accents** and dialects – both real and perceived – can make people nervous. About twenty years after the passage of California's Proposition 227, the Arizona Department of Education also began enforcing new rules on the linguistic practices of teachers, sending monitors into classrooms to make sure that teachers were pronouncing English words free from any noticeable foreign influence. Veteran teachers, with excellent credentials, who local school officials had already assessed as being fluent in English were singled out to attend accent reduction classes – even though the efficacy of such programs is debated (Lippi-Green 2012). The enforcement of these new accent rules came shortly after the Arizona state legislature passed a highly controversial law giving law enforcement unprecedented power to stop and require identification from anyone who seemed to have the "look" of an undocumented immigrant. While this law represented an obvious case of racial profiling, the accent policing of Arizona teachers represented a more subtle form of xenophobia. State Department of Education monitors who carried out these evaluations were operating under the assumption that a teacher who spoke with a **foreign accent** would pass on that accent to students, but everything we know about language acquisition tells us this is incredibly unlikely. Instead, it came out of a culture of fear of the increasing Spanish-speaking Latinx population in Arizona and represented an attempt to control that group by controlling their language use.

People in the United States can be so troubled by foreign accents that we even imagine them when they aren't really there, a phenomenon sometimes called "**accent hallucination.**" A famous study conducted in 1992 by communication scientist Donald Rubin revealed that people would perceive an accent that wasn't there when they assumed the speaker was foreign. In Rubin's (1992) study, a group of undergraduate students at the University of Georgia listened to a recording of a native English speaker from Ohio reading a short passage. One group of students heard the recording paired with a photograph of a white woman; another group of students heard the *exact same* recording alongside a photograph of an Asian woman. Students who heard the recording with the photo of the Asian woman evaluated the speaker as having an accent – even though it was the same recording, made by a native speaker of American English! In 2015, linguists Molly Babel and Jamie Russell (2015) replicated this study with undergraduate students in Vancouver, Canada and found similar results, so we know this phenomenon has not disappeared and is not unique to the United States. We refer to this study often throughout the book, so keep it in mind as you read on!

The "intense monitoring of the speech of racialized populations" that the cases here illustrate are one way of constructing what the Jane Hill (1998) termed **white public space**. In white public space – which Hill argues characterizes much of US public discourse – the language of non-white and non-native English speakers are deemed "disorderly." Laws, policies, and norms attempt to police and control speakers of non-English languages and non-white speakers of English (whether or not they "really" have an accent!). This attempt to control how people speak is, of course, based on fear. Fear that Spanish is "taking over" English in public education, fear that foreign-accented instructors are teaching our children how to speak English poorly, and fear of neighbors that don't talk (or look, or think, or act) like us drive much of the linguistic discrimination we see in the United States. We dig further into these issues in later chapters, especially as they relate to the education system (Chapter 8), the workplace (Chapter 10), and the legal system (Chapter 11).

5.5 And Sometimes One Language Tries to Wipe Out Another Completely

Sadly, sometimes one language community is so frightened of or hateful toward members of another language community that they try to completely abolish it. The rationale for such actions can range from overt hatred to delusional beliefs about linguistic and cultural inferiority to deep fear that people who speak an unfamiliar language might be able to use it to rebel or overthrow established systems of power. In the US, Canada, and Australia, the attempted murder of languages and cultures has been undertaken in the name of both colonial expansion via forced removal of speaker populations from their traditional homelands and "education" via forced removal of children from their homes and families into state- or church-run boarding schools.

Forced removal of populations can certainly cause people to shift their language: although the new language may be unfamiliar and not well adapted to its new speakers, it can also provide safety and survival of its speakers in the new location. Extraction of children into forced education in a school system run by those who hope to extinguish a child's connection to their family, culture, and community can create multigenerational traumas that can lead to **language shift**. Language shift occurs when communities stop using a marginalized **heritage language** and switch to a language with more economic and political power. This can result in monolingualism in a dominant language rather than multilingualism or mixing language resources. We discuss issues of language shift – as well as communities' efforts to retain and reclaim heritage languages – in more detail in Chapter 12.

As a linguist in your community, you must learn more about the heritage of languages in your area – and if you live in the US, Canada, or Australia, and many other places around the world, this will mean that you will learn about removals, forced education in monolingual English boarding schools, and various forms of attempted genocide aimed at native peoples. You will also learn that in spite of these policies, in many cases the speaker communities survive, as does the language: it may be spoken by people in your community, or it may be spoken by people outside of the community, in the area to which they were forcibly removed. The languages that are indigenous to your community may exist in documentation such as written records and audio recordings, and they may exist in the knowledge and practices of your neighbors. In communities that have suffered this type of linguistic trauma, though, it is common that people are uncomfortable sharing their language with those who are not members of the community (or even sharing it with other community members who might criticize them or be upset or offended by their ways of speaking). You may yourself be a member of a speaker community that is grappling with attempted genocides, past or present – and if so, studying your language may come with very complex and difficult emotional, intellectual, and practical concerns.

Language shift, and **language loss**, can be painful, but they are also often reversible. A linguist who wants to work with a speaker community that has been or is being threatened with violence must be careful to not compound the trauma and must sometimes step aside so that community members can exercise autonomy in their decisions about how the language should or should not be used, whether it should or should not be shared, and even how it should or should not be described. We have some ideas for you to think about in our methods chapter, Chapter 3, and some guiding principles in Chapter 4 about research ethics.

At heart, attempts at **linguicide**, the elimination of a language, are always attempts to eliminate the community, culture, and people for whom the language is home. Fortunately, eliminating a language is not so easy to do, and speaker communities can and do fight back. Learning about these battles is a critical part of your education as a linguist in your community.

Linguist in the Community

- Spend some time reflecting on, and observing, your own language behavior and that of your family and friends. Make some notes about your observations:
  - What are the rules (stated and unstated) of linguistic engagement in your community?
    - What languages do you use to speak to family, friends, coworkers, and other members of your community?
    - Are the rules or norms of language use in your home different from the linguistic rules/norms you follow at work, school, church, or other settings?
    - Does your workplace, church, school, or any other group you are a member of have an "official" language? How do you know?
  - Have you noticed examples of linguistic discrimination in the news or in your community?
    - What was the stated complaint? What aspect of language were the complainants focused on?
    - What nonlinguistic forms of discrimination might these ideas point to?
  - What are your rules and experiences regarding language contact in your community?
    - If you are multilingual, what rules and practices have you internalized about when you can use which language, and how or whether the languages can be mixed? If you are monolingual, what rules and practices have you internalized about how other languages can or should be used in different domains (school, work, social activities)?
    - Rate your knowledge of the language contact situation in your own community. Do you feel like you're very well aware of multilingualism, language mixing and language contact in your area? Why do you think your level of knowledge is as it is? Have you had opportunities to learn about the language landscape in your community?

- Do some research about the language history in your community. Find out what languages are indigenous to the place you are living right now. For readers in the Americas or Australia, we recommend this resource: https://native-land.ca/, which is created and maintained by a not-for-profit organization in Canada called Native Land Digital.
    - See if you can identify all of the languages that are located in your area and whether the language communities have treaty rights to your community, or are still found there.
    - Use what you learn to find out more about these languages, and see if you can discover whether the communities have active programs in language teaching and learning, repatriation of language materials, community language events, and such.
    - If you are interested, see whether there are opportunities that are open to noncommunity members to volunteer, participate, or contribute. Be careful, though – communities may well determine that their language work should not be accessible to outsiders.
- See if you can find information about languages spoken in your community. In the US, census data can be useful for this purpose. What are the most commonly spoken nondominant languages in your area? Do you hear or see these languages in your daily life?
    - Seek out public venues where people may be more likely to use nondominant languages. International markets, restaurants, or similar venues are often good opportunities for this. Give yourself a few minutes to make a few notes. Do you hear or see languages used that your research suggests are common (note that it is not always possible to know what language a person is using just by observing them, but you might be able to make some educated guesses)? Can you see any patterns to when and how these languages are being used, or who is using them (are they being used by younger people, older people, are there apparent patterns of gender identity or ethnic presentation)?
    - Watch the people who are not speaking. Do you see any reactions that suggest how community members feel about the nondominant language and its speakers in this venue? Do you see evidence of linguistic prejudice or discrimination in the area?

Linguist in the Classroom

- Take a poll of your fellow students in the class and find out what languages are represented there, and how the languages are likely to interact with each other.

- Are both spoken and signed languages represented?
- Are both multilingual and monolingual speakers represented?
- Are there any Indigenous languages represented?
- Can members of the class engage in codeswitching?
- Do students feel comfortable using all of their languages in class or at your school? Have students been criticized or shamed for using languages other than the dominant one(s) or for engaging in codeswitching at school? Have students criticized or shamed peers for doing this? Note that many of us have done this, especially if we grew up in a community that had negative beliefs about non-majority languages.
- How do students feel about hearing or seeing languages that they don't themselves understand?
* Set up a class debate about language policy! Debates can be great ways to explore topics that people feel strongly about because they allow us to get feedback on our ideas in a structured way, and they can require us to take the perspective of people with whom we disagree.
    - Identify a language policy proposal: perhaps to adopt a language as the "official" or only language of a community, or to require multilingual instruction in all public schools ... something relevant to your situation.
    - Split yourselves into two or more teams, and randomly assign teams to "pro" vs. "con" positions on the proposal. This is important: debates work best when we don't just get to argue for the side we naturally agree with.
    - Identify a procedure for "judging" the debate, where "judging" doesn't have to mean identifying a winner. Think about what the rules should be for the debate: Do you want rules for "civility"? What are the criteria for a strong argument? Will you structure the debate to allow both proposals and rebuttals? How long will each team have to present their arguments? If you want to have a "winner," what will be the criteria by which a team would "win," and who would decide?
    - Give the teams some time to prepare their arguments, and then run the debate in class.
    - Follow up. Be sure to take some time to discuss the arguments each team presented, and talk through any difficult or untenable claims.
* Learn in a multilingual class! If your instructor is multilingual, your class might be able to do this straightforwardly. If not, consider inviting a guest teacher or inviting multilingual students to help. If your school teaches a signed language, you may be able to enlist the help of a guest teacher who also has skills already as a sign language interpreter. Have

the leader of this class session prepare a presentation on any topic in at least two languages. Then, get ready to participate:
- Allow your presenter to speak for a short while without providing translations into your class' dominant language. Then talk as a class about the experience of trying to participate in a classroom that is run in a language you don't speak. This is an experience that many minority language speakers have had. How does this affect your thinking about the use of multiple languages in school?
- Next, have the speaker share their presentation while also providing translations. Then talk to the class about how the different languages worked in order to communicate the class content. Are there insights about the topic that seem easier or harder to communicate in one language or another?

- Test a machine translator! Students who are taking classes in a language that is not their first language are increasingly turning to technology to help. Instructors who are trying to engage multilingual audiences are also turning to tech. And the technology behind machine translation applications (such as Google Translate) is changing all the time.
  - First, have a discussion with your colleagues in class about the role of technology in helping languages get along. If a computer can translate for you, does that change the ways in which languages might relate to each other?
  - Then, test a machine translation application against a multilingual person. Using the results of your class language poll (from the first exercise in this section), select a nondominant language that at least a few of your fellow students speak (it is ideal to use one that is spoken by lots of students, and/or by the instructor!). Then try using the machine to translate from your dominant classroom language into the selected nondominant one. Try:
    - Instructions for an assignment; or
    - An imaginary office hour discussion; or
    - An imaginary study group session.
  - Let the human speakers of the nondominant language rate the machine translations. In what ways might they be good enough, and in what ways might they fail?
  - Importantly, discuss as a class the effect of using machine translation on the communicative process. Did it benefit the communicators in building the relationship they needed in order to communicate effectively? Did it hinder that process? How might the intervention of machines affect the ways we communicate with each other across language boundaries?

Glossary

accent A way of pronouncing a language that indicates affiliation with a social or geographic group. "Accent" differs from "dialect" in that accents are primarily patterns of pronunciation (including rhythm and intonation), while the term "dialect" refers to patterns of word choice and grammatical constructions, not just pronunciations.

accent hallucination A phenomenon in which a listener hears an accent that isn't actually present, usually based on nonlinguistic social cues.

blended languages/varieties Ways of speaking that draw vocabulary, pronunciation, and grammar from more than one source language and interweave the sources in conventionalized ways.

codeswitching The practice of changing between two languages that you and your conversation partner speak mid-utterance or mid-sentence.

corpus (pl. corpora) A collection of language examples (corpora can be collections of text and/or audio or video examples) organized to facilitate linguistic analysis and usually meant to be approximately representative of a language/speech community or genre (web pages, conversations, newspapers, etc.).

creole A blended language that originated as a pidgin or jargon and became a first language of some speech community.

***de facto* language** The language that is taken to be the norm for official government business, the law, education, business, and other facets of public life, despite not being formally designated as the official language.

diglossia A situation in which a bilingual community uses one language in certain social contexts and a different language in other social contexts.

etymology The history and origin of a word; the study of word histories and origins.

foreign accent A way of pronouncing a language that shows influence from some other language. For many people, if we learn a new language as adolescents or adults, our pronunciation of the new language will always be influenced by the pronunciation system of our home language or languages, and we may be said to have a "foreign accent" in the new language.

heritage language A language of your family or community, whether or not you have had access to learn or acquire that language.

intersentential codeswitching Switching from one language to another at sentence boundaries.

intrasentential codeswitching Switching from one language to another within a sentence.

Inverted Spanglish A term coined by linguistic anthropologist Jonathan

Rosa to describe hyper-Anglicized pronunciations of Spanish words to mock or critique structures of linguistic, racial, and ethnic inequality.

language loss A process in which a community loses access over time to their heritage language. Language loss can be a result of language shift.

language shift When a language community adopts a new language in place of, rather than in addition to, their heritage language. Language shift can lead to language loss.

Limited English Proficiency A designation sometimes assigned by education officials to students who are not fluent in "mainstream," "standard" varieties of American English.

linguicide The act of eliminating, or trying to eliminate, use and knowledge of a language. Linguicide has been a component in attempts at genocide in the US, Canada, and Australia, among other places.

linguistic discrimination Prejudicial treatment of a group or individual on the basis of their language, dialect, accent, or other elements of their language behavior.

linguistic exogamy The practice of marrying someone who does not speak the same language as your community does, and who is also not affiliated with your community.

monodialectal An individual who only knows one dialect of their language.

monolingual Used to describe a person or population who speaks only one language.

multidialectal An individual who speaks multiple dialects of their language.

multilingual Used to describe a person or population who speaks more than one language.

official language The formally designated primary language of a particular government or organization, used to conduct official business.

pidgin A simplified communication code, often blending words and grammar from multiple source languages. Pidgins may also be called "trade jargons" and are not used as anyone's first language. In some situations, pidgins may develop into full-fledged languages, and when they do, we refer to them as "creoles" rather than "pidgins."

Spanglish A particular variety of codeswitching between Spanish and English in the US. This term is sometimes used pejoratively, so please use it with care.

translanguaging The blending of features from two or more languages to maximize communicative potential or to deliberately shape identity.

virilocal Used to describe a situation where, after marriage, the married couple lives in or near the husband's place of origin.

white public space A term coined by the linguistic anthropologist Jane Hill to refer to the ways that the linguistic practices of minoritized people are criticized and devalued in public discourse.

Recommended Readings

Languages have been getting together and splitting apart for centuries and centuries! If you'd like to learn more about the social effects of some of these linguistic events, check out our recommended readings below. And remember, if you can't access these resources for free on your own, reach out to your local college or university library for help.

Babel, M., & Russell, J. (2015). Expectations and speech intelligibility. *Journal of the Acoustical Society of America, 137*(5), 2823-2833. https://doi.org/10/f7c68x

Heath, S. B. (1981). English in our language heritage. In C. A. Ferguson & S. B. Heath (Eds.), *Language in the USA* (pp. 6-20). Cambridge University Press.

Hill, J. H. (1998). Language, race, and white public space. *American Anthropologist, 100*(3), 680-689. https://doi.org/10.1525/aa.1998.100.3.680

Lippi-Green, R. (2012). *English with an Accent: Language, Ideology, and Discrimination in the United States* (2nd ed.). Routledge.

6 Linguists Meet Babies

6.1 But Why Babies?

At first glance, it may seem like adults are the ones doing the interesting language: We are the ones who work in the media, write books, blogs, social media posts, and articles, communicate with the world, and are generally producing a lot of language all the time. But then we have to ask ourselves how we got to this place. We had to figure out everything that we know about language, and we do a lot of that figuring out in the first six years (or so) of our lives!

Developmental language researchers, who study our early language capacity in many ways, typically characterize the period of language development as that which occurs between birth and the beginning of the school years – although we do still keep refining our linguistic skills throughout our lives. Babies and children also use language in creative, clever, and masterful ways, always understanding much more complex messages than they can produce, and you may not expect that their use is as linguistically and socially sophisticated as it really is.

Our language development occurs simultaneously with what linguists term "language socialization." This is the process of learning how to use all those newly developing linguistic skills – the ability to produce the sounds, words, and sentences of our first language – in ways that make sense within our family, community, and culture. If you've ever heard a young child use a curse word to the shock and surprise of the adults around them, you've seen firsthand evidence of a child who has mastered key parts of the vocabulary of their native language but who has not been fully socialized into the language norms of their community.

Typically, language development is treated as a result of certain cognitive faculties and processes, whereas language socialization is viewed as a process "external" to the brain, identifiable largely in social processes. In fact, language development and language socialization are closely interconnected, and both our language development and language socialization can be deeply affected by our specific situations. For those of us who are not neurotypical, or for those who grew up in the context of violence or threat to our wellbeing or without access to language input from our caregivers starting at birth, our paths may be different than those described in this chapter. Even for neurologically typical babies raised in a loving and language-rich environment, there is a tremendous amount of healthy individual variation in the timing of our language development processes. On top of all this, what we perceive as "language-rich" can be influenced by sociocultural norms. Too often, the real-world implication of these perceptions is the development of educational policies that reflect stereotypes about certain kinds of language socialization practices rather than our scientific knowledge about language development.

This chapter has two main parts. In the first part, we will explore some of the stages of typical language development. You will learn the general characteristics of each stage of language development, including which parts of language are acquired when, and at what age children tend to develop mastery of each of these elements. We'll also mention some common misunderstandings about language development. Understanding why these misunderstandings are so common will be an important learning to carry over to the next part of the chapter, which focuses on language socialization. The language socialization section will take you on a tour through several different language communities all around the world to highlight the many different ways that humans successfully figure out how to use their language or language(s) like a bona fide member of that community. As you take this tour, you'll want to keep what you learned about language development in the back of your mind – this will help you see that language development can happen successfully in many many different cultural contexts. We put language development and language socialization together at the end of the chapter, with sections on the misunderstandings sometimes referred to as the **"word gap"** and on the importance of literacy in language development and socialization. These are two areas in which people's stereotypes about and biases against certain forms of language socialization end up shaping what we tell parents to do in order to ensure good language development. By the time you reach these sections, you'll be able to assess for yourself why such beliefs don't hold up under scientific scrutiny.

If this sounds like a lot to cover in one chapter, don't worry – recalling our microscope-binoculars-telescope metaphor from Chapter 1 can help you follow along. We won't get too much into the *microscopic* details about the phonology or syntax of language development because we want to focus on a bigger picture. So instead, we start out with a telescopic overview of the general stages and trajectory of language development, and then we zoom in to our binocular-level observations for language development in different communities. At the end, we'll adjust the focus just a bit to zoom out a little bit more – still looking at specific case studies, but ones that highlight the interconnectedness of language development and language socialization. If you're ready, read on!

6.2 A Rough Timeline

In Figure 6.1, you can see a rough overview of the typical language development timeline. As you review this timeline, we need you to keep two key things in mind.[1] First, please do not use this timeline as a tool for diagnosis or a cause of anxiety about the language development of any particular baby or babies. There is a great deal of perfectly healthy individual variation in the rates and dates of the stages and phases outlined here, and variation in language development is uncorrelated with individual properties like "intelligence" or adult language capabilities. Babies may go slower or quicker through these stages and still end up as linguistic super users. Interestingly, there is not much variation that we are aware of in the order of stages, or in the stages themselves – not in terms of individual variation, and also not across speech communities – in spite of the large amount of variation in the ways in which we human adults think about our babies' healthy development, or in the ways in which we provide them with loving and supportive care. Similarly, babies learning one or more natural human languages do not seem to be phased by the differences among those languages. A three-year-old raised in a monolingual English-speaking environment, a three-year-old raised in a multilingual environment in the Vaupés in Brazil, and a three-year-old raised with a signed language will all be at approximately the same stage in their language development.

Second, always remember that this timeline tells a story about language development for babies who are neurotypical and who are born and raised in an environment in which they are physically and emotionally safe, and in which they have continuous access to language input from caregivers. If you are interested in learning more about atypical development, we would encourage you to seek out experts and literature in the academic field of speech, language, and hearing sciences. This scholarship tells us that atypical development is much more variable than typical language development, but we do not have the space in this textbook to say much more about it than that.

---

[1] The timeline presented here is drawn from the literature cited in the paragraphs that follow it, and especially from Lillo-Martin and Henner (2021).

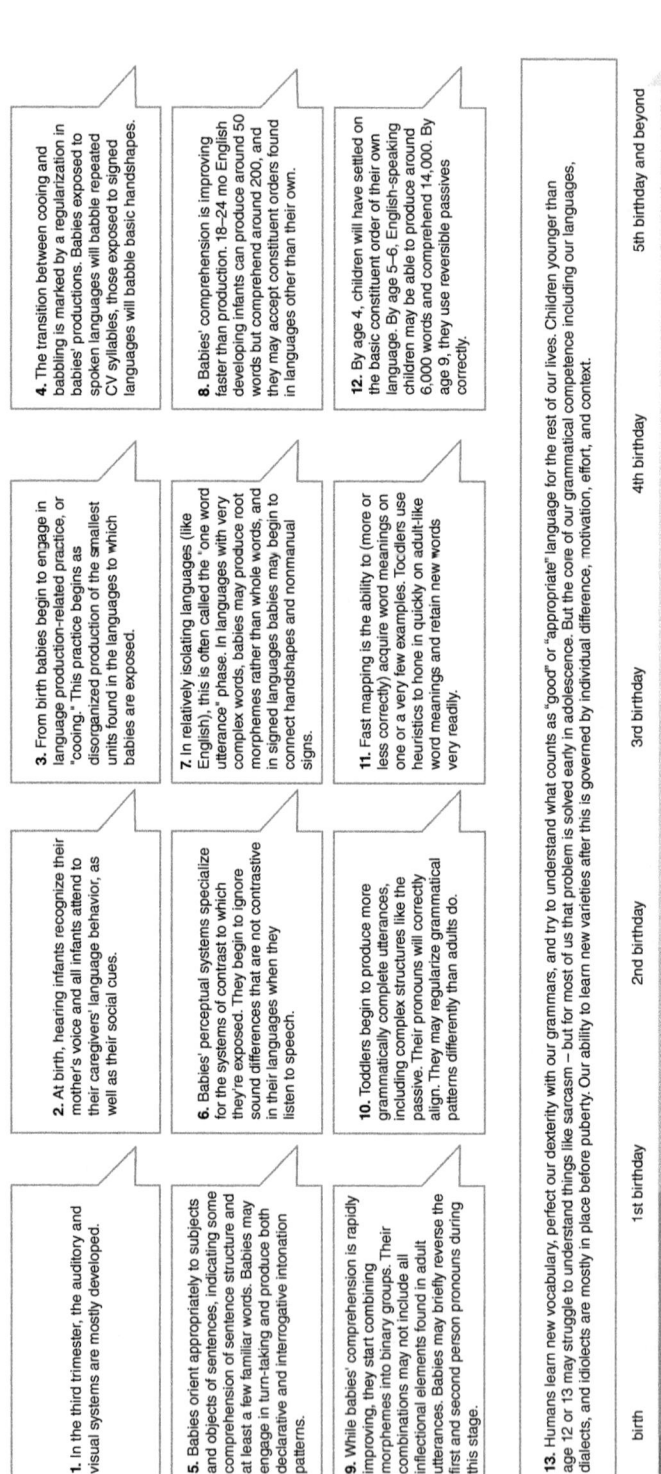

Figure 6.1 Typical language acquisition timeline.

Finally, because of the very early start humans get in language development, scholars of language often use the term "**native language**" or "**first language**" to describe languages that we have been exposed to since infancy. However, it is possible to grow up with multiple "first" languages – this is common for children who grow up in multilingual households or communities. Our "first" or "native" language(s) are distinguished from what you will often hear referred to as "**second languages**" or "non-native languages." These are all the additional languages one might learn after developing whatever language or languages we learn from birth. This means that we will all have one or more first language(s), and zero or more second language(s). We tend not to refer to "third" or "fourth" (or whatever) languages in our discussion because there are more differences between *developing* a first language and any additional languages than there are between *learning* your second, third, or fourth language. That said, there is much research to be done on ways in which our learning of additional languages is similar to, or different from, our development of first languages that you may wish to investigate. While that scholarship is developing, we are restricting our discussion here to first language (also called native language) development.

Children acquiring more than one language at once is the norm throughout the world, and multilingual development tends to progress at roughly the same rate as monolingual language development (Nicoladis & Genesee 1997, pp. 263–265). Because of this, we have opted to focus this chapter very generally on language development and social issues surrounding it without limiting discussion to monolingual or multilingual contexts. However, this is also a rapidly developing and changing field of research, and there are many alternate resources that you can seek out if you do become interested in the specifics of bilingual, multilingual, or monolingual language development specifically!

6.2.1 The Very Beginning

Our journey toward having a fully fledged language system begins **prenatally,** a short while before we are born. Our auditory system is estimated to be fairly developed by the time we reach a **gestational age** of twenty-five to twenty-eight weeks, or the beginning of the third trimester of pregnancy, and our visual system is maturing at about the same time (Eswaran et al. 2004; Litovsky 2015). What we "see" before birth is probably just shades of light and dark, but hearing develops a little earlier: by about thirty-five weeks gestational age we can differentiate between different pitches (250 Hz tones and 500 Hz tones) and between the sounds /ba/ and /bi/ (Shahidullah & Hepper 1994). Two-day-old newborns even recognize passages of storybooks that their mother read to them before they were born (DeCasper & Spence 1986).

To get a better idea of what we might hear before birth, dunk your head underwater and have someone above the water speak to you. There are some sounds and words that are easier to distinguish and some sounds that get completely muddled. You can probably understand the intonation that people are using: you can tell if they're happy, angry, excited, sad, and so on. If they start to sing a familiar tune, you might also recognize that. This is how DeCasper and Spence (1986) hypothesized that the infants they studied were able to recognize passages from storybooks – infants recognized the intonation and rhythmic patterns of the stories that they heard while in the womb, even though they would not necessarily be able to pick out every individual word. Visually, newborns typically can only focus on things close to them and it may take more time for them to sort out things like faces and backgrounds, but there's enough visual, auditory, and tactile information available to newborns to allow them to begin to focus on caregivers' communicative behavior, and that is exactly what they do.

Beginning in the days after birth, infants are off to the races in acquiring the languages that they are exposed to. Shortly after birth, infants can distinguish between their caregivers' spoken language(s) and a language(s) that they have not been exposed to based on the different stress patterns that the languages have, like English and Japanese (Nazzi et al. 1998). Babies' cries even show rhythmic patterns consistent with the spoken languages to which they have been exposed (Mampe et al. 2009). A few months later, they can also distinguish their native language from a language with very similar stress patterns, like English and Dutch (Nazzi et al. 2000), or use visual cues from people's faces when they speak to discriminate between familiar and unfamiliar languages (Weikum et al. 2007). It does not take long for hearing infants to tune into the contrastive segments (phonemes) that are important for distinguishing meaning in the languages that they are exposed to. After about ten to twelve months, hearing infants go from being able to distinguish between every possible speech sound to attending just the phonemes of their language (Werker & Tees 1984). That is, infants know which sound distinctions they can safely ignore and which they need to focus on in order to distinguish words. There is evidence that babies exposed to sign language also begin distinguishing between the gestural elements that matter for language and those that do not (Lillo-Martin & Henner 2021), although considerably less research has been devoted to development of sign language in babies than to babies acquiring spoken language.

You may have been around infants who are talking to themselves, but it's all gibberish to you. Babies **babble** to practice using their language production systems and the units of contrast present in their languages, as well as conversational norms like turn-taking (Kuhl 2007; Kuhl & Meltzoff 1996). It doesn't much matter that you do not understand them, but it is a great opportunity to engage with them – and social groups differ in the ways in which this kind of engagement should be done. For example, in your authors' own speech community, we often engage in close, face-to-face oral or signed communication with infants well before the time when they can respond appropriately, and we even often act out both sides of the conversation. We might say something like "how are you, little one?" and answer in a pretend baby voice, "I am hungry, mama!". But there are speech communities in which that kind of "conversation" would not be considered normal, and instead caregivers might engage with babies in a more parallel way – with the baby being a less directly active participant in our interactions. These different norms do not generate different outcomes for babies, although being cruel or isolating such that babies are stressed or lack opportunities to closely observe our communicative behavior is both inherently evil (we think) and certainly not healthy for babies' language (or other types of) development. We will come back to this topic in Section 6.3 later in this chapter.

When caregivers use language around babbling infants – whether or not they talk directly *to* them as conversational partners – infants are able to extrapolate both linguistic and social cues from the interaction, from basic patterns of sounds or contrastive units in signed languages (that is, phonological patterns; Goldstein & Schwade 2008; Goldstein et al. 2003) to appropriate responses (Goldstein & West 1999). Deaf babies and hearing babies babble similarly, imitating the languages that they are exposed to: babies exposed to spoken language will babble vocally,[2] while babies exposed to signed language will babble manually (Petitto & Marentette 1991; Petitto et al. 2001).[3] The jury is still out on what, exactly, the mechanism is that allows infants to acquire a language so completely – it could be a more general mechanism used in other cognitive domains, like being attuned to the frequency of parts of the input around them (e.g., Ambridge et al.

---

[2] Both hearing and deaf babies will babble vocally at first, but hearing-impaired babies may persist in the vocal babble stage longer (Oller & Eilers 1988), especially if they are exposed to signed languages.

[3] To our knowledge, there is less research to confirm whether hearing babies' early manual and other kinesic practice is similar to the manual babbling of babies exposed to signed languages, although Petitto and Marentette (1991) suggest that babies exposed to signed languages gesture and move their hands in ways that are different (and more like babbling!) from babies who are not exposed to signed languages. Future scholarship should address this question.

2015; Lieven 2010), or it could be a part of our cognition that is dedicated specifically to acquiring a language, such as Chomsky's Language Acquisition Device (Chomsky 1965), or it could be something in between, or neither option, or ... well, you get the idea. There are many ways infants could be going about the task of acquiring their language(s), and regardless of how they do it, they tend to end up being stellar language users.

6.2.2 First Words

Infants also start picking up on words and phrases in their language right away. In spoken languages, they use the predominant stress patterns found in their language to segment words from speech (Jusczyk & Aslin 1995; Jusczyk, Cutler, et al. 1993; Jusczyk, Friederici, et al. 1993) – remember, we do not speak with convenient gaps between words like the orthographic spaces between written words, so infants have to do something to learn words and figure out how their language groups sounds together. For signed languages, the rhythmic cues to word and phrase boundaries are visual rather than auditory – and often include nonmanual signs (facial expressions and other body movements) that help punctuate signed utterances. By the time infants are about a year old, they have usually started saying their first word-like units (Benedict 1979; Fenson et al. 1994). In English-type languages, where there are a lot of individual words that are also individual morphemes, babies will produce whole words. In Quechua or Navajo-type languages, where it typically requires lots of morphemes to produce a whole word, babies produce bare roots – despite the fact that they will not have heard adults use them (Courtney & Saville-Troike 2002) because they are not really "words" in the language – they are parts of words. Even in English-type languages, early words may be different from those that babies are exposed to – systematically and smartly different. This shows that we begin our first language development process as tiny linguists: not just perceiving the language behavior of those around us, but engaging in processes of linguistic analysis as we develop the ability to communicate with those around us.

As we learn more about how our language works and the units of meaning that our language depends on, we are able to use a variety of strategies to rapidly increase our vocabulary size. By the time a typical English-speaking child enters school at around age six, they are estimated to comprehend about 14,000 words and produce about 6,000 (Templin 1957)![4]

---

[4] Measures of vocabulary size are really hard to generalize across languages of different types – so when we give word counts, it is important to remember that we are talking about words in the types of languages that are most often included in language development research. English is certainly well-represented, as are many of the majority languages of

To get to this large vocabulary, infants and children have to be able to associate some string of sounds, or set of gestures, with some kind of concept or meaning. To think about this, it is helpful to refer to a classical view of the linguistic "sign," which is often attributed to Ferdinand de Saussure. The "sign" is a two-part thing – it includes a "signifier" (a pronunciation or gestural form of some sort) and a "signified" (a meaning or concept of some sort). Think of, for example, *a tree*. You might have a mental image of a thing with a trunk, branches, and leaves. That's the *signified*. If you're an English speaker, your signifier is a thing that is pronounced with a string of a "t," "r," and "ee" sounds. When you write it, your signifier is "tree."

But how do children figure out which labels go with which concepts? After all, language includes labels that identify individuals (like "Ferdinand de Saussure"), and labels that identify kinds of individuals (like "arbor"), and labels that identify qualities of things (like "leafy"), and on and on. Consider the following thought experiment from philosopher W. V. O. Quine (1960) to get a real sense of the problem faced by children in mapping labels to concepts: Imagine that you are documenting a language, and in doing so, you are trying to communicate with a native speaker consultant who does not also speak your language. The two of you are walking along a beach when suddenly a rabbit runs by, and then your consultant looks at it and shouts "gavagai!" You then have to figure out what a "gavagai" is.

Your first instinct might be to say that "gavagai" must refer to the rabbit that went running by – a mammal with long ears, a small tail, that moves by hopping, and so on – but keep thinking. "Gavagai" could also refer to the action of running or hopping, it could refer to different parts of the rabbit (like rabbit ears), it could refer to that specific rabbit (who is named Gavagai, like a dog named Gracie or a turtle named Butch), it could refer to the action of something unexpected occurring, and more. This is the kind of decision-making that infants are faced with when they are trying to learn new words: When we say "Look! A bunny!", the infant has to figure out that "look" is something to grab their attention, "bunny" is the whole animal that we see, and "bunny" with "a" in front of it means it is one of many possible bunnies – and nothing more than that! We are making no comment about the color of the bunny, how it is moving, or that we are surprised by its presence. Fortunately, children seem to operate with strategies and assumptions that help them determine what a word refers to.

Europe, and increasingly research on other major world languages is being published. But language types like Navajo or Quechua, referred to above, are not currently well-represented in this research, and in those languages what counts as a "word" can be much more difficult to define.

One of these assumptions is the **whole object assumption,** where a child assumes that a word they have not heard before refers to the entire object that they are paying attention to, not any of its properties. However, if they hear a new word in reference to something they already know the word for, they will use the **mutual exclusivity** assumption to assume that the new word refers to an object they do not already have a name for, so that every object they encounter has only one name. The **Principle of Contrast** also helps infants out here: using this principle, they assume that different words have different meanings (so if "gavagai" means "rabbit," it does not also mean "boat").[5]

6.2.3 Combining Meaningful Elements

Once children are a little older, somewhere between eighteen and twenty-four months old, they begin putting multiple words together. Even though some elements of their speech are missing, like function morphemes, the words that they use are generally in the correct order for the language that they are using. For instance, you might hear a sentence like "doggie sleep" from an English-acquiring child to refer to the napping pup. Even at this early age, they have figured out something about the structure of their language: generally, the subject of a sentence in English precedes the verb. As children continue to acquire their language, they put together more and more pieces of the lexical and syntactic puzzle.

One of the strategies that infants and children can use to figure out the morphological and syntactic properties of their language is to use **syntactic bootstrapping**. The idea behind syntactic bootstrapping is that once infants know enough individual words in their language, they are able to figure out some of the syntactic properties of their language (Gleitman 1990; Landau & Gleitman 1985; Naigles 1990), like whether a verb requires an object (Naigles 1990) or the minute differences in how to refer to objects as opposed to substances (Soja et al. 1991). They also know something about the morphemes that are commonly used to express some kind of grammatical meaning, like the past tense -ed – and all this is happening before they start using these words (Figueroa 2018; Figueroa & Gerken 2019).

---

[5] Importantly, these assumptions are not always correct – and we see that in babies' early use of words. It is not unusual for babies to learn a label like "dog," and then get confused and maybe a little mad when someone calls it a "hound" or a "mutt" (violating mutual exclusivity). Eventually, we all have to sort out learning the concept-label mappings that our languages use that violate these assumptions, but the assumptions seem to help us get a reasonable start. There is even some evidence that these assumptions might be available even to some dogs – you can read about two border collies named Rico and Chaser if you are interested in learning more about how these assumptions play out in that context.

6.2.4 Talking, Talking, Talking!

Typically developing children have, for the most part, assembled the building blocks of their language (or languages, if they grow up in a multilingual environment) by the time they are five or six years old – in fact, their mental grammar is nearly adultlike at this point. Some of the last parts of our languages that come into place include particularly complex or rare syntactic constructions, such as reversible passives like "the dog was chased by the cat" (Borer & Wexler 1987; Gordon & Chafetz 1990; Messenger et al. 2012). Since either cats or dogs can chase according to our knowledge of the real world, it is harder[6] for us to comprehend this type of passive than nonreversible passives, even as adults. Nonreversible passives like "the kibble was eaten by the cat" are easier for us to understand because we know that kibble is not able to eat! Some of us are still working on improving our motor skills at this point too, so the finer points of articulation can still be a little less than completely adultlike. English-speaking children may still show some difficulty in producing a clear distinction between "s" and "sh" sounds (so they might be characterized as "having a lisp"), for example. In some societies, professionals in speech and language sciences may work with these children in school providing "speech therapy." From a linguistic perspective, though, these motor-skill issues are not really problems with language – and an adult speaker of English who "lisps" is understood to be a fully competent speaker.

Another aspect of language that we continue to refine throughout our lives is our **sociopragmatic knowledge,** or how we use language appropriately in everyday situations. In some speech communities (including one we will discuss later in this chapter, and perhaps even your own!), people will remark that young children "have no filter" or are especially honest; they have not quite mastered how and when (and whether or not!) to express their thoughts and opinions. Children develop nuanced understandings of, and values toward, the languages that they are exposed to – and may take different strategies depending on their understanding of the relative values and functions of the languages around them. These different values can result in apparent differences in language development for languages that children learn might be "shameful" or "stigmatized" – and these differences can play a complex role in minoritized and Indigenous language communities especially (see Meek 2019 for a thorough review). Many scholars argue that this element

---

[6] When we say "harder" or "easier" in this context, what we really mean is that it takes a little longer ("harder") or a little less long ("easier") to get it. And when we say "a little" what we really mean is "by a few milliseconds." There are genuinely *hard* to understand sentences too, like "The mouse the cat the dog chased ate died," but we leave these to the
readers' investigation.

of **language acquisition** is more closely tied to cultural constructs of childhood vs. adulthood rather than stages of cognitive development. In any case, it is clear that humans can continue to learn new techniques for communicating and interacting in different contexts throughout our lifetimes – there is no true "endpoint." Just like our vocabulary expands throughout our lives, we continue to learn and change how we interact with people.

A common series of questions for caregivers centers on how they can positively influence children's language development: What are the tips and tricks you can use to give your child the best possible start in life? Should we avoid speaking to them in "baby talk"? If we are raising a child in a multilingual environment, should we pick one language to avoid confusing them? What about using one language per parent? What about this "thirty-million word gap"; is that something that caregivers should be concerned about?

These are reasonable questions to ask. Infants and children, however, seem to acquire a language differently than adults do. And there is no human society in which children regularly fail to acquire their community languages, or do so more slowly, or in some way that's "worse" than what we observe in other human societies – even though human communities differ (a lot) in their child-rearing norms. In the rest of this chapter, we discuss some of the questions posed in the previous paragraph and debunk some of the pernicious misconceptions about how babies develop their linguistic skills in a social environment.

6.3 Language Socialization

Another way that scholars can approach the study of how babies learn and develop linguistic skills that are appropriate to the speech communities they grow up in is through the study of **language socialization**. In this framework, scholars are less interested in the stages and timeline over which babies acquire the structural components of language and are more interested in how older members of a speech community model and teach appropriate communicative norms to babies, and in the different ways in which babies' and children's communication patterns affect and are affected by these practices. Just as language and culture are closely entwined, language development and language socialization feed into each other in the process of how a child develops into a full member of a culture.

In the case studies that follow, we discuss some of the ways adults interact with children and how those interactions change as the children develop language – and how the way adults interact with children does not affect how quickly or accurately children develop language. We also discuss how adults' interactions affect how children understand the ways they fit into a society. The language socialization framework also allows us to explore how different communities orient to questions of **literacy** as a part of linguistic practice, and how policies can be enacted to promote children's success in formal education systems. In the sections that follow, we will explore some of this cross-cultural variation in language socialization. After that, we will explore how ideologies about how much language children are exposed to and how literacy intersects with language shape the way different communities engage in language socialization and policy-making.

Our discussion of language acquisition in Section 6.2 pointed out that all neurotypical babies (raised in a safe environment with language continually being used around them) will go through all the same stages of language acquisition – regardless of the language(s) being used in their speech community. On the other hand, there is a great deal of variation in how different speech communities socialize their children into the linguistic and communicative norms of their communities. As we mentioned earlier, you may have noticed that adults have a rather unique way of talking to infants and children. "Baby talk" or "motherese" – most often referred to by linguists as **infant-directed speech** – is a widespread phenomenon across language communities (though *not* universal). When you hear a parent, caregiver, or other adult member of a speech community interacting with a baby, you may hear them use a unique intonational pattern, often described as "sing-song-y," with slower pace and greater pitch dynamism. Adults may also simplify the pronunciation of certain words – for instance, by using the term "baba" for "bottle."

When this topic arises in the popular media and in other public forums, people often wonder what the purpose of this register is. Does speaking "motherese" help infants figure out their first languages? Or does using baby talk limit a child's linguistic and cognitive development? Scholars from a range of disciplines have explored this question. From linguistic anthropology in particular – most famously in a paper by Elinor Ochs and Bambi Schieffelin (1994), but also in works by Lourdes De León (1998), Elise Berman (2014), and others – we have gained a cross-cultural perspective that puts these questions to the test. The work of these scholars investigates how parents, caregivers, and other community members talk *to* and *about* infants and children. Let's review some of the findings of their work!

6.3.1   ... In US American Families

The many dimensions of diversity across families in the US means that it is tricky to identify one core set of "US American language socialization" practices. Indeed, several scholars have noted differences in the ways that parents from different racial and socioeconomic backgrounds socialize their children into community norms of language use. We'll explore a few of those dimensions of difference in this section.

Ochs and Schieffelin described language socialization practices among what they called "Anglo-American White Middle-Class" families. They reviewed language development research from both British and American families in which the primary conversations analyzed are between mothers and children. The authors pointed out that the typical parent–child conversational context is inside a house, with just the caregiver and the infant as the primary interactional parties. Because of this, caregivers spend a lot of time gazing directly at their infants and trying to hold their infant's gaze. Not only that, but caregivers "have been observed to address their infants, vocalize to them, ask questions, and greet them," in turn interpreting the infant's noises and movements as "meaningful" (Ochs & Schieffelin 1994, p. 479) – in other words, caregivers "richly interpret ... what the young child is expressing. Here, the adult acts *as if* the child were more competent than [their] behavior more strictly would indicate" (p. 480). Ochs and Schieffelin refer to this communicative strategy as a "child-raising" ("no pun intended") strategy for accommodating infants' limited ability to fully participate in adult-like conversations. They also note another strategy – one they refer to as "self-lowering" (p. 480) – in which the caregiver "takes the perspective of the child," by "simplifying [their] speech to match more closely what the adult considers to be the verbal competence of the young child" (p. 480). This is what you might have heard referred to as "baby talk," or "motherese." Through the combination of these two strategies, Ochs and Schieffelin argue, infants are socialized into the "dyadic, turn-taking model" of conversation that is normative in white American culture, while at the same time being socialized into a sort of dependence on and separation from the rest of the adult community.

We can contrast these studies with the socialization work that linguistic anthropologist Shirley Brice Heath conducted with white and Black families in the Piedmont regions of North and South Carolina in the southern US (Heath 1983). We discuss more of this research later in this chapter and in others. But in terms of language socialization, Heath's research found that white families interacted with their children in ways that were similar to the white families studied by Ochs and Schiefflin. However, Black families in Heath's study interacted with their children in a very different way. She observed that Black adults tended not to address babies directly, nor did they engage in the faux-conversation of asking what the babies needed when they fussed – instead, they would simply provide for the babies what they needed (pp. 76–77). Babies aren't good conversational partners, and it is regarded as strange when adults would carry on a conversation with them (p. 86); however, they receive a lot of attention from adults and are typically not excluded from any adult conversations. While these different language socialization practices were found to have consequences in terms of participation in the mainstream education system, Heath attributes these differences to the ideologies surrounding different ways of talking as well as socializing children into language use. As our discussion of language development in Section 6.2 makes clear, there is no reason to believe that these different socialization practices provide cognitive advantages or disadvantages to children as they develop their first/native language skills.

Sociologist Annette Lareau, who conducted in-depth ethnographies with US American families of various racial and socioeconomic backgrounds, noted a similar pattern of difference along class lines. In her research, middle-class families engaged in what Lareau termed **concerted cultivation** (Lareau 2011, p. 111). This is an orientation toward child-rearing in which parents actively encourage their children to develop certain vocabulary and learn particular interactional norms – similar to the observations Ochs and Schieffelin made in their study of (specifically Anglo-American) middle-class families. Lareau also documented the practices of working class families who engaged in a parenting strategy she referred to as the **accomplishment of natural growth**. This technique largely parallels the way Heath describes the language socialization tactics in her study described above: it relies less on socializing children into extended verbal discussion and practicing of different kinds of verbal routines and more on using language as a "practical conduit of daily life" (Lareau 2011, p. 146).

These studies show that there are distinct differences in how cultures within the US believe infants and children should be interacted with and how they should talk to each other and the rest of their community. The children described in these studies grew to become fully proficient users of language in their communities, although it is true that certain linguistic styles are perceived more favorably in classrooms and workplaces. But again, these differences are rooted in language ideologies and not in the inherent superiority of one style or another, or a failure of one style of language socialization to properly "teach" a child their first/native language. Let's take a look at some more cultures and see even more differences in patterns of language socialization around the world.

6.3.2 ... Among the Kaluli of Papua New Guinea

In the highlands of Papua New Guinea – a country just north of Australia (see Figure 6.2) – a small community of speakers of the Kaluli language have a rather different perspective on communicating with and about infants. This is where anthropologist Bambi Schieffelin of (in Ochs & Schieffelin 1994) conducted her investigation into cross-cultural language socialization practices.

Much like white American parents, Kaluli parents often keep their infants close by while the caregivers take care of the chores of everyday life, such as gardening, cooking, or just sitting around and chatting with other adults. Unlike white American parents, though, Kaluli caregivers are not often preoccupied with directing their gaze toward their infants. As the primary infant caregivers in Kaluli society, mothers are attentive to infant vocalizations – cleaning or feeding a baby that cries, as necessary – but their vocalizations are not treated or interpreted as having "meaning" in any particular way. Indeed, as Kaluli babies are often described as "soft," "helpless," and "having no understanding" (p. 482), this would simply not make sense to Kaluli parents. Sometimes, Kaluli mothers will address vocalizations to their infants or greet them by name, but more frequently, babies sit facing

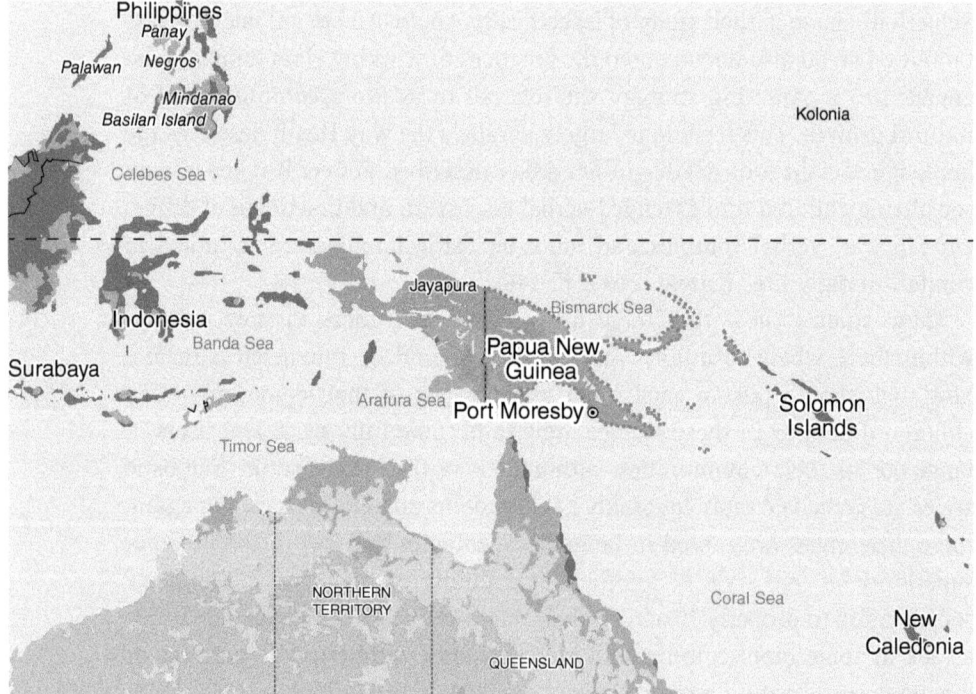

Figure 6.2 Map of Papua New Guinea (Google Maps).

away from their mothers, where "they can see, and be seen, by other members of the social group" (p. 482). If an older child addresses the baby, the mother might take on the "voice" of the infant, using a high pitch and nasalization to mark the baby's voice as different from her own – a sort of "child-raising" interactional strategy. But, overall, caregivers of Kaluli infants and other adults generally do not talk to infants in the way that white middle-class American families tend to do. Nevertheless, Kaluli infants become fully proficient Kaluli language users at about the same time as English-speaking children become fully proficient English speakers (and the same for each of the communities we discuss in this chapter).

6.3.3 ... In Samoa

The Independent State of Samoa – known at the time of anthropologist Elinor Ochs' research as Western Samoa – is an island nation situated about 2,000 miles north of Aotearoa (New Zealand) in the South Pacific Ocean (see Figures 6.3 and 6.4). In a traditional village on the island of Upolu, in the western region of Samoa, Ochs studied how Samoan-speaking families socialized their children into the language practices of their community (Ochs & Schieffelin 1994).

In these communities, social status and hierarchy – based partially, but not entirely, on age – is very important. It even shapes how infants are cared for.

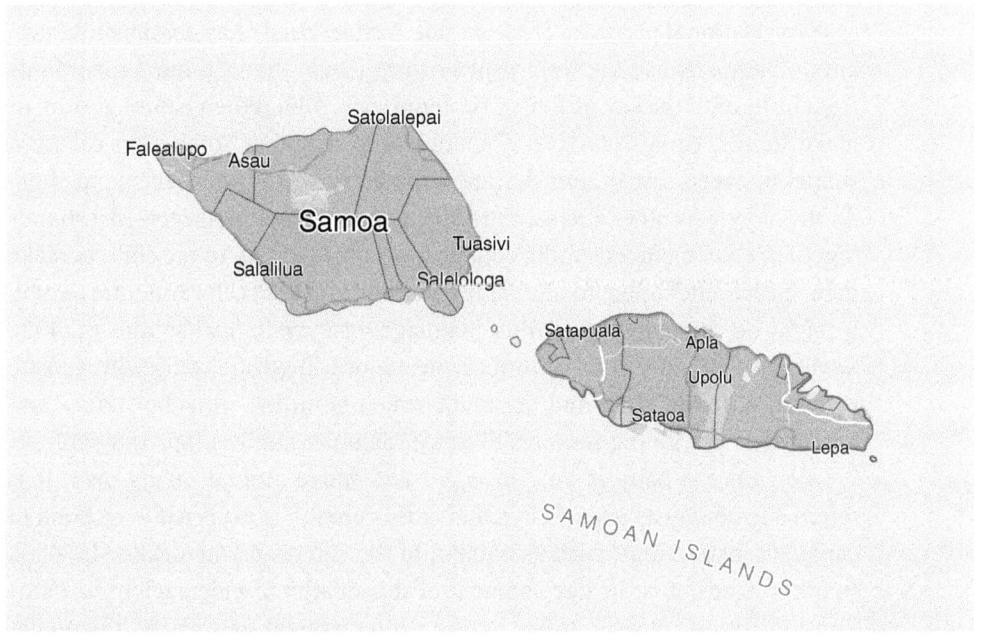

Figure 6.3 Map of Samoa (Google Maps).

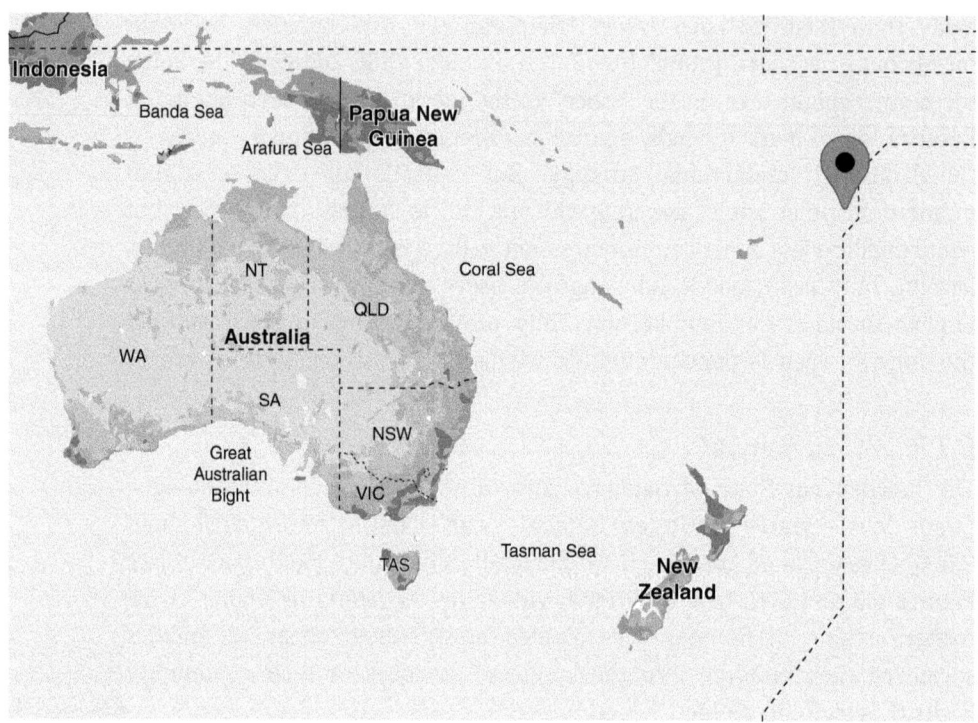

Figure 6.4 Location of Samoa in regional context (Google Maps).

Newborns and very young babies who, after all, cannot talk, are not treated as conversational partners. They are not even *referred* to as possible interactants – Samoans use the term *pepemeamea* ("baby thing thing") for infants from birth until the age of five or six months (p. 489). When babies gesture or make noises, caregivers take it simply as a sign that some physical need should be taken care of, not that the baby is trying to communicate (p. 489). As the baby gets older and starts to string more complex, speech-like sounds together, elder members of the community consider it up to the child to make their speech intelligible to adults: if a young child's speech cannot be parsed, it might be compared to another language, or even animal sounds (p. 492). Sometimes an older child with more developed linguistic skills will mediate between a young child and an adult, which is in line with the status- and age-graded caregiving responsibilities in Samoan families (pp. 488–489).

Later, once a baby is able to crawl and move around on its own, it is referred to simply as *pepe* (baby), and at this point it is expected to respond to caregiver instructions, such as coming to the caregiver when called (p. 489). In other words, it is the development of this quality of independent locomotion that transforms the infant into an interactional partner. At this point, young children are expected to practice producing "certain speech acts that they will be expected to produce later as younger (i.e., lower-ranking) members of the household" (p. 490). Through this kind of language socialization, "the cumulative orientation is one in which even very young children are ... encourage[d] to meet the needs of the situation, that is, to notice others, listen to them, and adapt one's own speech to their particular status and needs" (p. 491) – an entirely different strategy than the "child-raising" or "self-lowering" strategies that Ochs and Schieffelin (1994) described for Anglo-American families and Kaluli families. Despite these differences in language socialization strategies, Ochs found no evidence to suggest that these Samoan children developed fluency in their native language at a lesser rate than their English-speaking US American peers – or vice versa! While the natural progression of language development shapes ideologies about what kinds of language practices are worth doing with whom, in the end, both Samoan and US American babies hear and see language being used all around them, and thus end up as fluent members of their language communities.

6.3.4 ... Among Tzotzil Speakers in Southern Mexico

Linguistic anthropologist Lourdes de León investigated how infants are socialized into the communicative norms of a Maya community in southern Mexico. De León conducted ethnographic fieldwork in the town of Nabenchauk, Zinacantán, a village in the Mexican state of Chiapas that held about 3,000 inhabitants at the time of her fieldwork in the early 1990s (see Figure 6.5). Residents of Nabenchauk speak Tzotzil, a Mayan language with

Figure 6.5 Location of Zincantán, Chiapas, Mexico (Google Maps).

over 250,000 speakers, and many of them are bilingual in Spanish (De León 1998, p. 136).

When infants are born in Nabenchauk, they are initially restricted from interacting with individuals outside the household – babies are not frequently taken out of the home, and when they are, their faces are covered. This is due to cultural beliefs about keeping the child's soul safe before baptism at one year of age (De León 1998, p. 137). During this time, and even after the child is formally introduced to the wider community, the life of an infant in Nabenchauk looks in some ways quite similar to that of an infant in Samoa or among the Kaluli. Their "constant physical co-presence with a caregiver" (p. 137), often situated at eye-level with other adult members of a household or family group, means that children are immersed in paired and group social interactions from the earliest possible age (p. 132). While adults do not seem to address children directly (p. 133) and use only a very limited "motherese"-style vocabulary (p. 145), the way adults talk *with* and *about* their infants in this community illustrate that they see their children as competent participants even before they produce language. In particular, parents interpret their infants' gaze and gesture as communicative acts, using rhetorical questions and a quotative verb frame to "voice" the child's contribution to an interaction (p. 151). As the child develops greater mobility and linguistic competence, parents scale back the interactional "guidance" they do for their children, thus allowing their participation as full contributors to conversational interaction to slowly emerge as they age. And, just as we see for the other cross-cultural language socialization practices we have reviewed thus far, the strategies that Tzotzil parents use to habituate their children into the language norms of their community has no adverse or delaying effect on the development of full fluency in Tzotzil.

6.3.5 ... In the Republic of the Marshall Islands

The Republic of the Marshall Islands (RMI) is located in the Central Pacific Ocean, roughly northwest of Samoa, where Elinor Ochs' research was conducted, and roughly northeast of Papua New Guinea, where Bambi Schieffelin studied (see Figures 6.6 and 6.7). Here, on an outer atoll called Jaikon, linguistic anthropologist Elise Berman (2014) conducted fieldwork among speakers of Marshallese, a language of the Micronesian family and indigenous to the islands (p. 113).

Berman spent a total of twenty-six months in Jaikon across a period of several years, living with a local family and learning through firsthand participant observation how children in this community are socialized into age-appropriate language use. But more than wanting to understand how

6.3 Language Socialization 165

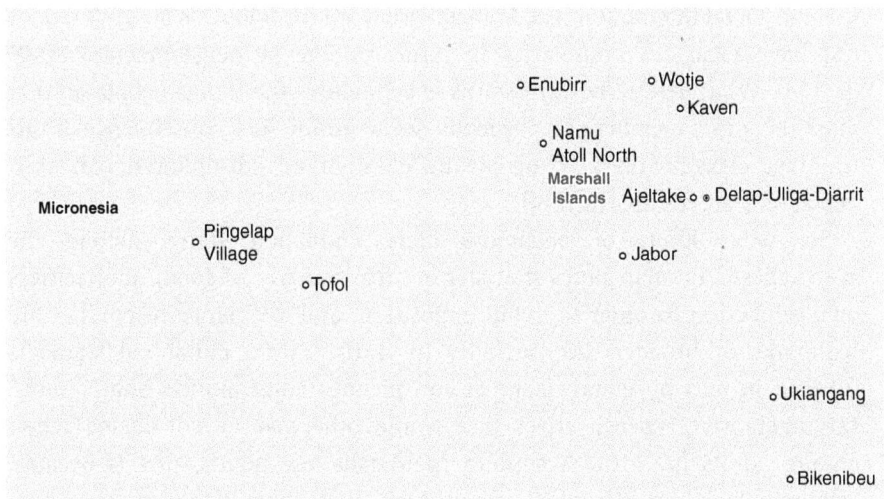

Figure 6.6 Map of the Republic of the Marshall Islands (Google Maps).

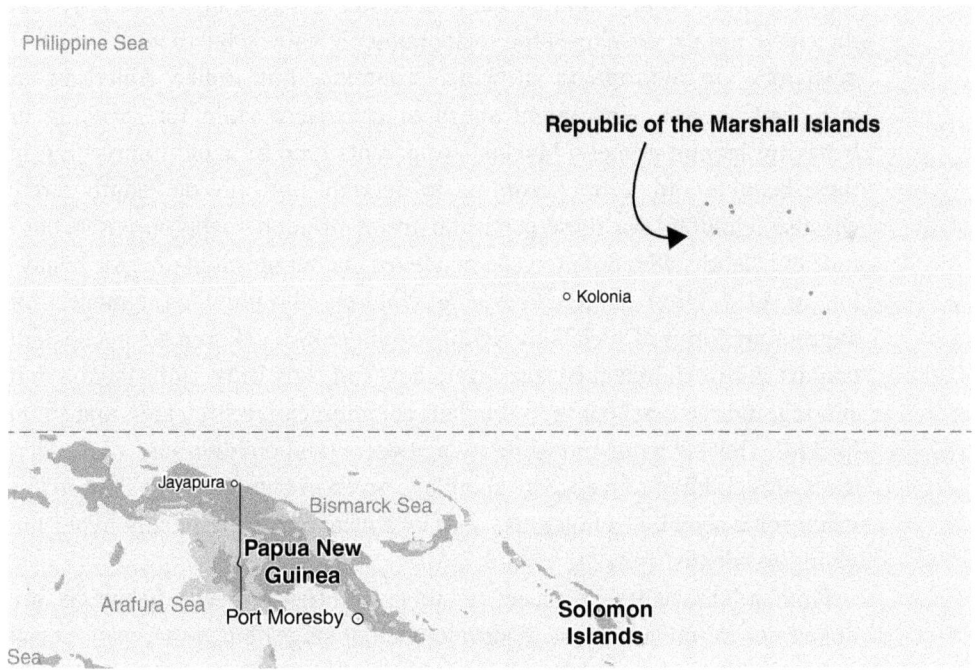

Figure 6.7 Location of the RMI in regional context (Google Maps).

Marshallese children are socialized into community-appropriate norms of language use, Berman wanted to understand Marshallese notions of "childhood" as a cultural category itself, and how the Marshallese version of "childhood" shaped the way adults interpreted and reacted to child language use and social interaction. The Marshallese word for "child" is *ajri*, but it does not have clear-cut boundaries in terms of age or developmental stage (p. 114). What determines *ajri* status is behavior – the things people do that mark them as a member of a particular social group. As a consequence of this framing, classifications of people as children or not-children can shift depending on context (p. 114).

So, what kinds of behaviors mark childhood status among the Marshallese? Berman notes that sharing (particularly of food), indirectness or misdirection in order to avoid imposition, and avoidance of conflict are hallmarks of broader RMI sociality (p. 116) – thus, childhood status is inferred in part by engagement in conspicuous consumption and "direct," "argumentative" speech styles that would otherwise be considered taboo among adults (p. 110). According to Marshallese adults, this is because "children lack the 'thoughts' and 'shame' that compel their acts of not-giving, asking, and demanding" (p. 110). This may sound similar to ideologies of children's speech that many American and European families hold – the belief that young children have "no filter" or, put more precisely, that they have not yet developed the sociopragmatic knowledge of what topics or behaviors are appropriate in which contexts. But unlike American or European parents, who might shush or chastise a child for speaking or behaving inappropriately, Marshallese parents tend to avoid intervening in these behaviors (p. 125). According to Berman, not only do "adults rarely chastise [children] for these particular forms of adult-inappropriate behavior," but "adults who do intercede may even encourage child-specific behavior" (p. 125). Why? Largely, it is older children who provide the models for appropriate forms of social interaction. Younger RMI children are in constant contact with children their age and older, and thus learn from them about sharing, indirectness, conflict-avoidant communicative strategies, and so on (p. 124). This behavior-modeling by age peers (and children just a bit older) leads RMI children to realize by about age seven or eight that not sharing (for instance) is socially "dangerous," and by this age they "explicitly avoid not giving to friends" (p. 124).

From a Marshallese perspective, then, children's speech behaviors are linked not to immaturity as a "developmental stage" but rather as a "social status" (p. 110). Thus, learning to communicate as a grown-up in the RMI is a gradual process of socialization into norms of indirectness and conflict avoidance through sharing (p. 123). Moving from childhood to adulthood is, for the Marshallese, "a process of gradually gaining … the modes of thinking that eventually compel people to engage in" adult-like interactional and communicative behaviors (p. 123). This tells us that if RMI children are more direct, less polite, or "hide and lie" less, it is because this is how childhood is constructed as a social category in this culture, rather than due to some developmental inability for children to be less direct. As we discussed in our mention of sociopragmatic development in Section 6.2.4, socialization into sociopragmatic knowledge is an ongoing, life-long process rather than a developmental stage with a clear-cut beginning and ending. In fact, this case study of Marshallese children illustrates that sometimes the notion of what is developmentally "appropriate" or "inappropriate" is itself determined more by social and cultural context than by some measure by which some might "succeed" and others might "fall short." Yet again when we look cross-culturally, anthropologists and linguists both find that there is a tremendous amount of difference in how caretakers teach their young ones how to use language and how to interact according to community norms and that all of these approaches can lead to children who are proficient users of their native language(s).

6.3.6 Some Takeaway Points

Despite all of the cross-cultural ethnographic evidence we have just reviewed, a major misconception persists – particularly in Western, English-speaking contexts – that children *must* be exposed to a certain style of speech in order to properly acquire their first languages and in order to be properly socialized into the language norms of their community. Certain forms of this myth also tend to assume that exposure to written forms of language is necessary in order for full and proper language acquisition to happen. Let us put simply what you now know: this is untrue. Like we've said throughout this chapter, infants acquire language and become completely proficient users of their language(s) regardless of how they are interacted with and spoken or signed to (so long as they aren't victims of abuse, or have a developmental or neurological condition that might impede this process). Rather than just disregard these misconceptions, though, linguists who aim to study language within its social and cultural context believe it is crucially important to understand the logic behind these myths and how belief in these myths shapes the way we approach language socialization practice and policy. Thus, in the next sections, we will dig deeply into the misconception of the so-called "word gap," and how that myth ties into the way we perceive socialization into literacy norms in communities that have a written form of their language.

6.4 The Misconception of the "Word Gap"

In 1995, researchers Betty Hart and Todd Risley published the results of a longitudinal study that they had conducted with English-speaking families in

Kansas City, Kansas, US. Over two and a half years, they followed forty-two families at different socioeconomic status (SES) levels and tracked the number and types of words used by the parents when speaking to their children. Based on what they had found and extrapolated from their own data, they suggested that the children of families with a higher socioeconomic status were exposed to nearly thirty million more words by the time they got to school than the children of families with lower SES. This has been termed the **thirty million** word gap, sometimes shortened to just the "**word gap**" or the "**language gap.**" Since its original publication, the claims of this study have circulated widely as fact. National political initiatives in the United States have even been formed in order to address the "word gap" in schools and in the community.[7] But, as scientists, we cannot take this claim at face value – we need to examine it further (Figueroa 2024a, 2024b).

The claim behind the word gap is situated in psycholinguistic spoken language development research[8] focusing on how interaction between caregivers and children facilitates language learning. For example, typically developing infants seem to need social interaction with another human being to learn their first languages and cannot learn one just through listening to audio, or even audio accompanied by a video of a person speaking (Kuhl et al. 2003). Similarly, deaf children whose parents do not sign to them or who otherwise are not exposed to a language modality that they can understand until later in life also do not sign like deaf individuals raised with a signed language from birth (Newport 1990).

These lines of research suggest that infants cannot just *listen to* their caregivers to learn a language, but they need to be talked to as well. More specifically, this type of research suggests that children from families of lower socioeconomic status must be lagging in their development since they are not being talked to as much (or hearing as many words, for that matter) as the children from families of higher socioeconomic status. Based on the cross-cultural case studies we reviewed in the previous section, though, we know that the social interaction necessary to learn a language does not need to be directed at the child or take any particular form, or include any specific pieces of vocabulary. Given the research discussed above, we need to go deeper into Hart and Risley's study and ask: Is it really just language?

---

[7] Former US President Barack Obama, for instance, gave an impassioned speech in 2014 describing "closing the word gap" as one of his key educational policy priorities.

[8] Importantly, this research does not consider signed language development at all – in fact, it doesn't even discuss the possibility of signed languages. We hope that you never forget that language development happens in signed and spoken languages, and note that our description of their work clearly refers only to spoken language.

Hart and Risley (1995, 2003) claim that differences in educational achievement between the high-SES children and the low-SES children that they followed can be traced back to the number of words that they are exposed to early in life. Since children in poverty seemed to be behind their peers academically and also heard fewer words from their parents than children of "professional" parents who were more academically advanced and heard more words from their parents, they argue that the cause of the perceived deficit must be due to the amount and quality of language that they are exposed to.

But think about these claims in comparison with the sections you just read about language socialization practices across several different cultures. From Papua New Guinea and Samoa to Mexico, the Marshall Islands, and the United States, all neurologically typical children in these speech communities became proficient language users and members of their community regardless of the style of language socialization used. If we accept this claim, the Hart and Risley assertion that the number of words spoken to a child can affect their educational achievements becomes suspect.

Hart and Risley's claims become even more suspect when we look into the particulars of their research design (Hart & Risley 1995, pp. 30–32). They recorded and transcribed interactions between parents and children from forty-two families over approximately two years and grouped the families according to socioeconomic status. They did this because they had seen in a previous study that more affluent children had larger vocabularies than their peers who were less affluent. However, their SES groupings are not evenly balanced across races: their highest SES "Professional" group had only one Black family with twelve white families, and their lowest SES "Welfare" group had six Black families with no white families. Only their middle SES "Working-class" group had a more or less even number of white and Black families (thirteen and ten, respectively). This sampling confounds socioeconomic status and race, so we can't be sure that the differences between the groups are due to race, SES, some combination of the two (and if so, how much difference can be attributed to each factor), or something else entirely (such as education level, caregiver health, and so on). We briefly discussed in Section 6.3.1 how white and Black families socialize their children differently and have different expectations about their linguistic input and output, so this is a further dimension where the number of white and Black families in the "Professional" and "Welfare" groups really matters.

When thinking about sampling, it is also important to consider who is able to participate in these studies. As much as Hart and Risley comment that "parents' schedules completely determined [the researchers']" and feeling as if they, the researchers, were "being held prisoners by a longitudinal study"

(Hart & Risley 1995, p. 41), there are only certain types of caregivers whose own schedules would allow them to participate in and complete a twenty-eight-month-long study. Professors' children might be overrepresented in behavioral studies because they are in a population that professors have easy access to, and professors generally value contributing to research. Families where both parents are working full-time may not be able to participate in studies at all, or may not know that such studies exist, or may simply not want to because they have higher-priority demands on their time. This study focused only on parents as the primary caregivers, but in other households, extended family, babysitters, nannies, or daycare providers may be the people who are spending the most time with a child. With this type of sampling, the results obtained are not generalizeable to the world's – or even the US's – entire population, but are only representative of these forty-two families and their particular circumstances.

Blum (2017) points out that Hart and Risley's study and others focusing on this "word gap" rely on language ideologies of Western, educated, industrialized, rich, and democratized (or WEIRD) cultures – like white North American middle-class families. In doing so, not only do they come to incorrect conclusions, but they also emphasize the idea that there is only one "normal" way to use and acquire language, and all other ways of using language are not good enough. As linguists, we know that this simply is not true. What about, for instance, children who are exposed to multiple languages or dialects from infancy? García and Otheguy (2017) note that children who are raised bilingually or bidialectally only seem to have a gap if only one of their languages or dialects is accounted for. However, if children are allowed to express themselves using all of the linguistic tools at their disposal rather than just the white, upper-middle-class American English verbiage that is expected of them, they are just as linguistically sophisticated – if not more so! – as their peers. Rather than restricting children and their parents to a false idea of the "correct" way to speak, there are distinct and obvious benefits to be had – and no word gap to be found – if researchers acknowledge and move beyond the WEIRD language ideologies that are so pervasive throughout our society and our scientific thinking.

Many word- or language-gap researchers point out that what is tested in formal language evaluations is only one facet of the linguistic capabilities that we use every day. For example, Blum (2017) notes, "In settings where joking is the common key of interaction, children may develop sophisticated tools for punning and storytelling – traits highly valued in higher education, the arts, and even business. But that isn't tested, and thus doesn't count" (p. 32). Standardized tests that measure the number of words a child uses do not necessarily measure the ability to use wordplay or relate facts and stories in ways that are entertaining to others, which are skills that are arguably *more* valuable in the long run than the sheer number of words a person can use. More generally, asserting only one communicative style as appropriate, normative, or correct can itself lead to lower educational outcomes for young people.

The groundbreaking research of Susan U. Philips (1982) – which we discuss in detail in Chapter 8 – describes this problem. In classrooms run by Anglo-American teachers, Native American students from the Warm Springs Reservation were perceived as understanding less, and performance assessments even rated them behind their Anglo peers. But these educational assessments were all built around the assumption that children express knowledge and skill in the same way – by responding quickly to direct questions from teachers, by making eye contact when they communicate, and by being excited to share all they know. Yet in the culture of the Warm Springs children, it is considered highly impolite to respond in such a way – their community socializes them into carefully and slowly considering any responses to questions, and to avoid the gaze of elders or people in positions of authority (such as teachers!) as a mark of respect. Thus, it was not that Native American children were learning or retaining less than their Anglo peers. Rather, it was that their Anglo-American teachers only saw one style of communication as properly expressing knowledge and learning, whereas the Native children were just following their community's norms for communicating respect. These same assumptions – that only one style of communication or language use is appropriate – underlie the myth of the word gap.

In exploring the empirical failure of the "word gap" claims, a team of researchers attempted to replicate Hart and Risley's (1995) study, but they did not find the same results. Sperry et al. (2019) used a variety of existing corpora covering different communities to tabulate the number of words that children were exposed to in their everyday interactions with their families and other caregivers and proceeded to examine the data using similar factors to Hart and Risley's twenty years before. Sperry et al. combined their data with that collected by Hart and Risley. They found that there was no significant difference between the number of words used by "primary caregivers" in the middle-class families vs. the poor families. Furthermore, they found no statistical patterns suggesting that there was an increase in the words that middle-class children heard compared to poor and working-class children when data from all caregivers to a given child was examined, not just the primary caregiver. Finally, when the speech in the child's ambient environment was examined, children in the lowest socioeconomic status heard *more* words than the children in higher socioeconomic status ranges. All of this suggests that social class really has nothing to do with the amount of language a child is exposed to, and further, that children from lower socioeconomic status backgrounds are actually hearing just as many words – if not more! – than children from higher socioeconomic statuses. It is important to remember, after all, that children are exposed to a great deal of speech, and they are not just paying attention to speech that is directed to them specifically. When examined more closely, the supposed "word gap" between high- and low-SES children disappears.

These results help clarify that it is not speech and language use around children that contribute to "achievement gaps" between low-SES and high-SES children as they enter school; there are other important factors at play as well. In a response to Sperry and colleagues' work, Golinkoff et al. (2019) note in an aside that nonlinguistic factors known to affect low-SES children more often than high-SES children include higher levels of air and noise pollution, food insecurity, and lead poisoning. These are factors that we are not able to control for in linguistic studies and factors that are also crucial determiners for educational success. Further compounding these circumstances with discrimination against different practices of language development certainly does not help!

Claims about the existence of a word gap, in which scholars try to suggest that a person's social status or wealth are somehow causal factors in their success or failure at language acquisition and development, are implausible on their face and disconfirmed by the data that we can observe in broad, cross-cultural research. Similarly, claims that focus on things like "word count" are always problematic, since – as we have discussed in previous chapters – the unit "word" is not clearly definable in a way that allows us to compare units across various types of languages (spoken and signed). Even trying to describe "high quality" as opposed to "low quality" language input gets tricky, as decisions about what counts as "quality" are inevitably based on the language norms of the dominant culture rather than some objective truth. We encourage the reader to remain skeptical of any such claims and to always see whether the scholars who make them have complied with the Bender Rule and the Lanehart Rule (as discussed in Chapter 4) in their published work.

6.5 Literacy Socialization

Although literacy – the ability to read and write – is not a necessary component of fluency in a language,[9] many language communities do see

---

[9] Refer back to Chapter 2 if you need a refresher.

mastering the written form of their language as a key step in developing communicative competence. Just as children must be socialized into the interactional norms of their community with respect to spoken language, so too do communities teach their children – in direct and indirect ways – how to use and understand writing. And just as is the case with spoken and signed language, what literacy skills look like in practice varies tremendously, in terms of what skills and forms count as literacy skills, who is expected to have them and to what degree, and how the social and cultural dynamics a given community is embedded within evaluate and interpret these skills. In other words, "each society or community is literate in ways that differ from the ways in which other societies or communities are literate" (Besnier 2001, p. 136).

As you think about this section, keep in mind that one of the differences between developing a language and developing literacy skills is that the literacy skills must be taught. Language development will simply happen through the normal course of being a human, and we do not need to be taught how to use language (though we might need a little bit of coaching on how to adhere to our community's communication norms). You may remember having to learn how to read and write, though, and it's a very different process than learning to talk or sign! However, communities in which literacy skills are highly valued can sometimes conflate the learning of reading and writing skills with the development of language – and in this conflation, ideologies about how reading and writing might shape our language development emerge.

One example of the variability in how children are socialized into different forms of literacy comes from linguistic anthropologist Shirley Brice Heath, whose work we mentioned earlier in the context of language socialization among US American families. The findings we reviewed above came from a decades-long ethnographic research study on four communities in the Piedmont regions of North and South Carolina in the United States (see Figure 6.8).

When her research began in the early 1970s, her aim was to understand how the Civil Rights Movement of the 1960s had affected the ways children and families were "adapting to classroom life in newly desegregated schools" (p. 1). She began by studying four communities in the Piedmont region: two predominantly Black communities, and two predominantly white communities, with one community in each racial group consisting mostly of upwardly mobile middle-class professionals and the other consisting primarily of manual laborers and other working class wage earners (p. 1). This mix of communities allowed her work to specifically investigate the relationship between class and race in local classrooms. And as she continued her

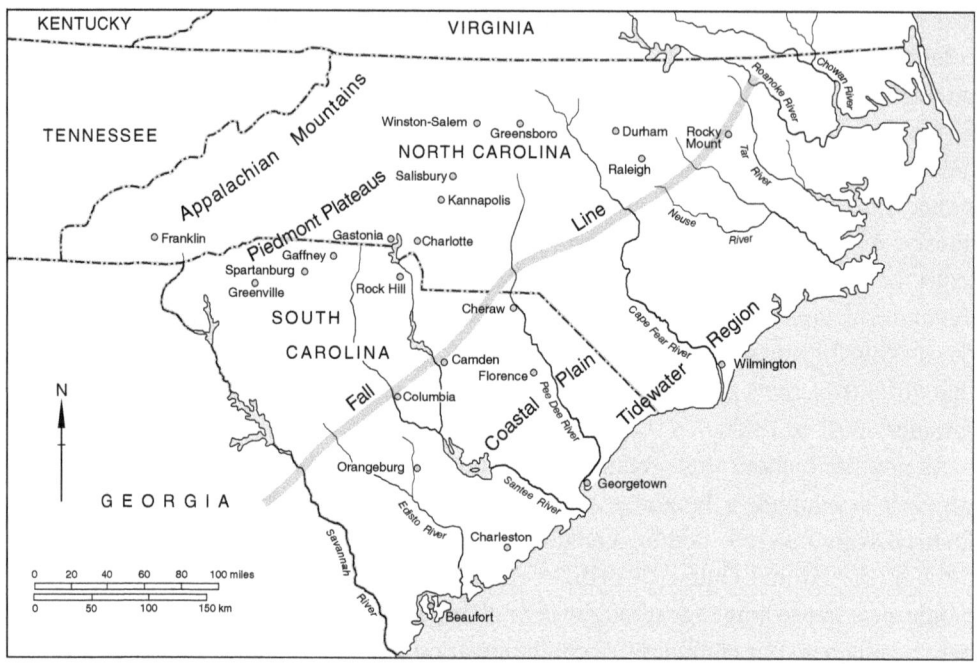

Figure 6.8 Map of Shirley Brice Heath's research area (Heath 2012, p. 2).

research and relationship with these communities, the economic changes brought about by the recession of the early 1980s and the way different experiences of labor and work life shaped how families socialize their children into literacy skills were highlighted as well.

"Maintown" was a predominantly white, upper-middle-class town. Adults in Maintown worked as teachers, lawyers, and businesspeople. Children in Maintown households were exposed to books from an early age, and thus were socialized into an orientation to literature that foregrounded the type of reading and writing associated with children's literature. Adults and children in Maintown would often read books together, with the adult asking leading or guiding questions that invited the child to connect the elements of the story to their own life.

"Roadville" was another predominantly white town, but these families were more working class than those in Maintown. Adults in Roadville had historically taken jobs in a local textile mill (p. 57), and children in Roadville homes tended to have comparatively fewer books than children in Maintown homes. Not only that, but the ways in which parents read to children was rather different here – rather than reading together, with parents frequently asking children questions about the unfolding of the story, children were required to sit still and listen carefully. In general, the orientation to the written word in Roadville homes is focused on getting children to focus on labels, features, and straightforward explanations of plot events (p. 71). Children in Roadville homes are not socialized to look for connections to other stories or events – rather, they are taught to "look for a specific moral in stories and to expect that story to fit their facts of reality explicitly" (p. 71). Meanwhile, children from Trackton – a working-class Black community where adults had historically worked as farmers (either on their own land or for other landowners) but more recently had begun working in the textile mills like Roadville adults (p. 57) – had an entirely different experience with literacy in their early years. Trackton children were immersed in almost constant human contact from the time they came home from the hospital, with language and communication happening around them virtually non-stop. Books for children were uncommon in Trackton homes, and adults typically did not sit and read to children – though adults did read in their homes, typically "newspapers, mail, calendars, circular ... school materials ... brochures ... and the Bible and other church-related materials" (p. 65). Instead, Trackton children were praised and rewarded by adults in their community for their oral storytelling skills, and more generally for their ability to participate in robust practices of oral communication in their community.

The different orientations these communities had to reading, writing, and literacy more generally led to very different experiences for children from each of these towns when they arrived in the public school setting. Maintown households often described themselves as "typical," "middle-class," and "mainstream" (Heath 1982, p. 52) – and this is reflected in what was considered normative and appropriate in public schools. When children in all three of these communities reached school age, they were confronted with literacy expectations from teachers that children should actively respond to questions about stories taught in class – Maintown kids were already experts in this kind of literacy behavior, as it was part of how their parents socialized them into language and literacy in their home!

Kids from Roadville homes tended to do all right, but not as well as their Maintown peers, as their home literacy socialization emphasized a more task-oriented approach to reading rather than building connections between narratives and their everyday lives. Heath reported that Roadville homes struggled a bit more in adapting to the literacy norms of classrooms that expected children to know how to engage in these question–answer routines about stories in books.

Finally, Trackton students entered school with a major disadvantage: while their white, middle-class teachers expected them to perform the same kind of responses to stories in books that Maintown kids did, Trackton kids had never been socialized into that kind of engagement with reading. Let's be clear, though: this is not to say that Trackton kids were "deficient" linguistically in any way. Indeed, they came from communities where oral language skills were highly valued and practiced from a very early age! Had schoolteachers asked students to dissect contextual clues in a story, or tell their own fictional stories, their home literacy practices may have put them at an advantage. But because literacy norms in the mainstream educational system only saw the value in a Maintown-style orientation to literacy, Trackton kids were perceived as less gifted and often struggled with learning this new approach to literacy in their early educational years.

Many other scholars have pointed out how children from speech communities whose languages are racialized or minoritized in other ways are often made to feel inferior by the ideologies of literacy in mainstream American schooling. April Baker-Bell, for instance, has shown that when children from Black Language–speaking households enter mainstream US schools, they are "falsely positioned as linguistically inadequate because their language practices do not reflect White Mainstream English" (Baker-Bell 2020, p. 20). While Baker-Bell's work focused more specifically on spoken language skills, it is clear how this same finding could be derived from Heath's work on literacy socialization. Since Trackton children were not socialized into the same relationship with literacy and narrative storytelling as Maintown and Roadville kids, the teachers assumed they were intellectually or at least linguistically deficient, despite the fact that they grew up in homes and communities with robust and complex oral linguistic norms. Per Baker-Bell's research, Trackton kids would have met with much more success in their classrooms if all kinds of linguistic and literacy skills were valued. These same patterns can also be viewed in Philips' research in classrooms with children from the Warm Springs Reservation – and in many other sociocultural contexts besides. Shirley Brice Heath (1982) puts most succinctly what this chapter's exploration of the relationship and distinction between language development, language socialization, and literacy socialization highlights: "Each community's ways of taking from the printed word and using this knowledge are interdependent with the way children learn to talk in their social interactions with caregivers. There is little to no validity to the time-honored dichotomy of 'the literate tradition' and 'the oral tradition'" (pp. 50–51).

6.6 Conclusion

This chapter has covered many different elements of the ways in which linguists approach babies. We have covered the cognitive stages that neurotypical infants raised in healthy environments typically go through as they figure out the patterns and structures of the languages used around them. In doing this, we learned that children become fully competent members of their language communities no matter how much their caregivers speak directly "to" them or "with" them, no matter how many different languages, dialects, or varieties are used in their families, and regardless of whether the languages used around them are spoken or signed. It is true that different language communities approach the task of socializing their children into their communicative norms differently – but in the end, the results are largely the same. While learning to read and write is not a required element of language development – with many contemporary and historical language communities worldwide not having any writing system or literary tradition – when communities *do* have a literary practice, they are often shaped by the same beliefs that shape socialization into the norms of spoken and signed language use in a given community. All in all, this shows us how important infants, babies, and children are as a site for learning about language and social issues!

Linguist in the Community

- Language acquisition intersects with language socialization in many ways, but one of the most humorous places to observe this connection is when children discover – and start using – "bad" words. These are usually cases when a child has heard a word in their speech community but has not yet been fully socialized into the norms/rules of appropriateness for who uses that word, and when. Draw a comic or write a short story about the first time you, or a child you know, used a word that is considered bad, inappropriate, or taboo in your community. Discuss what kind of word it is, what semantic domain it fits into, and the reactions of adults.
- Reflecting on your own memories from childhood, jot down some notes about your earliest memories of your own language development. These might be times when an adult or peer told you that you were using a word incorrectly or your pronunciation was wrong – or even times when you were praised for using language well! Then think about the ways in which those early experiences might have contributed to your values and attitudes about your language today. How might those early experiences have reflected your own pattern of development (as it relates to the language acquisition timeline we've described in Section 6.2)? How might they be related to the practices and values embedded in language socialization processes in your own communities of practice?

Linguist in the Classroom

- Parents often share cute videos of their children's language development on platforms like YouTube and TikTok. You may even have some videos handy yourself of children in your own family! Find some of these and (after receiving permission from caregivers when appropriate/possible) share them with small groups in your class. Try in particular to seek out videos of children using signed languages or using multiple languages in the same communicative instance. After watching them, take note of what features appear in their language use. Using the "typical language development timeline" chart and other knowledge from this chapter, try to describe where in the process of language development this child might be. During your discussions, keep in mind all of the natural and healthy variation in this process!
- Individually, or in small groups, critically consider our definitions of "first language" and "second language." These definitions may not be sufficient to describe humans' relationships to the languages in our communities – see if you can come up with situations (from your own experience, or hypotheticals) in which it's not clear that these definitions really fit. Are there cases in which a person might be said to have no first language? Are there situations in which a person may have access to a language that doesn't fit either definition? Share your thoughts with the class, and see if you can create a more comprehensive set of terms to describe our relationships with the languages we acquire or learn.

Glossary

accomplishment of natural growth A practice of socializing children to use language as is practical and necessary for daily life, but not necessarily encouraging the learning of specific vocabulary items or interactional norms.

babble A stage in infant language development in which babies experiment with different sounds and sound patterns in their languages without yet using any recognizable words.

concerted cultivation A method of child-rearing in which parents encourage children to learn specific pieces of vocabulary and other interactional norms that are perceived to offer benefits in terms of social mobility.

first language Any language that one has been exposed to since infancy. Healthy infants who have access to a caring speech community will have at least one first language, and humans are perfectly capable of acquiring many first languages.

gestational age A measure of the age of a pregnancy, usually in terms of weeks.

infant-directed speech A special register that adults in some speech communities use to speak to infants and children, often referred to as "motherese" or "baby talk."

language acquisition The naturally occurring process by which human infants, exposed to one or more first languages, gain the ability to understand and use that/those language(s).

language gap The fallacious notion that children from marginalized communities receive lower "quality" linguistic input in the first few years of their life than children from more privileged communities, with "quality" usually being determined in vague and shifting ways.

language socialization The culturally specific process by which children are taught the communicative norms in their speech community.

literacy The ability to read and write, which is taught overtly and explicitly and is not a necessary part of the language acquisition process.

mutual exclusivity A cognitive assumption made by children acquiring their first language that assigns only one word or label to a concept and only one concept to a label.

native language See first language.

prenatal Occurring before birth / during gestation of a fetus.

Principle of Contrast A cognitive assumption made by children acquiring their first language that different words have different meanings.

second language Any language that a person learns through exposure or effort after puberty. Humans may have one or more second languages, or no second languages at all.

sociopragmatic knowledge Linguistic knowledge shaped by sociocultural and contextual factors rather than by phonological, morphosyntactic, or semantic factors.

syntactic bootstrapping A cognitive strategy used by children acquiring their first language in which learning some individual words in their language allows them to start to figure out the syntactic structures of the language.

thirty million word gap The fallacious notion that children from lower socioeconomic backgrounds and other marginalized communities hear fewer words in the first few years of life than children from higher socioeconomic backgrounds or communities that are more privileged in other ways.

WEIRD A term used to describe research participants who come from communities that are Western, educated, industrialized, rich, and democratic.

whole object assumption A cognitive assumption made by children acquiring their first language that a word they have not heard before refers to an entire object rather than a property of that object or a group of objects.

word gap See **thirty million word gap**.

Recommended Readings

If you just can't get enough of the cuteness of babies and kids developing language skills, we have plenty of recommended readings to deepen your knowledge. The selection below represents some of our favorite work in this topic, but you can find every study we cite in this chapter in the reference section at the end of the book! Ask a local college or university library if you need help finding access to any of this work.

Baker-Bell, A. (2020). *Linguistic Justice: Black Language, Literacy, Identity, and Pedagogy*. Routledge.

Courtney, E. H., & Saville-Troike, M. (2002). Learning to construct verbs in Navajo and Quechua. *Journal of Child Language, 29*(3), 623–654. doi.org/10.1017/s0305000902005160

Figueroa, M. (2024). Language development, linguistic input, and linguistic racism. *WIREs Cognitive Science, 15*(3), e1673. https://doi.org/10.1002/wcs.1673

Heath, S. B. (2012). *Words at Work and Play: Three Decades in Family and Community Life*. Cambridge University Press.

Lillo-Martin, D., & Henner, J. (2021). Acquisition of sign languages. *Annual Review of Linguistics, 7*, 395–419. https://doi.org/10/gjrnzk

Meek, B. A. (2019). Language endangerment in childhood. *Annual Review of Anthropology, 48*(1), 95–115. https://doi.org/10.1146/annurev-anthro-102317-050041

Ochs, E., & Schieffelin, B. B. (1994). Language acquisition and socialization: Three developmental stories. In B. G. Blount (Ed.), *Language, Culture, and Society: A Book of Readings*. (2nd ed., pp. 470–512). Waveland Press.

7 Linguists Meet Computers

This chapter focuses on developments and opportunities in **computational linguistics**, including the ways in which digitally mediated language plays a variety of roles in contemporary communities. From the development of **machine-reading** and **"augmented intelligence"** for cancer researchers, to the creation and detection of "deepfakes" in text and voice, we hope this chapter will invite you to consider investigating language use in, on, and with computers.

We are writing this chapter at a time when a particular type of language technology, the **"large language model"** (LLM), is rapidly gaining prominence in both the popular media and in academic circles as a possible means of achieving true **"artificial intelligence."** LLMs form the architecture under systems including Microsoft's "Copilot," Google's "Bard," OpenAI's "GPT4o," and many other highly anticipated applications. We'll focus here on the basic building blocks that can be used to understand systems like these, in the knowledge that by the time you're reading this there will be many larger, fancier, and more powerful systems built on even fancier versions of this kind of technology.

In this chapter, we use the term **"computer,"** and sometimes the term **"machine,"** to refer to a wide variety of devices and networks – including, but not limited to, laptop and desktop personal computers, industrial servers, "smart" appliances, smartphones, and tablets, whether or not they're connected to the internet, and whether or not the systems and programs that control them are inside the hardware you're using or "in the cloud" (which is really a euphemism for industrial server farms that are situated all over the world). These devices and networks all share certain properties: first, they are digital processors – at their beating electronic hearts, they process information in binary form, and whether it's ones and zeroes, or simply on and off, at some level that's all they know; second, they are controlled by programs written for them by humans, using one or more of a large inventory of "programming languages," including operating systems, control systems, and applications; and third, humans "interact" with them linguistically by means of some input form – text typed on a keyboard, audio input through a microphone, and/or video input through a camera. Humans are talking to and with machines in an increasing variety of contexts and technologies, and these technologies are quickly growing into things that resemble human interlocutors. One of our key threads in this chapter is to consistently remind you, and ourselves, that this resemblance is illusory; if there's anything we linguists know, it's that machines are not doing language the same way that humans do language. Not yet, and maybe not ever. Since our colleagues in disciplines like computer science and electrical engineering are often unconvinced of this, we'll focus on examples that illustrate the kinds of divergence we see between humans using language and machines using language – at least as of the time of writing.

Google is one tool that we can use to see how small changes in the language we use affect what is returned to us by a machine. Take a moment, if you are willing, and open up a Google search in a private browsing window. We'll do three searches. First, type in "who were the first humans to come to America," and see what results you get. Then type in "who were the first people to come to America," and similarly, see what results you get. Are they different from the "humans" search? Finally, type in the following stem: "careers for." Stop there, and see what options you get as the top autocompletions for that search. Figures 7.1, 7.2, and 7.3 below show what we got when we did these searches in a private browsing window in Firefox on January 15, 2022, from a computer in Tucson, Arizona.

Figures 7.1 and 7.2 show that Google search gives dramatically different results to the question "who were the first _____ to come to America," depending on whether that blank is filled with the word "humans" or the word "people." If we ask after "humans," Google directs us to scholarly sources about the arrival of homo sapiens in North America. If we ask after

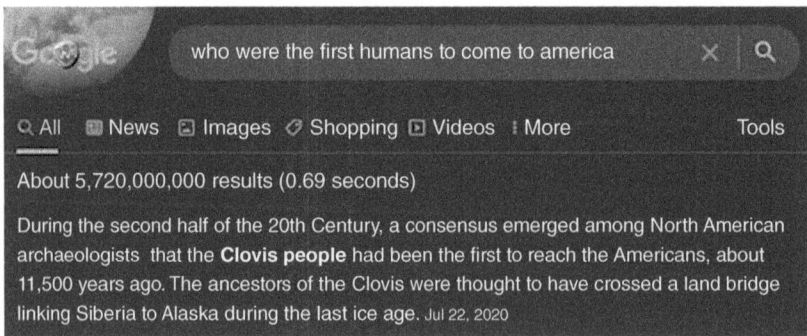

Figure 7.1 "Who were the first humans to come to America" returns a top result describing current scholarship on the arrival of Homo sapiens to North America.

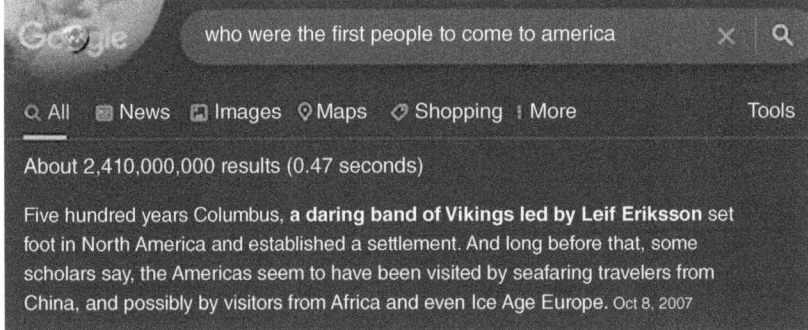

Figure 7.2 "Who were the first people to come to America" returns a top result describing current scholarship on the arrival of Europeans to North America.

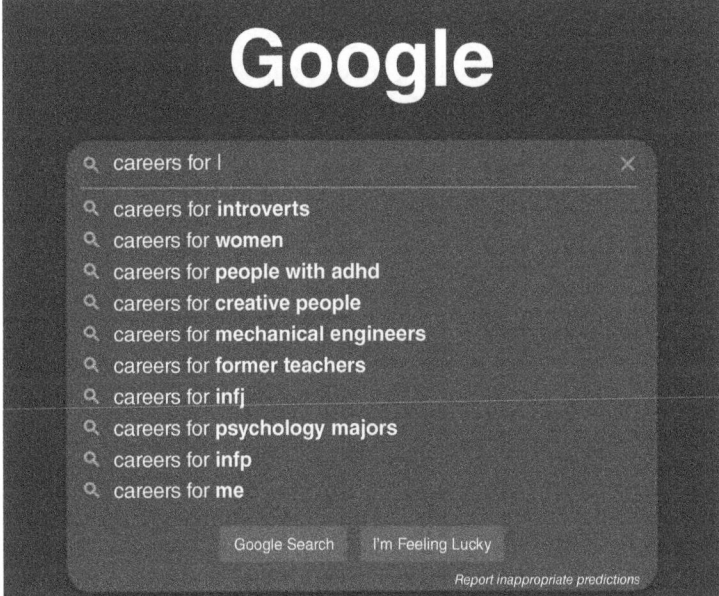

Figure 7.3 "Careers for" autocompletion in a Google search.

"people," Google directs us to scholarship about the arrival of European settlers to North America. These two words might be viewed by English speakers as roughly synonymous, such that swapping one for the other should not generate such a radical difference in answers. So why does the machine treat these questions as substantially different?

This strange behavior does not show up only in search results, but it also shows up when Google tries to guess the next word in our search as we type. Figure 7.3 shows the auto-complete suggestions for a search that begins with the words "careers for....".

The top three auto-completions were:

careers for...

- introverts
- women
- people with ADHD

Your results will almost certainly vary, but let's spend a moment thinking about why and how automatic completion in Google might produce these results.

First, it's important to know that there is no human providing these search results or suggested completions. They are based on patterns produced by a machine that keeps track of how lots of humans have been doing Google searches in the past. Crucially, these machines only track patterns – they have no direct access to language meaning. Google searches, and many computer technologies, are powered by a set of technologies called "**natural language processing**" or "**NLP**,"[1] and these technologies are developed, engineered, and refined by computer scientists, software engineers, and **computational linguists**. NLP is a very important strand in the development of "**artificial intelligence**" or "**AI**," but it's also used in an ever-growing set of technologies that we use every day at work, in school, and at home.

NLP technology is changing very rapidly. So rapidly, in fact, that almost anything we write in this chapter about the specifics of the technology might be obsolete by the time you read it. We can't predict how things will change, but we'll try to stick with topics and concepts here that are unlikely to change much. We'll have to see whether or not we are right about those!

Now let's get back to your Google searches and the auto-complete suggestions. Conceptually, you can understand how the auto-completes are created by thinking of Google as a giant, ever-growing database of stuff that people have typed into that search box, coupled with a kind of computer program that takes in all those examples and spits out new examples that "match" in some sense. This type of computer program is not written with sets of human-generated rules, though. Instead, it's a kind of program that lets the computer generate the rules it needs to make those matches, and to keep changing its internal rules as it gets more data in its database. This kind of program uses **machine learning** in order to "predict" what you're likely to want to type next.

---

[1] This should not be confused with NLP when it refers to "neurolinguistic programming," which has a scientific-sounding name but is in fact a discredited approach to "treating" a variety of mental, social, and physical ills.

Let's walk through a simplified example of how such a machine might work. Let's assume that the machine is working in English. First, the machine collects and saves all the things that have ever been typed into it. It's a machine, so it doesn't understand anything about the meaning or significance of what's been typed into it. It just keeps track of stuff like this: if I get an input of the character "c," it's statistically most likely that the next character will be either an "h," "l," "a," "i," "e," "o," or "u" – almost certainly not a space or a "q" or whatever. When it has gotten "caree" without any spaces, it can predict with pretty good certainty that the next character will be "r." The more stuff it gets, the better it can be about predicting the next thing.

The machine will also have access to information that tells it, "Hey, this is a language in which the things between spaces count as whole units, we'll call them 'words.' So when you produce your suggestions, put them in terms of strings of characters bounded by spaces." It may also have access to a directive that says something like, "Make your predictions have more than one thing that's a string of characters between spaces." This machine can also probably predict that when there's a space character, it can start producing suggested next sequences of words.

Once it's gotten the string "careers for," it's going to give options that it's seen before in this context – maybe seen before a lot. It's not going to give options that it's never seen before. This is why you probably won't get auto-complete suggestions like these on a stem "careers for":[2]

- kangaroos
- paint colors other than white
- a shallow grave on the dark side of the forest

Importantly, the reason we don't get these auto-complete suggestions is *not* because the suggestions are stupid or make no sense. It's only because the machine hasn't seen them often enough to predict that they will be likely to come next.

This means that we can use the auto-complete suggestions from the machine to tell us something about what other people are searching for, and what they're not searching for. If we go back to the top three auto-complete suggestions produced by Google for us on our test ("introverts," "women," and "people with ADHD"), we might notice that included among them are not very sensible possibilities like "extroverts," "men," or "neurotypical people."

---

[2] Honestly, we might be able to get the machine to generate these as auto-completes if we just type them into Google often enough. Students willing to join us in these efforts should please contact the authors.

Why not?

One reason is that we tend to search only for things that we can't readily find. If we see lots more searches on "careers for women" than "careers for men," that tells us that more people are having to work to find information about careers for women than are having to do the same thing for men. Linguists sometimes use the term "**markedness**" for this kind of phenomenon – the taken-for-granted things (e.g., that all careers are for extroverts or men or neurotypical people, unless designated otherwise) are "unmarked," and the special cases (like careers for women, careers for introverts, careers for people with ADHD) are "marked."

Machine learning systems can be "tuned" or "optimized" by human engineers, who make changes to the **algorithms** that the systems use to assess the goodness or badness of their predictions, but they can't actually be controlled by humans. Because they are set up to constantly change based on input and output pairings, there is no way for humans to know exactly how they will solve a particular problem or what their solution will be in future. Unlike rules-based programs (which are the kind you learn to build when you first learn to code), machine learning systems do not produce the same output every time, given the same input. In this sense, they are more analogous to biological creatures (though at the time of writing, the smartest machine-learning systems are about as smart as maybe an earthworm, and not nearly as smart as your average puppy or toddler) than to rules-based programs. They constantly grow and change.

There is one way in which machine learning systems are completely predictable, though – if there is a pattern in the data they've collected, ANY pattern, they will find it and amplify it. This is good news if the pattern in the data is something you want them to use, but it's terrible news if the pattern is something you'd just as soon they ignored – or worse, something that you need them to ignore because it's a pattern that is deeply racist, sexist, violent, or harmful. These kinds of patterns are, in fact, deeply embedded in the data that drive things like Google search, as has been well documented by Safiya Noble (2018), whose work has inspired many scholars interested in language and machines.

Even the most benign or irrelevant patterns in the data will fool the machine. For example, Heaven (2021) reported on implementations of machine learning in the domain of **image processing** of chest x-rays of people. The goal of this work was to see if these machines could identify patients with COVID-19 damage to their lungs based on the x-ray images. But what the machines ended up "learning" was that 1) different hospitals' x-rays are labeled with different fonts – so x-rays labeled with the fonts used by high-COVID-rate hospitals were judged by the machine as likely to show

COVID; and 2) that x-rays that were taken on patients who were lying down were probably COVID positive compared to those taken on patients who were standing up – because patients who are extremely sick (with anything) are much more likely to have a lying-down x-ray than those who are less sick. In these ways, the machines were tracking and reproducing biases in the data – biases that were not directly correlated with the patterns that humans hoped the machines would learn.

Data scientist Janelle Shane (2020) has made a small industry out of tricking machine learning systems in order to demonstrate the shortcomings of AI, including AI for language – NLP applications. In one brilliant exploration of the shortcomings of machine learning, she used a system called GPT-2 to create recipes based on 1) its giant database of material, including recipes, web pages, and (literally) billions of sentences in written English, and 2) a set of recipe titles for gelatin desserts from 1970s cookbooks. As an example of a recipe that this machine wrote, consider something called "Fair and Moose," which was created with the following list of ingredients:

- 3 cans (8 ½ oz) crabmeat, drained and cut in half quarters
- 1 ½ green beans, chopped
- 1 tablespoon grated onion
- 1 can (10 ¾ oz) condensed cheddar cheese soup
- ¼ cup cottage cheese
- ¼ cup brown sugar
- 2 tablespoons mustard

And this procedure:

1. Remove all internal rinds.
2. Prepare crabmeat according to package directions.
3. Transfer to a bowl of ice cold water and chill.
4. Remove all internal rinds.
5. Prepare cottage cheese according to the package directions.
6. Pour in crushed ice and dissolve in 1 ½ cups boiling water. Stir the cheese with the crushed ice for 4 to 5 minutes. Pour into a lightly sprayed 2-cup mold. Chill for 4 hours.
7. Unmold and fill with crab mixture. Serve with brown sugar and mustard. Garnish with cucumber. Chill.

Obviously, the machine does not know what it's talking about. But we can use this output to show quite clearly what Shane's AI *was* able to learn. First of all, it seems to have gotten a good sense of common ingredients in 1970s cookbooks – using jello packets in savory dishes, like those with seafood, was quite common. It also clearly learned the "form" of recipes: that they often have a title, a list of ingredients and quantities, and step-by-step instructions. It did *not* learn how to craft instructions that followed an intuitive or clear order, or even instructions that refer to all of the ingredients. So, we don't recommend you try AI-written recipes like these, but they are quite amusing to read.

We've used the acronym "GPT," and mentioned large language models (LLMs), and now might be a good time to unpack these terms and talk about how they're used together in the currently expanding world of language-based "AI." "GPT" stands for "**generalized, pretrained, transformer**" model, and GPTs are a special kind of large language model. A GPT is "generalized" in that it's put together not to solve any particular linguistic or engineering problem; it's meant to be able to be applied to any kind of task or problem that humans might want to use it for. A GPT is "pretrained" in that it has already learned a massive number of statistical patterns about the language information it has access to. And a "**transformer**" model uses a particular kind of statistical analysis (described for the first time in Vaswani et al. 2017) that's different from smaller, simpler, or more narrowly applicable systems used previously. Transformer systems can calculate statistics about a whole series of things at once and treat each series as though it were a basic or simple piece of information.

At the time of writing, most large-scale language technology systems we use are powered by machine learning using GPT models and aspiring to build "AI." But before we dive into some of these specific kinds of applications, how they work, and how a linguist in the community might use them to better understand language, let's explore a little bit about how we humans use language when we are communicating with each other via computers.

7.1 Studying Humans' Computer-Mediated Language Use

At the risk of sounding like the old people we are, we will begin with an example of a language pattern that showed up several years ago on various social media applications in the US, including Snapchat and Twitter,[3] after likely originating in texting. Spradlin (2016) wrote about this pattern, and her work was covered in the Washington Post (Guo 2016) using this tweet from a user whose handle was @bryanboy as an example:

---

[3] As of 2024, the social networking site we refer to in this book is officially named "X." Throughout this book, we'll continue to refer to the site as "Twitter," following many of the users of the platform and much of the popular discourse mentioning the platform.

(1)   "Bags ruin lewks!!! Y'all lewkin so fierce and ferosh in your new coat but that bag with its strap photobombing your lewks"

Example (1), like much of our computer-mediated talk, is produced in writing. The language is English, but the spelling and punctuation are different than you'd expect to see in formal writing. Spradlin showed that the innovative spellings are connected to innovative pronunciations, even for forms that wouldn't normally be spoken. In particular, her work focuses on the appearance of word forms like "ferosh" (< "ferocious"), where the innovation often includes two processes: shortening of the base word (which is always part of the pattern; linguists call systematic shortening of word forms "**truncation**"), and the addition of an "sh," "s," or other extra consonant sounds (which is sometimes part of the pattern) at the end of that base word. Other examples of this pattern, which Spradlin names "totes truncation," include those found in (2):

(2)   Totes truncations (Spradlin 2016, pp. 279–280)

"inf"	< "infamy"	(base word is shortened, no added material)
"profesh"	< "professional"	(base word is shortened, no added material)
"totes"	< "totally"	(base word is shortened, "s" is added)
"imposh"	< "impossible"	(base word is shortened, "sh" is added)
"jellies"	< "jealous"	(base word is shortened, "ies" is added)

Similar patterns certainly pre-date the emergence of these forms in texting and social media, with some (but not all) driven by language use over technology.[4] There's little doubt, however, that humans' use of text-based communication in venues like social media and texting is a significant and ongoing engine of change and innovation in English and other languages that are used in such venues.[5]

Not all of the changes involve written words, however. Text-based communication online increasingly includes the use of non-alphanumeric characters such as emoji, emoticons, and kaomoji. While we've seen many approaches to the ways in which people incorporate such characters into their online discourse, one prominent and fruitful approach might be to analyze these as something Gawne and McCulloch (2019) call "digital gestures."

---

[4] See, for example, forms of written English used in sending telegrams during the nineteenth and early twentieth centuries, when senders paid by the character. Shortenings such as "delish" < "delicious" and "nutrish" < "nutritious" are attested in British English "upper class slang" from the first years of the twentieth century in the works of authors such as PG Wodehouse.

[5] Which is surprisingly few. At the time of writing, English is the content language for approximately 63 percent of websites, with the next largest presence from Russian, at 6.9 percent (per W3Techs n.d. report as of January 24th, 2022).

Emoji are tools online interactants use to fulfill the kinds of functions face-to-face interactants fulfill by means of gestures. Their emergence can be illustrated in different genres of usage that Gawne and McCulloch describe. For example, **pantomime gestures** are those in which we use nonlinguistic movement to describe a situation or tell a story, often via some form of conventional rules (think of the game "charades" as a systematic use of pantomime gestures). Pantomime emoji are found in cases like (3a), which we've adapted from a tweet by Aaron Zamost (@zamosta) and which tells the story of the novel *Lord of the Flies*. **Emblems** are gestures that have specific word-level interpretations, as does the emoji in (3b), which stands for the word "peace." **Beat gestures** are those that emphasize the stream of speech rhythmically – you might, for example, repeatedly point at someone while yelling at them. The emoji in (3c) seem to function similarly for text-based communication. **Co-speech gestures** are less easy to clearly define, but include various idiosyncratic ways of using hand and body movements while engaged in speaking or signing. The emoji string in (3d) might qualify as a co-speech usage.

(3)   Emoji as gestures (from Gawne and McCulloch 2019)
    a.   pantomime:
        ✈🧒⭐️👦🏻👬👬🌊🍎🐷🔪🐚🐷🎖🐷😂😆🤣💬➖🌀🔥🐷👦🏻1🔥🕯🐻🗡😭😭😭
    b.   emblem: ✌️
    c.   beat gestures: don't 👋 count 👋 us 👋 out 👋!
    d.   co-speech gestures: I love that story! 💕😻🤗🤟🎬

Using language in technology also differs from other contexts of use in that it naturally creates large (sometimes very large) records of language behavior that can and often are used by scholars as well as corporations as corpora with which to investigate language usage. The social media platform Twitter provides ways by which investigators can create and use large-scale corpora to study things like how people's online language use might help provide insights into their health and diet (Fried et al. 2014; Herongrove et al. 2018), their politics (Starbird et al. 2018), how they spread or stop dis- and misinformation online (Starbird et al. 2014), and how they construct and maintain public personae that create alignments and disalignments with various constituencies of interlocutors (Valentinsson 2018).

These records of language behavior are created in a variety of ways by interactions with computers. If you've used an online translation machine such as Google Translate, you'll see that users are invited to "correct" translations or provide additional possible translations in the application. You'll also see that as you continue to use it, the application will change its behavior slightly – based on the kinds of things you've asked it to do. Behind the scenes, all of these translation tasks that you set for these systems can be and often are transmitted back into the companies that run them to be used as "training data" for this and other kinds of machines. And if one company is providing lots of different kinds of applications, you can bet that they are collecting your language data and using it whenever and wherever it might help them to update or improve all of their applications. At the time of writing, for example, Google Translate uses data collected on Android phones when you use Google's speech-to-text features (automatic captioning) in any of its apps. You gave them permission to do this when you signed their terms of service, which also specify whether your data are "de-anonymized" in the process.

Digital assistants such as Apple's Siri, Amazon's Alexa, and Microsoft's Cortana serve as conversational partners for lots of people around the world today. These machines take in acoustic data, transform it into text (this is called "**speech-to-text**," often abbreviated STT), feed the text into a number of different "**language models**" (in order to try to determine the meaning of your utterance), and then feed those results into systems that allow the application to take certain kinds of actions. The applications then produce text responses, which are fed to **text-to-speech** (TTS) models in the target language, so that they can synthesize a voice and respond in a way that sounds almost human. If you use a digital assistant, you'll be familiar with both the ways in which it successfully mimics a human conversational partner and the ways in which it fails. You might not have considered, though, whether it fails in similar ways or at similar rates for speakers of all linguistic varieties (it doesn't), and why virtually all digital assistant applications are launched with voices and names that (at least in North America and Britain) are clearly gendered female and sound white. In 2019, the United Nations Educational, Scientific and Cultural Organization noticed this fact and took issue with it in a report titled "I'd Blush If I Could: Closing Gender Divides in Digital Skills Through Education" (UNESCO 2019). A linguist in the community can find a variety of really interesting and important questions to investigate in the interactions we have with virtual assistants (where by "we" we mean any of us who use them, including, increasingly, young children). Your interactions with virtual assistants are, like your interactions with other language tech applications, almost always captured and provided back to (at least) the company that develops the app, and once they leave your mouth there's no telling where in the world of machines they'll end up.

There is a great deal of scholarship being done about the ways in which we humans are incorporating technology in our interactions with each other. Excellent work exploring the ways in which online interactions are used to manage group moral and ethical norms (Garcés-Conejos Blitvich 2022), invite and hear, or exclude and silence, core and peripheral members of communities (Safadi et al. 2020), and construct and manage individuals' identities (Zhang & Zhao 2020) is helping us to better understand the potential effects of technology on our patterns of interaction. The set of tools we use to communicate with each other online is constantly changing – and changing extremely quickly. Companies that create and maintain web-based applications generally see "long term" planning as anything that might happen more than five years from now, and the typical lifespan of a phone app is less than one year. In addition to this, the rate at which new and existing platforms rise and fall in patterns of usage, and the way they are often limited to small or very small demographics of users, makes the study of how humans use language online particularly exciting and also frustrating.

But we actually think that the things you're learning from the other chapters of this book are equally applicable to the study of how humans talk to machines. So rather than focusing our efforts here on applying those terms and methods to computer-mediated human language behavior, we have chosen to look at the computer itself – or at least to the ways in which computers manipulate and manage language as we interact with them.

Brave reader, let's talk about tech.

7.2 Studying Language Technology

We started this chapter with a Google search and used the predictive text to help illustrate something about how the search engine works. A linguist in the community can certainly use language technology to study language technology and better understand where that technology plays a part in our experiences talking with each other online.

Natural language processing (NLP) is an interdisciplinary field involving computer scientists, software engineers, linguists, data scientists, and other social scientists working to provide technologies that can correctly handle human language inputs and create appropriate human language outputs. NLP is behind a huge inventory of technologies we use daily – not only in search engines such as Google search, as described in the introduction to this chapter, but also in predictive text generation, content moderation on social media platforms, digital assistants, automatic captioning (speech-to-text), and voice synthesis (text-to-speech). The specific tools and approaches found in NLP are rapidly changing, but the challenges are long-standing and are still very far from solved. Here we'll first present a very high-level overview of how NLP systems work and why NLP is so different from human language, and then we'll discuss a couple of specific case studies in NLP. We hope that the material in this section of the chapter is of use to a linguist in the community who'd like to understand interactions between NLP and humans, but also to any readers who are interested in contributing to the development of new and better NLP systems.

7.2.1 How Do NLP Systems Work?

While the particular systems are always changing, the following structures are found today – and we think might have to be used in the foreseeable future – in NLP processes. First, NLP systems have to be able to convert human-generated inputs (text/image, audio, or video) into a form and structure that can be understood by the computer. Then, the computer needs to be able to find patterns and make calculations about that input. Finally, those patterns and calculations need to be translated back into some form of human language (text/image, audio, or video) that can be understood and perhaps used by humans.

The first step – converting inputs into something the machine can manipulate – is a complex undertaking in itself. If we take the example of text inputs, like this paragraph, the human who enters the text sees it appear on a screen as they type – using some kind of text input device (like the QWERTY keyboard mapped to a US-English character set that we're using to type with now). Under the covers, the computer has to be able to map each character – the letters, the punctuation marks, the spaces, and the line returns – to some form of **machine language**. And machine language is not like human language: it, at a very fundamental level, is a binary system of electrical pulses which can be thought of as either a 1 (electrical charge) or a 0 (no electrical charge). This mapping system needs to know all of the possible characters, and how to relate each character to some sequence of 0s and 1s.

You might be surprised to learn that this very basic process was not available widely in computation until the 1960s, and that its first and still most influential implementation – called the **American Standard Code for Information Exchange (ASCII)** – was created in the US by Bell Data Systems and others, standardized from telegraph code, and consisted of 128 possible characters (7-bit chunks of binary). The US ASCII chart in Figure 7.4 shows the system that was standardized by 1971. Note that the available characters include: the letters of the Latin alphabet in upper and lower case; the Arabic numerals 0 through 9; various kinds of brackets and arithmetic operators; punctuation marks like the question mark, comma, and period; a space; and "control characters" such as "ESC" (escape) and "DEL" (delete). Note that this character set does not include any of the characters necessary to write in major world languages such as Chinese or Arabic, and it also does not

194   7 Linguists Meet Computers

USASCII code chart

b7 b6 b5 →					0 0 0	0 0 1	0 1 0	0 1 1	1 0 0	1 0 1	1 1 0	1 1 1
B_{i16} b4	b3	b2	b1	Column / Row ↓	0	1	2	3	4	5	6	7
0	0	0	0	0	NUL	DLE	SP	0	@	P	`	p
0	0	0	1	1	SOH	DC1	!	1	A	Q	a	q
0	0	1	0	2	STX	DC2	"	2	B	R	b	r
0	0	1	1	3	ETX	DC3	#	3	C	S	c	s
0	1	0	0	4	EOT	DC4	$	4	D	T	d	t
0	1	0	1	5	ENQ	NAK	%	5	E	U	e	u
0	1	1	0	6	ACK	SYN	8	6	F	V	f	v
0	1	1	1	7	BEL	ETB	'	7	G	W	g	w
1	0	0	0	8	BS	CAN	(	8	H	X	h	x
1	0	0	1	9	HT	EM	)	9	I	Y	i	y
1	0	1	0	10	LF	SUB	*	:	J	Z	j	z
1	0	1	1	11	VT	ESC	+	;	K	[	k	{
1	1	0	0	12	FF	FS	,	<	L	\	l		
1	1	0	1	13	CR	GS	-	=	M	]	m	}
1	1	1	0	14	SO	RS	.	>	N	^	n	~
1	1	1	1	15	SI	US	/	?	O	_	o	DEL

Figure 7.4 USASCII chart by an unknown officer or employee of the United States Government. Public Domain, https://commons.wikimedia.org/w/index.php?curid=63485656

include "combining diacritics" such as accent marks needed to write in Spanish or French. The first ASCII standard was introduced in 1963, and until 2007 it was still the most common character encoding used on the internet (Dubost 2008).

As of 2022, standards for character encoding allow a much larger range of mappings than just the ASCII set – with a new standard often referred to as **unicode**. The rise of the Unicode Consortium (https://home.unicode.org/) has expanded the text and control characters available to computers to a much larger character set – including emoji and other non-alphanumeric characters. But although machines can support larger character sets, many systems are still built on and with ASCII as the primary and most convenient mapping. If you use any language other than English on a computer, you'll be familiar with lingering issues around support of orthographies (writing systems) that use characters other than those in the ASCII set. They can be difficult to input, and they can break when used across different systems and platforms. For example, your authors can attest that at a large southwestern university in the US, one that is a Hispanic Serving Institution[6] at the time of writing, anyone whose name contains the character "ñ" must choose

---

[6] In the United States, the title "Hispanic Serving Institution" is bestowed by the federal Department of Education on colleges and universities whose student population is made up

either to replace it with a plain "n" or see it replaced for them in our enterprise email systems with a "?". Think about all the other ways in which people's writing systems differ from each other – Arabic's right to left order, the fact that in written Chinese there need be no spaces to separate words – and you'll start to understand many of the ways in which going from simple text input to machine processing is challenging for most language communities around the world.

To some extent, character encoding and text input is really a subset of image processing for machines. Anything that a human sees on a computer screen is mapped to pixels by the computer, and the computer has to know what each of those pixels should be doing and how they are related to the systems that computers actually use for calculations. When machines accept input from audio or video materials, they have to do signal processing on those materials in order to characterize them as mathematical matrices.

ASCII encoding and the primacy of English orthographic implementations in machines has an outsized impact on language technologies. But let's move to the next step in NLP – in which the machine processes the input data, perhaps with the help of humans.

7.2.2 Tokenization, Annotation, Labeling, Lemmatization, and Named-Entity Recognition

When a machine is given text to process, it needs to identify characters, and it needs to find out what bundles of characters count as meaningful units such as morphemes and words. In some writing systems, such as those used for English, a machine might use spaces as "delimiters" of character strings to use as words; but in other systems different strategies will be needed. Even in English, spaces-as-delimiters don't really work, because "words" are more complicated than that. This processing step, called "**tokenization**," is illustrated in this brilliant case study from the Digital Tolkien Project (Tauber et al. 2022, currently housed at https://digitaltolkien.com/).

The question the project authors ask sounds simple – how many words are there in Tolkien's novel *The Hobbit*? The answer is not at all straightforward. This apparently simple question is actually a combination of two related ones: how many tokens are there (that is, how many words if you count each word once for every time it appears) and how many types are there (that is, how many unique words did Tolkien use)? We'll return to this distinction as we discuss ways in which language technology computes indices of

---

of 25 percent or more of individuals from Hispanic/Latinx backgrounds. You can find more information by doing an internet search for "White House Initiative on Advancing Education Equity, Excellence, and Economic Opportunities for Hispanics."

"complexity" or even "reading level" over spans of text. Next, the linguist needs to determine how to count things that might be one word or might be two – contractions (which in spelled English usually have a medial apostrophe, like "don't" and "must've"), compounds (especially those that in spelled English are typically written with spaces in between, like "hot dog" and "White House"), and idioms (which are multi-word units that act for all intents and purposes as single meaningful elements, like "pay up,"[7] meaning to pay an amount in full, and "take the cake," meaning something like "win"). Finally, the linguist needs to determine how to handle various kinds of punctuation – in spelled English, it's not just things like apostrophes, but also em-dashes and hyphens, for example, that could be used to either separate or combine elements into "words."

Depending on the decisions made, Tauber (2021) reports the following possible token counts for *The Hobbit*: 95,137, 95,390, or 95,643. None of these is the "correct" count, because we don't necessarily have right or wrong answers to the questions asked above. And this is an example of the easiest form of tokenization used in NLP applications at the time of writing: it's tokenizing clean text documents that use almost entirely spelled English[8] (which, remember, uses all and only ASCII characters) and that are in a single work by a single individual.

For some systems (such as email spam filters), the bundles of information – which for ease of reference we'll call "words," even though they may or may not correspond with units that a human would identify as words – can then simply be counted so that the machine can keep track of the number of times a given word appears in a given text. This number is called a word's frequency. For some applications, just being able to count the word frequencies gives the machine enough information to do the thing that the application is designed to do. For example, in the 1990s in the US, email spam filters needed to know if the subject line of an email contained the word "Viagra." If it contained that word, and if it contained that word multiple times, it was very likely to be spam.

By counting the frequencies of each word in a text and the total number of words in a text, the machine can also calculate a "**type/token ratio.**" Type/token ratios give a mathematical expression of how internally diverse a text is, and this number can be used to (imperfectly, but in some cases reasonably)

---

[7] OK, this is a verb-particle construction which we could think of as idiomatic, but could also analyze as some sort of phrasal constituent. Whatever we call it, the "up" in "pay up" doesn't actually mean "up," and "pay up" is pragmatically distinct from "pay."

[8] Tolkien's invented languages cannot be said to use spelled English, but in *The Hobbit* they apparently only recruit one non-ASCII character, ä.

calculate reading difficulty, complexity of writing, and the like. Let's work through an example of a type/token ratio calculation, comparing two very short texts. One comes from a first grade reader (Peterson 1996, pp. 2–3), the other from a scholarly book (Chomsky 1957, p. 3).

(4) "It is very, very big, but it is not a dinosaur. It has no legs, but it is not a snake. It lives in water, but it is not a fish."

(5) "This study will touch on a variety of topics in syntactic theory and English syntax, a few in some detail, several quite superficially, and none exhaustively."

Example (4) contains thirty-one words (tokenized by spaces, with punctuation ignored). Example (5) contains twenty-six words. A machine might store these texts as in (6–7), where curly braces say "this is an unordered set" and each element in the set includes a specific word (a "type") and the number of times that word appears in the passage (the number of "tokens").

(6) {it: 6, is: 4, very: 2, big: 1, but: 3, not: 3, a: 3, dinosaur: 1, has: 1, no: 1, legs: 1, but: 2, snake: 1, lives: 1, in: 1, water: 1, fish: 1} = 17 types

(7) {this: 1, study: 1, will: 1, touch: 1, on: 1, a: 2, variety: 1, of: 1, topics: 1, in: 2, syntactic: 1, theory: 1, and: 2, English: 1, syntax: 1, few: 1, some: 1, detail: 1, several: 1, quite: 1, superficially: 1, none: 1, exhaustively, 1} = 23 types.

The type/token ratio for passage (4) is therefore 17/31, or (about) .55, and for passage (5) it is 23/26, or about .88. A higher type/token ratio means that the passage is more internally diverse, and this typically[9] correlates with more complex writing and higher reading levels. Calculating type/token ratios for even quite long passages of text is something that's quite easy for a machine to do, and it does not require that the machine knows anything about the words in question, where they come from, or what they mean.

The sets of words in (4) can also be called "**unigrams**," and language models that use them are sometimes referred to "**bag of words**" models. Bag of words models can help us identify some important things about what texts might mean. But of course we know that words are not used in isolation, and some of the meaningful aspects of language are created by combining words into larger structures like phrases and sentences. Humans encode and interpret meaning in these larger units by (among other things) relying on hierarchical relationships among the words. Consider Example (8), and don't stop considering it until you have found at least two possible meanings – one probably intended, the other probably not.

---

[9] But of course not always. And in real life, computers use more complicated math than simple type/token ratios in order to account for the distributions of function vs. content words, and other factors that can skew the numbers in unhelpful ways. This simplified example is to give you the idea of how it works, not all the specifics.

(8)   There is a parasite that only occurs in cats called Toxoplasma gondii.

As a human, you might have immediately understood the sentence using the bracketed structure in (9). We use square brackets to group parts of the sentence together to illustrate a specific meaning. This is intended to show that you understand that the unit "there is a parasite that only occurs in cats" acts as one part of the sentence, and that the unit "called Toxoplasma gondii" is a modifier, telling you the name of the parasite.

(9)   [there is a parasite that only occurs in cats] [called Toxoplasma gondii]

But the sentence could also mean that there is a parasite that only occurs in cats who are named "Toxoplasma gondii." This is represented by the bracketed structure in (10).

(10)   [there is a parasite] [that only occurs in cats called Toxoplasma gondii]

As a human, you'll understand that this would be a very weird scenario indeed – parasites probably have no way of knowing the name of your cat. But the structure in (10) has some interesting properties. First, it's completely possible in English, and second, it's the only structure that a reasonable human could use to interpret a sentence like (11). Example (12) illustrates why grouping the sentence in the same way as (9) doesn't work.

(11)   [there is a parasite] [that only occurs in cats with compromised immune systems]

(12)   *[there is a parasite that only occurs in cats] [with compromised immune systems]

A pretty good explanation for the patterns in (9) and (10) in terms of humans is that when we understand language, we apply both our knowledge of the world and our knowledge of the possible organizations of meaning in language. In terms of that second thing, we know that meaning is organized in language in a way that's sensitive to groupings of words, not just their order.

But machines don't have their own "knowledge of the world," and for them, considering different groupings of words is expensive. So, how do machines try to understand sentences like these?

One simple approach is for them to take that unigram model and expand it a little bit. Instead of only identifying one word at a time and keeping track of how many times they see that word, some language technology systems take in two or more words at a time. This helps them keep track of at least some of the linguistic contexts of words. A common implementation is to use bigrams rather than unigrams; the example in (13) is what sentence (8) would look like in a **bigram model**, while (14) shows what it would be in a trigram model.

(13) {there is: 1, is a: 1, a parasite: 1, parasite that: 1, that only: 1, only occurs: 1, occurs in: 1, in cats: 1, cats called: 1, called Toxoplasma: 1, Toxoplasma gondii: 1}

(14) {there is a: 1, is a parasite: 1, a parasite that: 1, parasite that only: 1, that only occurs: 1, only occurs in: 1, occurs in cats: 1, in cats called: 1, cats called Toxoplasma: 1, called Toxoplasma gondii}

Unigram, bigram, and trigram models are examples of "bags of words" approaches that can collectively be referred to as "**ngram models**" – where the "n" can be any number we wish. You can see that increasing the "n" in your "ngram" model is a way of making the computer aware of larger language chunks, which might be useful in helping it process language in a way that's a little more human-like. But there are some problems with ngramming sentences. First, these systems will always produce interpretations where words right next to each other are modifying each other. This will always produce the wrong result for the intended meaning of Example (8). Second, as the n increases, the number of elements the machine has to store increases – and this kind of system becomes really expensive really quickly. We think that at the time of writing, you'd be unlikely to find anyone using anything bigger than a trigram model for a "bag of words" application.

So we need to move on to more complex ways for computers to store and process language if we want them to be able to do more complicated things than just filtering out spam messages or telling us how much more often writers of English have tended to put male pronouns in the "subject" position and female pronouns in the "object" position (but see Figure 7.5 for a quick view of these patterns using Google's Ngram Viewer, a very handy implementation of a bag of words model in language technology).

These more complex systems in natural language processing do more than just counting and keeping track of word or character lists. Instead, they look

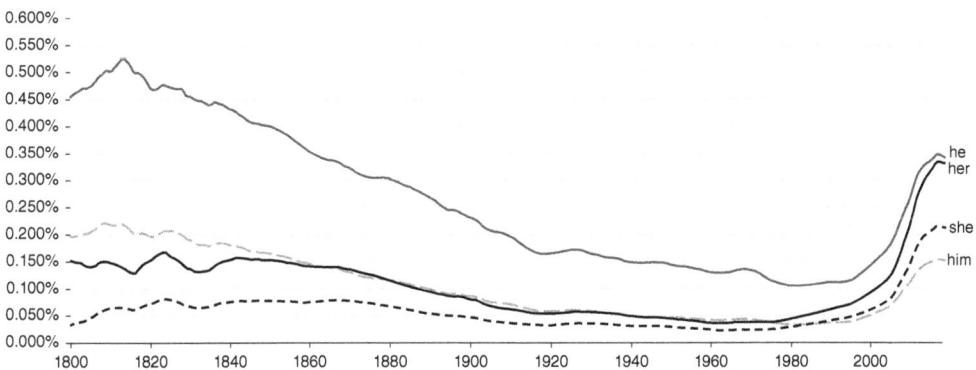

Figure 7.5 A visualization of how often male and female pronouns appear in object and subject positions; retrieved from https://books.google.com/ngrams/, August 30, 2024.

for statistical regularities among elements of various lengths, often using a computational system called a **neural net**. A neural net is a computer program that consists of "nodes" and "connections" and that is modeled on at least some people's idea of how human brains work. Each "node" is really just a mathematical formula. Each "connection" is really just an instruction that tells the output of one node whether or not it should go on to be processed by another node.

For example, let's imagine we want to have a machine learn some fact about a language, like that if you have a "p" at the beginning of an English word, it's more likely that the next letter will be an "r" than it is that the next letter will be a "c." You can give the system an example "pr" and tell it to calculate a "1" when it sees that pair, and an example "pc" and tell it to calculate a "0" when it sees that pair. Then you can teach another node that "pra" is more likely to happen than "prs." When an input hits the first node, if it gets a "1," instruct the machine to send that output to this second node. But if the first node gets a "0," instruct the machine to throw that input away and not pass it on any further. Repeat the process until some node has the instruction *not* to keep passing stuff to other nodes, and it spits out a result.

Now, imagine a system with a very large number of nodes – lots of nodes that get to calculate an answer based on some input (an input layer), lots of nodes that only get to calculate an answer based on something that was already kicked up to them out of the input layer (a hidden layer), and lots of nodes that get to spit out final results (an output layer). And imagine that the calculation each node gets to do is a statistical calculation called a "linear regression." Finally, imagine that the threshold for passing a result from one node to another can be changed, automatically, by the machine as it's figuring out the patterns it's looking at. What you've just imagined is, in fact, a neural net.

Machine learning and neural nets are often used to do lots of different kinds of processing of language data. Three important tasks they accomplish are **labeling, lemmatization,** and **named-entity recognition.**

Labeling means that the machine figures out the part of speech of each word that it identifies. Lemmatization means that the machine figures out what the "core" or "root" words are (the "lemmas" – these are like the headwords in a dictionary entry) and separates that information from strictly grammatical information like the tense of a verb, whether a noun is singular or plural, and so on. "Named-entity recognition" means that the machine has to figure out which words are actually proper nouns, or at least proper noun-like, and then identify what kind of thing they're naming – a person, a place, a corporation, and such.

Part-of-Speech:

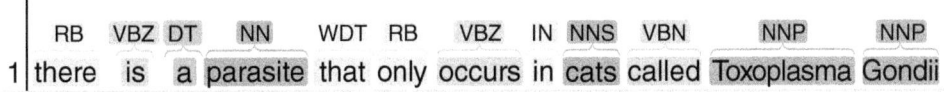

Figure 7.6 Part of speech labeling; retrieved from https://corenlp.run, March 4, 2022.

Lemmas:

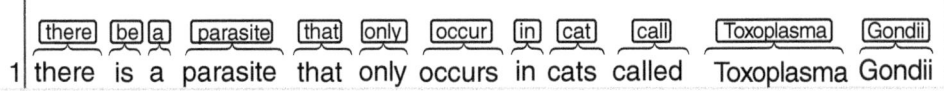

Figure 7.7 Lemmatization; retrieved from https://corenlp.run, March 4, 2022.

Let's look at how our sentence (8) fares in a state-of-the-art language processing machine that is developed out of Stanford University's computational linguistics group: https://corenlp.run (Chen & Manning 2014[10]).

First, the labeling step, with results shown in Figure 7.6. This parser has a set of abbreviations for parts of speech that might be unfamiliar, but you can probably figure out what some of them mean. For example, "VBZ" and "VBN" are labels for different types of verbs, and "NN," "NNS," and "NNP" are labels for different kinds of nouns. "DT" means "determiner," a word class that includes articles.

Next, is lemmatization, shown in Figure 7.7. Here we can see that the machine knows that "is" is actually a form of the base verb "be," "occurs" is a form of the base verb "occur," "called" is a form of the base verb "call," and "cats" is a form of the base noun "cat."

Finally, Figure 7.8 shows that named-entity recognition notices that we've capitalized "Toxoplasma Gondii,"[11] so the machine labels that as some kind of proper noun – in this case, it incorrectly labeled this as the name of an organization.

Once a machine has access to these initial pieces of information, it can also construct a "dependency parse," which is the machine's way of figuring out which elements modify which other elements. Figure 7.9 shows the dependency parse for our sentence.

---

[10] Between the time of writing and the time of publication of this chapter, https://corenlp.run has been superseded by https://stanza.run (Qi et al. 2018).
[11] When we didn't capitalize these words, the system did not recognize them as a proper name at all.

Named-Entity Recognition:

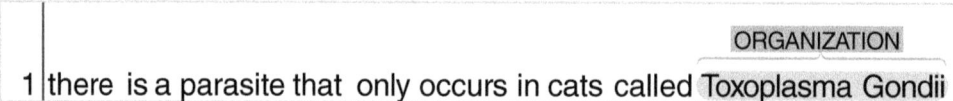

Figure 7.8 Named-entity recognition; retrieved from https://corenlp.run, March 4, 2022.

Basic Dependencies:

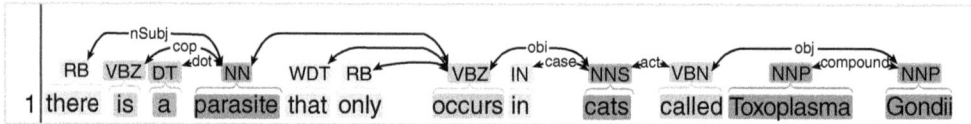

Figure 7.9 Dependency parse; retrieved from https://corenlp.run, March 4, 2022.

Figure 7.9 is a little complicated, but you don't need to understand all of it. We hope you can see that the system has divided this sentence at the verb "occurs," and that the chunk "called Toxoplasma Gondii" is attached to the element "cats." This shows that the CoreNLP system interprets the sentence incorrectly, as a sentence about cats who are called Toxoplasma gondii, rather than as a sentence about parasites who are called that.

Current implementations of NLP seldom produce multiple parses – even though humans do this all the time. This is one of the ways in which machine processing of human language is distinctly unhumanlike – at least for now.

At the time of writing, CoreNLP (version 4.4.0) had data and models for Arabic, Chinese, English, French, German, Hungarian, Italian, and Spanish. This is another way that machine processing of human language is deficient – humans are able to learn and work with any natural language, with or without written materials. In the world of language technology, languages other than English are often totally ignored, and languages that do not have a practical writing system (which is still the majority of languages, including all signed languages) are excluded by design. At least until more language models are added to these projects, the things they can tell us about language (in general) or languages (in particular) will be limited to the specific contexts in which these NLP systems are used.

7.2.3 How Machines Do "Meaning": Vector Semantics and Word Embeddings

So far, we've talked about how computers in natural language processing analyze linguistic form, and we've asserted that in most implementations of NLP today machines only operate over form – not meaning – of language. There are a few exceptions to that rule, and some systems you encounter may be using "**vector semantics**" in order to better model elements of meaning in language.

7.2 Studying Language Technology

Vector semantics is derived from the hypothesis that one can understand what words mean by understanding their distribution – that is, what words and phrases they appear next to – in language use. Machines can characterize word distributions mathematically and store those numbers, so they can also sort linguistic elements into sets based on similarities in their environments.

For a student new to this idea, it might be that the best way to understand how it works is by playing a game. Semantle (https://semantle.novalis.org/) is an English-language online word guessing game created by David Turner that uses vector semantics to provide feedback to a human about their guesses. Each day, a new game appears – with a single input box called "guess." A player types in a word, clicks "guess," and gets back a result that looks something like this:[12]

1
happy
5.43
(cold)
1

The "1" means that this is the player's first guess. The "happy" is the word that the player guessed. The "5.43" is the similarity score, calculated using a popular vector semantics implementation for English "word2vec."[13] A low number indicates that the word the player guessed is not very similar to the secret word; negative numbers indicate that the guess is very far from the target. "(cold)" means that you were nowhere near close to the secret word.

When the guess is within the 1,000 nearest synonyms to the target word, the game gives the player more contentful feedback – in this case, the word "give," the player's 85th guess, was the 993rd closest word to the target. Only six words were closer.

85
give
47.31
993/1000

---

[12] Examples taken from Semantle game 85, from April 21, 2022.
[13] The word2vec library was created by Tomas Mikolav and others at the Czech Institute of Informatics, Robotics and Cybernetics. Word2vec data in Semantle is taken from Google.

The player wins a game of semantle when they pick the secret word – that word will have a similarity index of 100.

One of the FAQs in the game's home page asks, "Why is the similarity so different from what I was expecting?," and this gets at the ways in which vector semantic systems still don't match human judgments about word meanings. If you play a game or two of semantle, and stick with it long enough to win, you'll likely be very surprised about which words count as near synonyms and which words don't. Vector semantics treats words as synonyms if they appear in the same context as each other – and as Turner notes in his answer to this FAQ:[14]

> By "similarity," we really mean "used in similar contexts." The principle was articulated by John Rupert Firth, who wrote, "You shall know a word by the company it keeps." So, "love" and "hate" may seem like opposites, but they will often score similarly. The actual opposite of "love" is probably something like "Arizona Diamondbacks," or "carburetor."

This tells us that even when machines are programmed to try and "understand" meaning in language, they're definitely understanding things differently than humans do. It may be the case that linguistic meaning cannot, in principle, be reduced to the kinds of mathematical expressions and algorithms that computers (currently) are bound by. Or it may just be that the machines and their programmers haven't yet figured out exactly the right calculations. Only time will tell. Until then, be sure to critically assess any claims you hear or read about NLP systems and other kinds of machine learning. If they claim to represent something fundamental about how language, in general, works, but are only trained on Indo-European languages, it probably doesn't understand as much as the creators think it does. Similarly, make sure you have a clear understanding of how the creators of a piece of technology are using linguistic terminology – even seemingly basic concepts like "similar" and "different" can be operationalized in very different ways, leading to very different assumptions about language use in a social context.

7.2.4 Types of Language Technology

In this chapter, we've referred to a variety of different kinds of language technology. Let's collect them here, and then add to the list as needed. We'll also be able to cluster these technologies into groups based on how much "language" they really need to "know."

7.2.4.1 Group 1: Optical Character Recognition Systems, Image Processing

Group 1 applications are those that allow a computational system to convert visual components of language (letters or characters in print resources) into

---

[14] https://semantle.novalis.org/, accessed April 22, 2022.

the kind of text encoding that a computer can process (ASCII, unicode). These systems need access to electronic images (which they process as pixels) from image or video materials, and an algorithm for converting arrangements of pixels into the letters or characters in the target orthography and encoding. Typically, the latter means that the machine has to have access to the set of "characters," or the symbols that have a value in that system, and to rules about how characters can and cannot be combined. One very early implementation of **optical character recognition** in the US was a system that was trained to recognize the five-digit zip codes on hand-addressed envelopes. The system had to learn to recognize each of the numerals reliably, regardless of the handwriting style of the person who wrote out the address. This application was highly successful, in part because of the very small set of characters (any one of the ten Arabic numerals 0 through 9) and the limited number of them (exactly 5).

Optical character recognition today is mostly advanced by scholars and engineers in mathematics and engineering, with some limited assistance from linguists. It is primarily an image processing problem, rather than a linguistic one.

That doesn't mean that a linguist in the community shouldn't care about or be interested in optical character recognition, though. At one of your authors' universities, a new application was licensed recently that would allow instructors to grade students' handwritten assignments by passing them from hard copy to pdf format, and then through a system that tries to find everything they've written and understand it in a structured way (for example, figuring out what material is paragraphs of text and what material is equations or other figures). There are significant linguistic challenges in doing so, and while there's not evidence that linguists have provided advice and expertise to the development of this product yet, we suspect they'll need to as the system begins to be used more broadly.

7.2.4.2 Group 2: Spam Filters, Spell-Checkers, Search Engines

Group 2 applications are those that need to know a little bit more about linguistic units like words and morphemes but don't necessarily need to be very aware of the meanings or pragmatics of larger units of language. Spam filters, for example, really only need to be able to identify frequent patterns of characters or larger units that are commonly associated with bad or fraudulent emails. They need to be "trained" by having constantly updated access to corpora or databases of these kinds of patterns, but they don't need to know the difference between, for example, "Viagra" and "you've won a prize,"[15] nor

---

[15] As the popularity of email grew, so too did the popularity of spam email – that is, unsolicited and usually unwanted messages sent to a mass list of users. Such emails often promote dubious financial deals or offers, so early email users often found words and

do they have to connect those terms to language-external domains (medicine, social groups). Spell-checkers need to know about frequent/allowable and infrequent/disallowable character combinations within words, but not about what the words mean or what part of speech they are (grammar checkers are more complicated and also less accurate than spell-checkers, at least for English). Massive, commercial search engines like Google are much more complicated than either of the previous two applications – and probably don't belong in this group at all, because a good search engine will be able to collect more data about context of use of search expressions in order to improve its results. But the basics of the kinds of search you use within a webpage or inside a document like this one is a relatively simple implementation of string matching algorithms, often allowing some wildcarding (*walk** can find any of "walk," "walks," "walking," or "walk") or boolean operators (like "and," "not," and "or"). Again, this doesn't require much knowledge of language in terms of meaning or pragmatics of use.

7.2.4.3 Group 3: Sentiment Analyzers, Content Moderators, Machine-Reading Systems, Automatic Captioning (Speech-to-Text), Voice Synthesis (Text-to-Speech)

Group 3 applications involve machines that *do* need to work with something akin to linguistic meaning, or at least be able to infer meaning. Sentiment analyzers are machines that take in text and determine what kind of emotive or subjective meanings are being expressed in that text. For example, a company may want to know whether their product's online reviews are mostly positive or mostly negative; sentiment analysis can provide a mechanized way to assess that. Most sentiment analyzers at the time of writing are based on libraries of words in the target language with their emotive associations (i.e., reviews using words like "bad," "upset," and "poor" are likely to be negative reviews, while words like "love," "excited," and "great" are likely to be found in positive reviews). Content moderation – in which machines help humans to identify language that's contrary to terms of service, hate speech, or other forms of community standard violation – is approached in a similar manner, at least currently. Again, the applications focus on lists of words or word-like elements in a target language that are likely to be associated with the relevant forms of speech. These forms of content moderation are far from perfect, but they are widely used and do not take into account meaning in units much larger than individual words.

---

phrases like this throughout their inbox. As a result, phrases that indicated these sorts of things became useful patterns for spam filters to recognize.

Speech-to-text and text-to-speech also rely on language models that need to know more than just what the possible units are – they need to be able to map acoustics to possible utterances in a context, so they rely on language models that sometimes include units larger than a word. They do not necessarily attempt to "understand" or "produce" their own meaningful utterances for humans to respond to. For this level of language tech, we move on to Group 4.

7.2.4.4 Group 4: Predictive Text Generators, Chatbots, Digital Assistants, Machine Translators

Group 4 applications are the ones that, if they work well, require the machine to understand language at the level of the sentence, utterance, or even conversation. In predictive text applications, chatbots, and digital assistants, the goal of the application is to understand our intended meanings so well that the application can engage in conversation with us, predict what we're most likely to want to say, and answer our questions (note that large-scale, corporate search engines like Google search try to do all of these things). Machine translation systems like Google Translate typically work with linguistic units at all levels, and the most relevant unit for quality translation in connected texts is no smaller than the sentence.

And it's Group 4 technologies that are most frequently subjects of "AI Hype," or the production and sharing of broad claims that technology has reached such a pinnacle that it has, in some sense, "learned" language. Such claims sometimes refer to a particular technology performing well in some version of a "**Turing Test**." The Turing Test, named after British mathematician Alan Turing who first proposed as a thought experiment this method for assessing artificial intelligence, is a test in which a human interacts with a machine without being able to detect that their interlocutor is a machine. Turing proposed that at the moment when a machine can fool a human into believing in its humanity, we will be witnessing the birth of a truly "artificial intelligence." Turing's concern was with a hypothetical human and a hypothetical machine, and so of course did not consider the diversity and creativity of humans and language tasks. There have come to be many types of "Turing Tests," but none comes close to being able to confirm that a machine has developed the capability to either understand or produce language at the level of competence found in any healthy and speaking or signing three-year-old human.

7.2.5 Addressing AI and Language Technology Hype

Most of us are using language technology in a lot of different ways, and if we're paying attention, we're likely seeing steady improvements. But we're also likely to see overly broad and hyperbolic claims about the state of the art and the nearness of a future in which machines will be as good at, or better than, humans in producing and understanding language. For example, in 2020, the newspaper *The Guardian* ran an op-ed column with the headline "A robot wrote this entire article. Are you scared yet, human?" and gave the byline to GPT-3 (GPT-3 2020).

In truth, the article was assembled by humans from chunks of text produced by GPT-3 based on human-generated prompts. The article drew from eight different GPT-3 responses, and the assembly was done by human editors who wanted an article that would "convince us robots come in peace." That is, humans had the idea, humans wrote the stems, humans assembled the machine responses to support their idea, and then humans edited the result so that it would read as if it were written by humans. The editors reported that the editing required was similar to what would be required to edit an op-ed written entirely by humans, but this of course does not take into account that a human author would not need to be fed prompts by an undergraduate computer science student, nor that a human author would not necessarily be willing to produce an output entirely supportive of an editor's preconceived argument.

We see news reports on applications such as machine translation that have claimed that the vision of a universal translation machine had already come true because Google Translate had been able to list more than two or three supported language pairs. At the time of writing, Google Translate supports – to some extent – 104 languages; but all of its translation tasks are mediated by text, in English, and there are more than 7,000 languages on earth. So, we are pretty far away from a "universal translator."

Even the 175 billion parameters of GPT-3 are not sufficient for that system to know that "you have the most beautiful fangs I've ever seen" is probably not going to be a successful pick-up line (Shane 2021), nor that "classy comma" is not a great name for a paint color (Shane 2022). Whatever is happening under the covers of this kind of system, it sure doesn't look like the system is "intelligent." It is, clearly, artificial.

Very large systems like GPT-3 and the largest available model (at the time of writing), the "Pathways Language Model" or PaLM (Chowdhery et al. 2022) – a transformer-based system that, at 540 billion parameters, boasts an order of magnitude more "neurons" than GPT-3 – are not without costs. Bender and colleagues (2021) note that these models are extremely costly – in money and in carbon footprint – to build and train and also extremely risky in that their basic architecture as systems that "learn" and reproduce linguistic forms without any access to meaning ensures that they will always pose a risk to humans by being able to produce linguistic forms that *seem* to make sense without being constrained by any connections to reality. We have seen this kind of danger in, for example, the Google search results that we discussed at the beginning of the chapter, in which the machine provides different answers when asked about "humans" vs. "people" and presents these answers as if they are objectively and unassailably correct.

Another area in which linguists in the community might be able to help combat language technology hype is the relatively frequent coverage of "sign language glove" projects. These typically come out of university research units that focus on bioengineering and/or medical engineering, typically from teams who do not include deaf people. The most recent of these, at least at the time of writing, came out of the Wearable Bioelectronics Research Group at UCLA (Zhou et al. 2020). The wearable device, a glove with a number of sensors on the fingers – and even a few sensors that could be worn on the face, was promoted as a tool that could provide "an easy way for people who use sign language to communicate directly with non-signers without needing someone else to translate for them" (Chen, quoted in Chin 2020). Devices such as this, however, would not in principle be able to "translate" from a signed language to, for example, spoken English, because signed languages use more than handshapes and facial expressions as meaningful elements in their grammars. Eye gaze, handedness, and body movements such as shoulder shrugs, for example, can all be incorporated into the grammar of signed languages. Furthermore, there are many signed languages and many varieties of every signed language – just as there are many spoken languages and many varieties of spoken language. These devices are often imagined by engineers who believe that providing this kind of technology would aid inclusion and equity for deaf and hard of hearing people, but who are not themselves users of a signed language nor members of relevant communities. After one such press release from the University of Washington, an interdisciplinary group of scholars wrote an open letter (Forshay et al. 2016) in response. The Forshay et al. letter identifies not only structural problems as outlined above, but also the social and cultural harms that come when one (comparatively privileged and well-resourced, but isolated) group promotes technological innovation as "help" for less privileged and more poorly resourced others without consulting them. These harms include continued reinforcement of inaccurate stereotypes about signed languages and their speakers and the extraction of important resources away from useful, well-informed, community-based projects toward those that have more obvious allure to an uninformed public.

Whether or not it's in theory possible for machines to manage language in a human-like way remains to be seen. Whether it is possible for them to do so using the tools and strategies currently in vogue (deep learning and neural nets, wearable devices) is even less clear. A linguist in the community can help others to understand why it can be damaging to people when misleading and overly expansive claims about the abilities of language technology are shared uncritically.

7.2.6 Using Your Knowledge for Good

There are good news stories about ways in which natural language processing and language technology are being used in ways that we think can be seen as "good." One example comes from an area often described as "machine reading for scientific discovery." In this paradigm, linguists and computer scientists join forces with subject area experts to provide access to scientific findings that are published across many articles, from many journals, from many disciplines. As Valenzuela-Escárcega and colleagues (2018) describe, even if we limit our interest to scientific research that is published in scholarly journals, in English, and in an area like biomedical science (and so indexed by PubMed), there are more than one million new articles per year. Furthermore, these articles are in fields and journals that are highly specialized, such that a researcher in (for example) biochemistry may not be able to access and find relevant research published in (for example) plant sciences. This results in a problem of the production of "undiscovered knowledge" in science – work that has found a crucial causal link between relevant units in one area of science is unknown to other researchers, whose work it might be expected to help. Of the one million plus papers published each year and indexed by PubMed, less than 5 percent are ever even cited (Valenzuela-Escárcega et al. 2018).

Linguists are in a unique position to be able to help solve problems like this because we study and try to understand the ways in which people in a community make linguistic meaning, and the kind of meaning that we need to be able to find in order to assist in scientific discovery is relatively narrow – it's the language of causes and effects. A machine that can quickly ingest – and then label and parse – written language, especially written language that is relatively homogenous in its dialectal and contextual properties (i.e., the language of scientific papers in the US) can be put to use mining those texts for the kinds of parses that are most likely to reflect claims of causes and effects. Those claims can then be extracted by the machine and organized so that human readers can find both relevant causes and effects and also the chains of cause and effect that can help us to solve really hard problems.

As your authors were drafting this chapter, a story emerged in the US news that gets to the heart of key issues in language technology. Hicks and Lawler

(2022) reported that an organization called "Crisis Text Line," which is a privately funded, not-for-profit company, had issued an apology to its users over data sharing with a for-profit startup company called Loris.ai. Crisis Text Line (CTL) provides access by text for anyone experiencing a mental health crisis to anonymous counseling and support, and it uses AI and NLP to assist in routing incoming texts to counselors. CTL is also a shareholder in Loris.ai, a company started by CTL founders, whose mission is to use AI and Big Data to "make customer service more human, empathetic and scalable."[16] The story? Data from CTL was being shared (anonymized and scrubbed) with Loris.ai without the knowledge or consent of CTL users.

A linguist in the community with an interest in language technology might look at this story from any of several angles. For example, what could the analysis of CTL texts tell us about how its users (clients, counselors) negotiate very difficult topics in this modality? What specific linguistic features and patterns would an AI pick up on from such an application, and how generalizable are they? Do the patterns that the AI uses to route and manage clients in the CTL workflow work better for some categories of clients or counselors than others? Can these patterns turn out to harm CTL users whose linguistic behavior might not be correctly identified by the AI?

But the story also might cause us to think about issues like who can or should be able to profit from our language use. Language technology leverages the digital tracks of many millions of online interactions – and in many cases, the speakers who produced those tracks are not aware of how their language data is being used and who is making money from it. In the case of CTL and Loris.ai, how would you feel if texts from your worst, darkest moments turned up in training data for a model that fed a chatbot you have to interact with to pay a bill, buy a sofa, or make an appointment?

Contrast this kind of technology development, which is proprietary, for-profit, and often secret with open-source and open access development efforts, such as Mozilla's Common Voice project (https://commonvoice.mozilla.org/en). Common Voice is a project that asks participants to "donate" their voice to a data set that is then made available at no cost to various technology developers. In crowdsourcing voices, developers – for-profit or not – can create language technology that better reflects actual language variation in the world. Would knowing that someone was making money off of your voice be more acceptable to you than having this happen without your knowledge?

---

[16] https://loris.ai, accessed February 3rd, 2022.

7.3 Computers, Meet Linguists!

Reader, we hope that what you've learned in this chapter inspires you to get involved in the creation, oversight, and possibly even regulation of language technology, including the kind of technology that we've described here as running most of the really powerful language-related applications as of the time of writing – like machine learning, and particularly deep learning, models. You may not think of yourself as a technical person, but it turns out that you are likely to be engaged with very complex and important technologies virtually all the time. And we know that these technologies are learning from a relatively small subset of humans (i.e., those who use language online, where it's mostly English and mostly written; and those who are working in computer science, engineering, and tech – who are mostly male, mostly white, and mostly without any training in linguistics at all).

By the time you read this chapter, some of the specific information we've included here will be obsolete. How do the technologies that you're using right now work? Who do they serve, and who do they leave out? What linguistic biases and patterns of discrimination do they perpetuate, and what do they help combat?

As a linguist in the community, you know a lot about language – and your knowledge is absolutely foundational to the development of good technological tools. Computers need us to help them interact with us in ways that strengthen us rather than simply amplifying our historic patterns of bias.

Linguist in the Community

- Consider participating in technology projects like Mozilla's Common Voice (https://commonvoice.mozilla.org/en) that allow you to contribute to meaningful efforts by scholars and engineers to decrease linguistic discrimination in technology.
- As you use language technology in different forms, note ways in which the technology gets things wrong – for example, by keeping an informal journal of strange auto-complete, auto-correct, or predictive text suggestions you get. See if you can discover patterns in the errors, and share them with others. Think about why the errors are occurring, and how a smart linguist might be able to join forces with engineers to fix them.
- When you're able, turn on "closed captions" as you watch videos on your computer or your television. Pay attention to things that the captions get

right and what they get wrong, and share those observations with others. Why are the errors happening, and what do they tell you about the machine that is creating the captions?

Linguist in the Classroom

- If your class uses technology to meet virtually (i.e., applications like Zoom, Webex, Google Teams, or similar), turn on the live captioning features and test them in class. Invite different students to speak, and see whether the system is more or less error prone for different speakers. A really fun game to play with these systems is to say proper nouns (names of prominent people, companies, places, and the like) that are often used in your area but that might not be famous nationally or internationally. Be sure to include at least some proper nouns that are not from English. See if you can put together a description of the patterns of errors that you find.
- Work in small groups and select a web-based machine translation tool such as Google Translate to use during this exercise. Groups that have one or more multilingual students who are happy to lend their language skills to others can follow the multilingual path in the activity; groups that do not can follow the translation ping-pong path in the steps below. At the end of the steps, come back together and share your findings – what do they tell you about the differences between how humans do language translation and how machines do it?
    - Step 1: Translate each of five words of the class's language of instruction, selected at random, into another language and evaluate the results.
        - Multilingual path: Use a target language that group members know.
        - Ping-pong path: Use any available target language – and after translating each English word into that target language, use the system to translate the result back into English.
    - Step 2: Identify three to five idiomatic expressions from the class's language of instruction – these are expressions that everyone uses but are not understood literally. For example, US English speakers might call someone a "backstabber" to mean that the person is mean in a sneaky way, not that they actually stab anyone; or they might say that you "raced against the clock" to mean that you tried to go really fast, not that you actually had a clock running in the next lane on the track as you ran the 100 meters. Translate each into the group's target language and evaluate the results.

- Multilingual path: Use a target language that group members know – you could even use idioms from your target language and translate them into the language of instruction if you wished.
  - Ping-pong path: Use any available target language; translate from your language to it, and then back to your language. You can even ping-pong-wander by doing this process multiple times if you get an example where the translations shift with each turn.
  ○ Step 3: Translate a passage of text – at least a few sentences – and evaluate the results.
    - Multilingual path: You know what to do.
    - Ping-pong path: You know what to do.
- Hold a class-wide write-with-a-robot competition! Find a text completion demonstration online (there are currently excellent ones for English at https://huggingface.co/docs/transformers/en/index) and make sure everyone knows how to use it to generate text. Then co-author a story or essay with the machine. You should track or mark the machine's contributions so that a reader can know what material came from the bot and what you wrote yourself. Collect the stories or essays and distribute anonymized versions to the class and ask everyone to vote for their favorites (no voting for your own contribution!). Collect the winners and share them in a celebratory manner with others!

Glossary

algorithm In mathematics and computer science, a set of steps to solve a well-defined problem such that the steps are unambiguous and the output is always the same given the same input. Data scientist Cathy O'Neil (2016) defines algorithms as "opinions expressed in code."

American Standard Code for Information Exchange (ASCII) A standard set of 128 character encodings used in most electronic devices, ASCII includes the letters of the Roman alphabet (upper and lower case), the Arabic numerals 0 through 9, and a number of punctuation and mathematical symbols, as well as control characters (such as end of line and space).

artificial intelligence A state in which a machine could be said to demonstrate human-like reasoning, an interdisciplinary field of research that aims to produce machines that can show evidence of "learning," "awareness," and/or "cognition." Artificial general intelligence (AGI), in which a machine is able to demonstrate intelligence across any domain, is the goal of many scholars, engineers, and entrepreneurs in the realms of computer science and engineering, among others, although attainment of this goal remains remote at the time of writing.

augmented intelligence An approach to artificial intelligence that seeks to provide systems that will assist humans in undertaking important tasks, but will not work independently. In augmented intelligence systems, the human decision-making process is prioritized.

bag of words models Computer systems that count individual words (types) and keep track of how many times each word appears in a text (tokens), but do not parse texts to find hierarchical relations among the words.

beat gestures Gestures (hand and arm movements, body orientations, facial expressions) that are used as we talk and that emphasize or modulate the rhythm of our discourse.

bigram model A bag of words model that keeps track of adjacent pairs of words in a text, rather than just counting individual words.

computational linguist A linguist who focuses on the use of computational methods to study language.

computational linguistics The subdiscipline of linguistics that focuses on the computational modeling of language, and the use of computational methods to study language.

computer Any of a number of digital electronic machines (laptop, desktop, hand-held, tablet, etc.) that can be used to carry out calculations automatically.

co-speech gestures Gestures (hand and arm movements, body orientations, facial expressions) that accompany our utterances, but don't necessarily organize them (e.g., raised eyebrows that accompany a question in a spoken language).

emblem gestures Gestures (hand and arm movements, body orientations, facial expressions) that stand in for an actual linguistic unit (e.g., the peace sign).

GPT A generalized, pretrained, transformer model, which is a machine-learning system that uses so-called neural networks in order to be able to provide predictions that are consistent with the (usually very large) amounts of data it has been trained on. GPTs are "generalized" in that they are built to be useful to solve virtually any kind of problem. They are "pretrained" in that the machine learning steps required for their use have largely been completed before they are used on a new problem. And they are "transformer" models because they use a particular type of statistical modeling that goes by that name (and is described in Vaswani et al. 2017).

GPT-2 A computational AI system created in 2019 by Open-AI, a corporation funded by Microsoft, Google, and others. GPT-2 is an implementation of natural language processing, trained on a very large, mostly English corpus and using 1.5 billion parameters, that is used in a wide variety of language technology applications in the US.

GPT-3 Is like GPT-2, only with more computational power (175 billion parameters). Its performance is slightly better than that of GPT-2 on a limited set of tasks.

image processing Any computational task in which a machine analyzes visual data (from image or video input). Language-related uses include optical character recognition, image recognition (for automatic alt-text generation, for example), and text-to-image operations.

labeling A step in computational natural language processing in which the machine tries to identify the part of speech for each linguistic unit and tag that unit with its appropriate part of speech label.

language model A theory of a language, and/or a set of examples of a language, that humans give to a computer to help it with NLP tasks.

large language model (LLM) A very, very large set of examples of language over which various statistics have been calculated. LLMs are typically multilingual and, as of 2024, also multimodal (including audio and video data as well as text).

lemmatization A step in computational natural language processing in which the machine tries to abstract away from an inflected form of a word (such as "walked" or "cats") to identify the root or stem (such as "walk" or "cat").

machine A mechanical tool.

machine language The lowest-level system that computers rely on. Machine language is binary and digital (it consists of sequences of 0s and 1s, or "off" and "on") and not (readily) human readable.

machine learning A branch of computer science in which machines are programmed with algorithms that are designed to allow the computer to use large amounts of input data, along with input–output pairs, to self-adjust these algorithms until their categorization approaches that intended by humans. It is used in AI research and applications. Machine learning systems "learn" from their training data such that they reproduce any patterns found in those data.

machine-reading Used to describe machines analyzing written human language, which can then be used either to assist humans directly or else as input to other machine learning models.

markedness An element is "marked" in some system if it is infrequent and/or unexpected in some way. In linguistics, a "marked" form is one that is less common than other analogous forms. For example, in English we know that the expression "male nurse" is more marked than the expression "female nurse," while the expression "female astronaut" is more marked than "male astronaut" at least at the time of writing. One consequence of markedness of expressions is that the "unmarked" version can often be unstated, while the "marked" version must be explicit.

named-entity recognition A step in natural language processing in which the machine tries to identify proper nouns and distinguish these from common nouns.

natural language processing (NLP) A branch of computational linguistics and computer science that focuses on using machines to create, manipulate, and understand human language. Fundamental to most work in AI.

neural net A type of computer program often used in machine learning and based on some people's theories of how human brains work. A neural net consists of "nodes," which are really mathematical equations, and "connections," which are really threshold values that determine whether or not the output of one equation gets sent to another node in the system. Neural nets typically have many nodes, which are described as belonging to an "input layer" if they take inputs and perform the first calculation on them; a "hidden layer" if they only take the outputs of another node, and only send their outputs to another node; or an "output layer" if their outputs are the end of the processing queue.

ngram model Any bag of words model, whether it keeps track of tokens one at a time, two at a time (bigrams), three at a time (trigrams), or more.

optical character recognition The process by which a computer tries to convert image data of orthographies (handwritten, typewritten, etc.) into text that the machine can understand and process.

pantomime gestures Gestures (hand and arm movements, body orientations, facial expressions) that we use as we talk to literally act out the events we're describing.

speech-to-text (STT) NLP programs that take in audio data and convert it to orthographic representations.

text-to-speech (TTS) NLP programs that take in orthographic data and convert it to audio outputs.

tokenization A step in natural language processing in which the machine tries to identify individual "words" and other meaningful elements (such as punctuation or partial word forms such as English "-n't").

transformer model A type of system used in NLP that primarily "learns" sequences of characters, spaces, and words and uses some amount of preceding material in order to predict the next character(s), space(s), and tokens. Transformer models such as GPT-2 and GPT-3 have shown modest success in some NLP applications when provided with massive amounts of training data and unimaginably large and energy intensive training.

truncation A process in which something is removed from a word in order to create a new word, for example "telephone" < "phone."

Turing Test A way of imagining the evaluation of artificial intelligence, inspired by Alan Turing, who mused that humans would be able to know that AI had occurred if we could talk to a machine and be fooled into believing that we were talking to another human.

type/token ratio A ratio that describes how often a particular linguistic form (type) is used across a whole corpus or subset of a corpus (tokens).

unicode An information technology standard for encoding (in principle) all the characters used in the writing systems of the world, including letters, syllabics, logograms, diacritics, punctuation, and images (such as emoji). The most common encoding standard in unicode at the time of writing is UTF-8, which allows 8 bytes per character, but UTF-16 is increasingly common.

unigram A bag of words model that takes individual words (tokens) one at a time.

vector semantics An approach used in NLP to provide machines with some operationalization of word-level meaning. Vector semantics is built on an hypothesis that words that appear in similar contexts are likely to have similar meanings. In a vector semantic approach, words that are considered opposites by humans (i.e., "good," "bad") are often analyzed as "roughly" synonymous, because they appear in the same syntactic and lexical environments as each other (i.e., "that was a bad movie" probably occurs with about the same frequency as "that was a good movie").

Recommended Readings

The relationship between language and computers is likely to be a hot topic for years to come. If you want to have the scientific linguistic background in this area to make you a master at dinner party conversations about AI and language, make sure to take a deep dive into our recommended readings below. A local college or university library can help you source access to these studies if you need help!

Bender, E. M., Gebru, T., McMillan-Major, A., & Shmitchell, S. (2021). On the dangers of stochastic parrots: Can language models be too big?. *Proceedings of the 2021 ACM Conference on Fairness, Accountability, and Transparency*, 610–623. https://doi.org/10.1145/3442188.3445922

Forshay, L., Winter, K., & Bender, E. (2016, May 23). Open letter to the office of news & information, University of Washington. *University of Washington*. https://faculty.washington.edu/ebender/papers/SignAloudOpenLetter.pdf

Gawne, L., & McCulloch, G. (2019). Emoji as digital gestures. *Language@Internet*, *17*(2). https://scholarworks.iu.edu/journals/index.php/li/article/view/37786

Noble, S. U. (2018). *Algorithms of Oppression: How Search Engines Reinforce Racism*. New York University Press.

O'Neil, Cathy. (2016). *Weapons of Math Destruction: How Big Data Increases Inequality and Threatens Democracy*. Crown.

Starbird, K., Dailey, D., Mohamed, O., Lee, G., & Spiro, E. S. (2018). Engage early, correct more: How journalists participate in false rumors online during crisis events. *Proceedings of the 2018 CHI Conference on Human Factors in Computing Systems*, (105), 1–12. https://doi.org/10.1145/3173574.3173679

Tauber, J. (2021, March 14). Tokenizing The Hobbit. *Digital Tolkien Project*. https://digitaltolkien.com/2021/03/14/tokenizing-the-hobbit.html

Valentinsson, M.-C. (2018). Stance and the construction of authentic celebrity persona. *Language in Society*, *47*(5), 715–740. https://doi.org/10.1017/S0047404518001100

Valenzuela-Escárcega, M. A., Babur, Ö., Hahn-Powell, G., Herongove, G., Hicks, T., Noriega-Atala, E., Wang, X., Surdeanu, M., Demir, E., & Morrison, C. T. (2018). Large-scale automated machine reading discovers new cancer-driving mechanisms. *Database*, **2018**, 1–14. https://doi.org/10.1093/database/bay098

8 Languages Go to School

This chapter focuses on the ways in which a linguist in the community might investigate the complex interactions between our languages and our experiences in the classroom. If you are reading this book as a textbook for a class, you've already experienced the ways in which your language may have been rewarded, penalized, shaped by, and shaped your educational experience. Much of what we learn in school about language is decidedly not linguistically informed – we learn (or are taught) a number of prescriptive rules about how we should and should not use language rather than learning about how our language actually works. For many of us, this process leads us to believe that the way we use language at home is not correct, not proper, and perhaps not acceptable. For some, it makes us feel that we're not really welcome in the world of academics. For others, these rules reinforce our notions of our own intelligence and superiority – and in this chapter you'll be invited to think about the harms that can happen in school as well as ways to remediate those harms and do better by students from all different linguistic backgrounds.

Most classroom work happens in and through language. Even math, science, and history classes – which aren't about language themselves – use language to communicate key ideas. Indeed, many societies expect schools to teach not only the content of the curriculum but also the "socially appropriate use of communicative resources" through which one displays mastery of content (Philips 1982, p. 73). For this reason alone, it should be clear that language is an important component of education and schooling. But language in schools is also important because many people and communities see their languages as core components of their identity. Studies have shown that when students feel supported and affirmed in their identities – including in the language varieties of their communities – they attain greater levels of educational success (Adair et al. 2017; García et al. 2021). In spite of this evidence, many educators and school officials treat language as a rigid set of rules that must be followed precisely rather than as a flexible set of norms that shape communication and interaction in unique ways.

Our beliefs about appropriate, correct, or proper forms of language – and how these beliefs intersect with our understanding of other social identities – can also impact teachers. You might recall our discussion in Chapter 5 about the phenomenon of accent hallucination, which we'll briefly review later in this chapter, and which happened in a school setting. As we further discuss these impacts in this chapter, you'll become familiar with a concept relevant for the subsequent chapters, too: **intersectionality**. While the term itself was coined in 1989 by legal scholar and civil rights advocate Kimberlé Crenshaw, the concept that certain social identities may be "privileged" in some contexts and "oppressed" in others has a long history in social scientific thought. In this chapter and the ones that follow, pay close attention to cases where language figures into intersectional analyses of identity and society.

Throughout this chapter, you should also keep in mind that when we say "language," rather than "languages," we are noting that many schools in the US and abroad operate under an **ideology of monolingualism**. **Bilingual education** (or **multilingual education**) is not as common in the US as it was in the 1970s and 80s, and it has never been the norm here. The enforcement of this ideology of monolingualism results in tremendous challenges for children who enter the educational system speaking a language other than the mainstream language – and even children who speak different dialects, or simply come from communities with distinct communicative norms. Worse still, our schools enforce this ideology of monolingualism in spite of lots of evidence that inviting multiple languages into the educational system – starting as early as possible and persisting through elementary, secondary, and higher education – is beneficial to students and communities alike.

In this chapter, we will explore how language and social issues play out in classrooms and educational contexts – not only the issues of discrimination against teachers and students we've alluded to above, but also how schools can be sites of language birth and language revitalization. Two key concepts inform how we approach these issues. The first is the theoretical lens of **raciolinguistics** – a concept which refers to the ways that language constructs race and racial difference (Alim et al. 2016) as well as how language and race are co-constructed (Flores & Rosa 2015; Rosa & Flores 2017). The second and closely related concept is called **critical language pedagogy** (CLP). You might hear this term used with the word pedagogies rather than the singular as it really is a term that incorporates a range of different approaches to teaching and learning about language. What all critical language pedagogies have in common, however, is that teachers and students are encouraged to think critically about how our sociocultural beliefs about language, dialects, and accents are connected to broader power structures within a society (Alim 2007; Godley et al. 2015). Putting both of these concepts together will allow us to see how language, education, and social issues are all intricately connected, so let's dive in!

8.1 Raciolinguistic Discrimination against Students

Schools are not just places where we learn about the world. They also teach young people how to be in the world. In many parts of the world, students are required to dress a certain way, behave a certain way, and, indeed, speak in certain ways according to beliefs about what is "appropriate" or "inappropriate" for a classroom setting. Until you start to question where these beliefs come from, it can be easy to see them as "obvious" or "natural." One might think, "Of course students shouldn't interrupt their teachers," or, "It would obviously be disruptive if a student were to use their 'outdoor' voice inside the classroom." Or perhaps it seems "obvious" that students should promptly answer a direct question from the teacher, or that "standard" language is the only appropriate code for classroom communication. You might even think that measures of vocabulary size are related to a student's ability to be successful. If you've been paying attention in previous chapters, you probably won't be surprised to learn that none of these beliefs are natural patterns of communication across all speech communities.

In the late 1960s, sociolinguist William Labov undertook a variety of studies whose goal was to get a better understanding of the linguistic development of children entering schools in Philadelphia, where he lived. Previous work had used a variety of methods to assess this, and many of those methods resulted in findings that Black students – even those who had participated in Head Start[1] preschool programs – were coming to school with very limited linguistic (and cognitive) skills. Labov noted that these methods – standardized tests administered by adults, commands from teachers for students to "talk more," teachers repeating students' responses, teachers lying to students to elicit corrections, and moral instruction – systematically suppressed Black (but not necessarily white) children's willingness to speak at all. These children kept their answers as short as possible, tried to avoid disagreeing with the adult, and so on. Black students' interactional style choices were then used as evidence that they "did not have" complex language ability (Labov 1970).

---

[1] In the United States, Head Start refers to an initiative by the federal government to provide resources for early childhood education, particularly during the transition from preschool to kindergarten. It was initially conceived as a program to help children from low-income backgrounds better engage with their peers from more advantaged backgrounds.

8.1 Raciolinguistic Discrimination against Students

Labov developed a different methodology that produced very different results. Instead of following the above mentioned scripts, he entered the classroom carrying a pet rabbit[2] hidden in his trenchcoat.

> The children wanted to know "what's under your coat?" At first I wouldn't tell them, but I finally said: "Look, I've got a rabbit here. Can any of you help me out? Somebody's got to take care of him while I'm talking to the teachers." ...
>
> They were told "He's kind of nervous, so just keep talking to him. He's used to people talking to him: talk to him and he won't get nervous." (Labov 1970, p. 24).

Labov's recordings of the children's dialog with the rabbit showed that their language (and cognition) were every bit as well-developed as their white counterparts'. All children produced more complex and nuanced language structures when talking to the rabbit than they did in any of the tests.

We do not mean to suggest that talking to a rabbit is a universal interactional pattern that we can expect all children to naturally feel comfortable with[3]; only that the experiment Labov performed was sufficient to show that how we structure conversation in schools has a differential effect on different populations of children because our practices depend upon unstated and unanalyzed notions of "natural," "proper," or "correct" language behavior. Similarly, Figueroa (2024a and 2024b) describes how it is that unstated assumptions about "correct" language mingle with unfounded beliefs about "vocabulary size" and that similar measures end up weaponized against children who come from backgrounds outside of the researchers' typical communities of practice.

A quick search of the scholarly literature via your institution's library or a search engine like https://scholar.google.com using the key term "**disproportionality**" in combination with other education-related terms like "special education," "speech language pathology," or "disciplinary patterns" will confirm the existence of a variety of scholarship from English-dominant countries showing that students who are English-language learners, deaf students, and those from economically, socially, ethnically, or otherwise stigmatized speech communities are disproportionately diagnosed as intellectually disabled and/or behaviorally challenged, are disproportionately diagnosed with disordered speech/language abilities, and are disproportionately disciplined

---

[2] Named Vincent. At the time of writing we do not know where Vincent came from, nor what color or type of rabbit he was. We only know that he was a very fine rabbit indeed.

[3] In the US in the 1970s, urban children probably had little or no experience with rabbits other than in storybooks and as potential classroom pets. We might expect different patterns from children raised in communities for which speaking to animals has different social meaning than it did for Labov's participants.

(and arrested) at school (see Annamma et al. 2014; Castilla-Earls et al. 2020; and Cooc & Kiru 2018 for helpful reviews of relevant scholarship).

While not all of this disproportionality is directly related to language, we have good reason to believe that much of it is – and as we've learned in previous chapters, we can't really extract bias against language from bias against the personal and group identities that language behavior indexes.

8.2 Language in School and the Illusion of "Standard" Language

North American schools tend to be breeding grounds for a language ideology that revolves around the existence of a **standard language**," something that can count as the (only) "correct" form of the language of instruction (English, Spanish, French, etc.). The same may be said about schools in other parts of the world that use an English-language medium of instruction – and, with a substitution of "Spanish" for "English," about Spanish-medium schools in Central and South America, and in Western Europe – and so on. The perceived "standard" is enforced at least on written language – with enforcement of spelling and punctuation rules that have little connection to actual spoken or signed language, as well as with enforcement of rules about vocabulary, phrase, and sentence structure that are more closely connected with language itself. In every case of which we're aware, this "standard" is derived from language behavior and linguistic ideology held by social groups who have power, status, and wealth; it does not accurately reflect anyone's day-to-day language use, and it indexes membership in or affiliation with those powerful social groups. In many places, including but certainly not limited to the US, the "standard" is also explicitly monolingual. This is in spite of research showing that bilingual and multilingual students almost certainly have cognitive (see, for example, Taboada Barber et al. 2021) and metalinguistic (Otsuji & Pennycook 2018) advantages compared with their monolingual peers.

School curricula and teacher training are often focused on mastery of the perceived "standard," and students, teachers, and staff whose home varieties are associated with marginalized groups are told that their language is "incorrect." Teachers and staff will almost always be very familiar with linguistic discrimination in the community but experience this discrimination as stemming from a "liability" that marginalized students bring and which instruction in the "standard" can fix. Have you ever been coached on how you should speak so that you'll be more employable? More successful at work or school? Treated more respectfully by others? Those who have offered you this advice have undoubtedly noticed that linguistic discrimination is a problem – and the solution that they've been offered, and offer to you, is to assimilate to the "standard." This is well-meaning advice, but it of course has damaging effects for everyone; most especially for those people who come to believe that their language is a liability, and that they can't be successful as who they are based on how they talk and write.[4]

In addition to the harm of teaching children that how they talk and write is deficient because of who they are, ideologies of "standard" language become double binds for marginalized students. Writing exercises in which students are asked to "write like you talk" regularly over-penalize students whose spoken language is marginalized (Charity Hudley & Mallinson 2011, p. 31; Smitherman-Donaldson 1987). Classroom teachers do not necessarily have any training with or experience of the linguistic varieties of their students, nor with the study of language generally – so rather than recognizing legitimate and useful linguistic variants, they may mark students' work as deficient or "incorrect."

This over-penalization can extend to classroom behavior and spoken or signed language as well. Teachers who are unfamiliar with the pragmatics and social norms surrounding, for example, Black English in the US may experience Black English through the lens of social stereotypes (i.e., Black English speakers may be stigmatized as "too loud" or "aggressive" or "disrespectful" based on teachers' conscious or unconscious biases about Black people; Charity Hudley & Mallinson 2011; Day-Vines & Day-Hairston 2005). On the other hand, Native American students may be stigmatized as "too quiet" or "slow" or "non-responsive" based on teachers' expectations that Native students will or should interact using white-preferred timing and intonation. Without necessarily being aware of their social biases and while operating in an institutional setting where white communication styles are prioritized, instructors mete out punishments where none are needed and thus negatively affect non-white pupils' educational experience in a variety of ways.

As we discuss in more detail in Chapter 12, in North America and Australia, and several other places around the world, schools have been an intimate part of a genocidal project against Indigenous people. In the US, for example, between 1819 and 1969,[5] the Bureau of Indian Affairs (BIA) was

---

[4] We cannot recommend highly enough the textbook *English with an Accent* by Rosina Lippi-Green (2012) for students in the US who are interested in better understanding all the ways in which the concept of a standard "English" is weaponised in schools, media, and the like.

[5] To put this into context, the eldest co-author of this book was born in 1963 and was a kindergartener in 1969. Because she is white, she did not have to go to a BIA Boarding school.

responsible for at least 408 boarding schools in thirty-seven states or territories (Newland 2022). Families were often forced to send their children to these schools on pain of imprisonment or starvation, and children were sometimes simply abducted from their families by the US Government and sent to boarding schools far away from home (Special Committee on Indian Education 1969). One explicit goal of the boarding school system was to forcibly assimilate Native children into white, Christian culture as manual laborers and domestic workers. The schools regularly engaged in such "identity-altering methodologies as renaming Indian children from Indian to English names; (2) cutting hair of Indian children; (3) discouraging or preventing the use of American Indian, Alaska Native, and Native Hawaiian languages, religions, and cultural practices; and (4) organizing Indian and Native Hawaiian children into units to perform military drills" (Special Committee on Indian Education 1969, p. 7). A similar system, referred to as the Residential School System, operated in Canada, with similar goals and practices (Truth and Reconciliation Commission of Canada 2015). By forcing children to attend school in a **majority language** that the children do not come to school with any knowledge of and punishing them for communicating using the language(s) that they have grown up with, BIA schools created a wide variety of social and cultural problems, including an interruption in intergenerational transmission of home languages for many communities – one that they are now working to mend and repair.

8.3 A Case Study: Antiblack Racism in the US Classroom

The historical antiblack and anti-Indigenous racism that we've just described continues to play out in its own way in terms of language in the classroom. Antiblack racism resulted historically in *de jure* educational segregation until the 1960s and *de facto* segregation that continues in many places into the time of writing. The system was established with only white linguistic varieties and white modes of interaction understood as "proper," and the privileging of white language and communicative repertoires is a continuing problem (see Wright 2021a for relevant history and policy).

Currently, there are fewer explicit educational policies that police students' language use in this way, but there is ample documentation that the varieties that linguist April Baker-Bell (2020) calls "White Mainstream English" are perceived as linguistically and intellectually superior in educational contexts while varieties of Black English are denigrated and oppressed. Baker-Bell argues these perceptions are rooted in a concept called Antiblack Linguistic

Racism, defined as "the linguistic violence, persecution, dehumanization, and marginalization that Black Language–speakers experience in schools and everyday life" (p. 11). Examples of this from this chapter, the rest of the book, and everyday life abound – teachers suggesting that the way students speak is not "accurate," "polite," or "appropriate"; school administrators telling students they won't get a job unless they change the way they talk; and even other students regarding Black students' language as just not good enough. At the same time, Black students and Black teachers both know that in order to navigate the world outside of their communities, students will need skills that allow them "to navigate and negotiate [their] language in spaces that will continue to uphold white linguistic hegemony" (Baker-Bell 2020, p. 97)

As a result of her fieldwork with students and teachers in Detroit, Michigan – plus the work of other scholars whose work documents these classroom experiences – Baker-Bell decided to use her work to advocate for implementing what she calls **Antiracist Black Language Pedagogy**. Antiracist Black Language pedagogy is a critical language pedagogy that seeks to dismantle the ideological underpinnings of Antiblack Linguistic Racism. Like other critical language pedagogies, Antiracist Black Language Pedagogy seeks to engage students and teachers in critical, reflexive, and challenging analysis of the "current sociolinguistic order of things" (Alim 2007, p. 166). Rather than teaching Black students that their language is sloppy, ungrammatical, "just slang," or wrong (as **deficit-based pedagogy** does) or following frameworks for language arts instruction that seek to position minoritized varieties as only appropriate in certain contexts (what Baker-Bell calls **Respectability Language Pedagogies**), Antiracist Black Language Pedagogy seeks to reframe how students who use Black Englishes understand their own varieties and help them build confidence in their linguistic skills.

This last item is particularly important because, as Baker-Bell found in her research with Detroit students, some young people feel "conflicted" about fully embracing their community language practices. This is a classic example of "linguistic double consciousness" (Baker-Bell 2020, p. 97), a term that draws on the broader concept of **double consciousness** developed by the African American sociologist W. E. B. DuBois. DuBois coined this term as a way to explain the unique psychological experiences of Black people in white supremacist societies like the United States. In this sense, it describes how racially minoritized individuals perceive themselves through the perspective of the oppressor groups and measure themselves against that perspective. In the case of the language arts classrooms that Baker-Bell studied, this is manifested in students' hesitation to fully embrace their community's language varieties out of an awareness that in broader society it may be rejected. With the abundance of deficit-based cultural messages surrounding Black linguistic practices, it is no wonder that many Black children enter their classrooms with this frame of mind. This is exactly what Antiracist Black Language Pedagogy seeks to counter. When teachers adopt pedagogical frameworks that don't just apologize for "the way things are" and instead support their students in "envision[ing] the way things can be" (Alim 2005, p. 173), students of all racial and linguistic backgrounds are affirmed in their linguistic skills – and this, in turn, leads to improved educational outcomes for everyone.

8.4 A Case Study: Investigating Schools on the Warm Springs Reservation (Oregon, US)

There is today a tremendous body of literature showing that for Indigenous communities, providing education in and with the community's own linguistic and cultural context produces academic outcomes for students that far exceed those found in English-medium and forced-assimilatory classrooms (see McCarty & Nicholas 2014 for an excellent review of this literature). At the time of writing, 95 percent of Native American / Alaska Native students attend public rather than community schools, graduation rates for these students remains the lowest of any ethnic group in the US, and, particularly in parts of the US with the most entrenched anti-Indigenous racism such as South Dakota, graduation rates for Native students are as low as 50 percent (Cai 2020). How have language scholars studied this problem?

Throughout the late 1960s and early 1970s, anthropologist Susan Philips undertook an ethnographic study of cultural differences between white students and teachers and Native American students in the classroom. Her research took her to the Warm Springs Reservation in central Oregon and to the nearby town of Madras, a majority white town. Community members had noted that Native students tended to perform worse than white students in school. Warm Springs residents felt this change was especially notable as their children entered middle school. At the middle school, Native students were outnumbered by white children at a ratio of five to one (Philips 1982, p. 19) – and all the teachers were white as well. This is an important detail because within these "mainstream" classrooms, there are often quite specific ideologies about the appropriate use of communicative skills. Indeed, mastery of a particular kind of classroom communication is often taken as a sign of higher-level understanding or mastery of content. While the sort of communicative styles that are presumed to demonstrate this mastery are ones that the children of Madras grow up learning, the communicative styles in the homes of Warm Springs children can be quite different.

Within their community, Warm Springs children are often cared for by many adults and even older children rather than just having their immediate parents as central authorities. In part because of this, Warm Springs kids are "expected to become more self-sufficient at younger ages," "to cooperate with older brothers and sisters in providing mutual companionship and care," and are discouraged from drawing attention to themselves or acting like they stand out as a "better" from their social cohort (pp. 118–119). If you have been to school in a predominantly white educational setting, you can probably already tell that this is quite different from the participant framework of a typical classroom. There's one central adult authority – the teacher – and while collaborative or group activities are often a part of learning, children are also expected to display their knowledge, understanding, and mastery by raising their hands when a teacher asks a question. In other words, many of the communicative behaviors that are rewarded by white teachers in classrooms are considered "unseemly" by the adults in the Warm Springs community (pp. 117–118). At the same time, white teachers interpret the lack of engagement in this kind of classroom communication as a sign that Native children are less intelligent, don't understand the material, or don't care. Thus, the issues faced by Warm Springs Reservation students in white, mainstream schools are largely due to "cultural differences in signaling attention" and also cultural differences in terms of which types of attention are noticed by the teacher as appropriate or inappropriate (p. 103).

These kinds of differences – and, more importantly, a lack of awareness of them in educational contexts – have material effects on students' education. Philips' research found that those who don't abide by mainstream communicative norms in the classroom may have their speech ratified less frequently by teachers (pp. 85–90), be less certain about their own mastery of course materials (pp. 98–99), and do worse on tests and graded material in general (pp. 96, 112–114). Lack of cross-cultural awareness about these sorts of classroom language differences can also result in over-penalizing minoritized students for language errors, leading to misdiagnosis of speech and language disorders and incorrect placement of marginalized English-speaking students in English as a Second Language curricula. In a recent class taught by one of your authors in a Native American community in the US, participants revealed that tribal members in local public schools were being systematically directed into ESL programs in spite of the fact that they are English first-language speakers and monolingual (Stacy Oberly, personal communication, July 15 2022). The variety of English spoken in that Native community has distinctive features that communicate a tribal identity, different from White English spoken in the surrounding communities – but it is clearly and undoubtedly American English. Leap (1993) describes myriad ways in which Native American varieties of English diverge from other ethnic and racialized ways of using English, and how both the structures and ideologies of Indigenous language communities can be penalized in schools dominated by community outsiders.

8.5 A Brief: Chicano/Chicana English in the US Classroom

As early as the 1970s, scholars in the US began to recognize and study a set of stigmatized varieties of US English that are heavily influenced by (particularly Mexican) Spanish but that do not rely on speakers having any Spanish language fluency at all (Metcalf 1974; Otto Santa Ana 1993). Often referred to as Chicano/Chicana English, these varieties have been misunderstood as poorly acquired or "broken" English (as a second or foreign language), which they are most certainly not (Fought 2002), and also misinterpreted as marking not only Mexican or other Central or South American heritage, but also low socioeconomic status and sometimes even criminality and gang affiliation, and as such they may draw reprobation, or even peremptory disciplinary action from school personnel (Mendoza-Denton 2008). Latina youth who find themselves discriminated against in school (among other places) may recruit features of Chicano/Chicana English as a means of resistance against such discriminatory patterns.

Studies on disparate impacts of education in the US and Canada also show that students from marginalized communities are over-represented in cohorts assigned to speech-language pathologists (Counts et al. 2018; Ford 2012; Hart Blundon 2016). But it's not just minority students who encounter problems with linguistic discrimination – minority teachers do too.

8.6 Raciolinguistic Discrimination against Teachers

A brief review of the "accent hallucination" study described in Chapter 5 might be helpful here. In 1992, a researcher from the University of Georgia published a study that compared undergraduate students' perceptions of lessons delivered by graduate students of purportedly different ethnicities (Rubin 1992). Rubin used an experimental method called a "matched-guise" procedure, in which each of two groups of participants (sixty-two undergraduate students, all of whom grew up in the US) were exposed to a stimulus (a brief audio lesson, accompanied by a photograph purporting to be the speaker) and then asked to respond to the lesson by taking a comprehension quiz covering the mini-lesson content and completing a survey asking about their perceptions of the similarity between the instructor and themselves, their perception of the "accentedness" of the instructor's speech, and their evaluation of the instructor. Both of the participant groups heard exactly the same audios – all of which had been recorded by a white, female graduate student who had grown up in the midwestern US. But each group saw a different picture – in one case, they saw a picture of a white woman, and in the other they saw a picture of an Asian woman. The matched-guise protocol allowed the researchers to test whether or not the participants' perception of the speaker's ethnicity would affect their responses.

The results showed that it did. Students who saw a picture of an Asian woman had significantly lower scores on the comprehension quiz, rated the instructor as less clear and competent, and rated the instructor's speech as accented more often than did students who saw a picture of a white woman. The matched-guise protocol means that these differences could not have been determined by the content of the lesson or the quality of the speech – they were instead driven by students' expectations (and stereotypes) about people who look like the person in the photo they saw.

This is a relatively small study, and it's old – but these findings have been confirmed by a variety of scholars in a number of different contexts (see, for example, Kang & Rubin 2009 for additional work of this sort). Our expectations and stereotypes about speakers affect our perceptions of their language behavior – and in schools, this means that teachers who are members of marginalized groups can be harmed by linguistic discrimination, no matter how they actually speak.

At colleges and universities in the US, one consequence of this fact is that Black, Indigenous, Latinx, Asian, L2-English and other faculty are predictably and disproportionately harmed by the use of student satisfaction surveys as part of the hiring and promotion process. Another is that some US students actively avoid taking classes taught by such instructors because of stereotypes about their linguistic "intelligibility" (among other things) – and even if they do find themselves in these classes, they may have poorer academic outcomes because of those stereotypes and expectations. We hope that as a linguist in your community, you'll consider linguistic diversity among your teachers, professors, doctors, lawyers, and so on to be a strength rather than a weakness and use any opportunities you have to help educate others on the importance of engaging with people from lots of different language backgrounds.

8.7 In Teaching English as a Foreign/Second Language

In many countries around the world, English proficiency – particularly, proficiency in forms of English associated with whiteness – is regarded as a tool for social mobility, educational achievement, and broader economic mobility. For this reason, the teaching of English as a foreign language (TEFL) or English as a second language (TESL) is quickly growing as a global industry. In North America, the UK, and various white-majority English dominant countries, TEFL/TESL is viewed as a way for immigrants, refugees, and others to gain access to educational, economic, and political capital in an English-dominant community. Outside of these communities, TEFL/TESL is often provided via costly private instruction often meant to provide children of economically powerful families greater access to global economic, political, and social capital (Porto 2014). In some communities, there are efforts to offer English language instruction to impoverished and disadvantaged populations as well (Barahona 2015; Porto 2014). In countries as diverse as Spain to South Korea to Oman, there's a rush to hire "native English speakers" into the TEFL/TESL industry.

As a linguist in the community, we know that the term "native speaker" is itself problematic, but in its most useful definition, a "native speaker" of a language is anyone for whom that language was included as a primary means of communication in early childhood through puberty, regardless of the child's racial, ethnic, or social category. In spite of this fact, we see evidence that the "native speaker" expected as a TEFL/TESL instructor is racialized as white. Scholar and educator Vijay Ramjattan (2019a, 2019b) documents the experiences of non-white instructors of EFL/ESL in Canada, who report students questioning their status as a "native speaker" of English and framing them as "invaders" in the TEFL/TESL classroom. Some students take the position that the money they are paying for this instruction ought to guarantee them a white (and perhaps male) instructor.

We see this in action from recent recruitment materials from a company looking to assist those who want to become EFL/ESL instructors (i-to-i 2021) that show how the industry conflates language and national origin in a manner that's very consistent with a racialized view of English as white. The text below is taken directly from i-to-i.com's FAQ page from mid November 2021 (www.i-to-i.com/tefl-faq/what-is-a-native-english-speaker/). I-to-i is a company specializing in training TEFL (Teaching English as a Foreign Language) instructors through certification courses and also provides a job board for TEFL positions throughout the world.

This page indicated that a "native speaker of English" must be a citizen of a small selection of majority-white countries. This criterion exists even though citizenship of a country and speaking a given language natively are not necessarily related, and even though many other countries use English as a national language and still more countries have large populations of people who speak English as their first or primary language.[6]

TEFL FAQ > Eligibility and Applying > What is a Native English Speaker?

A Native English Speaker is defined as someone who both speaks English as their first language **and** is a citizen of one of the following countries:

- USA
- UK
- Ireland
- Canada
- South Africa
- Australia
- New Zealand

If you're a citizen of a country such as India, the Philippines, or the Caribbean Islands, English may be your first language but you're still not technically defined as a native English speaker. Sorry!

After this information was shared on social media, where it received significant criticism, the company updated their discussion as below (quoted from the same URL as given for the above text, but on March 4, 2022). In this clarification, the company notes that the stringent definition of having citizenship of one of the countries listed is not their definition of a native English speaker, but rather one that is adopted by many TEFL organizations.

TEFL FAQ > Eligibility and Applying > What is a Native English Speaker?

When applying for jobs, you may hear the phrase "native English speaker," used a lot. So what does this mean? The Collins dictionary defines it as:

"Someone who speaks that language as their first language, rather than having learned it as a foreign language"

So, technically, anyone with English as a first language from birth is a "native English speaker." But in practice, with TEFL jobs, you will often find employers use this phrase to refer to people that are citizens of one of the following countries:

---

[6] All of the countries and territories around the world that fall into this definition would be too numerous to list in this chapter, but they can easily be found searching the internet. Some of the countries fitting the definition include Botswana, Guyana, Hong Kong, India, Jamaica, Malta, the Philippines, and even Antarctica.

- USA
- UK
- Ireland
- Canada
- South Africa
- Australia
- New Zealand

This TEFL employer interpretation of the phrase "native English speaker" is, unfortunately, widespread and is used by multiple countries in their visa requirements for TEFL roles. So, working visas for certain countries can be difficult to come by, if you don't hold a passport from the list above.

This can, understandably, be frustrating for native English speakers from other countries, such as India, the Philippines, or the Caribbean Islands; however, all is not lost! Although you may be considered "non-native English speakers" by some countries (we know you aren't!) there are still plenty of TEFL teaching opportunities out there for those that are fluent in English and hold accredited TEFL qualifications (like the ones we offer at i-to-i). Head over to the LoveTEFL jobs board where you can search for jobs by the passport you hold.

Support for i-to-i's emphasis on a hypothetical employer's description of what constitutes a "native English speaker" can be found in the scholarly literature. Researchers Todd Ruecker and Lindsay Ives, for instance, examined fifty-nine recruitment websites for TEFL instructors in China, Japan, Korea, Taiwan, and Thailand. They found that the language schools represented in those websites would prefer to hire a white native English speaker above other native English speakers, and certainly above non-native English speakers (Ruecker & Ives 2015). Anthropologist Shanshan Lan discusses cases of Black and Asian native English speakers being dismissed from positions and undergoing more scrutiny in the hiring process than their white (or white-passing) counterparts in TEFL settings in Beijing and Xi'an (Lan 2021). Photos are often required in application packets to be passed on to hiring managers to support this practice (Lan 2021; Ramjattan 2019b; Ruecker & Ives 2015).

The core idea that is continually expressed in TEFL recruitment materials, whether implicitly or stated outright, is that only white speakers of English are qualified to teach it (Lan 2021; Ramjattan 2019b; Ruecker & Ives 2015). And although many teachers in the EFL/ESL domain are highly trained and credentialed professionals, it is also the case that many in and outside of the industry believe that no particular training in linguistics, English language, language instruction, or anything else is necessary to be qualified to begin a career in TEFL/TESL. Only 14 percent of the job postings in Ruecker and Ives' (2015) study explicitly required teaching qualifications, and they note that in general, the preferred applicant is one who is enthusiastic above all else. Lan (2021, p. 126) further notes that the ESL industry in China idealizes certain kinds of whiteness so much that an instructor's actual qualifications to teach English, or any other subject, may not have much effect on the kinds of jobs they receive or on their salaries. Instructors hired based on their whiteness rather than their qualifications may also be expected to teach other courses unrelated to their training, such as "History of American Culture" or "Introduction to Western Culture." That is, whiteness is constructed as a qualification – and non-whiteness an impediment – to participation in the TEFL/TESL industry.

Finally, it is important to note that many of these countries calling for increased English language education and seeking out these English language instructors do not fund public education especially well. Even when some amount of English language education is mandated in public schools, these education systems are often underfunded and understaffed, leading to an overall rather poor quality of English as a second or foreign language education. This is where the TEFL/TESL industry comes in – it ends up serving as a privatized version of the language education people are supposed to receive in schools. And privatizing the "better" form of English language education limits who can receive the benefits of learning English. In countries where this is the case, private TEFL/TESL classes can be prohibitively expensive, so achieving a certain degree of English proficiency comes to be seen as a marker of class status (Valentinsson 2020).

8.8 But Schools Can Also Be Places Where Good Languaging Happens

You may be reading this chapter as part of your formal education, and if you are, you might be thinking about ways in which school has been a happy place for you and your language. At least, we hope that you are. Schools can, of course, be places in which children's linguistic curiosity, brilliance, and creativity get nurtured and supported (and this might be a great moment to pause and think about any supportive and helpful teachers or staff from our own educational backgrounds who helped us feel empowered to expand our linguistic repertoires and celebrate our linguistic skills). Thank you to all those good people who work hard every day to ensure that school is a safe and happy place for students!

Here we celebrate ways in which schools become places for linguistic (re)birth, reconnection, solidarity, and reconciliation not only for those in the linguistic majority, but for everyone.

8.8.1 Schools as Engines for Linguogenesis

In addition to being places where language ideologies are born and reinforced, schools are also places where languages themselves are born by way of a wider community coming together when they may not have done so before. One of the best-loved examples of this type of language birth is Nicaraguan Sign Language (ISN; Idioma de Señas Nicaragüense), but there are likely to be other cases where languages are born and maintained in a school setting.

Languages are also maintained and revitalized at schools, where children are taught in the language that has historically been spoken in the region. We will discuss Māori, Hawaiian, and Sámi **language nests** in Section 8.8.3, but similar programs are in use elsewhere: language nests and **immersion programs** for Indigenous languages throughout the US and Canada like Mohawk and Cree, Welsh-medium education in Wales and Argentina (called addysg cyfrwng Cymraeg in Welsh), Gaelic-medium education in Scotland (foghlam tro mheadhan na Gàidhlig), Breton-medium schools in northern France (Diwan), Basque-medium schools in Spain (Ikastolak), Irish-medium schools in Ireland (Gaelscoileanna), and other similar schooling opportunities all work toward maintaining the speaker population of a variety of **minority languages**.

8.8.2 Nicaraguan Sign Language

In Nicaragua in the late 1970s, a special education school focusing on the needs of deaf children in the area was formed (Senghas & Coppola 2001). A few years later, a vocational school, focusing on the needs of deaf adolescents and young adults, was also formed (Senghas et al. 2005). Before the formation of these schools, deaf individuals tended to be raised in relative isolation: there was no Deaf community for them to interact with outside of their family, and most schools employed **oralist** teaching methods (that is, only spoken language was used with the students, not signed language). As a broader Deaf community coalesced thanks to the schools, however, the signing systems that children used to communicate at home with their families, **homesign**, began to intermingle. It's suggested that Nicaraguan Sign Language arose from all of the different homesign systems coming into contact with one another to form a more standardized signed language, and through the generations of students coming through the school, the language has been further refined by the students continuing to use it (Senghas et al. 2005).

The way that ISN has become more refined is reflected in how combinations of signs have changed as well as how the signs themselves have also changed. For instance, the overall variation in which sign(s) were used for a concept generally decreased from the first cohort of students at the school to the third cohort of students: for a concept like HORSE, the first-cohort signers that were interviewed used four distinct signs, while third-cohort signers used just two signs (Pyers & Senghas 2020). It seems like later cohorts settled on one or two of the signs that were introduced by the first cohort: doing this makes the language more systematic, and, in a sense, more "standardized." Later cohorts also separate signs that indicate the manner in which an action is happening and the path that an action is taking, rather than combining the two, which allows for more combinations – and thus a change in the syntactic structure of the language (Senghas et al. 2004). Rather than using a sign that combines a rolling manner and a downward direction simultaneously to indicate something like "rolling downhill," signers in later cohorts can instead use the rolling sign and the downward motion sign separately. Senghas and her colleagues also documented shifts between early and later cohorts in ISN in terms of the size of the signing space (signs generally got smaller, and involved more subtle body movements, in later cohorts) and the addition of vocabulary in domains like mental states and processes (later cohorts had more complex sign sets for verbs like "think," "believe," and "know"), such that within three cohorts (a period shorter than a typical human lifespan) ISN went from a signed language that shared more properties with general gestural communication than other, older signed languages to one that is basically structurally indistinguishable from those older signed languages. The speed of **linguogenesis** – language birth to language maturity – found in the ISN case has helped linguists to ask better questions about the birth and early development of languages generally.

In addition to the genesis of new languages, schools are also places where languages can survive. These are typically places where parents must choose to send their children rather than being similar to mainstream school systems. In the next section, we will be focusing on language nests, which are schools that prioritize language education for young children.

8.8.3 Language Nests and Minority Language–Medium Schooling

One method of keeping your language alive and transmitting it to future generations is to use it in school settings, particularly with young children. In Chapter 6, you learned about how infants and toddlers make short work of acquiring their languages – so perhaps it will make sense to you about why these efforts are focused on them! Children are also required to attend school, which makes it a perfect place to expose them to linguistic and cultural practices that may otherwise be lost and may already be delegitimized in the wider community but are still important to the parents or other community members.

In this section, we discuss the revitalization and maintenance of languages in three regions through the use of language nests and other opportunities for language exposure. Māori language nests can be found throughout Aotearoa (New Zealand), while Hawaiian language nests can be found on the islands of Hawaiʻi. Sámi language nests can be found mainly in the northern reaches of Finland, Norway, and Sweden. Although we only discuss language nests that cater to these three groups, we would like to emphasize that language nests and similar revitalization and maintenance programs exist around the world to serve many different Indigenous and minority languages.

Let's take a peek into some of these schools and learn more about how they work and what they need in order to be successful.

8.8.3.1   Te Reo Māori: Te Kōhanga Reo and Kura Kaupapa Māori

We will start our tour of language nests in New Zealand, which is an island nation situated southeast of Australia. In recent years, efforts have been made to relegitimize and acknowledge the Indigenous inhabitants and reclaim the Māori language, which has led to the country being referred to interchangeably as "New Zealand" and "Aotearoa."[7] As we discuss this country, we will use the Māori "Aotearoa" to refer to the country to which traders with the Dutch East India Company gave the name "New Zealand." Te reo Māori, "the Māori language," is the ancestral language of the indigenous population of Aotearoa. Māori is typologically classified as a Polynesian language, which means that it shares many common structural, phonological, and lexical characteristics with other Polynesian languages, such as Cook Islands Māori,[8] Hawaiian, Samoan, and Tahitian.

English colonizers settled in Aotearoa in around 1840 and began efforts to establish English as the language used throughout the country. In 1867, these efforts were formalized in the Native Schools Act, which mandated that English was the main language in Aotearoa and banned Māori in schools.

---

[7] Pronounced /aɔ.ˈte.a.rɔ.a/. You can listen to a pronunciation in the Te Aka Māori Dictionary: https://maoridictionary.co.nz/search?idiom = &phrase = &proverb = &loan = & histLoanWords = &&keywords = Aotearoa.

[8] Cook Islands Māori, which is spoken on the Cook Islands, is closely related to te reo Māori, but is a distinct language (Nicholas 2018).

It wasn't until 1987 that the Māori Language Act made Māori one of the official languages in Aotearoa, and also allowed some limited use of the language in courts. Today, only about 20 percent of the Māori population can use the language for everyday conversation, and 11 percent report speaking Māori "very well" (Ministry of Social Development n.d.).

By the mid 1970s, only about 20 percent of the Māori population spoke Māori fluently, and in 1995, this number had decreased to only 4 percent of the population (King 2001). Due to this dwindling ability to use Māori and the risk of losing access to their history and culture, a movement formed to teach children the Māori language and cultural practices. This movement led to the first Kōhanga Reo opening in 1982 and the first kura kaupapa Māori opening in either 1985 or 1988 (King 2001; Tocker 2015).[9]

Two types of Māori immersion schools exist today: one for children from birth to age six, and one for older children. Kōhanga Reo immerse young children in the Māori language and culture, and about 10 percent of all children were enrolled in Kōhanga Reo in 2020 according to the annual Early Childhood Education census (Evidence Data and Knowledge & Ministery of Education 2021). The language nests were formed around the idea that not only should young children be taught completely in Māori, but the family should also be involved in the governance of the school. This took place largely through meetings called hui, where those involved in the Kōhanga Reo would meet and discuss goals and outcomes for the school.

The goal of Kōhanga Reo is to immerse children in Māori language and cultural practices, initially through the native speaker community elders teaching children. Second-language speaker instructors, who tend to be younger adults, may undergo a comprehensive training program that covers topics from the philosophy of Kōhanga Reo to the Māori language to child development. To take part in this training, the person must be supported by the community supporting the Kōhanga Reo to further emphasize that the community as a whole is engaged in the learning of the students.

Kura kaupapa Māori are immersion schools that enroll children through secondary school and were established to fill the need for further Māori-medium education after children aged out of the Kōhanga Reo (Tocker 2015). There are also bilingual Māori–English tracks in primary and secondary schools in Aotearoa, but kura kaupapa Māori continue the emphasis on both language and cultural practice that was emphasized in the Kōhanga Reo. They keep this emphasis while also incorporating the curriculum followed by mainstream schools and mandated by the government.

---

[9] Tocker (2015) discusses the controversy about what "counted" as the first kura kaupapa Māori, but suffice to say that kura kaupapa Māori were established in the mid to late 1980s.

Children enrolled in Kōhanga Reo and kura kaupapa Māori typically have much higher achievement in Māori cultural and language skills than children enrolled in mainstream Aotearoa schools (McKinley & Hoskins 2011), so by this measure the Māori immersion schools are reaching their goals. However, the language is still mainly spoken by elders and is therefore still very much endangered. While the schools are supported by the government, simply having government support does not guarantee survival (although it's certainly a big step!). The challenge is to continue growing the program and continue finding more ways to get the wider community to buy into maintaining te reo Māori.

8.8.3.2 Hawaiian: Pūnana Leo and Kula Kaiapuni

Hawaiian is a Polynesian language that is indigenous to Hawai'i, which is an island archipelago in the North Pacific Ocean. Much like what happened in Aotearoa, English was eventually established as the primary language in Hawai'i through the work of missionaries and colonizers. When first visited by Europeans in 1778, Hawai'i was a monarchy; a constitutional monarchy was established by King Kamehamea III in 1840, and the monarchy was overthrown by the US Government in 1893, annexed in 1900, and admitted as a state in 1959. Between 1778 and 1878, the population of native Hawaiians decreased 94 percent, from a population of approximately 800,000 to about 47,500, and Hawaiian went from the only language spoken on the islands to English being the majority language.

In 1820, missionaries arrived, and by 1826 a basic writing system had been developed. By 1850, Hawaiians were "universal[ly]" literate (Warner 2001, p. 134). However, this began to change when English was introduced first in government-sponsored schools, and then in all schools when the monarchy was overthrown. The Organic Act in 1900 both annexed Hawai'i as a territory and mandated that all government business and education in at least 50 percent of the schools be conducted in English. In 1896, English-only instruction became mandated for all schools in Hawai'i except for those on the island of Ni'ihau, which is a private island where Hawaiian is spoken to this day.

Finally, in 1978, Hawaiian was designated as an additional official language alongside English. By this time, there were only about 2,000 native speakers of Hawaiian left, and many of them were of the older generation. This legislation granted further legitimacy to the Hawaiian language, and also formed the Office of Hawaiian Affairs in the state government. The legislation also mandated that Hawaiian language and cultural practice be supported by the state, which would eventually support arguments that Pūnana Leo should be allowed to operate under the Hawaiian Board of Education (Nakata 2017; Warner 2001).

News of the success of the Kōhanga Reo in Aotearoa had also spread to Hawai'i, which inspired the creation of Pūnana Leo for Hawaiian with the same structure and goals. Hawai'i's first Pūnana Leo opened in 1984, two years after Aotearoa's first Kōhanga Reo. The first Kula Kaiapuni, serving children from kindergarten through twelfth grade, opened in 1987 to allow the children who had attended Pūnana Leo to continue their education in Hawaiian. Today, Pūnana Leo have grown to additionally produce educational materials, both for use in the schools and commercial use, including books, radio programs, and TV shows (Wilson & Kamanā 2001). As of 2015, there were twenty-one Kula Kaiapuni operating throughout the state (Nakata 2017).

Pūnana Leo are Hawaiian-only centers, even including a physical boundary around the school to further emphasize the separation between the primarily English-speaking outside and the Hawaiian-only grounds. Children between ages three and five are enrolled, and even children who did not grow up speaking Hawaiian at home are expected to move throughout the school day exclusively in Hawaiian. Children are in the same class, not separated by age, and the older or more experienced children are expected to help the younger, newer children navigate the daily routine and memorize the short phrases that are used throughout the school to ask permission to use the bathroom or be excused from the lunch table.

Parents are also expected to participate in the school community. Families provide service to the school while their child attends, they spend at least an hour per week in a Hawaiian language class, and also meet monthly with the instructors. These are similar to the expectations of families in Aotearoa who enroll their children in Kōhanga Reo and have the intention of creating a community where the children are able to use their language in situations other than those at school and to normalize the use of Hawaiian in the family (even if the family members did not previously speak Hawaiian) and throughout the island community.

Kula Kaiapuni continue the Hawaiian-only method of instruction from the Pūnana Leo. An hour of English instruction is introduced in fifth grade, when children are about ten to eleven years old, and the amount of English used in schools gradually increases through twelfth grade, when students are seventeen to eighteen years old. The gradual introduction of English is based on the French Canadian "super-immersion" model and cements the designation of a Hawaiian-monolingual program rather than a bilingual curriculum. Kula Kaiapuni have been struggling with the politics that attempt to classify them as bilingual programs rather than monolingual Hawaiian immersion programs, which would result in different educational policies and curricular decisions that run contrary to those that are currently in use.

Students who go through Pūnana Leo and Kula Kaiapuni tend to be high academic achievers and are recipients of scholarships and awards at a higher rate than students who go through mainstream schools (Wilson & Kamanā 2001). This is contrary to what the community and the government had expected of them, and is also a positive indicator of the effectiveness of the Hawaiian-medium educational system that was developed in response to community members wanting to preserve and maintain their language.

8.8.3.3 Sámi: Giellabeassi, Kielâpierval, Ǩiõllpie'ss

In Europe, there are many minority languages but only one Indigenous language recognized by the European Union: Sámi. Revitalization efforts of Sámi utilize the language nest methodology as well as community centers and other centers, schooling opportunities, and media outlets with programming directed toward adults (Aikio-Puoskari 2018; Laihi 2017; Pasanen 2018), similar to efforts to maintain Māori and Hawaiian throughout the lifespan.

"Sámi" refers to an Indigenous people who speak a collection of distinct but related languages spoken by the Sámi people in northern Finland, Norway, Russia, and Sweden. The Sámi languages are part of the Finno-Ugric language family, which also includes majority languages like Finnish, Estonian, and Hungarian. Today, there are nine Sámi languages with living speakers (Pasanen 2018), although at one point, there were more in use. The most widely spoken and studied Sámi languages include Southern Sámi, Lule Sámi, Northern Sámi, Inari Sámi, Kildin Sámi, and Skolt Sámi, with between 300 and 500 speakers (Inari and Skolt Sámi) to anywhere from 17,000–30,000 speakers (Northern Sami; Aikio-Puoskari 2018; Nilsson 2014; Steinfjell 2014). Sámi languages are recognized as either official or minority languages in Finland, Norway, and Sweden.

The Sámi languages are all endangered, the cause of which shares a similar story with Hawaiian and Māori. The indigenous Sámi people were forced off their lands by Scandinavian settlers in the eighteenth century, and, as with many Indigenous peoples around the world, were eventually enrolled in boarding schools with the supposed goal of assimilation (Pasanen 2018). The assimilation took the shape of adopting Christianity as their religion and forcing Finnish, Swedish, or Norwegian to be spoken. Furthermore, Skolt and Inari Sámi were forced off of their ancestral lands after World War II (Laihi 2017; Pasanen 2018) and moved to Finnish-speaking lands, where their connection to the language and cultural practices was weakened. By the 1960s, only a few children were learning the Sámi languages at home.[10]

---

[10] In 1980, there were only four native speakers of Inari Sámi who were under thirty years old (Leggett 2019).

Fortunately, movements for Sámi revitalization were also beginning at around the same time (Aikio-Puoskari 2018; Pasanen 2018).

The first Sámi language nest, where children would be exposed to Skolt Sámi, opened in 1993 in Finland (Aikio-Puoskari 2018).[11] In 1997, additional language nests opened, this time for Inari Sámi (Aikio-Puoskari 2018; Pasanen 2018). The expansion of and support for Sámi language nests in the late 1990s led to the slow reversal of the language shift that had taken place for the Sámi languages and is still ongoing as of this writing (Pasanen 2018).

As with Hawaiian and Māori language nests, Sámi language nests cater toward very young children to integrate cultural and linguistic practices early in life. As the language nests are situated under the jurisdiction of a country's government (such as Finland), there are requirements and expectations for what a daycare facility should provide that vary from country to country. Within those constraints, however, there is focus on traditional Sámi cultural practices woven into the children's daily life, such as making food from traditional Sámi recipes or visiting local reindeer herders, and, of course, focus on the Sámi language (Braut 2010; Harju-Luukkainen et al. 2022; Laihi 2017).

Several researchers note that because there is no or very little infrastructure outside of the language nests to use Sámi, especially if a child's parents do not speak Sámi or they live outside of the current areas that are more densely populated by Sámi, there is little incentive to use Sámi "on the weekend" (Braut 2010; Harju-Luukkainen et al. 2022). There are also only a few Sámi bilingual schools for primary and secondary schooling throughout the four countries with Sámi speakers, so unless it is used at home, children may not have an opportunity to continue using Sámi. Finland is one of the countries that has limited government-sponsored TV and radio programs in Sámi languages, most of which are directed toward adults, but there are a few for children (Leggett 2019).

The Sámi languages are still very much endangered despite the overall enthusiasm for revitalization in the Sámi community. Part of this is due to a lack of speakers of the Sámi languages to teach students at all levels, but part of this is also a lack of resources outside the language nest. When 70 percent of Sámi speakers live outside the areas that are traditionally occupied by Sámi people, it is difficult to connect to a broad community of other Sámi speakers as well. With forceable relocation of Sámi speakers continuing until very recently, and comparatively recent governmental support and smaller population than Māori and Hawaiian speakers, it may not be surprising that

---

[11] Braut (2010, p. 38) also notes that a small Lule Sámi daycare was established in 1989 by four parents in Norway.

it is difficult to gather a critical mass of Sámi speakers. However, revitalization is a long and slow process, so we shouldn't give up hope.

8.9 Conclusion

In this chapter, we've described schools as both dangerous and hopeful places for language communities. In many places in the world, people spend a significant percentage of their childhood in schools, and schools are a powerful force in the development of our self-perceptions, our identities, and our political and economic power as adults. Those school experiences are part of the complex of our human development, and what happens in school affects and is affected by what happens outside of them. We know, for instance, that when schools insist on ideologies of monolingualism, students who enter school systems speaking a different language or dialect than the mainstream can suffer. We also know that beliefs about how teachers should speak can affect who gets hired in schools – regardless of their skills or competencies. And we know that these ideologies of monolingualism harm monolingual children just as much as they harm children who enter the school system with other languages in their toolkit – these ideologies often lead to systematic defunding of foreign language education, which means that children get fewer opportunities to be exposed to languages other than their own and, as a result, deprives them of the known cognitive benefits of exposure to multiple languages.

For all of these reasons, what we have discussed in this chapter is intimately related to the topics we've investigated in previous chapters (particularly infants' language development in Chapter 6) and will continue to investigate in future ones. You might want to come back to this discussion as you read more about language and the law in Chapter 11 and learn more about the boarding school / residential school era in Chapter 12.

For now, consider reflecting on your own experiences of language at school. How has your linguistic repertoire fared in your education so far? How has your experience of teachers, professors, and teaching assistants been tinted by the lenses of your language experiences and ideologies? What kinds of schools are around you today, and how are they supporting the linguistic diversity in your community?

Linguist in the Community

- Start and/or engage in a social media campaign in your community that celebrates the advantages of many types of language practice in the classroom. You might be inspired by the work of Baker-Bell (2020, p. 86).

- Volunteer as a tutor or helper through a local organization to assist children or adults in literacy. You may find such classes at a local library or cultural center. Engage respectfully and openly with students to help reinforce the view that they are not deficient based on how they use language, and help them identify the systematicity and beauty in the way they speak, sign, read, and/or write.
- Find out about the language policies at schools in your area. Are there schools in which students are forbidden to speak certain languages? Are there schools that are particularly welcome to a linguistically diverse community? Get involved in local school board governance where you can advocate for linguistically informed policies and practices for both teachers and students.

Linguist in the Classroom

- Discuss excerpts from literature in which authors describe experiences with linguistic discrimination. Consider works such as "Mother Tongue" by Amy Tan, "How to Tame a Wild Tongue" by Gloria Anzaldúa, or "Discovering the Power of Language" by Malcolm X – most of which are freely available online. Discuss with your classmates how these authors help us better understand why it is important for schools to support the full linguistic diversity of their student and teacher populations.
- Create an "I sound like a scholar" campaign for your campus, inspired by this one at North Carolina State University: www.youtube.com/watch?v=cjfC-1lg0rY.
- Organize the class into small groups and ask each group to generate a list of things they remember being taught about language in school. As groups report out, create a master list that has the following categories: "spelling and punctuation" (for example, capitalize the first word after a colon), "words" (for example, don't use ain't), and "phrases and sentences" (for example, don't end a sentence with a preposition). Then pick items from each group and discuss: Where do you think this rule came from? Whose language does this rule privilege? Whose language does this rule stigmatize? Does the rule apply to both formal and informal language? Does it apply to writing and speaking and signing? Why do you think you were taught this rule?
- Investigate the linguistic diversity of instructors at your school or in your department, and collect publicly available student course evaluation information for these instructors. Do you find patterns that suggest that instructors who have particular types of language backgrounds tend to

have higher or lower student satisfaction ratings? You can also share notes about your and your peers' experiences in the classroom learning from instructors with unfamiliar patterns of language use. As you have had more experience learning from a variety of speakers, have you seen a difference in your ability to understand and focus on their language?

Glossary

Antiracist Black Language Pedagogy An approach to language teaching advocated by Baker-Bell that understands students' linguistic repertoires as well-formed, valued, appropriate, and correct. While Baker-Bell's approach is focused on antiblack racism, antiracist language pedagogies are well suited to communities harmed by traditions of racism generally.

bilingual education A system of formal education in which teaching and learning are conducted in two languages; in the US, this is typically (but not always) English and Spanish. In bilingual education programs, the goal is often to provide students who do not speak a majority or national language with instruction that assists them in learning that majority or national language.

critical language pedagogy A framework for teaching and learning in which students and instructors question, debate, and critically examine the taken-for-granted language ideologies, as well as the power relations that (re)enforce them, as part of the language arts curricula in schools.

de facto "Of the fact"; this refers to things that are true in the world, whether or not they are supposed to be.

de jure "Of the law"; this refers to things that are true by virtue of legislation or other official act.

deficit-based language pedagogies Teaching practices that presume that students' home languages are incorrect, impoverished, or inappropriate, and that the goal of instruction is the replacement of those language practices with some other standard, which is understood to be "correct," "proper," and "appropriate."

disproportionality A pattern in which some groups of people are more or less likely to be harmed, or to benefit, from a system – regardless of their prevalence in the overall population.

double consciousness A term developed by African American sociologist W. E. B. DuBois to describe how Black people came to perceive or understand themselves through the lens of the dominant white supremacist culture.

homesign A system of often informal gestural communication that develops in family or small social groups that include one or more deaf people. Homesign systems often emerge when these families or social groups do not have access to a signed language community.

ideology of monolingualism A set of beliefs, attitudes, and practices that support the idea that there is only one language that should be used within a community.

immersion programs Language programs in which 100 percent (or as close to 100 percent as possible) of the teaching and learning activities occur within the target language.

intersectionality The social scientific analytic framework that understands social identities and social structures of privilege and discrimination as overlapping and interconnected.

language nest A community-based educational practice that brings together very young children and community members of multiple generations and offers language immersion in the community language in an intergenerational context.

linguogenesis Language birth.

majority language A language that is at least believed to be spoken by a plurality or majority of people living in a given community; this will typically also be a language with high prestige and one that is connected to social, political, and/ or economic power.

minority language A language that is at least believed to be spoken by a smaller number of people in a community than the majority language(s). Depending on the social, cultural, and historical context, minority languages may or may not have prestige or be seen as connected to social, political, and/or economic power.

multilingual education An educational system that supports learning and teaching in a variety of languages, not necessarily as a means of moving students from a minority to a majority language.

oralist A perspective on language that privileges spoken over signed languages. In education, oralist traditions seek to teach deaf and hard of hearing students to function primarily through the local spoken language, using techniques such as lip reading and speech therapy.

raciolinguistics An approach to linguistic research that investigates the ways in which communities use language to construct concepts of race and how communities' ideas about race affect their linguistic practices and concepts (Alim et al. 2016).

Respectability Language Pedagogies Language instructional approaches that present assimilation to a particular set of linguistic norms as a key or necessary path to "respectability" within a larger speech community. Minority or stigmatized language behavior is not necessarily seen as broken or bad, but it is seen as an impediment to "success."

standard language A variety of a language that is perceived to be or is treated as a mainstream form of communication, often having undergone some degree of formal codification of grammatical rules and norms of pronunciation.

TEFL/TESL Teaching English as a Foreign Language / Teaching English as a Second Language. These are labels for a set of academic specializations and an industry that is built around the teaching of some varieties of English (typically White American English or White British English) to students who did not grow up with those languages. TEFL/TESL programs are found in schools in the US, where they are meant to serve immigrant students, but also around the world in both public and private educational contexts.

Recommended Readings

Whether you're reading this book as part of your own formal schooling or as an independent project, you'll have a great deal of personal experience about the use and teaching of language varieties in educational settings. If you'd like to learn more about how your own experience might align with or be different from some of the case studies we covered in this chapter, we recommend you use your local college or university library to check out some of the recommended readings listed below.

Alim, H. S., Rickford, J. R., & Ball, A. F. (2016). *Raciolinguistics: How Language Shapes Our Ideas about Race.* Oxford University Press.

Baker-Bell, A. (2020). *Linguistic Justice: Black Language, Literacy, Identity, and Pedagogy.* Routledge.

Charity Hudley, A. H., & Mallinson, C. (2011). *Understanding English language Variation in U.S. Schools.* Teachers College Press.

Figueroa, M. (2024). Decolonizing (psycho) linguistics means dropping the "language gap" rhetoric. In A. H. Charity Hudley, C. Mallinson, & M. Bucholtz (Eds.), *Decolonizing Linguistics* (pp. 157–172). Oxford University Press.

Fought, C. (2002). *Chicano English in Context.* Springer.

Labov, W. (1970). Finding out about children's language. In D. Steinberg (Ed.), *Working Papers in Communication* (pp. 1–29). Pacific Speech Association.

Leap, W. L. (1993). *American Indian English.* University of Utah Press.

Lippi-Green, R. (2012). *English with an Accent: Language, Ideology, and Discrimination in the United States* (2nd ed.). Routledge.

Philips, S. U. (1982). *The Invisible Culture: Communication in Classroom and Community on the Warm Springs Indian Reservation.* Longman, Inc.

Valentinsson, M.-C. (2020). English and bivalent class indexicality in Buenos Aires, Argentina. In S. Brunn & R. Kehrein (Eds.), *Handbook on the Changing World Language Map* (pp. 1–18). Springer.

9 | Languages Meet Genders and Sexualities Where They Are

Imagine you have a human-shaped doll in your hands that you want to make look like someone you know. To make this doll have any kind of appearance, you will need to make several decisions: What clothes should it wear? How should its face and hair look? How should it speak? As it is currently, the doll is a blank canvas and could be anyone at all. You would make different choices depending on who you wanted to model the doll after – your cousin Gracie probably makes different choices than your friend Butch.

Now you might imagine yourself as the doll, because you make similar kinds of decisions every day. You end up deciding the type of clothes you want to wear, how your hair and face should look, and how you speak – and all of these decisions are influenced by how you want to present yourself to the world. They may also be influenced by the physical characteristics of your body and how you were brought up by your family: if you were assigned female at birth, your caregivers may have clothed you in dresses and bows, while if you were assigned male at birth, your caregivers might have avoided the color pink and dressed you in jeans and t-shirts.

As you grew up and could begin dressing yourself, you probably chose clothing that was different from that which your caregivers dressed you in (and, maybe, this was shocking to your caregivers). You also adopted or created slang that was used among your peers and preferred social groups, you wore your hair and makeup in a particular way, and you may also have changed how you speak, dress, and act depending on who you socialize with. In short, you are constructing an **identity**. While there are many facets of an identity, the one that we'll focus on in this chapter is the linguistic facet.

In this chapter, we will discuss how people use language to construct identities and identify with different social groups, particularly with regard to gender and sexuality. Studies in communities around the world and with individuals across the lifespan have documented patterns of people using language in different ways depending on whether they want to convey a more masculine, feminine, or androgynous persona, or to mark an affiliation with different sexual identities. You may already be familiar with people using different types of pronouns based on which gender they are, but in addition to the pronouns people use, there are other ways of using language to construct an identity both on and off the gender binary. We hope that you might begin reading this chapter by thinking about your own experiences, values, and definitions of "gender," and your ideas about how the social categories of gender in your community have matched (or mismatched) your observations.

9.1 Grammatical Gender Bumps Up against Social Gender

You may already be familiar with the concept of **grammatical gender** in language: not only humans and animals, but also inanimate objects, are associated with certain articles and word endings depending on which gender they are. If you're an English speaker, it can be very odd to think of a bridge (*eine Brücke*, German) and a rock (*une pierre*, French) and an apple (*una manzana*, Spanish) as taking the same "feminine" distinction as a human woman. This is just one of the reasons why linguists tend to think of grammatical gender as a classification system rather than anything based on social gender.

In languages that have true grammatical gender, every noun in the language will belong to one of some number of categories. In languages of the Indo-European family (the one that English, Spanish, Russian, Hindi, and many others belong to), the categories are typically called "masculine," "feminine," and (sometimes) "neuter," and they're sort of associated with those concepts. There are also different systems of grammatical gender crosslinguistically, not all of which use categories associated with genders or sexualities. For example, languages of the Algonquian family of the Northern US typically sort nouns into two categories that are translated as "animate" and "inanimate." Niger-Congo languages of Africa may have as many as twenty noun classes, such that the categories are referred to by linguists as, for example, "class 1," "class 2," ... "class 20" (see Corbett 2013 for more detail). All grammatical gender systems pose a problem in that no matter what the set of categories is, there are always nouns that don't fit naturally into one category (or that might fit naturally into more than one) based on their meanings. But these systems impose a one-to-one mapping of nouns to categories – and this results in lots of semantic weirdnesses (for example, in the Algonquian language Blackfoot, the word for "strawberry" is grammatically inanimate but the word for "raspberry" is grammatically

9.1 Grammatical Gender Bumps Up against Social Gender

animate; in German[1] the word *Mädchen* "girl" is grammatically neuter instead of the expected feminine, etc.).

In the grammatical gender systems with which you're likely familiar, the grammatical genders are conflated with social gender. In those cases, how do we talk about non-binary people or groups of people where more than one gender is represented in languages that require you to pick a gender, either masculine or feminine?

There are, fortunately, many solutions to this. In Spanish, you might refer to *mis amigues* "my friends" rather than *mis amigos*,[2] and in Swedish, you might use the pronoun *hen* "they" instead of the masculine *hon* or the feminine *han*. You might have seen "Latine" and "Chicane," or "Latin@/Chican@," written out. There are other options, too, such as using singular "they" or **neopronouns** like xe/xem/xyr[3] to more accurately reflect a person's gender identity when it does not fit within the bounds of "he" or "she."

Accurate gender representation is also important outside of pronoun use. In a study on German, research participants named more famous women when they were asked to name three famous people with a "capital-I form" (where the feminine ending is denoted by a capital letter "i") like *PolitikerInnen* "politicians" instead of a masculine generic form like *Politiker* "politicians" or a combined form like *Politikerinnen und Politiker* "politicians (fem.) and politicians (masc.)" (Stahlberg et al. 2001). The study's authors interpret this to mean that masculine generics include a component of "maleness" in their meaning and are therefore not truly generic.

Linguist Lauren Ackerman (2019) is, to our knowledge, the first person to clarify the different types of "gendered language" that we work with on a daily basis, and then to propose a model of how all of the different types interact with each other and our linguistic cognition. Briefly, her model outlines three types of gender: grammatical gender, **conceptual gender**, and **biosocial gender**. Grammatical gender is what we outlined above – cases like *eine Brücke* being feminine in German. Conceptual gender is the gender that we usually associate with a noun: cowgirls are usually female, while

---

[1] It might be helpful to note that English is closely related to German. As such, English used to have a very similar system of grammatical gender. This system has been almost entirely lost in modern English.
[2] In many languages, including in Spanish, the "default" grammatical gender to use when you're referring to a group of people with multiple genders represented is masculine.
[3] These neopronouns are ordered in the same way as "she/her/hers" or "they/them/their," so you might use them like so: "Xe loves xyr cat named Whiskers. Whiskers snuggles with xem every night." We have generally heard this set of neopronouns pronounced /zi, zɛm, zɚ/. There are also many other examples of neopronouns!

bikers on motorcycles are stereotypically male. Biosocial gender is the "actual" gender of someone in conversation, which affects the pronouns they use and, in many languages, some of the morphemes that are added to words that describe them (for instance, a female politician in German is a *Politikerin*, while a male politician is a *Politiker*).

Ackerman argues that each of these types of genders, and how they are represented in various languages, affect how we process language. For example, we should see differences in how quickly we read a sentence or differences in brain activity if we read something like "the cowgirl forgot his lasso at the party," and the cowgirl is actually your friend Teddy (who uses he/him/his pronouns) dressing up for Halloween, as opposed to a cowgirl who uses she/her/hers pronouns forgetting her lasso and being misgendered.

The details of Ackerman's model are more nuanced than this brief overview, but her definitions of different types of gender in language are helpful for us as a starting point. We frequently find ourselves in a space between grammatical gender and conceptual or biosocial gender, and being able to clarify what we mean and which piece of language in gender we're talking about is useful.

Another place in which grammatical gender bumps up against social gender is in the use of pronouns in languages such as English. English and some other Indo-European languages are unusual crosslinguistically in providing an at least four-way distinction in its third person pronoun series, as seen in (1):

(1)   Third person singular pronouns, nominative forms:
        "he"   = conceptually or biosocially animate and male
        "she" = conceptually or biosocially animate and female
        "it"   = conceptually or biosocially inanimate
        "they" = conceptually or biosocially animate

English is particularly unusual in that it has retained these gendered forms at the same time as it has lost virtually all of its grammatical gender. Old English (spoken before about AD 1066) had a three-way grammatical gender system, much like German's. But during the centuries between 1066 and 1600 – the Middle English period – that system had fallen away. As a result, English no longer assigns common nouns like "sun," "book," and "table" to any grammatical gender category.

Note that the English system in (1) includes not just information about the conceptual or biosocial gender of the referent of the pronoun, but also about its **animacy**. Animacy is a term that, when used in grammar, typically refers to a referent's aliveness, and/or its ability to think and choose, and/or its

9.1 Grammatical Gender Bumps Up against Social Gender

ability to move independently.[4] For example, some English speakers will prefer (2) over (3), depending on our notions of "animacy":

(2)   That cow is kissing her new baby.

(3)   That cow is kissing its new baby.

But we won't (most likely) find speakers who are willing to say (5) instead of (4) if we're talking about humans.

(4)   That new mom is kissing her new baby.

(5)   *That new mom is kissing its new baby.

In fact, (5) is tantamount to claiming that the new mom isn't human, and may not be alive at all. When it comes to the mapping of conceptual gender onto third person pronouns in English, we've already had to associate the referent of those pronouns with animacy. Within the domain of living, or cognizant, or independently mobile entities, English gives us the option to either also identify the referent's conceptual or biosocial gender or not do so when we choose the pronouns we'll use.

Linguist Kirby Conrod (2020) has written a great deal about the interaction of the grammatical function of these pronouns and their implications with regard to gender. In their 2020 chapter in the Oxford Handbook of Language and Sexuality, Conrod points out that each of the four forms in (1) have functioned as singular pronouns in English for at least the last few hundred years. "Singular they" in particular has been used in a variety of contexts even by the most prescriptive grammarians, who, for a time in the late nineteenth and early twentieth centuries, began to emphasize the stylistic practice of using "he" as a singular pronoun when referring to a hypothetical or otherwise gender-ambiguous referent. This fad has now largely passed, but there are still in the US at the time of writing some groups who are actively advocating that pronoun choice in English is some kind of politically controversial action (see, for example, Hillard 2019).

---

[4] Grammatical animacy is used in some languages Indigenous to North America, particularly those of the Algonquian family. In these languages, each noun is assigned to one of two classes in which most (but not all) of the referents that are, e.g., whole living things are assigned to the "animate" class and all others to the "inanimate" class. That these classes are in some way truly grammatical rather than referential is confirmed by comparisons between, e.g., the nouns for "strawberry" and "raspberry" in Blackfoot, which assigns one to the "animate" and the other to the "inanimate" class (Bliss 2017). Diné Bizaad (Navajo, Willie 1991) and other languages in its family utilize a conceptual/biosocial notion of animacy based on the ability of a thing to move independently as part of their grammars, though not as a way of organizing noun classes.

Conrod notes that honoring speakers' gender self-presentation when using pronouns to refer to them is easily understood as a politeness issue rather than as a political one; contrary to claims that using a gendered pronoun could constitute an "error" because of some imagined mismatch between the gender of the pronoun and the referent's "biological sex," we know that gender is a social and cultural construction rather than a biological one. And in a community in which people are targeted for violence based on sex, sexuality, and gender, it's easy to understand the need to manage our linguistic resources in a way that is helpful rather than harmful to others.

9.2 Languages and Genders

In 1973, linguist Robin Lakoff wrote what many consider to be the foundational paper that defines markers of feminine language in white, middle-class, English-speaking communities, particularly North American English: "Language and Woman's Place." In the decades since, people have continued to research and define what linguistic practices make someone seem more feminine, and how these practices differ in a variety of locations, populations, and other contexts. Lakoff wrote this paper in the middle of the second-wave feminist movement in the United States, where women were agitating for the ability to obtain the same level of schooling and employment as men, equal funding in institutions that were provided with federal funding (which became Title IX), and many more issues.[5]

Lakoff's (1973) primary argument was that there are different ways that men and women use language,[6] as well as different ways that language is used with reference to women as opposed to men, and that these differences lead to discrimination against women and viewing them as lesser than men (p. 46). One of the differences that Lakoff highlights is the use of precise color terms and "gentler" epithets – it's unremarkable when a woman describes something as "mauve" or "lovely," or says "Oh dear!" in response to an emotionally charged event or statement, but when a man does so, it's noteworthy at best, and potentially also seen as grounds for bullying and teasing at worst. Why? Because this type of language is reserved for women and men who can be classified with women, like gay men, hippies, male

---

[5] It should be noted that these issues are by no means resolved fifty years later, particularly for transgender people and people of color.

[6] These differences are framed more as differences in degree rather than differences in kind. Lakoff does not posit that women's and men's language are categorically different, but that they are gradiently different.

academics, ministers, and upper-class British men, who are similarly "'uninvolved [in business or political affairs]', or 'out of power'," or otherwise "shielded from harsh realities" (Lakoff 1973, p. 53).

Lakoff also points out that when women enter the masculine sphere of having a career, their position must be modified: woman doctor, saleswoman, and so on. Words that should have the same meaning except for gender, like "master" and "mistress" or "bachelor" and "spinster," also have very different connotations. The feminine word in the pair often has negative connotations, while the masculine word typically has neutral or positive connotations. Lakoff even points out that activities that are seen as less serious, or even trivial, tend to be modified by "lady" rather than "woman": she compares "one-woman shows," put on by a single female actor, to rarer (or perhaps nonexistent) "one-lady shows," which strike her as being put on by a dilettante rather than a serious actor – or even "*Ladies' Lib" or "*Ladies Strike for Peace" (instead of "Women's Lib" or "Women Strike for Peace"), both of which she marks with an asterisk as ungrammatical (Lakoff 1973, p. 60).

You may have noticed that although some of the language Lakoff used to discuss her points feels antiquated in the current time, we are still feeling our way out in terms of gendered language use today. Women's voices and ways of speaking are continually criticized by people of all genders in these English-speaking communities, and are also blamed for holding them back in the workplace. Linguist Lisa Davidson briefly described the various dimensions along which women's voices are thought to be annoying or deficient; namely, women are perceived to be shrill, use uptalk (where statements might sound like they end in a question?), use "sexy baby voices" that are nasal, high pitched, and full of uptalk, and use vocal fry (Davidson 2017).

On the bright side, Lakoff's work has generated additional questions and refinements to her original claims. The notion that men and women use language differently has evolved into a broad field of study within sociolinguistics and linguistic anthropology where women's language use continues to be analyzed and theorized and is also compounded with other facets that shape an identity of "female" or "woman" or "lady" for different groups in different cultures and societies. In several of the sections that follow, we discuss some of the ways that people claim gendered identities, focusing mostly on how language is used in these situations.

9.2.1 Gendered Expressions Differ across Communities

Lakoff's scholarship about "women's speech" in English, and work by related scholars produced in the 1970s and beyond almost always focused on the language behavior of white women in white contexts (Morgan 2015).

African American Women's Language (AAWL) emerges from a system of multiple constraints – some that have been imposed on all Black Americans' speech by the particular form of violent racism that marks US history and culture, with the additional expectation of subservience to white and male forms, particularly when speaking in spaces where white people are listening. These include expectations to "use formal address when speaking to a White person ... do not speak unless spoken to ... do not speak assuredly (use hedges), and do not make statements (overuse tag questions), and so on" (Morgan 2015, p. 821). But AAWL also draws on a full and rich pool of linguistic and extra linguistic features indexing solidarity, joy, and strength: like innovative usage of reported speech ("my momma always told me..."), culturally significant diminutives ("sista," "girl"), collaborative and multivocal speech styles. It should not be surprising that constructions of Black femininity draw from a more variable and diverse reservoir of cultural and social resources than is often discussed in scholarship by and about white people, nor that speakers develop complex repertoires that draw from and index the intersectionality of Black and female identities.

Importantly, Lakoff's work and the literature that has followed focuses on gendered language in North American English-speaking communities. While their findings may also be relevant elsewhere, they would not claim to be describing "women's language" universally. The roles and expectations that are connected with constructing and sharing one's gender are far from universal; instead, they vary in all the same ways that other cultural patterns vary. We think it's useful to compare the findings for North American English with those found in a variety of other language communities of North America, so here we'll provide a few brief case studies on the linguistic construction of gender in several Indigenous communities. The examples that follow are short sketches, and we intend them as examples that help us to understand some of the ways in which the linguistic construction of gender can occur.

In the Tohono O'odham community, an Indigenous nation of the American Southwest, women's and men's language varies, but not in the same ways – and not with the same consequences – described in Lakoff's and Davidson's work. Tohono O'odham is a member of the Uto-Aztecan language family and is spoken at the time of writing by something like 15,000 people in the US and Mexico (Ethnologue 2023). According to work by Ofelia Zepeda and Jane Hill (1998) O'odham speakers share a general understanding that speaking at a low volume is appropriate for adults, and speaking too loudly is indicative of childishness or rudeness. Women, particularly those of middle age or older, utilize a distinctive speech style involving a pulmonic ingressive airstream – essentially speaking on an inhale rather than on an exhale. This style is not used by men, but in contrast to the situation in English-speaking communities in the same geographical area, women aren't criticized for using it.

Women's speech in Koasati, a Muskogean language of the US Southeast spoken by the Coushatta tribe, as well as men's varieties, have been the subject of anthropological research since at least 1944, when Mary Haas discussed differences between men's and women's speech that includes both lexical differences and pronunciation differences. Haas' (1944) work shows that in that community, the base form of words and pronunciations is the women's form – and men's speech varies based on a set of rules for deriving the men's forms from the women's. Similarly, in Gros Ventre, an Algonkin language spoken in Montana in the US, women's and men's speech has been shown to involve different pronunciation of certain phonemes (Flannery 1946), with the "women's" form also being used by men when they are speaking carefully or clearly to outsiders (Taylor 1982).

The Indigenous California language Yana had distinctive forms of speech that are identified as "men's" and "women's" speech, but the variety one used was determined primarily by the gender of the addressee in relation to that of the speaker (Silver & Miller 1998): "Men's speech was used by men when talking to men. In all other cases, women's speech was used, that is, in men talking to women, and women talking to either men or women" (p. 157). Women used men's speech in some cases, for example when directly quoting men who were speaking to other men.

We note that in describing the Yana example, we used the past tense. Yana was spoken in Northern California and is one of the many language communities that was destroyed during the Gold Rush of the middle nineteenth century. We do not at present know that Yana is being spoken in any contemporary community, but it could be – many Indigenous California peoples are in the process of recovering languages that might otherwise be lost. Cushatta and O'odham are definitely not discussed in the past tense; both are language communities that are continuing to change and grow over time.

We further note that all Indigenous communities in the US were subject to extensive and often brutal missionization by white Christian denominations starting in the earliest years after first contact with Europeans. Missionization may have played a role in the reification of binary gender categories in a number of communities who had formerly and traditionally identified more than two genders – a practice that is found in a variety of cultures around the world, and likely existed in many communities in Indigenous North America (Roscoe 1987). Far from being a universal property of human societies, gender binarity is a profoundly social construction specific to particular cultures and historical periods (Herdt 2020).

On Madagascar, an island off the southeast coast of Africa, Elinor Keenan (later, Elinor Ochs, from studies we discussed earlier in this book) described a community of Malagasy speakers that sharply differentiates men's and women's language (Keenan 1974). Men are praised for their ability to "twist words" and speak very indirectly, with many metaphors, idioms, and proverbs, and will use a lot of effort to avoid any face threats.[7] This happens even when someone causing trouble is caught in the act – being nonconfrontational is the norm, and men in particular are expected to show no open expression of anger or any direct criticism. Women, on the other hand, are the community members who can speak openly and directly and can engage in confrontation. Women, therefore, are the members of the community who keep order, reprimand children, and do the bargaining at market, all of which require some form of straightforwardness and confrontation.

In doing our research for this chapter, we noticed an important gap in scholarly work on language and gender – that is, we found little or no work that focuses on language and gender in signed language communities. How might speakers of a signed language index their gender identities or those of their interlocutors? We would certainly expect this to be a rich area of research, and would be delighted if readers of this book might be inspired to explore that question.

The most important thing to understand from this discussion is that any ideas we have about peoples' genders "naturally" or "normally" leading to particular linguistic practices are wrong; instead, the relationship between our linguistic practices and our gender identities is complicated, culturally specific, and to some extent arbitrary. The good news is that this means the study of language and gender will provide many fascinating research findings from many different speech and language communities. In the next section, we'll review several cases in which the performance of gender identities is conducted via specific linguistic behaviors.

9.2.2 Gendered Linguistic Performances Also Differ
9.2.2.1 Is There a Phonetics of Gender?

It is not uncommon for us to hear or read about "typical" or "natural" differences between men's and women's voices – for example, men might be said to have deeper voices (lower pitch) and perhaps less pitch variation than women. These presumed differences are often thought to be driven by

---

[7] If you don't remember what "face threats" are, they threaten the social status of people in conversation. For a more detailed reminder, review Chapter 2.

our biology. Zimman (2018) points out the following problems with such a perspective:

1. Different social and cultural groups have different ideas about what constitutes "sounding like" someone of a particular gender;
2. Gendered differences in the sounds of our voices seem to emerge when we're being socialized into our gender identities, not from early childhood;
3. The phonetics of "gendered" speech can differ between individuals within a single social or cultural group; and
4. Speakers who wish to do so can change their vocal performance to take on different gender identities at different times.

These factors suggest that whatever we're doing when we're using language, it is not primarily determined by our biologies, nor is it necessarily fixed during our lifetimes.

9.2.2.2 Conversational Shitwork

In the late 1970s and early 1980s, sociologist Pamela M. Fishman recorded three couples' conversations in the home for a total of fifty-two hours. When analyzing these conversations, Fishman found that, indeed, the men and women in the couples interacted differently. In this case, men were typically able to introduce a topic of conversation successfully, while women were less successful in changing topics; women asked more questions and introduced topics differently than men did. Women seemed to do more of the support work and maintenance to keep conversations going after men introduced and pursued topics. Fishman deemed women the "'shitworkers' of routine interaction" (Fishman 1978, p. 405), and the work of maintaining conversational interactions has since been termed **conversational shitwork**. Conversational shitwork (or **maintenance work**, if you prefer), is so thoroughly associated with women's speech that phone sex fantasy narratives espouse many of the qualities of it to be relatable to male audiences: the recording of the woman on the other end of the line will ask questions, show that she is agreeable, and show that she enjoys listening – presumably to her male "interlocutor" (Hall 1995).

9.2.3 We Teach Toddlers to Be Girls and Boys

Where exactly does this difference in language use come from? The specifics of language use, as we hope you have seen, aren't biological imperatives. Instead, we can exploit how we use language to show that we are a member of one social group or another. How we show that we are part of a social group may (and indeed, *does*) change throughout our lives as we move fluidly between social circles.

Much like we don't explicitly teach infants to use language, we also don't sit children down and say, "If you want to sound like a woman, do this. If you want to sound like a man, do that." (Occasionally an adult might say something like "Little girls don't talk like that!", but explicit dictums like that are not how children internalize these norms). However, the ways that adults interact with children, the behaviors they praise, and the things that are valued by society *do* implicitly teach children how to act based on their assigned gender. Even toddlers are treated differently depending on whether they're little boys or little girls: boys are encouraged to introduce new topics of conversation and participate in public displays of quick-wittedness with both their peers and adults, while girls are encouraged to "fuss at" community members as a way to practice asserting themselves, or to make themselves scarce, depending on the culture of their surrounding community (Heath 1983). Parents use different forms of language with their children, depending both on the gender of the parent *and* on the gender of the child (Gleason 1987). Children even do things like manipulate their vocal tracts to attain lower and higher pitches depending on their sex well before any physical changes of puberty change their voice (Sachs et al. 1973).

These gendered expectations show up in how children interact, both with others of the same gender and in mixed groups. In many North American and West European communities, girls' interactional style tends to be more collaborative in nature, while boys' tends to be more competitive (Maltz & Borker 1982; Mulac et al. 2001). This was first suggested by anthropologists Daniel Maltz and Ruth Borker after having observed groups of children playing in same- and mixed-gender groups. They (and subsequent papers) discussed that the children had been socialized into such different gendered expectations that it was as if they were engaging in the same kind of cross-cultural communication that adults from different social contexts do, resulting in similar types of miscommunications and misunderstandings.

All of this work, however, looks at children in Western contexts (and mostly white Western contexts). Based on some of the research we review in this chapter, we can expect that children are essentially expected to – and do – perform like the adult counterparts of their assigned gender. We see this because we tend to think of children as miniature, inexperienced adult members of society, and therefore expect them to behave like members of the society they live in (Ochs & Schieffelin 2017). As children acquire language, they also acquire other facets associated with community membership, like styles, dialects, conversational norms, and so on. As the child grows, they become more adept at using different linguistic mannerisms to index (or socially point to) their multifaceted identities as a community member – gender, socioeconomic status, age, and so forth. Thus, the specifics that we have talked about so far for children refer to mainly white, middle-class, Western populations, but we can expect that a Kaluli girl in Papua New Guinea, for example, will grow up emulating other Kaluli women in her language use.

9.2.4 Is Every Girl a Valley Girl?

Parody and satirical performances can be used to highlight and exaggerate features of speech that are associated with a particular group. "Valley Girl" speech is one example of this. You may have heard it used by female characters in TV and movies who are meant to seem vapid, materialistic, wealthy, vain, and so forth. You might think of Cher Horowitz in the movie *Clueless* or Elle Woods in *Legally Blonde* as characters with this stereotypical speech pattern. The key in both of these movies is that each woman has a storyline where, despite their Valley Girl speech, they are shown as smart and successful, and care at least as much about their loved ones as their appearance.

Valley Girl speech is characterized by several different features, like vocal fry, uptalk, shifted vowels compared to canonical productions of English vowels,[8] using words and phrases such as "like" or "oh my god" frequently, using tag questions like "you know?", and having a more variable pitch throughout an utterance (Slobe 2018). In addition to these linguistic features, the persona of a Valley Girl includes other identifying features like an attachment to their phones (landlines in the 1980s and 90s; cell phones from the 2000s to present), Starbucks drinks, Apple products, blonde hair, and a propensity for taking selfies and rolling their eyes (Slobe 2018). More recently, **creaky voice** – sometimes called **vocal fry** – has also become associated with the speech of young women. Creaky voice occurs when a person is speaking with low airflow and very relaxed vocal folds at the lowest pitch of their vocal register, which results in a voice quality that has been described as "guttural," "rough," or "gravelly" by non-linguists. The frequency of a speaker's voice is much lower when they are using a creaky modality, which in many Western linguistic contexts would index a more masculine way of speaking. Indeed, some vocal coaches suggest that transgender men who want to sound more masculine use more creaky voice (and more on this later). But throughout the first two decades of the 2000s,

---

[8] You might remember the Northern Cities Chain Shift from our discussion of phonetics and phonology in Chapter 2 – there is also a vowel shift occurring in California English, which has been descriptively termed the California Shift.

we have seen this modality of voice increasingly being used to index the stereotypical Valley Girl persona. As you'll see a bit later on, however, creaky voice is highly flexible in what kinds of gendered identities it can index.

When someone is parodying a white girl, they have this large array of features to draw on, including those that aren't associated with language that a person is using. This means that they may draw on some subset of features to create a character that effectively indexes a Valley Girl persona without saying anything at all, like a blonde white girl taking endless selfies on her iPhone while she sips a Starbucks beverage. You might notice that these features are used not only by cisgender women, but also by people of all genders. Valley Girl speech is so intricately tied to a single gender, though, that even if a cisgender man were to use each of these features, he would likely not be categorized as a "Valley Girl" but as another identity entirely.

Valley Girl speech and its related characteristics are so thoroughly associated with girlhood and female youth in general that anthropologist Tyanna Slobe argues that it's become the expectation not just for white girls, but for *all* girls (Slobe 2018). When girls, particularly girls of color, do not conform to the expected, mainstream way of speaking, they are not conforming to "normal" behavior standards. If they do not conform to "normal" behavior standards, this can lead to punishment – including by instructors, from harsher grading to suspensions from school (Charity Hudley & Mallinson 2011; Day-Vines & Day-Hairston 2005; Harris-Perry 2011; Onyeka-Crawford et al. 2017; Slobe 2018; Smitherman-Donaldson 1987). We discuss this type of discrimination more in Chapters 8 and 11.

9.2.5 "Muy Macha" in the Bay Area

Linguist Norma Mendoza-Denton spent several years in the 1990s doing field work in a high school in the California Bay Area, near Stanford University. There, she investigated how Latina girls who were members in one of the two primary gangs in the area constructed their identities as people who were members of one gang or another. The girls Mendoza worked with formed a **community of practice**, a group of individuals who, in joining together to engage in a set of activities or practices, cocreate a system of linguistic and other norms that are influenced both by the individuals' identities and the particular practices in which they participate (Meyerhoff & Strycharz 2013). As you may guess, there are telltale linguistic signs that Mendoza-Denton was able to identify through hundreds of hours of recorded interviews with the girls.

To be a credible member of one of the gangs, the girls had to combine both linguistic and physical signifiers: To be a member of the Norteñas, not only did you have to be a fluent speaker of Chicano English (to emphasize your identification with both the American and Mexican sides of your culture), but you also had to wear red clothing, baggy pants, and dark red lipstick, and wear your hair in a feathered hairstyle. In contrast, members of the rival Sureña gang spoke much more Spanish (emphasizing their affiliation with their Mexican heritage and Mexican pride), wore blue clothing and brown lipstick, and wore their hair in severe, slicked-back high ponytails (Mendoza-Denton 2008).

Members of both gangs placed great emphasis on being Mexican and, even more, on being "macha": taking charge of yourself, your actions, and their outcomes, not being controlled, and being able to take care of your own affairs. Mendoza-Denton (2008) notes in this section that, in describing what being macha means, her informant "T-Rex" walks a fine line between what are usually seen as typically feminine values and typically masculine values while also rejecting outright that being macha has to do with being masculine (pp. 169–170). Mendoza-Denton also speculates that the ideals of being macha may protect the girls from consequences arising from the feminine ideals that they had heard from their mothers – to accept infidelity and a disproportionate amount of the burdens of housework and domestic life from their partners, depend financially on their partners, and otherwise give up their own personal power.

In later work, Mendoza-Denton (2011) notes that an important aspect of the "hardcore" gang member persona, for both women and men, is the use of creaky voice. One member of the Norteñas used creaky voice when she wanted to express toughness, silence, and hardcoreness, particularly when she discusses knowing who her true friends are in tight situations. Similar emotions and qualities are expressed when Chicano rapper Kid Frost uses creaky voice in particular stanzas of his songs, or when voicing his character, a gang member, in the 2004 *Grand Theft Auto: San Andreas* video game. Unlike the way creaky voice indexes a sort of vapid femininity for Valley Girls, here it's part of the construction of a gendered identity that is shaped by ideals of toughness.

9.2.6 Talking Like a Man?

In 1975, Jean Berko Gleason wrote the following in a developmental psycholinguistics textbook:

> To date there have been essentially no published studies of men's speech to children. In fact, for a while there was some question as to whether there was such a thing as men's speech to children: in a study of fathers' speech to their 3-month-old infants, Rebelsky and Hanks found that fathers spent an average of only 37.7 seconds a day engaged in this activity. (Gleason 1975, p. 290)

This claim, undoubtedly true with regard to the relevant scholarly literature, helps us to understand the ways in which scholarship on language and gender in many communities seems to have long-standing gaps when the topic is "men's speech" or "masculine" language. Might the embedded statement, that the fathers of 1975 in the US spoke to their babies for less than forty seconds per day, really be accurate? Or is it perhaps more likely that social constructions of masculinity and femininity caused both researchers and parents to disregard the ways in which men might be engaging in interactions with their children?

As we've discussed the ways in which "women's speech" or "feminine language" styles have been described and discussed by scholars of language, we've only occasionally mentioned styles associated with men or masculinity. Often, especially in work that focuses on language use in public spheres, scholars have conceptualized men's styles as ungendered or default, with women's language requiring special analysis or discussion. Again, we can think about why this might be, and how it relates to our general conceptualizations of gender roles and expectations. We should also not be surprised that much work in the US that focuses on "men's speech" centers on the language practices of white men in particular. Construction of masculine identity in Black communities is connected to different sets of resources and structures (Kirkland 2015), and we find that in this context it is often Black men's varieties associated with music (jazz, hip-hop) that are the engines that generate ways of sounding "cool." These linguistic practices are often co-opted by others to create discourses of youth, coolness and hipness–an example of a linguistic practice sometimes referred to as **crossing**, "the use of a language or variety that feels anomalously 'other' for the participants in an activity, involving movement across quite sharply sensed social or ethnic boundaries, in ways that can raise questions of legitimacy" (Rampton & Charalambous 2012, p. 482).

In early work on regional dialect variation and language change, men's speech – particularly that of nonmobile, older, rural men – was constructed as a reservoir of linguistic conservatism (Lawson 2020). Indeed, the acronym for this demographic was "**NORMs**"! This belief made men's speech important data about local varieties, with the language of women in these same communities being seen as leading indicators of language change (see, for example, Labov 1990). Social expectations of heteronormative masculinity in North America, particularly among whites, include beliefs that men talk less, are less expressive or variable in their speech styles, and are likely to use less educated, elaborate, or fancy vocabulary. Men are constructed as more likely to use profanity or stigmatized language than women are, and as more verbally competitive; with masculinity often being expressed by language that is explicitly misogynistic.

Careful study, however, often shows that these features are not consistently confirmed. Mehl et al. (2007) studied US college students by providing them with audio recorders that they could wear and that would turn on at random times during the day without the students' knowledge. The recordings were then transcribed and analyzed, and it was confirmed that there was no statistically significant difference between male and female students in terms of how much they talked (by word counts). This finding – that women do not necessarily talk more than men – was so surprising that it merited an article in the journal *Science* (a venue that does not generally publish scholarship on language). In addition to this, Deborah Cameron's (1997) work showed that it is possible to "correctly" analyze the same conversation in US English in a way that confirms it as a genuine example of stereotypically men's speech styles (based on beliefs about gender differences in conversational topics, for example) or in a way that confirms it as a genuine example of stereotypically women's speech styles (based on beliefs about gender differences in conversational structure, for example). Even claims about whether or not a particular utterance contained "gossip" could be determined not so much by the content of the utterance but by the expectations of the analyst about who was talking (if the talk was between men, relevant passages might not be identified as "gossip," but if it was between women, they would be).

So how do individuals in different speech communities "talk like a man," and how might we investigate masculine gendered language without creating caricatures or imposing a definitive analysis on ambiguous data? One concept that might be particularly important here is that of indexicality, which we first mentioned back in Chapter 2 as the idea that certain linguistic features can "point to" or index certain social qualities or identities. Two prominent scholars of language and gender – Penelope Eckert and Sally McConnell-Ginet (2013) – explain the relationship between gender and vocal pitch through this lens. Because on average adult males are somewhat larger than females, males might be expected to have a lower overall vocal pitch. This expectation is not particularly clearly borne out in reality, but a lower-pitched voice might nevertheless invoke or communicate a more masculine identity. The expected relationship between a lower-pitched voice and a more masculine speaker can then be used by speakers to index or point to a masculine identity by lowering the pitch of their voice. Vocal pitch then becomes a symbolic resource that we can use in order to build our gendered identities.

It would be genuinely surprising to find a speech community in which "men's speech" was characterized by an obligatorily high vocal pitch; though we do find communities in which an artificially lowered voice can index a particular type of femininity ("vocal fry" as discussed above generates lower pitch than modal voicing does). And it is not the case that men generally or always have lower pitched voices than women do. Instead, lowered pitch can be assigned a gendered meaning, which can then be indexed by people as they use a spoken language.

Other indices of "masculine" or "male" speech in (particularly white) US English-speaking communities include the *avoidance* of vocabulary items associated with women or femininity – for example, describing all of the hues in the pink-purple part of the spectrum as "red" rather than using more nuanced color terms like "raspberry," "crimson," "rose"; or restricting terms for emotions to those on the stoic-angry continuum; or the use of misogynistic language and "locker-room" style joking (see Ahearn 2012 for excellent examples and discussion).

These are not connected to any particular physical or physiological standard of "male"-ness – their indexical value is completely culturally constructed. It would not be at all surprising to find a community in which stereotypically male speech included a vast and nuanced color-term vocabulary or the ability to name and discuss positive and affiliative emotions. It would not be surprising at all to find a community in which neither color terms nor emotion words play a role in the construction of masculine identities, either.

And has been discussed in previous sections, speakers' gender identities do not necessarily drive their use of gender-associated linguistic features. Sa'ar (2007, p. 413) describes the common and potentially unconscious use of masculine-marked pronominal forms by Arabic-speaking women in describing themselves, even as they associate themselves with feminine activities. In this example from their work, a thirty-four-year-old woman says the following to the researcher, in Arabic, where the bolded words of English correspond to the Arabic masculine forms: "One day **you** suddenly **realize** that **you are** a mother and all **you wish** to do is stay home with the children" (Sa'ar 2007, p. 413).

As Ahearn (2012) points out, it's important to understand gender not as something we "have," but as something we "do." And we are not limited in our performances of gender in language to only the traditional Western "masculine" and "feminine" categories – sometimes referred to as the "gender binary."

9.2.7 Trans and Non-Binary Gendered Language

The idea of the gender binary is sometimes presented as if it were a natural fact, but of course it is not. "Nature" does not give us two neatly divisible biological categories that align with Western European notions of "male" and "female," but instead presents – in humans and other organisms – a variety of expressions of genders and sexes at the molecular, genetic, physiological, and social levels. As Agustín Fuentes (2022) writes, from insects to fish and birds to mammals including humans, the facts of nature provide a variety of ways of being "male," "female," "neither," or "both."

In spite of these facts, many of us today live in communities in which human infants are assigned one of two genders at birth – we are presented to the world as "a boy" or "a girl." This gender assignment may or may not be one that maps with our own physical, social, or cultural selves. People whose gender identities differ from those assigned at birth are transgender. Transgender people include transmen and transwomen, but also people whose gender identities are agender, polygender, genderfluid, or genderqueer. People whose gender identities align with those assigned at birth are cisgender. At the time of writing, the Pew Research Center (Brown 2022) estimates that the percentage of people in the US who are transgender is around 1.6 percent of adults of all ages, but more like 5 percent of younger people. It's not clear what the "normal" or "natural" numbers should be, as the US, and many similarly situated communities, have long been places in which it is dangerous to be "out" as a transgender or gender nonconforming person. Given this, it's possible that many transgender individuals don't feel safe identifying themselves as such, and therefore it would not be unreasonable to assume that these numbers are significant undercounts of trans people.

Are there particular linguistic styles or features that are associated with transgender identities? This question is an important one, and it's difficult to answer because of the stigmatization of gender nonconformity and the systematic erasure of trans people in linguistic, sociolinguistic, and anthropological research (Becker & Zimman 2022). By "erasure" we mean that trans people are literally not mentioned or discussed in the literature at all. This doesn't mean that trans people have not been included in sociolinguistic research in the past, but only that where researchers have kept track of participants' gender, they almost always did so based on the gender binary "male" and "female." A trans person participating in such a study would simply tick the box that best fits their gender identity – so transmen are likely included in research on men's language behavior, and transwomen in research on women's language behavior. That is, people have been categorized based on their lived gender expression, not their gender assigned at birth.

Over the last few years, scholars have begun paying better attention to transgender identities in their own rights, and on the ways in which transmen and transwomen may self-consciously adapt their linguistic and other self-presentation to transition publicly from "male" to "female" or vice-versa. Some trans people have access to gender-affirming medical care,[9] which may include hormone treatments, surgeries, and the like – and for some of these people, voice coaches are a component of that care. Voice coaches assist their clients in adopting speech styles and vocal qualities that index their gender identity effectively, which can include for example learning to lower the pitch of their voice or increase their pitch range, among other phonetic variables.

Note that transgender language is not at all the same as the language of drag. Drag is a style of performance in which the performer exaggerates and stylizes a type of stereotypical or socially recognized gender expression. "Drag queens" are usually (though not always) people who identify as men and who develop and perform a hyper-feminine character for purposes that include entertainment. The language behaviors of drag queens (Calder 2019) can give us valuable information about the content and structure of stereotypically female gendered language (especially that associated with a particular style of hyper- or "fierce" femininity). "Drag kings," on the other hand, are usually people who identify as women and who develop and perform a hyper-masculine character, often in a way that parodies the limitations of traditional masculinity (Basiliere 2019). The language behavior of drag kings can tell us about the content and structure of stereotypically male gendered language. Neither drag queens nor drag kings intend to trick or fool an audience into believing they are really women or men, respectively – instead, the art of drag is an art of playing with, holding up for examination, and manipulating the gendered stereotypical expectations, biases, and beliefs of the community in which the performers work.

Some drag performers may also be transgender or gender nonconforming in their non-drag personae, but many are not. The exploration of language behavior associated with gender nonconforming, non-binary, and trans people is an important area of work that is only now beginning to be disentangled from discussion of "men's" and "women's" language. The study of the language of drag helps us to better understand the social and cultural meanings associated with gendered language behaviors, and possibly to subvert them. (See Barrett 2017 for more details on this and related topics).

---

[9] Cis people, of course, have access to gender-affirming healthcare almost all of the time. This care may also include hormone treatments, surgeries, and the like.

9.3 Languages and Sexualities

If our gender identity is part of how we design and present our "doll" (that we asked you to imagine at the beginning of this chapter), our sexuality is an underlying quality that may interact with or affect that self-presentation, or might not – but it's a part of each of us. Sexuality refers to one's sexual feelings about others, including gendered sets of others. We suspect that human sexualities vary across individuals more than they vary across cultures (in that there are individuals who belong to all positions on the sexuality spectrum, most likely, in all reasonably large human communities), although cultures differ dramatically in their habitual attitudes and practices around sexualities. Heterosexuality, homosexuality, pansexuality, bisexuality, and asexuality are some of the labels we can attach to sexual identities.

Like everything else that we are, sexuality can be expressed or concealed in language, and a linguist in the community may explore the tools and repertoires that are used by different kinds of people to do this. Language and sexuality is an area that has received somewhat less research than has gender and language, and this may be at least in part due to the more elemental, and perhaps therefore more dangerous, nature of sexuality – at least as it is understood in the cultures of your authors. In any case, we are acutely aware that sexuality and sexual orientation are seen as dangerous and highly sensitive topics in our and in many (but certainly not all) human communities.

9.3.1 Gay and Queer Sexualities

In 1993, linguist and anthropologist William Leap organized the first "Lavender Language and Linguistics Conference" as an international conference on LBGTQ+ language research (Leap 2019). Lavender linguistics is a focus on the study of language practices in various gay and queer communities by the use of small-scale case studies, work that acknowledges the differences among communities of practice around the world. Lavender linguistics and queer linguistics continue to be important and growing fields within the study of language, sexuality, and gender. Within the domains of lavender and queer linguistics are studies not only of the linguistic practices of communities of LBGTQ+ people, but also the heteronormative practices that promote and facilitate homophobia and gender- and sexuality-based violence.

Hazenberg (2020) emphasizes the following facts about how language and sexuality intersect in communities like those of your authors. First, when we talk about language and sexuality, the expectation is typically that we're interested in language and homosexuality or queer identity, not heterosexuality – though we note that the study of the language of heterosexuality is of at least equal importance and interest, and is by no means "neutral" or "default." Second, marginalized sexualities are associated with linguistic stereotypes associated with, for example, gay men or lesbian women. These stereotypes – in the US they are things like differences in the pronunciation of "s," with gay men's "s" sounds being fronted (as noted in Calder 2019), differences in characteristic pitch and intonation, with lesbian women expected to have lower pitch and less pitch range, and the like – then become resources that individuals can use to communicate their sexualities through the way they speak. People are generally very, very good at languaging, and this includes being very skilled at taking on different speech styles and adapting our language to different situations. So we are able to use the linguistic resources related to gender and sexuality stereotypes in order to communicate these things about ourselves to others. Calder (2019) notes that if you can tell a person's sexuality from how they speak it's because that person is *allowing* you to tell their sexuality from how they speak.

9.3.2 Straight Sexualities

In the communities in which your authors live and work, heterosexuality is considered the norm and is the sexuality most of us are socialized into from a very young age. Because it is considered the norm, like we previously discussed with masculine language, scholars have only relatively recently started investigating how we construct or index a heterosexual persona, and how this persona might differ between other parts of our identities. However, heterosexual speakers still draw on particular linguistic styles and forms when they want to emphasize their heterosexuality (Coates 2013; Kitzinger 2005) and have to work to provide their "heterosexual credentials" to interlocutors (Coates 2013, p. 541). Like the other parts of our identity, we must incorporate it into our humanoid doll form: it is not simply a given that our blank state of human sexuality is heterosexual.

There is a great deal of value placed on heterosexual relationships, particularly the heterosexual couple, and one metaphor that has been used to describe this value is of a marketplace – one called the **heterosexual marketplace**. Social status and social value are derived from a person's position within the heterosexual marketplace and among the relationships maintained there. Heterosexuality is therefore something that preadolescent girls in the US use to define their perceived maturity and departure from childhood (Eckert 1996, 2011). As they enter into the heterosexual marketplace, girls begin to discuss boys as objects and also make efforts to further differentiate themselves from boys (as well as younger children). This differentiation takes the form of using makeup, dressing differently, and no longer engaging in rough play on the playground – and also using language differently. They gossip more and may even "just talk" with other girls instead of playing games during recess (Eckert 1996).

Men in North American college fraternities are also notoriously beholden to the idea of the heterosexual marketplace as a way to define their own sexual and gender identities. Just as they emphasize their masculinity by the types of stories they tell and the words they use to tell them, they also use these tools to emphasize their heterosexuality (Kiesling 1998, 2002). When linguist Scott Kiesling observed the fraternity men he writes about, he noted that their derogatory remarks and displays of dominance above other men relied on knowledge of the normative heterosexual script. In other words, to understand why one man might taunt another with "Hi honey, I'm home" during a game of Monopoly, you also need to understand that normative couples in this cultural script are made up of one woman and one man, and the woman is typically considered subordinate to the man.

Another of the ways that the young men Kiesling studied worked to maintain or display their heterosexuality was to discuss their sexual conquests during weekly fraternity meetings (Kiesling 2002). The fraternity brothers called them "fuck stories," and it was taken as a point of pride among the brothers to be involved in one. They portrayed women as sexual objects for the consumption of men. Even outside the "fuck stories," heterosexual sex and attraction was highly valued, whether at parties or even in making an entire city more appealing.

9.4 Us and Them?

We've focused this chapter on ways in which each of us creates and manages our "doll" self, and in doing so builds, changes, grows, and adapts our own identity. It's also worth noting that scholars have found many cases in which the identity of our interlocutor, the person or people with whom we're communicating, is a factor that plays a role in our language behavior. We've noted that gendered speech styles in the California language Yana were conditioned by the gender of the listener. In your speech community, do you speak differently to people depending on (your perceptions of) their gender or sexuality? Do you think that people speak differently to you depending on their perception of your gender or sexuality? We suspect that there may be differences of both types in many of our linguistic repertoires. A linguist in the community might be able to develop methods to investigate and describe these patterns.

9.5 Conclusion

In this chapter we have discussed genders, sexualities, and language and how we communicate, or conceal, our gender identity and sexuality through language. We hope that you come away from this chapter with at least these few key understandings: that humans use language as a way of expressing or hiding lots of aspects of our identities, and that genders and sexualities are aspects of our identities; that the social and cultural norms surrounding genders, sexualities, and language are remarkably diverse across different communities within the same social or cultural group, and across different social and cultural groups; that the idea of gender binary is a cultural construction rather than a biological fact; and that there's no one way to be a "man" or a "woman," a "girl" or a "boy" in terms of our language or in terms of any other aspect of our self-presentation.

As we write this chapter, we are less than a week after the passage of a set of laws in Uganda that will penalize homosexual behavior in that country with imprisonment and potentially death (Akinwotu 2023), and less then a year after the controversial hosting of the World Cup of football (soccer) by Qatar, in spite of that country's draconian laws against homosexuality (Sullivan 2022). In the US, a number of states are considering legislation that targets transgender people (a gender identity) and drag performers (neither a gender identity nor a sexuality) for punishment that seems to be related to the proposers' values about sexuality (although these might be proxy for other interests in social control and disempowerment of groups seen as "other"). At this historical moment when it is becoming more rather than less dangerous to express non-binary or nontraditional gender and sexual identities, your authors think it's particularly important that we understand these facts and at least consider using our knowledge to ensure that each of us can be safe in our own skin whether we are at home or abroad.

Linguist in the Community

- Look at the ways in which characters with different gender identities or sexualities talk in fiction, film, or other media. See if you can identify linguistic features that you think are most salient in the actors' portrayal or the author's depiction of a person with that gender identity or sexuality. These are likely to be features that index that kind of identity. How do the features differ between media that take place in different communities or at different points in history? How do the artists who create the work utilize these linguistic resources to build a persona of their character? And how do these features relate to the ways in which you or others around you use language?

- If you're comfortable adopting visual and vocal cues that range between different gender identities, consider a matched-guise approach in which you, for example, dress and otherwise try to self-present first as a kind of stereotypical example of the gender identity with which you identify, and second as a less stereotypical one – perhaps moving your presentation closer to something like androgyny. Under each of these two guises, as you go about your daily business, pay attention to and note any aspects of the ways in which others speak to you that you find interesting. You could keep track of things like politeness forms, how often people of similar or different gender presentations want to speak to you, for how long and on what topics – anything that strikes you as interesting. Then revisit your notes to see if you can find differences between people's talk to you in each guise – these would be very interesting hypotheses to pursue in a more formal study (one that would of course need to be vetted for human subjects protections and research integrity!).

Linguist in the Classroom

- This activity is described by Hazenberg (2020). Begin by jotting down the language features you associate with a gender/sexuality stereotype (for example, gay men's speech, heterosexual women's speech, etc.). After a few minutes, ask other students how many features they were able to list. The length of the typical list tells us something about the detail of the stereotypes associated with that identity – long lists mean we have a very detailed stereotype, short lists mean we have a more general one. Then work in small groups and combine your individual lists into a group list. Assess how similar your lists are to each other. If a particular feature shows up on many people's lists, this indicates that it is a strongly shared element of the stereotype. In your groups, discuss the level of detail and sharedness in the stereotypes that you discovered in this process, noting that features that are strongly shared might be features that individuals would deploy in order to communicate their gender identity or sexuality to others, or to ensure that others view them as having a gender identity or sexuality that is safe. If you are able to repeat this activity for different gender identities or sexualities, you will likely find that some stereotypes are less detailed than others, and some have more shared elements than

others. What might these differences tell us about the perceptions of a "default" gender identity or sexuality?
- Using sock or paper bag puppets (which you may construct in class or bring from home), create a play in small groups. Give the groups a very basic plot for their play (for example, two students meet in the cafeteria after class, and one tries to ask the other out on a date), and randomly assign genders to the puppets such that in some groups puppet A is the "boy" and B is the "girl," and vice-versa in others. Make it very clear to the audience what the gender of the puppet is. Then ask each group to perform their play, with the class taking notes about the properties of the gendered speech of the puppets. Collect the linguistic features used by the groups to indicate the puppets' genders, and compare them to what we might expect from each other in more natural conversation.
- Create a transcript of a conversation between two or more people in which you do not label the participants' genders. Provide the same transcript to different groups of students, and ask them to analyze the gendered language patterns in the transcript. Tell half of the groups that the conversation is between men, and the other half that the conversation is between women (or between a man and a woman, or use additional gendered categories of speakers if you wish). Then collect the analyses done by the different groups and discuss whether, and how, the groups' gender stereotypes may have influenced their analysis of the text.

Glossary

animacy Whether an object is alive (animate) or not (inanimate). Turtles are animate, rocks are inanimate.

community of practice A group of people who, in engaging in shared activities, cocreate a set of linguistic and other norms that distinguish them from others and that signal both the individual's own identities and that of the group.

conversational shitwork Continuing the flow of conversation by asking questions, bringing up new topics, and so forth. Also called maintenance work.

creaky voice A way of producing sound for speech during which the vocal folds are relaxed and vibrate more slowly than a speaker's usual way of speaking. In English, it does not make a difference in meaning whether someone says a word in creaky voice or not, but in other languages, it does. Also called vocal fry.

crossing The use by a speaker of a linguistic variety that is associated with an identity different from the speakers' own, in ways that might raise questions of authenticity or appropriateness.

femininity The use of physical attributes and linguistic styles to appear more like a stereotypical woman.

gender The socially constructed associations between a person's phenotype or outward appearance and a role in society. Not confined to a binary and may change over time.

grammatical gender A classification system in language where words are arbitrarily classified and must be used with morphemes of a type matching the classification. For example, the word "gata" in Spanish is feminine and must be used with feminine articles ("la," "una") and feminine affixes ("-a" in "rayada"), as in "Ártemis es una gata rayada" (Artemis is a striped (female) cat).

heterosexual marketplace A concept discussed by Penelope Eckert (1996 and elsewhere) based on field work in US schools; Eckert discusses sets of social practices in which boys and girls, largely by socializing within same-gender groups, begin to orient themselves around notions of heterosexual couplehood, and the norms surrounding that practice. This definition has also been extended to young people more generally.

identity How you perceive yourself, the steps you take to create that perception, and how other people around you perceive you.

index (an identity) To use a characteristic or combinations of characteristics to imply that a person belongs to a group: for example, long hair typically indexes a feminine identity.

intersectionality The social scientific analytic framework that understands social identities and social structures of privilege and discrimination as overlapping and interconnected.

maintenance work Continuing the flow of a conversation by asking questions, bringing up new topics, and so forth. Also called conversational shitwork.

masculinity The use of physical attributes and linguistic styles to appear more like a stereotypical man.

neopronouns Pronouns that have been developed for use to represent other gender identities more accurately than "she/her/hers," "they/them/their," or "he/him/his," such as "xe/xem/xyr" or "fae/faer/faer."

nonbinarity Not being part of a two-way classification. For example, people who do not feel they identify as a man or a woman may use "non-binary" as a broad descriptive term for their gender identity.

NORM Nonmobile, older, rural male; a demographic that early variationist studies in sociolinguists sought out for speech that was more resistant to changes in progress.

sex A set of biological attributes in humans that results in a particular phenotype. May include physical or physiological features, such as hormone levels, chromosomes, or expression of genes.

sexuality The relationship between a person's own gender and the gender(s) of people they are attracted to.

vocal fry A way of producing sound for speech during which the vocal folds are relaxed and vibrate more slowly than a speaker's usual way of speaking. This is a more casual term than "creaky voice" and is frequently used to denigrate young women's use of it in speech.

Recommended Readings

We can learn so much about ourselves and others by studying language. Our focus here was on gender and sexual identities, and below we recommend our favorite readings for enhancing your understanding of this topic. However, don't forget that this is just one element of the relationship between language and identity writ large – many of these readings will highlight links between language, gender, sexuality, and other identity categories like class, race, geographical origin, and more! Reach out to your local college or university library if you need help accessing these materials.

Cameron, D. (1997). Performing gender identity: Young men's talk and the construction of heterosexual masculinity. In S. Johnson & U. Meinhof (Eds.), *Language and Masculinity* (pp. 8–26). Blackwell.

Charity Hudley, A. H., & Mallinson, C. (2011). *Understanding English Language Variation in U.S. schools.* Teachers College Press.

Eckert, P. (2011). Language and power in the preadolescent heterosexual market. *American Speech, 86*(1), 85–97. https://doi.org/10.1215/00031283-1277528

Heath, S. B. (1983). *Ways with Words: Language, Life, and Work in Communities and Classrooms.* Cambridge University Press.

Herdt, G. (2020). *Third Sex, Third Gender: Beyond Sexual Dimorphism in Culture and History.* Princeton University Press.

Mendoza-Denton, N. (2008). *Homegirls: Language and Cultural Practice among Latina Youth Gangs.* Blackwell Publishing.

Ochs, E., & Schieffelin, B. B. (2017). Language socialization: An historical overview. In P. A. Duff & S. May (Eds.), *Language Socialization* (pp. 1–14). Springer International Publishing.

Zepeda, O., & Hill, J. (1998). Collaborative sociolinguistic research among the Tohono O'odham. *Oral Tradition, 13*(1), 130–156.

Zimman, L. (2018). Transgender voices: Insights on identity, embodiment, and the gender of the voice. *Language and Linguistics Compass, 12*(8), e12284. https://doi.org/10.1111/lnc3.12284

10 Languages Get a Job, Get Rich

In this chapter, we will explore several of the ways in which language and the economy are entwined. With that relationship in mind, you may first think of the typical advice given to job seekers, to speak in a "formal," "professional" sounding voice when they go for an interview. What counts as "formal" or "professional" language in these settings – and, crucially, by whose definition? Our discussion of this relationship will start here with an exploration of linguistic gatekeeping and the value of different kinds of linguistic skills and features in the labor market. We'll then explore the relationship language has with **socioeconomic class** more broadly – both how linguistic variation patterns change along class lines, and how the way we describe products can be a signal of class identity. At the end of this chapter, we'll encompass all of these case studies and ideas within the larger concept of the **"linguistic marketplace."** By the end of this chapter, we think you'll find that these relationships are quite complex – certainly more so than any list of "rules" about how to talk, or not talk, in the workplace.

10.1 Language and Getting Hired

You may have been given advice about how to find and secure a new job, and some of that advice may have centered on language. How should you word entries on your résumé or CV?[1] How should you introduce yourself and answer questions? What are the linguistic features that might help you get hired? All of these questions speak to elements of **linguistic capital**. This term, coined by French sociologist Pierre Bourdieu, describes all the language-based resources we use to convey our role in society, as well as

---

[1] In some countries, like the United Kingdom, this sort of document is referred to as a *CV*, or *curriculum vitae*. In common parlance you may also hear shortened forms like *vitae*. In the United States, where your authors are from, the term CV typically refers only to a specialized document used to apply for professorial jobs at universities – we call the sort of brief document that lists your professional accomplishments and work experience a *résumé*.

the values associated with our roles. In other words, it is the conglomeration of linguistic assets that we use to indicate to others information about our social station. By the same token, others may interpret certain elements of our linguistic capital – as well as any "gaps" in linguistic assets they may perceive – as information that can tell them about where they fit in the social order. Our linguistic capital shapes our success in the linguistic marketplace, the metaphorical space where our linguistic skills function as commodities that can be traded in exchange for access to certain financial prospects.

But just as in other areas of language study, the beliefs, attitudes, and values people have about language don't always line up with the facts. And a linguist in the community might want to investigate the facts around you so that they can better understand the role that language plays in securing economic opportunity.

We can begin by looking at aspects of language over which we have little or no control – like our names. For many of us, our names were given to us by our parents at a time when we had no say in the matter. Nevertheless, we take those names to school, to the job market, and, well, everywhere we go. Young parents may worry about whether the name they give their child will help or hinder that child in the adult world. In some cases, we hear stories about children whose parents purposefully gave them a challenging, odd, or difficult name (in the US recently at least two sets of parents who named their sons "Adolf Hitler" were in the news and in trouble with the law; see Goldberg 2010; Kolirin 2018), and there is of course the classic country song made popular by Johnny Cash but originally written by Shel Silverstein called "A Boy Named Sue"). What does your name add (or detract) from your linguistic capital? Might your name make you rich or leave you impoverished? What value does your name have on the linguistic marketplace?

In recent years, at least in the US, the big-picture answer appears to be "no," but there are lots of interesting details behind that answer that you might want to investigate on your own. For example, you could familiarize yourself with the methods used by Bertrand and Mullainathan (2004) to investigate whether résumés from job applicants with "white" or "Black" sounding first names are treated differently by employers.[2] They responded to job advertisements in Boston and Chicago with résumés that were matched

---

[2] To be clear, any person of any race can have any name. However, there are demographic trends that show that certain names are more common among certain racial groups, and there are also stereotypes about how certain names index race. The authors of this study used data from both of these sources to determine what counted as a "white" or "Black" name for the purposes of this study.

in terms of qualifications but different only in the applicant's first name (for example "Jamal" vs. "Greg," "Emily" vs. "Lakisha"). They found that applicants with Black-sounding first names got called in for interviews 50 percent less often than did those with white-sounding names. This type of effect of applicant names on job callbacks has been found to result in significant patterns of discrimination by employers in the US, the UK, and Western Europe such that in each of those places, having a name that is associated with or perceived as being linked to non-white racial identities, and/or perceived as being linked to Muslim identity, results in significantly fewer callbacks for interviews on the same qualifications (Quillian & Midtbøen 2021). On the flip side, having a particularly popular first name might make you "more employable," at least in some communities (see Pascual et al. 2015 for evidence of this pattern in France).

Despite these effects, our names don't speak for us – many other linguistic behaviors shape how we are perceived as potential employees. Having as part of one's linguistic capital a proficiency or comfort in particular linguistic genres (e.g., greetings, public speaking, persuasion), speech styles (e.g., formal or casual), social varieties (e.g., the ability to use linguistic varieties that are associated with dominant social categories), and regional varieties (e.g., the ability to speak in a regionally prestigious variety rather than one that is stigmatized) are treated as job qualifications. Our linguistic self-presentations in job interviews, cover letters, and the like form a significant part of our pitch, and potential employers often (consciously or unconsciously) judge the "goodness of fit" of a job candidate based on linguistic features. For example, in the US there is a thriving accent reduction industry, including courses and programs offered by individuals, schools, and corporations, that claims to offer people an opportunity to add assets to their linguistic capital that conform more with community beliefs about how someone "should" speak (Thomson 2012). As linguists, of course we are fully aware that accent reduction is not possible; what really is at stake is the ability to shift one's "accent" to suit the preferences of others and the prevailing demands of the linguistic marketplace, often toward an idea of a "standard" or "proper" way of speaking.[3]

Similar methods as we described for the study of the effects of names on résumé responses can be used to explore possible patterns of unconscious bias or discrimination in other areas, such as grading/marking (Nick 2017) or housing (Carpusor & Loges 2006). Baugh (2018) explores such methods and

---

[3] A relatively recent discussion of one broadcast journalist's experience with "accent reduction" as part of his career trajectory can be found in the episode "Talk American" on the podcast *Code Switch* (NPR 2018). We also discussed it briefly back in Chapter 5.

the findings they have led to in the US, such as developing documentation of various forms of "linguistic profiles" in which goods and services may be systematically denied to individuals based on their linguistic self-presentation. For more detail on this work, check out Chapter 11.

For readers who are interested in exploring issues of employment and other forms of economic discrimination that have their bases in language, we recommend reading the material in Chapter 7 on language and computers as well as Chapter 11 on linguistic discrimination. Many of the areas in which we are seeing these forms of bias involve the use by employers, landlords, and other economic power holders of systems and applications that use artificial intelligence based in natural language processing and often machine learning. Automated résumé evaluations, pre-employment "personality tests," and other forms of automated screening, credit checks, and the like are increasingly managed by technological systems that use computers to find patterns in our language behavior.[4] We must remember that computers and their software are not neutral or unbiased: instead, they contain the same biases that their human programmers do, and they can magnify patterns that lead to increased bias for or against people seeking employment.

10.2 Language at Work

Once we find ourselves in the world of work, how does our language relate to our ability to retain our employment and even access promotions and other benefits of employment?

10.2.1 Language and "Professionalism"?

The concept of "**professionalism**" is one that we find in a wide variety of scholarly and vocational arenas. Professionalism consists of the behaviors and artifacts that a community expects from individuals who hold particular forms of employment. Think for example of what you would expect – linguistically and otherwise – from the individual who operates the bus or train you ride on, from the individual who checks you out at the grocery store, from your teacher or professor, your doctor, a lawyer, and so on. A linguist in the community might want to explore, describe, and analyze the components of "professional" language, how we add these components

---

[4] Interested readers may want to find Cathy O'Neil's (2016) book *Weapons of Math Destruction* to learn more.

to our linguistic capital, and how they are valued and exchanged on the linguistic marketplace.

"Many Black professionals in the United States ... report being under pressure, if not requirement, to assimilate to White Standardized spoken English. And for most of us, in our fields, equity in general is still a goal, not a reality," reports Kelly Wright (2022, p. 25), who goes on to investigate how Black Americans understand and implement the requirements of linguistic "professionalism" in their workplaces.[5] Wright finds strong support for the belief that professional sounding language is consistent with white standards, and that use of linguistic features inconsistent with white professional speech reduces many people's assessments of the credibility and professionalism of the speaker. Sociolinguistic labor includes the activity, concern, and effort we expend in trying to predict, manage, and appease the unconscious and conscious biases of those in power in the workplace, such as managers, colleagues, and customers.

How can we begin to investigate the linguistic underpinnings of this so-called professionalism? Wright's work provides some useful methods, including the "**Metalinguistic Method of Sociolinguistic Interview**" (MMSI; see Wright 2022, pp. 40–49), a revised and expanded version of the traditional sociolinguistic interview, which we discussed previously in Chapter 3. Before using the MMSI the interviewer first assesses their own positionality, community membership, and linguistic history and attitudes, as these factors will in part determine how the interview protocol should be designed. The MMSI proceeds through multiple stages, including stages that ask about participants' broad life and language experience, those that ask about particular vocabulary items or linguistic structures, and those that ask specifically about their experience with language in context. MMSI results can then be analyzed to better understand the sociolinguistic labor that individuals do as a part of their professional self-presentation.

We can also investigate the role we take as coworkers, supervisors, and customers by systematically assessing the perceptions of professionalism connected to various linguistic properties. Wright did this by recording speakers producing sentences with different elements associated with African American language alongside minimally different sentences with no such elements and asking listeners to rate each sentence as more or less "professional" than its pair. A clever linguist could devise a variety of ways to assess community members' judgments about professionalism in

---

[5] A 2018 film called *Sorry to Bother You*, a social satire written and directed by Boots Riley, takes on these requirements and expectations specifically as they relate to Black people in the US.

language. If you do, we hope that you'll think about the ways in which we might be able to reduce the sociolinguistic labor required of our peers, friends, employees, customer service representatives, and others to promote greater equity in the workplace.

10.2.2 More Languages, More Money?

Another link we find between language and labor has to do with whether there is an economic (and perhaps social and psychological) benefit to multilingualism. In a 2018 blog post from the World Economic Forum, Hardach (2018) used a number of statistics about bilingualism in order to bolster claims that high-bilingualism countries have better economic outlooks than lower-bilingualism countries. For example, Hardach states that overall, the EU includes 44 percent monolingual and 56 percent bilingual citizens, with Luxembourg having the highest percentage of bilingual citizens, at 99 percent, and Poland having the lowest, at just 57 percent. In that discussion, for example, Great Britain is said to have "lost out" on an estimated 3.5 percent of its gross domestic product (GDP) because of its "poor language skills." In this view, "languages" themselves are units of linguistic capital – and having access to more than one of them is valuable not just to individuals, but to national economies!

It turns out, however, that the measure of "poor language skills" was the number of university degrees in "foreign languages" conferred over time, which was declining; not the number of bi- or multilingual people in the country, and not the variety of languages spoken by people in their daily lives.

Also in 2018, the British newspaper *The Independent* breathlessly reported that Princess Charlotte, the daughter of the prince and princess of Wales, then two years old, was "already bilingual," and "adorable and smart" (Ritschel 2018). Charlotte's bilingualism reportedly came from her English-speaking parents and a Spanish-speaking nanny. While we leave the question of her level of general intelligence and her physical appearance to others to determine, at the time this article was published many noted that millions of parents in Britain had bilingual two-year-old children – virtually all young children of non-English-speaking immigrants would have achieved the same level of multilingualism as Princess Charlotte had at the same age. These children, whose bilingualism may have included first languages such as Arabic, Bengali, Lahnda, Hindi, or Urdu, are rarely described in the press as "adorable and smart." Instead, young children who are growing up bilingual in a household with monolingual parents, where the parents may have no or limited expressive ability in English, are typically described as a "problem" for communities and schools. In other words, it isn't just a question of how many languages you know that confers linguistic capital (although raw number is certainly a part of it) – it's which languages you know, as different languages are valued in different ways on the linguistic marketplace. This interpretation can be seen in journalism and research aimed at solving this "problem" (see, for example, Woods & Hansen 2016) of multilingual children whose linguistic skills are viewed as a deficit rather than as an advantage.

So is there economic, political, or social power to be gained by being bilingual or multilingual? Are some languages, and some language varieties, tied to economic success at greater rates than others? Are there properties of languages that might make them better or worse for use in business and commerce? A linguist in the community might want to investigate these questions – and you can read on for some of our thoughts on this.

One way of answering these questions might be to explore how multilingualism is discussed among groups with different social statuses. In their production of a limited-episode podcast called Nice White Parents (discussed in Larson 2020), journalists Chana Joffe-Walt and team from Serial Productions spent time talking with parents at a New York City public school that had traditionally served mostly Black and brown students but that in 2020 started seeing large numbers of white students enrolling for the first time. Many of the white parents began lobbying for a foreign language emphasis at the school, which would include study abroad experience, in French. The non-white student population already included many students who were multilingual – but it was the kind of multilingualism that grew from a home life of multicultural and intergenerational families. The white parents didn't see this kind of multilingualism as being as culturally, educationally, or economically advantageous as the study of and in (European) French would be.

What do these values tell us about different communities' views of the economics of languages? At minimum, it suggests that only certain kinds of multilingualism are considered valuable on the linguistic marketplace. Here, we might hypothesize that the parents at this school consider French to be a high-prestige language that would provide their children with valuable linguistic capital as they grow up and enter the workforce, which is precisely the white parents' argument in the podcasts. We might further hypothesize that this is due to the historical global prestige of French as a language of culture and the arts – recall our discussion of the Germanic and Latin roots of English words, and how the Latinate words that came to us from the French spoken during the Norman conquest of English are often perceived to be fancier, more elite, or even more educated. In any case, the attitudes of these parents show that the "value" of multilingualism varies depending on how a given community or individual perceives the worth of some language or set of languages. But we can also look at the ways in which multilingualism can "translate"[6] to different kinds of jobs, and even higher earning potentials – and we'll explore this in the next section.

10.2.3 Multilingualism at Work: Translation as a Profession

There is at least one kind of professional venue in which multilingualism can be a money-earning proposition: **translation** and **interpretation**. Translators and interpreters take language materials from one community and convert them into materials that can be understood by another community. Translation typically (but not always)[7] refers to doing this work asynchronously in the written modality, while interpretation usually refers to those who work in the spoken or signed modality with two languages simultaneously. As a student of language in the community, you'll be aware of the need for both translators and interpreters to understand much more than just the languages involved in the conversion process. In order for an audience in one language community to be able to understand an interaction, literary work, legal document, or other linguistic object, the language has to be appropriately contextualized and situated. For some genres of language use, the translator or interpreter also needs to be able to convert the patterns of sounds, rhythms, metaphors, and the like. These professions take the metaphorical concept of the linguistic marketplace to a quite literal level – the commodities being exchanged for money are, in fact, linguistic abilities.

And good translation or interpretation requires tremendous skill and knowledge. We hope that you've had lots of opportunities to see signed language interpretation in action at public events and in the media; you may have seen interpreters at music concerts, at technical or academic lectures, and during news conferences or public service announcements. You may have even served as a translator or interpreter for relatives or friends who don't have access to the language they need in order to function in your community. Another way in which the work of translators becomes visible is in the consumption of media in a language other than your own. We hope you've had the opportunity to read literature both in the original languages and in translation, and watch films made by people from all over the world with subtitles or dubbing that allow you to understand their speech – translators' work makes this possible! In fact, some people engage in this work just for fun, like fans of television shows or films who produce

---

[6] Pun intended.
[7] "Simultaneous translation" is a term used for live interpretation of multiple languages during, for example, meetings of the United Nations.

unofficial, fan-made subtitles for their favorite media (even when doing so might flout copyright concerns – see Park 2019). Whether a community prefers subtitles or dubs in their foreign language media can vary cross-culturally (e.g., Sherouse 2015; Valentinsson 2022), but both modes reflect complex processes of language-related work.

The US Bureau of Labor Statistics (2022) reports that the occupational outlook for interpreters and translators in the US is excellent, with significant growth expected in these areas in the coming years. The academic preparation to work as a professional translator or interpreter in the US is typically fluency in English plus at least one other language and a baccalaureate degree. More generally, it's likely to be the case that translators and interpreters must be able to use at least one large-scale or official language in addition to at least one non-local, small-scale or Indigenous one. Translation and interpretation are key resources needed in the medical and legal contexts and in areas such as engineering and technology. But there are cases and situations in which these needs are not taken seriously, or in which poor or unskilled translation and interpretation can lead to trouble, and a linguist in the community might find opportunities to learn more about how our everyday language behavior can influence the availability of these resources.

For example, during Hurricane Irma, which came ashore in Florida in September 2017, a local television station broadcast a news conference designed to provide residents of Manatee County with important safety information. The news conference included a "sign language interpreter" whose ASL was clearly not accurate. *The New York Times* reported that, rather than faithfully translating the spoken information, the interpreter signed "pizza" and "bear monster," tried to keep up with the speakers by fingerspelling[8] as much as possible, and otherwise failed to provide the necessary information to deaf and hard of hearing audiences. Afterward, it was revealed that the interpreter was not trained or certified as such, but was instead a man whose brother was deaf and who had grown up signing within the family unit only. Officials in charge of the press conference said that they had not had sufficient time to recruit a qualified interpreter (Caron 2017). Clearly, having communicative proficiency in two languages is not enough to make a person an interpreter or translator.

---

[8] Fingerspelling is a technique in which the ASL signer uses separate signs for each letter of a spelled (in this case, English) word – spelling out the words letter by letter rather than using the ASL words for things. Obviously, fingerspelling is not the optimal way to express concepts in ASL or any other signed language, but it is useful if the spoken language speaker uses a word or words for which the interpreter does not have an ASL sign or guesses that their addressee might not know the relevant sign(s).

We may think of translation and interpretation services as being necessary only between two different language communities, but there are contexts in which these services may be required even within a community we think of as speaking "the same language." Jones and his colleagues (2019) focused on the accuracy of court reporters in Philadelphia, Pennsylvania in transcribing the testimony of English-speaking Black witnesses. Court reports transcribe everything said "on the record" in a trial, deposition, or other formal proceeding, and their transcriptions form the official legal record of what was said. Even an audio recording would not count as the official legal record of a witness's testimony for purposes of things like appeals, so the accuracy of the court reporters is crucial to the appropriate functioning of the US system of justice. Court reporters must meet strict licensure requirements in which they must show accuracy rates above 95 percent in a test environment.

However, Jones and colleagues (2019) noted that licensure testing is done on the speech of white-sounding speakers, and that there is significant and systematic variation between white and African American English. And in their study, the researchers found that court reporters' accuracy when transcribing African American English was shockingly low – in some contexts less than 50 percent, and in no contexts anywhere near the 95 percent threshold required for licensure. The inaccuracies of court reporters were found to frequently introduce admissions of criminal behavior that were not in the actual testimony in a significant number of cases. Rickford and King (2016) found similar issues in their in-depth analysis of the testimony of Rachel Jeantel, a speaker of Haitian Creole influenced African American English, and its interpretation by an all-white jury in Florida.[9]

One way to begin to remedy this problem would be to require that interpreters be provided for African American English speakers in Philadelphia courtrooms (and, perhaps more broadly, in the US and elsewhere). The idea of hiring "translators" for African American English speakers has come up from time to time in the US media (see, for example, Netter 2010), but at the time of writing we do not have any confirmed examples that such policies or practices have been implemented.

10.3 Language and Socioeconomic Class

We often talk about groups of people within our community who differ from each other based on factors such as income and/or material wealth,

---

[9] We discuss this case in more detail in Chapter 11.

educational attainment, and profession – these are the kinds of factors that we group in the concept of socioeconomic class. How each of these factors group together into widely accepted class categories can vary cross-culturally. In the US, for instance, communities are often divided into groups such as "working class," "middle class," and "upper class" – but even within this one country, the precise definitions and measures associated with each grouping may not be explicit or universally shared. It's not uncommon, for instance, to read about families in the US whose incomes fall in the top 1 percent globally (see Shapiro & Long 2018) refer to themselves as "middle class," and there are of course many ways to think about "working class," "working poor," "blue collar," and other categories that may vary across cultures. But whatever the system – whether we think of it as a stratified set of groups defined primarily by income and material wealth, a more fluid set of interrelations defined by individuals' own perceptions and associations, or something closer to a Marxist view focusing on access of various groups to the control of means of production – we probably associate the properties and varieties of our linguistic behavior with some notion of socioeconomic class.

10.3.1 Grammar and Economics

Before proceeding to our discussion of ways in which our language may reflect and be reflected by our socioeconomics, let's start with an example of how things very clearly do not work. In spite of many scholars' efforts to demonstrate the contrary, we can conclusively show that the grammar of our language is in no way a determinant of our wealth, or rank, or power. There is no sense in which the grammar of, for example, British English, is directly related to the economic wealth of the British commonwealth. If you investigate patterns of global wealth and attempt to correlate them with language types or grammatical structures, the result is incoherent. At the time of writing, the World Bank (2023) lists the following countries (along with the most commonly spoken languages in each) as the top five in terms of per capita gross domestic product:

- Monaco (French, Ligurian, Italian)
- Liechtenstein (German)
- Luxembourg (Luxembourgish, French, German)
- Bermuda (Bermudian English)
- Ireland (Gaeilge, Ulster Scots, English)

What connects these countries to wealth is not that they share linguistic heritage (it's true that the languages of these countries are all members of the Indo-European language family), but that they are all relatively small communities with wealth-friendly banking systems, among other factors.

Nevertheless, in 2017 a group of economists (Chen et al. 2017) published a paper in the *Journal of Corporate Finance* titled "Languages and Corporate Savings Behavior" in which they argued that the kind of future tense marking a language uses determines the amount of savings corporations keep on hand. This paper followed a much publicized work (Chen 2013) that claimed to find that the same linguistic variable (speaking a language that has distinct future tense marking or not) explains why some groups of people "save more, retire with more wealth, smoke less, practice safer sex, and are less obese" than others. These claims, though linguistically nonsensical, incoherently argued, and statistically unsupported (as demonstrated in Pepinsky 2022 and discussed by Kennedy 2018), were (and are) accepted by many readers as valid and sensible. Why would people find it plausible that the grammar of a language might be so closely linked to financial well-being? Do we connect language behavior with wealth and economic success? Under what circumstances might language and money go hand in hand?

To be clear, even if there were some universe in which the existence of a future tense in your language could determine your savings habits, these studies could not – even in principle – have found it. Their empirical claims about how different languages encode grammatical tense are factually wrong and show a stunning lack of understanding of relevant findings in linguistics, anthropology, history, sociology, psychology, and cognitive science. Furthermore, we know to a very reasonable degree of certainty that we do not live in such a universe – there is no robust correlation between language structures in any language and any social behavior as complex as financial planning and banking. But we do know that we live in a community in which our language itself might be worth something (money, power, prestige), and we do see evidence all around us that language is linked to both prosperity and its absence because of the ways in which we perceive language as an index of social class, education, and well-being. Let's talk about some of the ways in which these connections play out in our communities, and in doing so outline some of the ways in which a linguist might go about investigating and understanding them.

10.3.2 Exploring Linguistic Correlates of Socioeconomic Class

In 1966, in New York City, linguist William Labov (2006) undertook an exploration of one aspect of the varieties of English used in three large department stores: the presence or absence of an "r" sound at the ends of words like "fourth" and "floor." The presence or absence of the "r" sound in that position, which we'll call **coda** position, in words has long varied among different regional varieties of English in the US and elsewhere, and, in the US, this variability encoded social and economic status differences as well.

10.3 Language and Socioeconomic Class

Before (approximately) World War II, the lack of coda "r" was a characteristic of elite social and economic status in the US, particularly in the Northeast. After the war, this dynamic shifted and the lack of coda "r" became more closely connected with lower socioeconomic status, especially among white speakers.

Labov investigated this phenomenon by creating a quick, anonymous survey protocol. He selected three different department stores in the city – Saks 5th Avenue, a store that catered to very high-income customers; Macy's Herald Square, a store that catered to middle-income customers; and S. Klein Union Square, a store that catered to low-income customers. Each store was housed in a multi-story building that had at least four floors on which merchandise was available. Labov's protocol was to enter each store, find some product that was sold on the fourth floor of that store, and then go back to the ground level and ask a store employee where he could find that product. The goal was to elicit the response "fourth floor" from the employee. After the employee gave that response, Labov would pretend he hadn't heard them clearly, and ask them to repeat the answer. This would produce a more carefully articulated "fourth floor" from the employee. Once he had completed the rapid interview, he would find a hiding place where he could note whether or not the employee had pronounced their coda "r"s in the first and/or second repetition.

Labov found an interesting pattern of results, roughly as follows:

1. In the wealthy and middle-income stores, employees produced more coda "r" sounds in the repetition (the "emphatic" pronunciation) than in the first utterance of the phrase.
2. In the low-income store, employees did not significantly change their pronunciation between the first and second repetition.
3. Overall, employees of the wealthy store pronounced more coda "r" sounds in the first repetition (the "casual" pronunciation) than did employees of the middle-income store. Employees of the middle-income store produced more coda "r" sounds in both the casual and the emphatic pronunciations than did employees of the low-income store.
4. The difference between the first and second repetition was greatest for employees at the middle-income store, where the emphatic pronunciations were as full of coda "r" sounds as were the emphatic pronunciations of the high-income store employees.

Finding 1 suggests that at the time, production of coda "r" sounds was a desired target for high- and middle-income store employees. Finding 2 suggests that production of coda "r" was not necessarily desired for low-income store employees. Finding 3 suggests that production of coda "r" was associated with high-income store employees. None of these conclusions was unexpected, though they were all, of course, received with interest. The most surprising finding was 4, and Labov interpreted this as indicating that the middle-income store employees were the most linguistically insecure – they changed their pronunciation to match a higher-status variety during careful speech only.

Note that the variation Labov observed was not straightforwardly connected to the social identities of the employees. In other papers on the subject (e.g., Labov 1972), he noted that salespeople may borrow prestige in the form of linguistic features from their clientele – that is, a salesperson in an establishment catering to high-income customers may use the most obvious features of their speech to "fit in," since they themselves may not be high-income (or speak a variety that is perceived as prestigious). The patterns he found resulted from a mix of employees' own linguistic repertoires as well as the institutional culture and community cultivated by each of the department stores.

Labov's department store study has become a mainstay of sociolinguistics courses over the last fifty-five years as much for its method – though it was not invented by him – as for its results. While there are many shortcomings to this rapid survey method (it relies on the judgment and memory of a single researcher, so it does not produce verifiable data, it does not allow the researcher to collect information about the identities of participants, etc.), it illustrates how much we might be able to learn from each other by means of strategic observation.

Many years later, speakers' use of "r"-like sounds were explored by linguistic anthropologist Qing Zhang (2018) in a very different context: metropolitan Beijing. An economically rising social group of young professionals, referred to locally by borrowing a word from English – **yuppies** – used the "r" sound in their speech in a characteristic way: by using more "r" sounds at the ends of many words than other speakers of Mandarin, and also by softening some of the word-initial sounds[10] in a way that produces an "r" like start of words. This pronunciation is distinct from more local dialectal features (Zhang 2005, 2008), and so Beijing yuppies who use this new form of "r" end up sounding more cosmopolitan and worldly. This is especially meaningful for those yuppies who work in international corporations, where being perceived as worldly via your language use can help improve your standing at work.

---

[10] Specifically, those sounds that have a "retroflex" consonant in them – /ʂ/, /tʂ/, and /tʂʰ/. Readers with some knowledge of articulatory phonetics might find this to be a sensible change; the phonological process at stake is called "lenition."

And many more contemporary investigations find links between peoples' economic position and their linguistic behavior, often including hypercorrection and other evidence of linguistic insecurity in the ways in which speakers construct, maintain, and manipulate their personae. Since Labov's work, the focus of the linguistic anthropologist and sociolinguist has been less on broad social categories with linguistic variables as indicators of membership in those categories and more on the ways in which individuals move through and among systems where they can signal membership in and/ or attitudes about various identities and affiliations. Micro-level linguistic differences, like the inclusion of more or less "r" at the ends of words in the Northeastern US, or like the increased use of "r"-like sounds at both the beginnings and ends of words by Mandarin Beijing speakers described by Zhang (2018), provide a great deal of information about how we view ourselves in relation to others and in relation to whatever social and economic systems we find ourselves in.

10.3.3 Language and Consumption: You Are What You Eat

If you've been to a grocery store any time recently, you will probably have seen lots of examples of companies using language in order to market a product as either "economical" (low-prestige) or "gourmet" (high-prestige). We can take coffee as an example. A couple of coffee varieties seen recently in a local supermarket in Tucson, Arizona, in the US are pictured in Figures 10.1 and 10.2.

Manufacturers and marketers are providing consumers with **semiotic cues** including color, size, and shape of packaging, photos, graphics, and, of course, language in order to signal social and cultural information about

Figure 10.1 House-brand coffee.

Figure 10.2 Starbucks-brand coffee.

the product to the customer. The low-prestige product in this example is labeled as "ground coffee, medium roast"; the higher-prestige product is given significantly more text. It is identified as "committed to ethical sourcing" (= virtuous, pure), with "notes of cocoa & rich praline" (using the vocabulary of wine tasters) and situated in "Pike Place" (= hip, niche source), all of which tap into a vocabulary of fancy coffee in the US. In this vocabulary, identifying the remoteness of the source of the product, identifying the product with the language of purity, and utilizing specialized terminology for flavor and aroma have all been presented as ways in which participants in "coffee culture" signal themselves as elite and high-status consumers of gourmet beverages (Cotter & Valentinsson 2018).

Although you are probably familiar with these kinds of descriptors for fancy coffee, marketers haven't always used this kind of language. In the late seventeenth century, coffee started as a beverage touted by Puritans and other similarly minded European Protestant groups as an elixir that, like other drugs, provided a form of mental and physical stimulation, albeit in a more restrained manner than, for instance, alcohol. Due to how difficult it was to obtain and prepare, coffee remained a beverage only accessible to the wealthiest sectors of society. But as European imperialism reached the corners of the globe where coffee was most easily grown, it became easier – and cheaper – to cultivate, refine, and sell. By the end of World War II, coffee in America was widely regarded as fuel for the working class – nothing elite about it (Cotter & Valentinsson 2018, pp. 490–491). It was in the mid 1980s when marketers discovered that advertising to increasingly niche groups of people could yield better returns on their advertisements that the specialty coffee discourse we're familiar with today began to emerge. This trend framed coffee not as a utilitarian tool for worker productivity, but as a "way of life" (Roseberry 1996, p. 767) for "urban, urbane, professional men and women who distinguished themselves through consumption" (p. 773) – folks akin to the Beijing yuppies described in Zhang's (2018) study. With your beverage of choice so tied to your identity, it is not surprising that these types of consumers became increasingly interested in not just the coffee itself but in all the features that could distinguish it from "bad," "cheap," or even just "regular" coffee. Hence, marketing language that labels coffee according to where it was grown, its flavors, its textures, and other such characteristics took off.

Today, high-end specialty coffee shops often hold "cupping" events, where customers and industry professionals alike can sample coffee grown in different regions, harvested in different seasons, and prepared in different ways. Through training with professional baristas, coffee drinkers can (ostensibly) learn to distinguish which sorts of coffees taste like "lavender," "peach fuzz," or "Italian plum," and what makes it have smells one might describe as "bright," "earthy," or "hollow." Specialty coffee producers also use this unique vocabulary to label and market their coffee – signaling to purchasers that this isn't just any old cup of joe, but rather something with a distinctive, unique flavor profile that only the most refined, educated consumers can identify. By purchasing coffee that frames itself with this language – and by using this language themselves – specialty coffee drinkers engage in what Cotter and Valentinsson (2018) call **bivalent class indexicality** – or, put more simply, the ability to suggest that they are both high-class and down-to-earth at the same time. More on this later in this section.

In fact, the link between new lifestyles and consumption habits emerging and changing linguistic resources to describe and market consumer products is not unique to coffee. Many scholars have investigated how lifestyle habits are linked to the consumption of different sorts of food products, from tea (Besky 2014), to meat (Cavanaugh 2016), to cheese (Paxson 2012), to tequila (Gaytan 2014), and even to certain kinds of water (Kaplan 2007). Perhaps most parallel with the case of specialty coffee is the case of craft beer. Beer, like coffee, is a beverage that has been historically associated with the working class. But in a study of contemporary craft beer breweries and drinkers, scholars found that using specialized technical jargon to describe flavors and smells was a tool the craft beer consumer could use to differentiate themselves and their products from the "average" consumer (Konnelly 2020).

We might be tempted to argue that these differences in marketing semiotics are about more than just the sociocultural status the brand wants to project onto the consumer. Instead, we would argue that they are signaling real differences in products, such as differences in quality and ingredients. While there may be cases in which that is true, we are sure you will find examples in which the thing being described and the words that are used to label it for marketing and sale are not so closely connected to each other. Research on the meanings of terms used by **oenophiles** to describe the flavors of wine, for example, has shown that there is little consistency between tasters/speakers – so little that one taster cannot generally communicate a wine selection to another equally sophisticated taster by describing the taste and aroma of the wine (Lehrer 2009). The vocabulary selected by each taster reflects their own underlying preferences rather than, for example, the percentage of sugars or tannins in the wine. What does this tell us about fancy wine jargon, then?

Instead of being (just) names of flavors or aromas, these words are labels that situate the speaker in a sociocultural relationship to the wine. Linguistic anthropologist Michael Silverstein calls this register of "talking about wine to show off how much you know about wine" **oinoglossia**. Oinoglossia essentially amounts to all the technical jargon that sommeliers and wine aficionados learn as they participate in communities where drinking fancy wine is an important marker of taste or class (Silverstein 2003, 2006; see also **brutoglossia** for a similar type of craft beer talk in Konnelly 2020. Cotter & Valentinsson 2018 might have also coined a term like "kokkoiglossia" if they were as clever as Konnelly or Silverstein[11]). But the crucial element is not whether or to what degree this register "accurately" represents the qualities of the beverage – instead, it has to do with showing off what kind of consumer you are. In the case of oinoglossia, it's someone who has specialized, technical knowledge of the kind of beverage that well-to-do, upwardly mobile people who care about social status drink – in other words, yuppies. For craft beer and craft coffee drinkers, it's about showing off another kind of upper-class identity: they are someone who is casual and down-to-earth

---

[11] And if Cotter and Valentinsson were *extra* clever in their 2018 paper, they would have carefully analyzed the Ancient Greek etymologies of all these technical terms, as well as the cultural context from which these words emerged – and would have ended up calling specialty coffee talk "oinoglossia" as well, as the standard "breakfast" drink in Ancient Greece was, in fact, wine.

enough to appreciate a beverage that isn't the usual purview of the upper-crust, but who are cultured and educated enough to know how to consume it in an "elite" way – some might call such individuals hipsters. In all of these cases, the importance of unique language to describe and market specialty products has less to do with highlighting particular qualities of the product itself and much more to do with highlighting class identity.

But what is the class identity that specialty food discourses highlight? And does it go further than snobby oenophiles sipping wine together in a private tasting room? Linguist Gwynne Mapes (2021) has explored the answer to both of these questions. Mapes uses the term **elite authenticity** to describe how the "lowbrow, simple, and authentic can be simultaneously refined, tasteful, and 'first-class'" (p. 26) – in other words, something akin to "hipster food discourse," which is a broader way of thinking about the kind of dual relationship encountered in brutoglossia and specialty coffee discourse. Tracing the history of elite authenticity and its relationship with **neoliberalism**, Mapes argues that over the last several decades socioculturally "elite" positions are coming to be crafted less through ostentatious, conspicuous consumption of luxury goods, but through a skillful blending of both high- and lowbrow consumer behavior (pp. 4–5). Her study of restaurant reviews in *The New York Times* (*NYT*) – an elite newspaper of record in a highly wealth-stratified cosmopolitan city – is an excellent example of this. Rather than highlighting how the hottest new restaurants are attractive by virtue of how expensive and luxurious they are, Mapes shows that *NYT* restaurant reviews tend to use language that frames the best restaurants as old-school, neighborhood haunts, serving up some kind of "traditional" or "authentic" cuisine (pp. 30–31). This framing is closely linked to the kind of reader the *NYT* restaurant review editors imagine is reading their newspaper. It's someone who has a high income, so they probably want to spend their money on elite dining experiences. But it's also someone who is highly educated and plugged into cultural trends, so they don't want to seem totally out of touch with the hip, down-to-earth crowd. *NYT* restaurant reviewers sell this balance of eliteness and authenticity through several rhetorical strategies. Reviews might emphasize when chefs are "natives" of the region whose cuisine an establishment offers (p. 56); describe dishes as "humble," and pair them with photographs that make it seem as if they've just come out of the oven (p. 58); and encourage "adventurous" eating by trying "exotic" ingredient combinations or traveling away from the city center to try a new restaurant (p. 62). Yet at the same time, this "authentic," "humble, "exotic" cuisine is often presented photographed with expert, precise food styling; served alongside extremely expensive ingredients like gold flakes and caviar; and cooked by celebrity chefs. It is this seeming juxtaposition of "high" and "low" linguistic description and images that produce "elite authenticity" which allows people to perform eliteness without being elitist (p. 71).

The research that we have reviewed in this section highlights how our socioeconomic status can be signaled by the language we use, as well as how we use language to interact with consumer goods and how goods are marketed to us. But the links between class and language go even deeper: in the next section, we will show how even language itself can be turned into a commodity.

10.4 Commodification of Language Itself

As we talk of linguistic marketplaces, we must also consider how language and language resources themselves turn into commodities that can be "exchanged" or "traded" (metaphorically or literally). **Commodification**, the process by which an object can be made available to the marketplace, has been argued to have been applied to language and languages, especially in the relatively recent past (Heller et al. 2014). We can find interesting examples of linguistic commodification in the street names of Tucson, Arizona, which is home to one of your authors. Tucson is a richly multilingual place in which the most frequently spoken languages are Spanish and English (not necessarily in that order). It sits in a part of the US that was Mexico until 1854, and it has experienced rapid growth over the years with a great deal of territorial expansion.

As noted by Hill (1993), the pattern of Spanish-language naming of streets and businesses in Tucson illustrates an interesting asymmetry between English names and Spanish ones. The pattern is not, perhaps, what you would expect – that Spanish names are used in parts of the city with more Spanish speakers, and English names used elsewhere. It's often the opposite. For example, there is a large area of the city that is today home to mostly lower-income people, where Spanish is spoken by many – but in which the street names are English words for US States ("Alaska," "Nebraska," etc.). Many of these areas were developed in the 1950s, 60s, and 70s during a time when the adoption of English-language names was seen as a way to reinforce the increasingly Anglo character of the city (Akros Inc. et al. 2007). In the wealthier areas of the city, Spanish street and business names are much more common, and they are often ungrammatical in Spanish (qualifying as "mock Spanish" in the sense of Hill 1993). For example, "Camino la Zorrela," a street name in a very affluent section of the Catalina Foothills, means nothing in Spanish; "Camino Ingresso" – another street in the same neighborhood – mixes Spanish and Italian for no apparent reason, and "Avenida de Paz" is used without the required article. These names seem to be constructed for sound rather than meaning, building an association of (mock) Spanish not with local (marginalized and often denigrated) varieties but rather with a mythical, Mediterranean influenced ambiance. And clearly developers have been successful in using these Spanish-sounding names as part of an effort to market locations and businesses to affluent white consumers.

This example highlights what linguistics like to call **linguistic landscape** – or, the way different languages are used visually as symbolic tools within human environments. In addition to these Arizona street signs, there are many other ways to investigate the role that visible language in public places plays in understanding the economics of language. A linguist in the community might investigate things like product and location naming practices that are intended to invoke "foreign" languages and analyze their correlations with price points, prestige, or community membership. The so-called "metal umlaut" in the names of heavy metal bands such as Blue Öyster Cult, Motörhead and Mötley Crüe is clearly part of a branding or marketing strategy associating these bands with a Germanic (or "Wagnerian") identity.[12] The ice cream brand name Häagen-Dazs was explicitly created to appear to seem (but not be) Danish[13] – based both on the desire to position the brand as more costly and exclusive than others, and on the wish to show affiliation with Denmark based on that country's resistance to Nazi persecution of Jews in World War II (Nathan 2012). And the linguist Jan Blommaert has documented the highly amusing example of a chocolate shop he encountered in Japan called "Nina's Derrière." One hopes the shop owners were hoping to use a visible display of the French language to index a sense of sophisticated elegance, and not, in fact, with the literal French translation of the phrase – "Nina's bum" (Blommaert 2012). Additional examples of excellent work relating to linguistic landscapes can be found in Leeman and Modan's (2009) work on Washington, DC's Chinatown neighborhood. We are sure you'll find interesting stories behind the language choices you see, and that some of those choices will be reflective of the ways in which we connect language with economic class.

10.5 Conclusion

In this chapter we've discussed a number of connections between language, money, jobs, and economics. We've described ways in which a linguist in the

---

[12] We base this discussion on remarks found in Liberman 2020.
[13] It is, in fact, originally from New York City.

community might investigate social biases and prejudices around hiring and promotion at work, and how we might connect our languages and linguistic varieties with prestige or affiliation to socioeconomic class. We've discussed how our views and attitudes toward our own and others' linguistic repertoires come up again and again in our economic life.

We trust you have been able to generate some ideas of your own to investigate, and we hope you will look to the tools and methods described here in order to do just that.

Linguist in the Community

- Using maps or your own travels through your community, take a systematic inventory of street names there. Look for patterns in which some neighborhoods or developments might have certain styles of street names, particularly those that reflect a certain language background. What languages are used to name streets and neighborhoods that are affluent and prestigious? Does this differ for streets and neighborhoods that are less affluent? What does this tell you about the history of your community?
- Consider a Labov-like mini-experiment in which you first identify a feature – it could be a vocabulary item, or a pronunciation pattern – that you would expect to differ among people of different socioeconomic classes. Then create a plan in which you might be able to elicit that feature from others. You could do it by asking people for directions, or asking where a certain section is in a library or bookstore, or even asking something like the time. Take brief notes after each interaction about a) the apparent socioeconomic class of the speaker – based on your knowledge of the context and locations where you're working – and b) the presence or absence of the feature in question – based on your impression immediately after the interaction. After you've collected some notes, see if any patterns emerge. If they do, use those patterns as a way to generate a hypothesis for a more carefully controlled study. If they don't, consider possible explanations as to why your experiment didn't go as expected. Were your preconceived beliefs incorrect? Did the method not work?

Linguist in the Classroom

- In pairs or small groups, discuss examples from students' experiences about advice they've gotten about how to behave – and especially how to speak – in job interviews. Share the different kinds of advice with the class as a

whole, and analyze them based on whose linguistic styles or norms are reflected in them. Are we being advised to speak in a way that's associated with a given gender, ethnicity, or geographic region? How might we work to adapt those expectations in order to make job searches more fair?
- In groups or as a whole, create a list of familiar languages and ask participants to assess each on the basis of how it is perceived socially and economically in your community: For example, does the language strike us as one that would make a consumer product name more prestigious and pricey, or less? Would a person who has that language as part of their repertoire be able to parlay that knowledge into a higher salary, or perhaps be likely to keep their knowledge secret in order to maintain prestige and professional power? Look for patterns in attitudes toward the economic valence of languages that might map onto other kinds of beliefs or prejudices about the speakers of those languages.
- Ask students to look at job ads in any open online forum, and collect information about how many and what kinds of job ads use language proficiencies in their required or optional qualifications for applicants. Pool the collected information together and look for patterns that might reflect the various economic values of different kinds of language proficiency.

Glossary

bivalent class indexicality The ability of a semiotic form to index both high-status class markers and low status class markers at the same time.

brutoglossia A social register of talk used by members of the craft/specialty beer community in which specialized terminology is used to to describe the qualities and characteristics of beer and beer production.

coda The consonant sound occurring at the end of a syllable.

commodification The process by which something can be made available for exchange or trade in an economic marketplace.

elite authenticity A product that is simultaneously everyday and also composed of first-class materials – for example, blueberry pancakes where it is highlighted that the blueberries are organic, the pancakes are made of organic wheat flour, and the syrup that comes with them is a high-grade real maple syrup.

GDP Gross domestic product, or the monetary value of all goods and services produced by a given country during a specific period of time.

interpretation A type of translation in which the meaning of a chunk of oral or signed language is communicated into the oral or signed form of a target language, usually live.

linguistic capital The language resources or assets available to a speaker that are imbued with cultural value and social power.

linguistic landscape The visual representations of language(s) and their relative salience within a particular geographic area.

linguistic marketplace The metaphorical space in which languages, varieties, dialects, accents, and linguistic resources are negotiated and exchanged for other forms of cultural or social capital.

Metalinguistic Method of Sociolinguistic Interview A type of sociolinguistic interview (see Chapter 3) in which the interviewer both explicitly accounts for their own language background before conducting the interview and also asks interviewees directly about their language practices and beliefs about language in context.

neoliberal(ism) A viewpoint or political stance that focuses on the free market, capitalism, and economic prosperity within a democratic state.

oenophile A wine connoisseur.

oinoglossia A social register of talk used by consumers of wine in which specialized terminology is used to to describe the qualities and characteristics of wine and wine production.

professionalism Having the characteristics, qualities, or skills that are socially perceived to be linked to particular kinds of jobs, roles, or titles.

semiotic (cue) Symbols and the meanings made out of them. Semiotic cues might include typography and graphics on fancy beverage labels (or the lack thereof) or the language we use to talk about them.

socioeconomic class A grouping of factors like wealth, education, and profession. The combination of these factors can account for systematic variation in how language is used.

translation The process of communicating the meaning of a chunk of language in one language to a target language, usually done after the utterance of the first language; or the result of this process.

yuppie An informal acronym for "young upwardly-mobile/urban professional."

Recommended Readings

We can't help you ace your next job interview, but if you want to dig deeper into the links between language variation, the economy, employment, and the job market, we have plenty of recommended readings listed below. We hope you'll take some time to explore some of the nuances captured in these studies that we only describe in passing here. Your local college or university library should be able to help you find access to these readings – and they may even be able to help point you to a local career center if you do want some help preparing for that upcoming job interview. As for us, we'll stick to the linguistics.

Bertrand, M., & Mullainathan, S. (2004). Are Emily and Greg more employable than Lakisha and Jamal? A field experiment on labor market discrimination. *The American Economic Review*, *94*(4), 133. https://doi.org/10.1257/0002828042002561

Cotter, W. M., & Valentinsson, M.-C. (2018). Bivalent class indexing in the sociolinguistics of specialty coffee talk. *Journal of Sociolinguistics*, *22*(5), 489–515. https://doi.org/10.1111/josl.12305

Hill, J. H. (2008). *The Everyday Language of White Racism*. Wiley-Blackwell.

Jones, T., Kalbfeld, J. R., Hancock, R., & Clark, R. (2019). Testifying while Black: An experimental study of court reporter accuracy in transcription of African American English. *Language*, *95*(2), e216–e252. https://doi.org/10.1353/lan.2019.0042

Labov, W. (1972). *Sociolinguistic Patterns*. University of Pennsylvania Press.

Rickford, J. R., & King, S. (2016). Language and linguistics on trial: Hearing Rachel Jeantel (and other vernacular speakers) in the courtroom and beyond. *Language*, *92*(4), 948–988. www.doi.org/10.1353/lan.2016.0078

Valentinsson, M.-C. (2022). Semiotic disruption and negotiations of authenticity among Argentine fans of Anglophone media. *Journal of Linguistic Anthropology*, *32*(2), 345–363. https://doi.org/10.1111/jola.12355

Wright, K. E. (2022). *Black Professionalism: Perception and Metalinguistic Assessment of Black American Speakers' Sociolinguistic Labor*. [Doctoral Dissertation, University of Michigan]. https://doi.org/10.7302/6091

Zhang, Q. (2018). *Language and Social Change in China: Undoing Commonness Through Cosmopolitan Mandarin*. Routledge.

11 Languages Get Fired, Get Arrested, Go to Jail

11.1 Linguistic Discrimination Is Alive and Well

In the fall of 2021, employees at a large southwestern university[1] in the US were asked to complete mandatory training in anti-discrimination and anti-harassment practices. The training was a short online "course," produced by a commercial vendor, requiring perhaps one hour of attention in which employees were asked to read and understand both legal and institutional statements and policies about what constitutes illegal discrimination and how the university community wanted to go beyond the minimal legal standard and really engage in earnest anti-discrimination efforts.

After reviewing law and policy emphasizing that discrimination based on a person's race, ethnicity, or national origin was never acceptable, employees were asked to consider the following scenario, and mark it as either "discrimination" or "not discrimination."

> Camilla is hiring a marketing manager who will be responsible for overseeing all external communication in the US, including working as a spokesperson who handles public speaking appearances at events where the audience primarily speaks English. She interviews a candidate who reports having moderate fluency in English. The ability to speak fluent English is a requirement of the job. That said, Camilla and the candidate can still understand each other pretty well. However, Camilla decides to move forward with other candidates.
>
> Is this possible discrimination? Yes or No.

On a "yes" answer, the test-taker receives the following feedback:

> Not Quite: It is OK to make employment decisions based on someone's capacity to do the job. Camilla does need someone who speaks fluent English for an external communications role that involves public speaking to an English-speaking audience. Try again.

---

[1] This story comes from the personal experience of one of your authors, who followed up with relevant advisory groups to try to address the problem described here.

The scenario asked employees to imagine themselves as hiring managers screening candidates for a position that involved customer support, and that therefore required "fluent English" from successful candidates. The manager interviews a candidate whose English is "foreign accented," but basically intelligible. The manager determines not to forward that candidate to the finalist pool.

Is this discrimination?

The keyed answer in the anti-discrimination training module was that it is not. The rationale given was that since the job requires fluency in English, the manager is allowed to screen out applicants whose English is not fluent.

But you might see that there are a few problems with this logic. Who gets to determine what counts as "fluent" English? Are we really able to be accurate in our assessments of fluency, or might our judgments about other people's fluency be affected by our preconceived notions of people's racial and ethnic identities or national origins? Since the interlocutors are able to understand each other, shouldn't this indicate that the "foreign accented" candidate is as fluent as they need to be for the job?

Research in sociolinguistics makes it clear that the answer to this question is "yes," and it's a very strong "yes." Our beliefs, attitudes, and perceptions of others' identities affects our perception of their language behavior and can even lead us to "hallucinate" speech patterns that aren't there. Furthermore, there are a variety of reasons why a job candidate might undervalue their own linguistic skills despite having the requisite knowledge to perform their job as well as, say, a monolingual US English speaker.

For example, Rubin (1992) conducted a study in which they audio recorded a white graduate student who grew up in Wisconsin and who was a monolingual speaker of US English, giving several short "lectures" on different scholarly topics. He then recruited several groups of undergraduate students to listen to the lectures and take a couple of brief tests afterward. One of the tests was on the content of the lecture (testing students' comprehension). One of the tests was on the students' perceptions of the lecturer.

For each of the lecture topics, there were two groups of student listeners. One group was shown a picture of the graduate student whose voice was actually in the audio. The other group was shown a picture of a person who appeared to be of East Asian ethnicity. Both groups heard exactly the same audio, but the only difference between them was that one of the student groups had visual cues to an East Asian ethnicity for the speaker.

Rubin's results showed several very interesting effects. First, the students who saw the picture of the white speaker scored better on the comprehension tests than those who saw the other picture. This pattern was found regardless of the academic topic of the lecture. Second, students who saw the picture of the East Asian person rated the lecturer lower in terms of intelligibility than did the students who saw the picture of the white lecturer. Some of the students even said that they found the East Asian–appearing lecturer to be hard to understand because of their "foreign-accented speech."

Of course, there was no foreign-accented speech – those students relied on visual cues in a way that affected their perceptions of the speaker's "accentedness." Results like Rubin's show us very clearly that our expectations and biases play a significant role in our perceptions of other people's language behavior.

Work from a variety of researchers (Babel & Russell 2015; Hanulíková 2018; Kutlu 2020; McGowan 2015) replicates and refines these effects and extends them to a much wider variety of contexts, many of which we'll discuss in this chapter. We find a troubling pattern in the linguistic biases that shape our perception of each others' language: if another person seems to belong to a stigmatized or low-prestige social group (for example, in the US, a speaker of Black American English, or Chicano/a English, or even the varieties of US English common among Native American communities) or from a region that we see as less prestigious (for example, Québécois French as opposed to Parisian French), we are likely to perceive these stigmatized varieties as less intelligible than they really are when measured by careful and qualified observers (Lindberg & Trofimovich 2020).

This means that a typical hiring manager in the US is not only a poor judge of candidates' fluency, but their judgment is likely to disadvantage some candidates based on those candidates' race, ethnicity, or national origin. Race, ethnicity, and national origin are known as **protected characteristics**, or qualities of a person that are protected by law from discrimination. In the US, you cannot deny someone a job based on their protected characteristics.

While we linguists wait for people in other professions, including the legal profession, to learn more about these problematic effects, we can at least assert with confidence that the correct answer to the question on that training – the one about whether the hiring manager's action was discriminatory – is "yes." It's very likely discriminatory, although it's also very likely that this type of discrimination will not be treated as illegal. Unfortunately, there are many avenues for linguistic discrimination in the legal system, including housing discrimination and attributing lack of credibility to legal witnesses and testimonies, as well as which languages people are allowed to use at work.

11.2 Language and Housing Discrimination

Wherever we are in the world, we all have to find a home – and often that means seeking an apartment or home to rent. Landlords may have preconceived notions about who would make a good or bad tenant, and these notions invoke stereotypes about the ways in which people use language. In the US, native speakers of English who use an accent or dialect of English that seems to differ in some way from our ideas of "standard" or "mainstream" American English are often at risk of discrimination when searching for housing. Linguist John Baugh documented this in his well-known study of how **linguistic profiling** happens in the housing market. As a native speaker of three different American English dialects – Chicano English, **African American English**, and mainstream US English – Baugh was able to directly test the effects of linguistic discrimination on the housing and rental market. Throughout the early 1990s, he would call apartment listings asking for information about the availability of the unit, each time using a different one of his native dialects. Overwhelmingly, when he spoke in African American English and Chicano English, he was told that the unit was no longer available, even when calling with his mainstream US English dialect led to offers to have the same apartment unit shown (Baugh 2003).

With his colleagues Thomas Purnell and William Idsardi, Baugh showed that most people were able to accurately guess the racial/ethnic identity of a speaker based on extremely limited auditory information – as little as a single "hello" – and research into how this played out in the housing market revealed that landlords were using this information to discriminate against potential renters based on their race in the San Francisco Bay area (Purnell et al. 1999). Since the Fair Housing Act (part of the United States' 1968 Civil Rights Act) prohibits discrimination in housing based on race, these studies offered important evidence that landlords were able to use accents as a covert way of enacting racial discrimination.

Using similar techniques, other researchers have also found a great deal of discrimination in the housing market: Douglas S. Massey and Garvey Lundy (2001) found similar occurrences in Philadelphia and, further, showed intersections with gender in addition to dialect and class. Andrew Hanson and Zackary Hawley (2011) also found interactions between perceived race and class even in emailed exchanges about rental properties.

More recent research has shown that linguistic discrimination in the housing market is still ongoing. Another multidialectal linguist, Kelly Wright, illustrated this through a series of experiments that extended and built on the work that Baugh and his colleagues conducted (Wright 2019). First, she evaluated whether property managers claimed they took the voice of a potential tenant into account when taking a phone call about a property, and how connected they are to the community they rent in – taking this as a measure of how aware they are likely to be of the language varieties used by potential tenants. Next, she tested whether her multiple dialects sounded enough like distinct people that she could use her own voice to call apartments and test for this sort of linguistic discrimination – finding that they did! This meant that when Wright began using the same methods employed by Baugh and his colleagues – calling apartment listings using three distinct dialects, each associated with a different racial or social group – she could reasonably assume that the landlords were perceiving the calls as coming from different people.

When calling apartment listings in Knoxville, Tennessee, she found that her different dialects fared better in receiving a strong commitment to show her the apartment when it was perceived as "matching" the demographics of the neighborhood (Wright 2019). Landlords were more likely to offer an appointment to view the property when she used her African American English dialect in a Black working-class neighborhood or when she used her Southern English dialect in a white working-class neighborhood. When she called landlords in a middle-class neighborhood, landlords were equally likely to offer her a showing appointment regardless of which dialect she used. However, the Southern English dialect was overwhelmingly likely to get a strong commitment overall, potentially because it was perceived as both white and local – more authentic than a mainstream US English voice would be. Furthermore, she found evidence of steering in her interviews, where landlords would suggest a different property for the speaker than the one they were originally asked about. Steering a prospective buyer or renter toward a property they did not ask about is a violation of the Fair Housing Act, so Wright's findings have similar legal implications to Purnell, Idsardi, and Baugh's work.

The Fair Housing Act mandates that housing discrimination is illegal in the United States. Many legal scholars have argued that the protections afforded by the Fair Housing Act extend to certain forms of linguistic discrimination – for instance, that landlords cannot discriminate against a potential tenant because they have a variety of speech that might be associated with a particular national origin. However, discrimination based on regional accents, or speech varieties based on racial or ethnic difference, are not as clearly protected under the law. The work of linguists like Kelly Wright and others shows just how pervasive this form of discrimination is and how much work is still needed to prevent it.

11.3 Language and the Legal System

Early sociolinguistic research on credibility in courtroom talk built on the tradition of language and gender research instantiated by Robin Lakoff through her foundational book, Language and Woman's Place (Lakoff 1975). As you might remember from Chapter 9, Lakoff described how language and gender ideologies intersect in ways that constrain how we view "feminine" speech in the United States. Broadly speaking, Lakoff argued that American women were expected to employ a range of linguistic strategies that mitigated, attenuated, or lessened the force of their opinion – thus constraining them to a role of powerlessness in interaction. Linguistic features included in Lakoff's analysis included (but were not limited to):

- The use of **tag questions**: "Great day today, isn't it?"
- The use of **hedging devices** such as "kind of," "probably": "That's kind of disappointing" or "It'll probably work out."
- The use of indirectness: for example, saying "Brr, it's a little chilly in here!" to convey a request to close a drafty window.
- Avoiding expletives.
- Rising intonation at the end of utterance such that a declarative sentence might sound like a question.

As we also discussed in Chapter 9, much of her claims were based on observations about the speech of upper-middle-class white women, and you can visit that chapter if you want to review some of those critiques. We mention her work again here because, just as she laid the groundwork for much of the contemporary work on the study of language and gender, her analysis also shaped a tremendous number of further studies on the social functions that linguistic forms like the above can serve. One notable study in this vein was conducted by William O'Barr and Kim Atkins in the 1980s, which studied the role of these features of "women's language" in the context of courtroom testimony across thirty different court cases. Rather than finding high rates of "women's language" features in the speech of female attorneys, judges, jury members, and witnesses, O'Barr and Atkins showed that these features were found most frequently in the speech of those occupying less socially powerful positions in the courtroom. For instance, if a female attorney were cross-examining a male witness, the witness might use more of these features as a reflection of his less powerful and less certain role in the courtroom. Thus, O'Barr and Atkins argued for a reframing of these features as elements of "powerless language," rather than as features of "women's language" (O'Barr & Atkins 1980). In later work with colleague John Conley, O'Barr further posited that avoidance of these features and use of features that might be deemed "powerful" (e.g., avoiding tag questions and hedges, being direct, etc.) could be a way of establishing credence and believability, particularly in contexts where these features are highly valued, like a courtroom (Conley & O'Barr 2005, p. 65).

Since the 1970s and 80s, further research has investigated the relationship between how linguistic style impacts courtrooms – in particular, how language shapes assessments of credibility for witnesses. Nicole Hildebrand-Edgar and Susan Ehrlich's work investigated these themes within the context of a Canadian rape trial from 2014 (Hildebrand-Edgar & Ehrlich 2017). Their work complicated the notion that "more powerful language" equals "more credible speech," specifically when gender ideologies are also at play.

While the complainant in this rape trial used features of "powerful language" – namely, using relatively few tag questions and hedges in her testimony – the accused used comparatively many more such features in his. Under a lens that only compares powerful vs. powerless speech styles in constructing courtroom credibility, we might expect that these differences in linguistic style led the complaint to be perceived by the jury as highly credible and trustworthy. In this case, the opposite was true. Hildebrand-Edgar and Ehrlich argued that this was because "powerful" language was at odds with gender ideologies about how female rape victims should behave. Under such gender ideologies, female victims of rape are not expected to assert powerful stances. Indeed, they are often expected to appear fearful, highly emotional, vulnerable, and defenseless. These beliefs are rooted in the culturally specific notion of the "ideal victim," who is expected to wear certain things, behave in certain ways, and react in certain ways to crimes committed against them in order for them to be taken seriously as a victim. Thus, the notion of "powerful" language and how it shapes credibility must always be considered in relation to sociocultural and pragmatic contexts – these stances and linguistic styles will not always be desirable or accepted for all speakers at all times.

Philipp Angermeyer (2015) explores issues of language and credibility in US courts for speakers who are multilingual, whether or not one of their languages is also the language of the court. In testimony given by multilingual participants, there is complex interplay between the processes of codeswitching, interpretation, and court reporting that can result in transcripts that omit or misrepresent key facts. Angermeyer describes an exchange between a defendant and the attorney of a plaintiff in which the defendant's use of Haitian Creole, their first language, which was being rendered into English by an official court interpreter, was challenged as itself evidence of unreliability or deception on the grounds that the defendant could speak English. Ceil Lucas (2014) discusses interactions between codeswitching and interpretation in ASL, particularly when deaf people are signing within an otherwise monolingual English context, that may offer challenges that differ still from those encountered by speakers of spoken languages other than English.

The cultural specificity of a "credible" linguistic style was also illustrated in the 2013 trial of George Zimmerman, a man accused of killing an African American boy named Trayvon Martin. During the trial, the prosecution called nineteen-year-old Rachel Jeantel to testify. Jeantel was a close friend of Martin's – in fact, she had been speaking on the phone with Martin until just moments before his murder. This made Jeantel a key witness, and it is no surprise that the prosecution called her to the stand. In the end, she testified for nearly six full hours. Ultimately, though, Jeantel's testimony made little difference in the case – one juror reported that her testimony was not mentioned once in the jury deliberations that took over sixteen hours (Bloom 2014, p. 148; cited in Rickford & King 2016, p. 950). By any legal standard, this seems bizarre. Multiple hours of testimony from the next closest thing to an eyewitness account, without even a mention in jury deliberations? Why would this be?

Linguists John Rickford and Sharese King argued that this disregard for Jeantel's testimony was a case of linguistically driven racism. Rachel Jeantel is a speaker of a dialect of English that scholars often refer to as African American English. Like all other regional and social dialects of English, this language variety has its own unique rules, structures, and styles. While certainly some of these structures differ from other dialects of American English – like using stressed BIN ("been") in utterances like "I BIN knew I was the last person to talk to Trayvon," which jurors would have been unlikely to understand as meaning "I had known for a long time that I was the last person to talk to Trayvon" (Rickford & King 2016, p. 958) – these features are just as systematic, rule-governed, and orderly as the unique features of other dialects of English, and in cases like this one carry important meaning about the temporal relationships between events – information that's crucial for the jury to understand what happened when. However, the use of this dialect is often highly stigmatized. This is due to the centuries of systemic racism that pervade many American institutions, which left a legacy of discrimination not just against Black Americans themselves but also against the language(s) they use.

Decades of scholarship in perceptual dialectology and sociolinguistics has illustrated how repeated negative portrayals of Black people have led to widespread cultural beliefs that Black language is "less than" (Lippi-Green 2012) – less orderly, less proper, less grammatical, and, crucially for Rachel Jeantel's testimony, "less intelligible" and "less credible" (Rickford & King 2016). Because of these beliefs, Jeantel, who used several features of African American English in her testimony, was denigrated in media coverage of the trial. It was not just jurors who disregarded her testimony, but reporters and political commentators arguing that their inability to understand her meant that she had failed to convince the world of the credibility of her story. We know this is not true: she was speaking under oath and therefore we must assume her credibility regardless of her speaking style.

Issues of linguistic credibility also come up when individuals interact with the legal system via the police. Interviewing victims of crime is often considered a key step in building evidence for a case. In England and Wales, police interviewing practices are laid out in an official document published by the Ministry of Justice in 2011, titled "Achieving Best Evidence in Criminal Proceedings: Guidance for Vulnerable or Intimidated Witness, including Children." A team of linguists – Charles Antaki, Emma Richardson, Elizabeth Stokoe, and Sara Willott – took to investigating how these guidelines were employed by police in the particular case of complainants alleging sexual assault, who also had intellectual disabilities (Antaki et al. 2015).

The standard guidelines for police interviewers in the "Achieving Best Evidence" document lay out specific methods of eliciting information from complainants and other witnesses that rely on a typical form of pragmatic reasoning. One such strategy is to avoid directly challenging witnesses over inconsistencies in their accounts and instead raise them as questions or issues of confusion on the part of the police interviewer. For instance, a police officer interviewing a complainant might ask, "If X was the case, how was Y possible?" This formulation implies that something was implausible about Y, given conditions laid out in X (Antaki et al. 2015, pp. 332–333). You can test how this works by imagining a case where Y seems "unchallenging, natural, and consistent" with X – for instance, if his hands weren't free, how was he able to use the steering wheel? (Antaki et al. 2015, p. 337).

Reporting a sexual assault to the police is an inherently stressful endeavor, and many individuals may find it extra challenging to perform in linguistically normative ways. We may stumble over our words, stutter, or get distracted as we recount these difficult experiences. However, as Antaki and colleagues point out, individuals with intellectual disabilities may be at particular disadvantage in these contexts, particularly when it comes to reasoning with the kinds of unstated assumptions produced by linguistic structures such as the formula discussed above (p. 345). The authors write that "not only might they simply not understand the question, but they might give an answer that failed to deal with the fault that it implied. Thus, for example, if the question is predicated on something that 'anyone' would do ... one could reply in a way that offered a countervailing account" (p. 345).

So, for instance, when a police officer asks, "Why didn't you run away when the attacker pursued you?", there is an implicit assumption that the "reasonable" response to an attacker pursuing you is to run. A countervailing account might offer a justification or explanation for seemingly "unreasonable" behavior, such as, "My coat was caught on a door and I couldn't get it free easily." Individuals with intellectual disabilities which affect their ability to follow these lines of pragmatic reasoning may not readily produce such answers. Antaki and colleagues found many cases where complainants with intellectual disabilities responded to such questions with phrases like "I don't know" or other phrases that evinced a lack of understanding of the purpose of the question (pp. 338, 345). This can create an implication that the complainant did not "do the 'reasonable' thing," which, in turn, can damage complainant credibility (pp. 345–346).

In order to have greater equity in police interviews with complainants alleging sexual assault, Antaki and colleagues argue that the "Achieving Best Evidence" guidelines should be updated to encourage police to concretely explain why they are asking certain types of questions in a way that best helps a complainant – in any cognitive or mental state – to best answer their questions. More broadly, this case teaches linguists that we should not assume a lack of "credibility," "honesty," or "believability" simply on the basis of whether an interviewee's responses are **aligned** or **disaligned** with the question posed to them (that is, whether their responses conform to what we expect for a given question).

For another example of the effects of different styles of victim interviews, let's turn to another case of interactions between crime victims, the police, and other parts of the legal system. In a 2003 article, linguist Ana Celia Ostermann explored how professionals in two different settings in Brazil – an all-female police station and a nongovernmental feminist crisis intervention center – negotiated interactions with victims of domestic violence. At each of these sites, crime victims appear in person to make reports about their experiences, begin legal proceedings (at the police station), and sometimes also be connected to legal and social support services (at the NGO feminist crisis intervention center). This can constitute a threat to the victim's **face**, or an individuals' public self-image. Ostermann notes that "disclosing and describing to strangers the violence that takes place in the private sphere of one's home constitutes a potential threat to one's public image or face. This holds even when those strangers are professionals whose job involves dealing with cases of domestic violence on an everyday basis. It is potentially face-threatening for the victim because it places her in an emotionally vulnerable position" (Ostermann 2003, p. 475). Thus, part of what workers at both the all-female police station and the NGO feminist crisis center do in considering how to take these reports is engage in **facework**; that is, discursive and interactional strategies that mitigate the potential face threat to a crime victim.[2]

Ostermann's research found that employees at the police station and employees at the crisis center used very different strategies for managing the face concerns of victims. The all-female police station, called Delegacia da Mulher, was established with the belief that female police officers were "naturally" better suited than male officers in dealing with cases of violence against women, and that female victims of crime would "naturally" respond better to requests to provide statements and evidence to female officers (p. 477). Whether or not this was true, few of the officers stationed at Delegacia da Mulher had chosen this particular line of work – most were assigned it simply on the basis of their gender, even if they showed aptitude for or interest in other kinds of police work. Meanwhile, the NGO feminist crisis center, called CIV Mulher, was founded and staffed by academics, activists, and organizers with the specific goal of "addressing root causes of gender violence without overt police intervention" (p. 477). Although neither the CIV Mulher nor the Delegacia da Mulher staff receive specialized training to conduct intake interviews with complainants, many of the CIV Mulher staff in Ostermann's study reported drawing on their academic and professional training in order to engage with clients.

In exploring the typical responses to intake interviews with clients at each setting, Ostermann looked for what interviewers – called *frentistas* at Delegacia da Mulher and *triagistas* at CIV Mulher – did when a client reached a **transition relevance place** (TRP). According to conversation analysts, a TRP is a point or moment in conversation when one speaker's turn is potentially completed, and thus another speaker may step in. Ostermann found some rather stark differences between what happened at TRPs in client intake interviews with *frentistas* at Delegacia da Mulher compared to interviews between clients and *triagistas* at CIV Mulher.

For example, Ostermann noted that *frentistas* remained silent at TRPs more often than *triagistas*.[3] That is, when a client was telling a story about their experiences and reached a point in their narrative when the officer could have taken a conversational turn, the *frentista* simply didn't. In contrast, *triagistas* at CIV Mulher use silence relatively infrequently at TRPs and instead engage with TRPs in a variety of ways. Most common for

---

[2] You can refer back to Chapter 2 for more information about face and facework.
[3] We will use *frentista(s)* when we are discussing the interviewers at the police station, Delegacia da Mulher, and *triagista(s)* when we are discussing the interviewers at the feminist crisis center, CIV Mulher, even though their role is essentially the same for the point of this research.

CIV Mulher *triagistas* at TRPs was the use of what Ostermann calls **topic-related responses** – that is, turns that show some kind of relation to what the client was saying in their previous turn, such as asking for further detail or requesting that the client retell some part of the story. The *triagistas* also used comparatively many more **continuers** – noises such as mmhmm, ah, or uh-huh that are commonly used to indicate to an interlocutor that we will pass up our upcoming turn of talk and that they should keep talking. Finally, Ostermann noted a difference in how workers at both sites used **topic-change responses** at TRPs: *frentistas* would more frequently use their conversational turn to completely shift to a different topic than the *triagistas* would (p. 482). You can imagine that changing to a different, unrelated topic might signal to you that your interlocutor isn't interested in what you had said. Thus, changing the topic can be seen as not cooperating with your interlocutor, especially when your interlocutor has placed themself in a vulnerable position as the victims had done.

Broadly, Ostermann interprets her findings to indicate that client intake interviews at CIV Mulher are more cooperative and solidarity-building as *triagistas* use more interactional strategies that encourage clients to tell their story with cooperation from the workers. These workers use various interactional strategies to show clients that they believe her story and want to support her. *Frentistas* at Delegacia da Mulher are interpreted as comparatively less cooperative since *frentistas* do less interactional work to build solidarity and show a client that they care about her story. According to Ostermann, differences in how cooperative each interviewer is perceived to be are reflective of the different institutional goals of each setting: at the police station, the goal is to begin legal proceedings against the abuser, so a police report must be filed; at the NGO, the goal is to establish rapport and support the client with a variety of resources (Ostermann 2003; Ostermann & Comunello da Costa 2012, pp. 209–211). The best way to put this is in the actual words of employees at each of these sites. A CIV Mulher coordinator described these intake interviews as "a crucial opportunity to set the relationship between institution and client 'on the right foot'," whereas a worker at the Delegacia da Mulher noted that she doesn't "give the victims more than the state can offer. And that is [an intake report]" (Ostermann 2003, p. 497).

This difference in orientation is critical in the context of reporting domestic violence or sexual assault: if one instution collaborates with and supports victims in preparing statements on abuse or violence, whereas another makes little effort to do so, it seems self-evident that the former institution will have an easier time working with these clients to accomplish these goals and seek justice. However, it is important to note, as Ostermann does, that employees at CIV Mulher and Delegacia da Mulher are not simply mouthpieces for these institutions. The way they approach these interactions is also reflective of their broader social positions in the community. *Triagistas* at CIV Mulher tend to be professional, highly educated, white, upper-middle-class women who specifically sought out this work and whose educational backgrounds complement the work. *Frentistas* at the Delegacia da Mulher tend to be of lower socioeconomic standing, typically with a high school diploma and no other relevant training, working in a traditionally male-dominanted system in a setting not of their choice and often with difficult family lives of their own (p. 499). In other words, the workers at CIV Mulher are able and motivated to provide better quality care because they have better resources to do so, relevant training prior to working at the CIV Mulher, and choose to do the work rather than being assigned to it regardless of aptitude or preference.

If we want to see victims of crime and injustice taken seriously and treated compassionately, we need to make sure that all of these sites of interfacing with the legal system – from juries, to witness testimonies, to the work police do and the ways that victims make reports – are shaped and governed by policies that reflect a rigorous understanding of how language shapes the crucial moments of interaction.

11.4 Trouble with Transcription

The story of Rachel Jeantel's court testimony, which we described in Section 11.3, is only one example of how beliefs about "proper," "correct," "intelligible," and "credible" language can affect our justice systems. We also see these beliefs intersecting with ideologies about oral/spoken vs. written language use.[4] As you know from Chapters 2 and 3, **transcription**, or the written representation of spoken or signed language use, is an important component of linguistic analysis. What elements of the language signal get encoded in a transcript depends largely on what features of language a linguist is studying. If you are a phonetician, for instance, you might narrowly transcribe all of the detail of the sounds in a word or utterance. On the other hand, if you are a conversation analyst, this level of detail is both distracting and unnecessary since the specific phonetic contours of the utterance are not part of the analysis. Instead, the conversation analyst's transcript will carefully notate when a speaker's turn is cut off by someone else, when multiple

---

[4] Interestingly (but not surprisingly), these ideologies always seem to leave out signed languages, though dialectal variation in signed languages is of course present and ideologically active in Deaf communities (Lucas 2014).

speakers overlap with one another, and other such elements of language in interaction.

Either way, as linguist Mary Bucholtz points out, "The transcription of a recording [of some instance of language use] is not a straightforward act" (Bucholtz 2000, p. 1441) – this difficulty is in part due to issues like the quality of a given recording, but it is also influenced by the language ideologies of the transcriber and the context. In the trial of Oscar Pistorius, the South African runner who was tried and convicted of killing his partner, Reeva Steenkamp, a recording of Pistorius was alternatively transcribed as either "she wasn't breathing" or "she was everything." Obviously, these two possibilities say very different things about Pistorius' statement (Fraser 2014). In the Rachel Jeantel example, the court reporters in that trial may not have accurately or fully represented Rachel Jeantel's speech if they were operating under the assumption that her variety of African American English was inherently "unintelligible." Bucholtz's own work as a pro bono legal consultant revealed such a discrepancy, where an official police transcript of an interrogation marked several key passages of speech as "unintelligible" – yet when Bucholtz attempted her own transcript of the recording, it was perfectly possible to recreate what the interlocutors said (Bucholtz 2000, p. 1442). In this same transcript, Bucholtz also noted that certain utterances were attributed to the wrong speaker and simply mistranscribed. This led her to conclude that the "official" transcript of record imbued the interrogating officer with more authority and credibility. See for yourself what you think of the comparison in Table 11.1: you might notice differences in the words used in each transcription or even the level of detail in the transcriptions.

In fact, another study on this topic (Walker 1990) has shown that transcribers will standardize the speech of individuals with institutional authority in legal contexts – such as police officers and lawyers – and represent the speech of those with less authority – such as witnesses and individuals accused of crimes – using nonstandard and even stigmatized orthographic features. These sorts of transcription choices lead, according to Bucholtz, to "self-fulfilling analyses" (Bucholtz 2000, p. 1459). Here's how it works: There is a pervasive myth in many language communities that the best versions of spoken language are ones that most closely model the written language. These versions of a spoken language might even be called "standard" versions of a language (Lippi-Green 2012, pp. 58–59). People often speak of "pronouncing words exactly as they are written" or "saying every letter in a word" as an ideal or appropriate way to speak (as if English orthography is obvious or transparent). For example, linguist Geoffrey Pullum wrote about an acquaintance pronouncing words oddly in a blog post. The acquaintance

Table 11.1 Two versions of a police interrogation transcript, reproduced from Bucholtz (2000, p. 1442).

Police transcript	Researcher transcript (simplified)
Q = Police officer, A = Client	Pol = Police officer, Cli = Client
1. A: I'll tell you every – every single thing.	1. Cli: I'll tell you every – every single thing.
2. Q: Okay.	2. Pol: Okay.
3. A: I mean what – *see you got to understand*	3. Cli: I mean what –
4. (unintelligible).	4. Pol: *See you got to understand.*
5. Q: (Unintelligible).	5. (unintelligible).
	6. Cli: *Do me a favor, man, that's it.*
	7. Pol: *Yeah?*
6. A: Yeah.	8. Cli: Yeah.
7. Q: Yeah. You've got to understand (unintelligible) *house?*	9. Pol: Yeah. You've got to understand (unintelligible).
8. A: Yeah.	10. Cli: Yeah.
9. Q: Okay. You've got to understand. I'm not going to make *you deal with anybody* –	11. Pol: Okay. You've got to understand. I'm not going to make *a deal with anybody* –
10. A: Well, I don't want to.	12. Cli: Well, I don't want to.
11. Q: Unless – unless I know what I'm *doing*. You know what I'm saying?	13. Pol: Unless – unless I know what I'm *dealing with*. You know what I'm saying?
...	...
12. Q: What's the (unintelligible)?	14. Pol: *Now are we going to talk about it? The other part?*
13. A: *(Unintelligible).*	15. Cli: *What are you guys going to do for me? Take care of what I ask you to do for me.*
14. Q: What are you going to ask me to do?	16. Pol: What are you going to ask me to do?
15. A: I want to give her a kiss.	17. Cli: I want to give her a kiss.
16. Q: I'll do that for you. (Unintelligible).	18. Pol: I'll do that for you.
	19. Cli: *Promise?*
	20. Pol: *Not before we talk.*
17. A: Huh?	21. Cli: Huh?
18. Q: You've got my word.	22. Pol: You've got my word.
19. A: I've got your word?	23. Cli: I've got your word?
20. Q: You've got my word.	24. Pol: You've got my word.

suggested they only sounded odd because "everyone simply ignores how words are spelled anymore" (Pullum 2010), implying that their way of pronouncing words was correct because they were pronouncing them as they were spelled. Speakers whose dialects are perceived as "cutting out letters" or "shortening/reducing words" in any fashion often find their speech criticized or demeaned for failing to meet these prescriptive standards – or, indeed, lead people to not speak their cultural languages because they are not able to use them in a way that matches the standardized, written variety (Lane & Makihara 2017).

We know too that conforming to prescriptive linguistic norms is often taken as a sign of moral rectitude, trustworthiness, and credibility. So when a transcriber – be they a linguist, a court reporter, or some other figure responsible for representing someone's speech in writing – decides to make one party's speech conform to the standards of written English and uses non-standard orthography to represent someone else's speech, they are engaging in an "act of power" (Bucholtz 2000, p. 1461) that "take[s] sides, enabl[es] certain interpretations, advanc[es] particular interests, favor[s] certain speakers, and so on" (p. 1440). "Objective" representation of spoken (and signed) language into a textual form is simply not possible, and to imagine it is allows for power differences to sneak past us.

In addition to this, it is very easy for our perception of what we hear to be changed by those in authority, such as police officers. Helen Fraser has shown this multiple times in her work, where she asks participants to transcribe speech. She also analyzes transcriptions herself from unclear and indistinct recordings[5] – like those that might be used as evidence in trials. Some participants are asked to transcribe "cold," without hearing the recording before and without additional information, and some were asked if they heard a particular phrase (which did not actually exist in the exchange) after having heard the passage but before transcribing it. While the cold transcribers were unlikely to include the phrase, the transcribers who were asked if they recalled hearing a phrase did include it (Fraser 2018a). This is one of the dangers of working with incorrect transcriptions. In additional work, Fraser describes trials where crucial pieces of evidence are police transcriptions and she, as a trained linguist, could not determine for certain that she had heard the phrase in question (Fraser 2018b).

In Australia, where Fraser works, police can be called into court to testify as so-called "ad hoc experts" when audio like this is included under the reasoning that they have listened to many such files and are therefore better than the average person is at understanding what is being said. However, as we have seen throughout this chapter, our expectations about what we hear are easily affected by many factors outside of and in addition to someone's language. If a police officer – or member of the jury – assumes that the

---

[5] You can hear for yourself exactly how unclear and indistinct the recordings are yourself by visiting Fraser's website and listening to the examples that she has uploaded: https://forensictranscription.com.au/audio/.

defendant has committed the crime they are accused of and then hears a recording, you can imagine that it would be an uphill battle to convince the rest of the courtroom otherwise. **Confirmation bias**, or the tendency to interpret new data as a reinforcement of your opinion or world view, is difficult to overcome, even when you are aware of it.

11.5 Language and Employment

In this section, we return to some of the issues we presented at the start of the chapter; namely, whether it is legal to insist on only using English in the workplace or to refuse to hire someone like the hypothetical interviewee in the scenario at the beginning of the chapter. Employment laws in the US, UK, Australia, and Canada restrict or forbid English-only policies in the workplace: employers cannot mandate that their employees only speak English at all times. At the same time, people are hired and fired based on their perceived English proficiency. As we see in the keyed answer feedback quoted at the start of the chapter, the legal line is fuzzy between what is considered discrimination and what is not even though the ethical line may seem clearer. We can explore this further using two examples from the state of Arizona, in the Southwestern United States.

In 2002, two employees at a drive-through restaurant in Page, Arizona, were fired because they would not agree to a company policy requiring them to speak only English at work. Two other employees quit rather than comply (Fischer 2002; Janofsky 2002). The employees and the Equal Employment Opportunity Commission (EEOC; an agency of the US federal government) sued on the grounds that this policy violates protections against discrimination based on national origin. After a settlement was reached between the parties, but before the settlement could be enforced, the owners of the restaurant were approached by a law firm and advocacy group, the "Mountain States Legal Foundation," which represents itself as a "free market public interest law firm," and attempted to rescind the settlement agreement so that the case could be taken to court. Their attempt failed on appeal, and the settlement agreement, which required the restaurant owners to discontinue this policy, pay a small amount of money to the fired employees, and engage in cultural sensitivity training, was finally enforced in 2007 (EEOC v. RD's Drive In/Exxon | Civil Rights Litigation Clearinghouse 2007).

In February 2012, in an auto parts store in the same city, an employee said she was fired based on rumors that she had been speaking a language other than English at work (Allen 2012). Unlike the previous case, the employee was not able to sue and instead found herself looking for work elsewhere.

In both of these cases, the language that was being used in the workplace was Diné Bizaad (Navajo) and the community was one in which there were, and are, many people who speak Diné Bizaad either as a first or second language. Some people, primarily elders, are more comfortable speaking in that language than in English or Spanish, which are also languages commonly found in the area. So why would speaking Diné Bizaad in the workplace be seen by anyone as a problem?

The city of Page was established in 1957, after a land swap between the state of Arizona and the Navajo nation, in order to house workers who were building the Glen Canyon Dam – a project that flooded a number of Native American communities and led to forced relocations of their residents. Prior to the swap, it had been a Navajo town, referred to as "Government Camp." The area is home to Antelope Canyon, and Old Oraibi – a Hopi community that is among the oldest continuously occupied towns in North America. This suggests that there might be sensitivities around language as an index of cultural and ethnic identity and deep histories of tension between speakers of local Indigenous languages and speakers of English who have no Indigenous background.

An interested scholar could approach this question by reviewing the reporting from Page about these events and reading the court filings. We find statements provided by the participants at the time, like those in (1) and (2):

(1) The owner of the restaurant in the 2002 case reportedly "imposed the rule in June 2000 after getting complaints from several employees that Navajo-speaking workers were insulting them. He said the workers could hear their names being spoken but were unable to understand exactly what was being said about them." (Fischer 2002)

(2) The employee at the auto parts store reported that she was fired "on the spot" after a new manager, who had implemented an English-only rule, found out that she had spoken Navajo to a customer. The employee had also been known to be critical of the rule, saying to a coworker that it "wasn't right," and asking what she was supposed to do if a customer only spoke Navajo (Allen 2012).

Let's take a moment here and ask ourselves some questions for reflection.

In (1), people who could not understand the language of their coworkers assumed both that their coworkers were talking about them (but were they?) and that their comments were negative (but were they?). Do you and others in your community make these kinds of assumptions about language use that you don't have access to? Under what conditions do you think that's likely to happen? If you were able to interview the people involved in these disputes, what would you want to ask them? Do you find any connections with the discussion of the Trayvon Martin case from earlier in this chapter where the way in which Rachel Jeantel spoke was experienced by white jurors as unreliable because they didn't understand Jeantel's variety?

In (2), do you think that the action of the manager might have been more driven by concerns about the language use of the employee, or more about a sense that the employee was being noncompliant in general? If this were to happen in your own community, do you think that there might be a similar result? What if the employee was caught speaking a very prestigious language to the customer (for example, what if they had conversed in Latin)? Or what if the employee had been using American Sign Language? Would, or should, the results be different?

Let's turn to another example: the case of Spanish and English use at a Mexican restaurant in Texas, in the United States. Linguist Rusty Barrett spent three years working as a bartender and server in this venue, which in his work he calls "Chalupatown." As a Spanish speaker, Barrett developed friendships with the kitchen staff, primarily Latino men, who primarily spoke Spanish. As a white American, Barrett also developed relationships with management and waitstaff, who were also largely white Americans, and, crucially, predominantly English speakers. Although there was little explicit company or workplace policy about which language was appropriate or correct to use in the workplace, Barrett nevertheless found that language played a major role in the discrimination that Latino workers faced in this restaurant, including in ways that led to outright racism directed toward the largely Latino kitchen staff and even to patrons (Barrett 2006).

The business of Chalupatown was largely conducted in English – menus were written in English (with some items written in Mock Spanish[6]), waitstaff took orders and communicated with guests in English, and management communicated with employees in English. While in some ways an English-dominant workplace makes sense for an establishment in the United States, the way this informal policy was practiced at Chalupatown led to major difficulties in communication at the restaurant.

First, while all employees were aware that the kitchen staff was largely Spanish-dominant, it was assumed that Spanish-speaking employees would simply "get used to" receiving instructions and **directives** in English. Barrett (2006) found that "despite recognizing that directives [in English] were not always understood, managers typically blamed failure to follow a given directive on the Spanish speaking employee" (p. 186). Spanish-speaking employees who failed to understand instructions given in English were

---

[6] They included phrases like "Not your *ordinario* hard-shell tacos!" and frequent use of ¡inverted exclamation marks! in otherwise English sentences.

deemed "lazy" and incompetent (p. 186). Even when management did attempt to communicate with Spanish-speaking employees in Spanish, it was often done with little attention to the actual communicative skills of the kitchen staff, and usually with little respect for Spanish as a language.

In terms of speech, Barrett found a significant reliance on what some scholars have termed **foreigner talk**, a speech variety often used in a (misguided) attempt to communicate when one assumes one's interlocutor is not familiar with the speaker's language. Some of the key features of this register are "exaggerated gestures and facial expressions, speaking at a higher amplitude, exaggerated pronunciation, and syntactic reduction" (p. 184). Rather than developing their own Spanish linguistic skills or offering resources for Spanish-speaking employees to develop their English skills,[7] management and waitstaff tend to rely on this exaggerated speech variety to communicate with kitchen staff, sometimes supplementing the foreigner talk register with a Mock Spanish accent as well.

The lack of linguistic effort made by management and waitstaff at Chaluptatown also extended to written communication. Barrett reports that he was once asked to check a Spanish translation of a written notice that management was preparing for employees. Written notices were one of the few contexts in which management would make any attempt to use Spanish to communicate with employees. But when Barrett was approached to provide a translation for such a notice, he was "explicitly told not to worry about whether the grammar and spelling were correct ... only to verify that the notice would be understandable to a monolingual Spanish speaker. I was told that the use of 'correct' Spanish was unnecessary because 'most of them can't read anyway'" (p. 187). Aside from the incorrectness of this assumption, according to Barrett, it illustrates a paradoxical line of thinking: If you are trying to communicate with someone who cannot read, why would you choose a written notice to convey your message? Barrett argued that this attitude revealed a more general disregard on the part of management for the linguistic needs and skills of Spanish-speaking Latino kitchen staff.

Unfortunately, this attitude contributed to conditions in which Spanish-speaking and racial minority patrons were also discriminated against by the waitstaff. At Chalupatown, Barrett experienced servers frequently discussing a belief that Latino, Black, or disabled patrons were unpleasant to wait on because they left bad tips. Many servers went so far as to describe these

---

[7] ... or offering Spanish courses for their English-speaking employees, for that matter.

clients using racial epithets and other offensive language (Barrett 2006, p. 175). This created a self-fulfilling cycle, where servers believed that minority customers would leave bad tips, which led the server to providing inferior service, which then led, unsurprisingly, to lower tips (p. 201). One day, Barrett was able to challenge this perception by taking on waiting duties for tables deemed "bad" by serving staff (i.e., in which Latino, Black, and other minority customers were seated). At the end of the day, it became clear that Barrett had received more tips than even the most experienced servers in the restaurant.

Despite the pervasively discriminatory atmosphere at Chalupatown, the Spanish-speaking kitchen staff at Chalupatown were still able to push back against these conditions in subtle ways. Barrett reported on one occasion when a manager's lack of Spanish knowledge was used against her:

> A manager who was having a particularly bad hair day told me that she had been receiving compliments from the kitchen staff. She said, "The cooks told me I look really pretty today. They said they liked my hair." Somewhat bewildered, given the state of her hair, I simply said, "That's nice" and remained silent. After a short pause, the manager asked, "Hey, what does escoba ["broom"] mean?" Clearly she had not understood the sarcastic nature of the cooks' compliments. (p. 196)

What this anecdote reveals is that although the disregard for Spanish on the part of English-speaking employees at Chalupatown made work difficult in many respects for Spanish-speaking employees, the Spanish-speaking employees also developed resources for openly venting "frustrations and criticisms without sparking reprimands from managers" (p. 196). Do you see any connections between these issues in Chalupatown and the reactions of white jurors to the speech of Rachel Jeantel in the Trayvon Martin case described in Section 11.3? If so, can you articulate those connections? And if not, what do you think are the crucial differences?

These cases give us a way to think about the role of languages in communities and to understand how and why languages and their speakers might find themselves in conflict – and what we can do to better address the needs, wishes, and human rights of everyone in our communities when we take on the role of linguists.

11.6 Discrimination and Modality

Linguistic discrimination also remains a problem in the interactions of community members who have access to different modalities of language – spoken or signed – and who use different language-related technologies such as writing (formal or informal), voice synthesis and voice recognition, and such. Consider for example the hypothetical interaction in (3), based on a real-life event reported on social media[8] by the parent of a deaf child in Britain:

(3)   Parent: I'm requesting an interpreter on my child's behalf.
    Receptionist: what kind?
    Parent: BSL.
    Receptionist: British speaking language?
    Parent: Er no ... British Sign Language.
    Receptionist: What's that?
    Parent: An interpreter who interprets spoken English into sign language.
    Receptionist: What's his nationality?
    Parent: British.
    Receptionist: And he lives in the UK?
    Parent: Yes ... hence why I am phoning.
    Receptionist: So he CAN speak English then, so it's not essential?
    Parent: He is deaf. He needs a SIGN LANGUAGE interpreter. It's in his medical records.
    Receptionist: ...
    Receptionist: I don't think we do that sort.

We invite you to consider all the venues in which community members who rely on signed language or language technologies in order to engage with others might be excluded. In many communities, institutional and governmental surveys about language use simply don't count the number of people who use signed languages such as American Sign Language (ASL, common in the US), British Sign Language (BSL, common in the UK), and many more. US Census data on language use in the community, for example, only lists spoken languages in its most recent reports. In this way, alternative linguistic modalities are often discriminated against by being literally erased or ignored in public venues.

    Linguists know, as do signed language speakers, that signed languages are not "alternatives" to spoken ones, and their use is not limited to deaf people. There are communities in which the most common language of the community – for hearing and deaf people – is a signed language, and spoken languages are seen as auxiliary or secondary. Nevertheless, for deaf speakers of signed languages, lack of availability of high-quality sign language interpreters is a significant barrier to full participation in their communities. In Chapter 10, we discussed one example of deadly discrimination that occurred in the US in 2017 (Caron 2017). As a deadly hurricane, Irma, swept ashore in Florida, officials in Manatee County conducted a press conference

---

[8] https://twitter.com/QueerCantHear/status/1464378049739333632?s = 20, November 26, 2021.

to provide important safety information to the community. They asked a county employee who used American Sign Language with family members to provide ASL interpretation rather than hiring a qualified ASL interpreter. The result was a disaster (and probably a violation of the Americans with Disabilities Act). The employee did the best he could, but his translation vacillated between unintelligible and wildly inaccurate. Community members who needed ASL were left without access to crucial safety information.

Most speakers of signed languages are multilingual. In the US and the UK they learn not only the sign language of their community but also at least written English. Many community members who are hard of hearing or have auditory processing deficits also rely on written modalities of language in order to be able to communicate effectively with others. Written language, unlike signed language, is never a primary linguistic mode – writing is a technology that allows some speakers to draw their message (which is actually encoded in a spoken or signed language) in a fixed medium of some kind. But for those community members who are not able to access language in its primary spoken or signed forms, writing can be a necessity. And in contemporary society, many of us are interacting with each other via mediated communication systems in which a written transcript, captions, or subtitles might be used as a way to make our language available to others. The technologies by which this can be done are explored in Chapter 7, "Linguists Meet Computers." We see there that even when we deploy machines to help us, we can create discriminatory practices and products that serve to exclude community members from our language use rather than facilitating accessible communication.

11.7 Conclusion

In this chapter, we've discussed many of the ways that linguistic discrimination surfaces in everyday legal situations and how it affects the ways we are all treated in the legal system. This is especially true when we speak a marginalized dialect or use language in different ways, as shown in situations throughout this chapter, including when searching for homes to rent, in the workplace, when interacting with law enforcement and the judiciary system, and more. As linguists, we know that there is nothing about a language or dialect that makes one superior to another. Instead, people in power use language to discriminate against people's protected characteristics when otherwise they wouldn't be able to get away with doing something like that.

Linguist in the Community

- News reporting often describes alleged criminal offenders and alleged crime victims quite differently depending on a range of sociocultural factors. Investigate what differences exist in the language of crime reporting in your regional news sources, including both print and broadcast media. Keep track of how they describe the sociocultural identities of the offenders and victims – noting gender, race, socioeconomic status, citizenship status, ability/disability, and other such factors. At the same time, keep track of the words used to describe offenders and victims. Are offenders described with words such as "thug," "gangster," "terrorist," "violent," or similar terms? Or are they described as "misguided," "disturbed," "ill," or "confused"? Look for patterns in how different sets of terms are used to describe different types of people in the context of crime reporting, and consider what broader sociocultural forces might shape these patterns of language use.
- Make some observations about which languages are used and the attitudes people have about them in the places you frequent. You might go to a cafe, restaurant, or bar – anywhere you can stay for an hour or two and people watch – and see what language(s) or dialect(s) the staff are using with each other. Do you recognize what the staff are speaking? Do other patrons interact with the staff in the same language or dialect, or is there one that seems to be used mainly by the staff and another mainly by the customers? Do patrons have any reaction to the language staff are using, and if so, how? Can you hear any of the patrons discussing the staff's language use? You might do this exercise in a few different locations around your town or in a variety of venues to get a better idea of the interacting language ideologies in your community.

Linguist in the Classroom

- The United States Supreme Court maintains audio recordings and transcriptions of all legal arguments brought before them, currently at www.supremecourt.gov/oral_arguments/oral_arguments.aspx. These arguments can be quite long (often over an hour) and the transcripts equally so (a hundred pages or more!), but they offer a unique site to compare what elements of courtroom language a court transcriber tries to capture vs. what elements of language a linguist might want to capture in their transcript. With a small group of your classmates, print

out a few pages from the transcript of a few different sections. Look particularly for places where attorneys are delivering prepared statements and where they are responding to questioning from the justices. Then, compare these transcript sections to the corresponding sections of the audio recording. What linguistic features are left out of the "official" transcript? Why do you think that might be? Present and discuss your findings with others in your class.
- Split into teams to debate the proposition that single-language policies in the workplace are inherently discriminatory. Make sure that you:
    - Randomly assign teams to "pro" and "con" sides – debates are more effective when you don't always argue on the side of the proposition that you naturally fall on;
    - Develop a set of guidelines to measure what constitutes a "good" debate, including how the debate should be structured, how much time each side will have to prepare arguments and to speak, whether the debate should have a "winner" (and if so, how to determine the winner), and so forth;
    - Give yourselves enough time to research your arguments and make notes;
    - Run the debate;
    - Debrief after the debate and, as a class, discuss each team's arguments, claims that may be untenable, or especially noteworthy claims.

Glossary

African American English (AAE) A set of linguistic varieties that are associated with African American identity in North America, and that are sometimes analyzed as varieties of English, and sometimes analyzed as originating with an English-based creole. Sometimes called Black English, Ebonics, African American Language, or African American Vernacular English.

aligned When a conversational response conforms to the expected conversational norms of a given community or setting.

confirmation bias The tendency to interpret new data as a reinforcement of your opinion or world view.

continuer A spoken or gestured cue that signals to an interlocutor that the listener has heard what they have said and that they should continue speaking.

directive An instruction, usually given by an authority figure.

disaligned When a conversational response does not conform to the expected conversational norms of a given community or setting.

face An individual's public self-image or self-presentation.

facework The interactional and conversational strategies used by speakers and listeners to construct and maintain the face of themselves and others.

foreigner talk A speech variety marked by exaggerated gestures, expressions, pronunciation, and amplitude, as well as syntactic reduction, often used in a (misguided) attempt to communicate when one assumes one's interlocutor is not familiar with the speaker's language.

hedging device A word or phrase that is used to inject some doubt or hesitation into a statement. This may be a way to show politeness or deference or to soften a command, as in, "Maybe you should check that answer again."

linguistic profiling A method of categorizing or characterizing a person based on the way they use language.

protected characteristics Innate characteristics of a human being which, by law, cannot be grounds for providing differential treatment. Examples of protected characteristics include age, race, sex, and national origin, and they may differ depending on the jurisdiction.

tag question A hedging device used to request confirmation at the end of a statement, like the "wasn't it?" at the end of "That was a good movie, wasn't it?".

topic-change response A response in a conversation in which the speaker changes the topic of conversation from the previous topic.

topic-related response A response in a conversation in which the speaker connects what they are saying to what the previous speaker said.

transcription A technical system for writing a language, designed to clearly identify some set of linguistic properties. Not the kind of writing we use in our day-to-day communication.

transition relevance place (TRP) A point or moment in conversation when one speaker's turn is potentially completed, and thus another speaker may step in.

Recommended Readings

If the material in this chapter shows anything, it's that language has the power to shape people's lives in material ways. We hope what you've learned here inspires you to further explore the use of language as a tool for discrimination – and at the same time, learn to combat linguistic discrimination! The recommended readings we provide below are a great starting point, and your local college or university library is a great place for getting access to these readings.

Babel, M., & Russell, J. (2015). Expectations and speech intelligibility. *The Journal of the Acoustical Society of America, 137*(5), 2823–2833. https://doi.org/10/f7c68x

Bucholtz, M. 2000. The politics of transcription. *Journal of Pragmatics, 32*, 1439–1465. https://doi.org/10.1016/S0378-2166(99)00094-6

Fraser, H. (2018b). Forensic transcription: How confident false beliefs about language and speech threaten the right to a fair trial in Australia. *Australian Journal of Linguistics, 38*(4), 586–606. https://doi.org/10/gd87q9

Lippi-Green, R. (2012). *English with an Accent: Language, Ideology, and Discrimination in the United States* (2nd ed.). Routledge.

Lucas, C. (2014). *The Sociolinguistics of the Deaf Community*. Elsevier.

Purnell, T., Idsardi, W., & Baugh, J. (1999). Perceptual and phonetic experiments on American English dialect identification. *Journal of Language and Social Psychology, 18*(1), 10–30. https://doi.org/10/c7rb4f

Rickford, J. R., & King, S. (2016). Language and linguistics on trial: Hearing Rachel Jeantel (and other vernacular speakers) in the courtroom and beyond. *Language, 92*(4), 948–988. https://doi.org/10.1353/lan.2016.0078

Rubin, D. L. (1992). Nonlanguage factors affecting undergraduates' judgments of nonnative English-speaking teaching assistants. *Research in Higher Education, 33*(4), 511–531. https://doi.org/10.1007/BF00973770

12 Languages Go to War, Languages Make Peace

We have discussed a variety of ways in which human communities seem to form connections between ourselves and our languages. The languages and linguistic varieties that we use provide information about how we think about ourselves, who we affiliate with, and what communities we belong to. It will not be surprising, then, to find that when communities of people are in conflict with each other, we often see conflicts playing out in ways that involve our languages. It will also not be surprising when we find out that languages can also help us to peacefully coexist in a multilingual world.

In this chapter, we discuss how language has been used as a proxy for national identity and as a colonial weapon, or even as a target of cultural violence and genocide. Similarly, we explore how language has been used to attempt to broker peace, promote a more unified world, and as a way to recover cultural practices to allow communities to survive a little longer. In this telescope-view chapter, we hope to show you how attitudes about language can encompass national values and identities on a large scale as well as on the smaller scales on which we have been focusing so far. In doing so, we hope you will better understand how language affects and is affected by society as a whole, and even how global conflicts alter communities' relationships with languages. We will ask you to consider how language has been used in all of these ways, which can sometimes be extremely painful and upsetting – particularly if you're someone who has experienced war on your language. We therefore ask you to explore this content mindfully.

12.1 Languages Go to War

When communities of people come into contact with each other in the context of aggression, whether as antagonists in civil wars, or in wars of territorial aggression, or in the context of settler colonialism, issues of language use and linguistic identity often take an outsized role. For example, the United States has always been a richly **multilingual** country, but there has also been a strand in US culture that claims some varieties of English as "ours," and other languages as "theirs." These tensions played out during the framing of the US Constitution when the founders determined not to name a national or **official language** for their new country and its citizens (Ruiz 1994).[1] The earliest US citizens expected, and perhaps hoped, that the variety of English spoken in North America would take on its own distinctive character, setting it apart from the language of the British government they had just violently separated from. Scholars such as Noah Webster (from the US) and Samuel Johnson (from England) sought to distinguish US English from British English by writing and compiling dictionaries – a practice called **lexicography**. These dictionary projects allowed for an authoritative, standardized perspective on spelling norms, pronunciation, and vocabulary to flourish. (See, for instance, Merriam-Webster n.d. for examples of both successful and failed attempts to differentiate US from British English spellings.)

That same US government, at its founding, understood itself to be a new community in an old land. The Indigenous nations of North America had undergone significant population loss and destabilization of their communities due to diseases introduced by European settlers (Mann 2006). During the first years after the founding, the new US found itself in a variety of relationships with Indigenous nations – some were allies, some were enemies, but all were viewed as "others." Thus, although languages such as Hebrew, French, and Greek were rumored to have been put forward as candidates for the US **national language** (mostly by anti-British extremists; see Baron 1990), no Indigenous languages were. Ultimately, rather than conflate language and national identity with each other, the framers of the US Constitution, in their first amendment to that document, identified "freedom of expression" as a core value, at least as it pertained to US citizens.[2]

Presumably, this move was meant to include freedom to speak in the language or linguistic variety of one's choice. However, this move did not, and has not, separated language from national identity for many people in the US, though the somewhat ironic result has been that "English" (not "American") is now the language that is mostly featured in discourse in the US as "our language." It also did not, and has not, protected minority and Indigenous language speakers from **discrimination** and **bias** in the US. But it

---

[1] "Citizen" status at the time was restricted to white, landowning men. All citizens of the US at its founding were settler-colonists.

[2] "Congress shall make no law respecting an establishment of religion, or prohibiting the free exercise thereof; or abridging **the freedom of speech**, or of the press; or the right of the people peaceably to assemble, and to petition the Government for a redress of grievances." emphasis added.

is worth reflecting on – and investigating – what you and your community members think about the connection between your languages and your national identities. It is also important to learn about the roles that our beliefs and attitudes about languages have played in cases of war and genocide, and in processes of peacemaking and healing.

12.1.1 Languages and National Identity

Many nations in the world do officially recognize one or more languages as "official" or "national" languages. In doing so, languages also become associated with national identities. As borders change, so too may the favored language so that it aligns with the majority or victorious party. We can observe this throughout the history of English, as one example. The position of English in the UK, and its development and growth as a national language, is a useful contrast with our discussion of English in the US. The English language developed as the result of Western European groups migrating to the British Isles and intermingling, starting in about the year AD 450. These groups, whose languages included Frankish, Gothic, Anglish, Saxon, and others, were mostly **Germanic**. They settled among the local inhabitants, who were mostly speakers of **Celtic** languages such as Irish, Scots Gaelic, Manx, and Welsh (van Gelderen 2014).[3] As the Germanic groups gained political and economic power, their languages became more influential and eventually emerged as a "new" form, now often referred to as "**Anglo-Saxon**" or "**Old English.**"

The British Isles were a multilingual region, with Old English well situated in the area by the early eleventh century. Around this time, invasions by another set of Europeans began – the Norman French. The Normans were victorious militarily, and their prestige was again reflected in language behavior such that between 1066 and 1400 or so, French was the language of the British king and court. It was not until 1399, with Henry IV, that a British king's coronation oath was spoken in English rather than French.

While most common people in England spoke English (and people in the territories that are now Ireland, Scotland, and Wales continued to speak their Celtic languages), they frequently learned French as a second language. Further, the English of the time was very strongly influenced by Norman

---

[3] "Germanic" and "Celtic" name both cultural groupings and linguistic ones. In terms of language, the "Germanic" languages included a number of languages of Western Europe at the time, the modern descendents of which include German, Norwegian, Fresian, Greenlandic, Swedish, Danish, and others. Both Germanic and Celtic languages share a common ancestor language called "proto-Indo-European," but by AD 450 these language groups had become different enough from each other that they would have been completely unintelligible across communities.

French, so much so that the English of the time is referred to as belonging to a new historical epoch – the epoch of Middle English, or Anglo-Norman English.[4]

During this period, French was not the primary language of government – instead, Latin was used for official written documents. By the 1500s, English became the official language of Parliament and legislation. But it wasn't until 1731 that English replaced French and Latin as the language of government, and there is still no "official" national language of the UK.[5] This has not stopped English from becoming the *de facto* language of British Expansion and a major colonizing language around the world.

Why would a multilingual community like the UK be widely perceived as "English-speaking," and why would English be the language of the colonies founded by the British over the eighteenth, nineteenth, and twentieth centuries – including the US? We have found no reason to believe that these facts have anything to do with the languages involved. They are driven instead by **ideologies of nationalism**, expressed in and through language. In the UK, English – emblematic of a particularly powerful class of elites – became an instrument of assimilation and a symbol of conquest. The English language traveled with English-speaking forces who invaded and took power in places like Scotland, Ireland, and Wales – and the exercise of English over the community languages in those places became an exercise of power. In the multilingual environment of the Anglo-Saxon period, English coexisted with other languages, but with military attempts at conquest, language became a way to assert a uniformitarian identity, sometimes by force, on a "defeated" population. Thus multilingualism gives way to **language shift** – and language becomes conflated with national identity.

This pattern is not inevitable and does not happen everywhere. It is a very strong component of the kind of military expansion characteristic of the European side of the Indo-European cultural complex. In other parts of the world, and under other circumstances, national identity is not so closely tied to language use or ideologies of monolingualism. In 2021, a quick internet search looking for "multilingual countries" returned a very long list of countries that recognize two or more "national" or "official" languages, and many that don't recognize any particular language as a national

---

[4] We talk about some of the lasting impacts of the influence of Norman French on English at the beginning of Chapter 5, so head there if you would like some examples.
[5] Welsh is the national language of Wales, by statute. There are substantial numbers of speakers of Indigenous languages of the UK such as Scots, Welsh, Scottish Gaelic, Irish, British Sign Language, Angloromani, Irish Sign Language, and Northern Ireland Sign Language.

language. For example, the country of Mali in northwest Africa has retained the colonizing language, French, as its official language of government but has also enshrined, in its 1992 constitution, protections of its cultural and linguistic diversity. Mali supports thirteen national languages, all of which have deep historical roots in the country. Skattum (2009) reports that only about 10–15 percent of the citizens of Mali speak French, and the largest population language, Bambara, is used by perhaps 40 percent of the population as either a home language or a **lingua franca**. Multilingualism is itself a source of national identity in Mali. In the Americas, Bolivia holds the record for the largest number of official languages. As a result of the ratification of the 2009 constitution, all Indigenous languages of the country, thirty-six of which are named, have become official languages in addition to Spanish (Wolff 2016). In the Bolivian context, recognition of multilingualism is a key component in the struggle against the colonizing power of Spanish. This is another example of multilingualism as a component of a single national identity.

But international aggression can and often does involve language policy components. For instance, efforts at linguistic unification and the suppression or elimination of regional or minority languages in countries such as China, and neighboring countries like Tibet, highlight the many ways in which language and national identity are very strongly connected. Fights that are really about people's national identity, citizenship rights, and the like are proxied by fights about language use in schools, in government, in the community, and sometimes even in the home (see, e.g., Erbaugh 2009; Roche & Suzuki 2018). We even see strong connections between linguistic and national identity in conflicts about **orthographies**. For example, the languages Serbian and Croatian are mostly mutually intelligible, but Serbian has often been written using the Cyrillic script, showing an affiliation with Russia, while Croatian is typically written with the Latin alphabet, showing affiliation with Western Europe.

Other examples are the discussions about the place of the Russian language vs. the Ukrainian language in Ukraine. These discussions have become increasingly prevalent since 2014, as complex geopolitical tensions between the two countries developed, and even more so since February 2022, when Russia launched a full-scale invasion of Ukraine. Even in translation to English, decisions about the spelling and pronunciation of words can point to the complex history between these two languages. The spelling "Kiev," the capital city of Ukraine which is transliterated from the Russian Киев, was used in the US until the Russian invasion of Ukraine, as was the pronunciation [kijɛv] or "kee-yev." Soon after that, there was a movement to encourage English speakers and others to use "Kjiv" (from Київ), pronunciation [kijɪv] "kee-yiv" or [kiv] "keev," which is closer to the Ukrainian pronunciation. At the time of writing, most English-language news media of which we are aware are using "Kjiv," not "Kiev" (Socolovsky 2022). In what may be a similar move, the English language transliteration of the country that has typically been written "Kazakhstan" has begun to appear in various media as "Qazaqstan," with the use of the letter "Q" marking a political shift from affiliation with Russia and Russian affiliation with the West (Keating 2017).

You may have also noted some of this debate pop up in your own country as journalists outside of Russia and Ukraine reckoned with how to refer to these countries in light of Russia's February 2022 invasion of Ukraine – is it "the" Ukraine, or just "Ukraine"? Some linguists have traced the etymology of the word "Ukraine" back to an Old East Slavic word meaning "borderland" or perhaps just "region" (Motschenbacher 2020; Zaleska Onyshkevych & Rewakowicz 2014). When we translate this word to English, the use of the definite article makes sense as using this sort of marker in reference to a particular region is common – think "the mountain range" or "the seaside." After Ukraine gained independence in 1991, however, many news organizations, governments, and individuals began referring to Ukraine without the definite article because using it with a definite article seems to suggest that it is "just" or "only" a region of Russia rather than a independent country in its own right (Taylor 2013). In the context of war, the presence or absence of "the" constitutes a political position on the conflict.

12.1.2 Languages as Targets of War

Sometimes, war is waged on populations in ways that specifically involve wars on languages. In many parts of the world, including the US and Canada,[6] wars waged by colonizing groups against Indigenous peoples have focused particularly on languages and the embeddings of languages in culture and religion. Here we will focus on the US context, but readers are invited to investigate their own histories to learn more about whether, and how, such warfare may have been conducted in the past, or is being conducted in the present.

At the founding of the US as an independent government by and for the white, property-owning male settler-colonists, the geographic reach of the new state consisted of thirteen colonies, now the states of New Hampshire, Massachusetts, Rhode Island, Connecticut, New York, New Jersey, Pennsylvania, Delaware, Maryland, Virginia, North Carolina, South Carolina, and Georgia (Figure 12.1).

---

[6] ... and Australia, and Russia, and China, and ... and ... and.

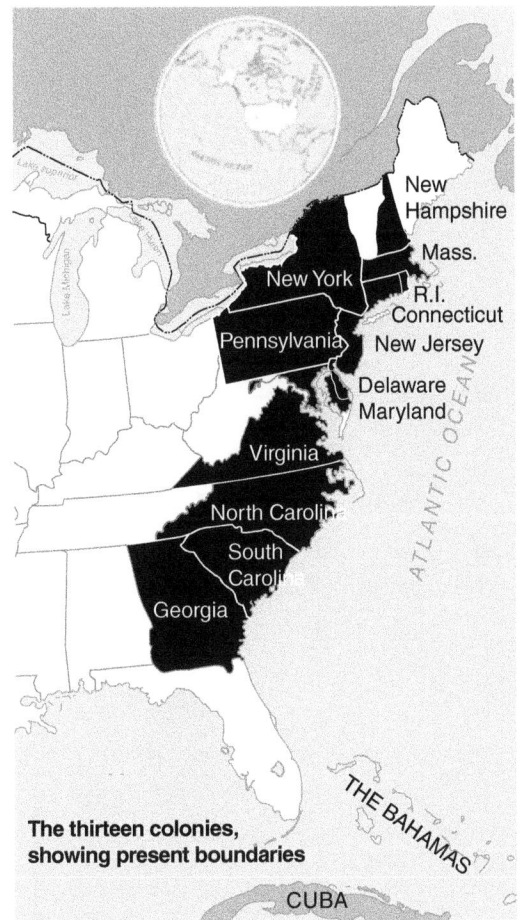

Figure 12.1 The present-day boundaries descended from the thirteen original colonies of the US. (Attrib. Jengod, Wikimedia commons, CC BY-SA 3.0).

The territory that is now the continental US was also populated by at least 300 distinct linguistic and cultural Indigenous groups (Mithun 2001; see Figure 12.2). At the time of the founding, these groups were seen by the colonizing powers as nation-states, insofar as they could negotiate treaties (government-to-government agreements) and declare war on each other. While there was significant interest on the part of some of the colonialists in learning about the languages of the Indigenous communities (Thomas Jefferson and Benjamin Franklin were both part-time linguists in addition to their other pursuits), the role of Indigenous languages was not seen as a real part of the establishment of the US government.

Over the years, though, colonial expansion progressed in a way that involved the US government taking a kind of ownership over Indigenous

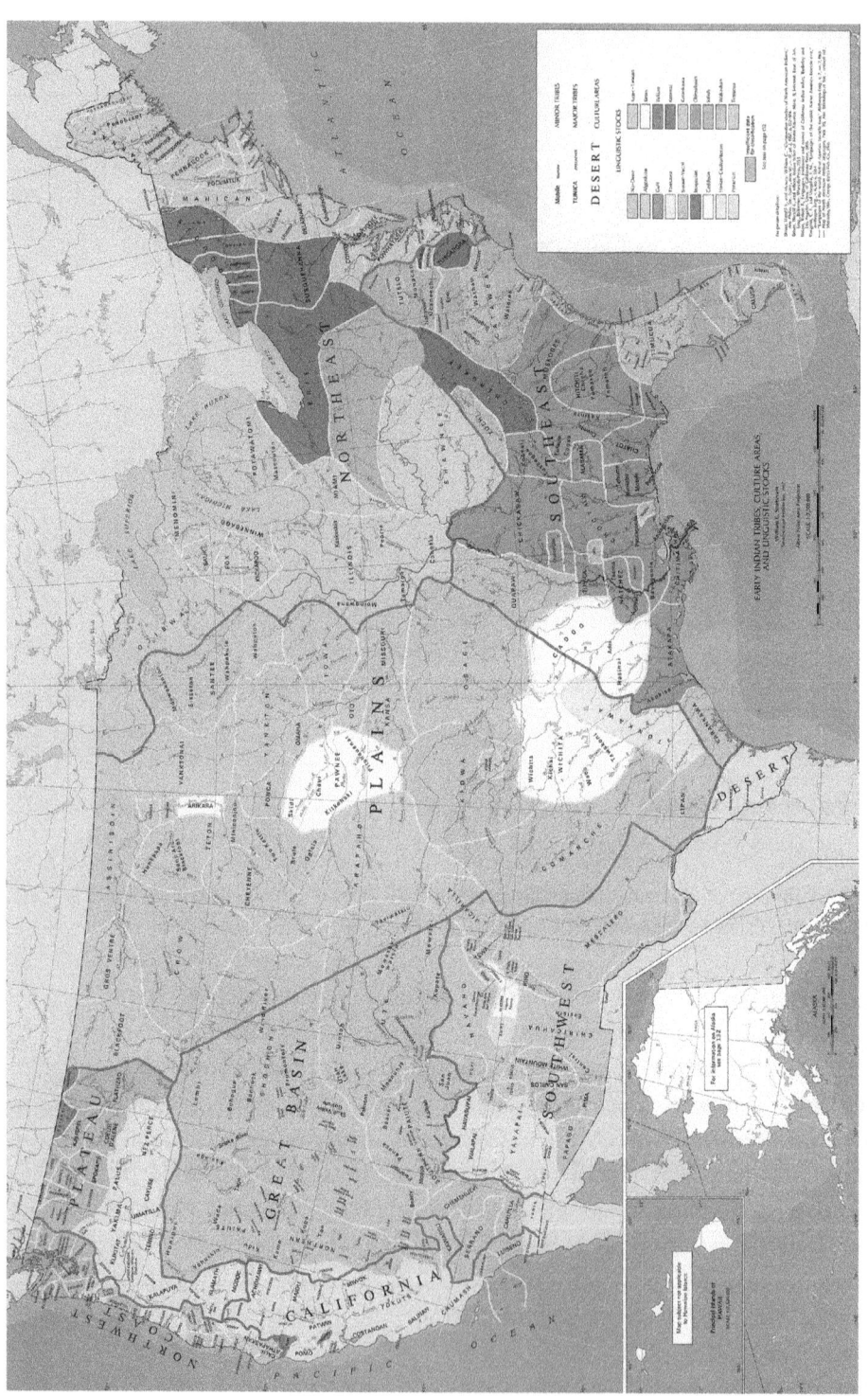

Figure 12.2 By USGS – 1970 USGS map., Public Domain, https://commons.wikimedia.org/w/index.php?curid=5824202.

communities. This happened through a complex interaction of warfare and forced relocations, missionization, and "educational" initiatives, but they all conspired to create a kind of multidimensional war on those communities. **Cultural genocide** – warfare whose aim is to either kill all members of a given community OR absorb those individuals into the aggressor's culture, religion, language, and society in ways that exterminate any trace of their own cultural, religious, linguistic, and social identities – against Native peoples in the US began soon after the founding and in some areas continues more than 250 years later.

Weapons of cultural genocide include language. In the US, as in many places in the world, a key component of cultural genocide is to induce (by violence or other means) language shift instead of cultivating multilingualism. Starting before the Civil War, and increasing during the 1860s and 70s, Christian missionaries established mission schools throughout "Indian country." Mission schools typically enforced draconian English-only policies on students with punishments for students' use of their own languages including violence so extreme that many children "lost" their family language, and some their lives.

Mission schools formed the backbone of a system of boarding schools, run by the 1870s by collaborations between the US Government's Department of the Interior (the Bureau of Indian Affairs, or BIA) and various Christian groups. The boarding school era's policies of forced assimilation did not officially end in the US until 1970, and this century-long war against Indigenous languages, cultures, religions, and lifeways is one of the primary reasons that every single Indigenous language of North America is currently classified as "endangered" by many academic and government groups (though not necessarily by the communities themselves – see for example Leonard 2008). The fact that in 2021 at least 200 Indigenous language communities have survived with at least some of their language, culture, religion, and traditional lifeways intact is a testament to the resilience of humans in the face of terror, war, and deprivation. A statement by Natives4Linguistics, a collaboration of Indigenous scholars of linguistics, is worth quoting at length in this regard:

> Many, if not all, Native Americans, First Nations, Inuit and Métis peoples have relatives who are survivors of boarding schools, residential schools, or day schools. Some were raised with stories of grandparents hiding from government officials who came to take the children away. Others were raised with their grandparents or parents not talking about their experiences at these places because doing so was too traumatic.

> These boarding and residential schools are once again in the spotlight, as they were during the time of Canada's Truth and Reconciliation Commission (TRC), "shocking" the world with the truths Indigenous peoples knew all along. The atrocities committed at these sites are not news to those who come from these communities. We know that our histories are not being taught (or not being adequately taught) in schools, contributing to the continued violence and discrimination against Indigenous peoples and to our invisibility and underrepresentation in society, in academia, and elsewhere.
>
> Over a decade after Canada's Truth and Reconciliation Commission began its work, there is finally some news that a similar process will occur in the U.S. It is also not surprising that it would take a Native American scholar such as Secretary of Interior Deb Haaland (Pueblo of Laguna) to call attention to these sites and advocate for the recently announced Federal Indian Boarding School Initiative. We are certain that it will confirm that these schools were the primary sites of our cultural and linguistic genocide.
> (Natives4Linguistics 2021)

One result of this war against language is the erosion of the cultural and social practices that are used by nations to identify themselves and to be identifiable by outsiders. Ironically, the fact that the languages of Indigenous communities in the US had been destabilized was and is used by the US federal government as a tool by which Native American tribes can be denied official recognition and the few legal protections that come with that recognition. Recognition is an acknowledgment by the federal government of the tribe's existence as a separate and sovereign nation, and it allows that nation to secure a land base, to be exempt from certain taxes, and to be eligible for a number of important benefits. However, in order to gain federal recognition, communities have to prove some forms of cultural continuity since 1900, and (along with blood quanta and other measures of descent) this can include linguistic continuity. Communities for whom intergenerational transmission of language and culture was most profoundly broken are the very communities who are often unable to now secure recognition and legal status as a "nation" (McCulloch & Wilkins 1995).

The BIA boarding schools provide an example of a kind of language of war in which the combatants conceive of a scenario in which they can "win" without literally killing the enemy – but instead somehow converting that population so that they no longer present themselves or think of themselves as "different" (McCarty & Nicholas 2014). In the US, a similar logic lies behind efforts in many spheres of influence to decrease sociolinguistic diversity by forcing some groups of speakers to abandon their language varieties and adopt the varieties of a powerful majority. **African American Language** (or AAL)[7] in the US has been the target of this kind of cultural and linguistic warfare since the beginning of the slave trade and continuing to the present (Wright 2021b).

As a well-known example of the "war" against AAL, consider the events of 1996 that took place in Oakland, California. Oakland was, and is, a multiracial and multiethnic city in which Black children in particular were viewed by the white community as "underachieving" academically. Indices of this "deficit" included poor outcomes in standardized testing, particularly in "language skills," as well as high dropout rates. The language of school was, and is, White English,[8] a set of varieties to which many young students had little access at home. Similar issues had been raised in other parts of the US, and educational policy experts, teachers, and parents were struggling to identify solutions that "worked." The people trying to solve this problem believed that successful students should be proficient in White English in both written and spoken venues. In reality, poor outcomes on standardized tests for non-white students are the fault of the tests themselves: they are written in ways that presuppose familiarity of children with relatively affluent white social and cultural practices and turn out to be better tests of children's familiarity with that social milieu than they are of anything like academic ability or readiness for school (Kendi 2016).

The Oakland school board considered this problem and understood it to be analogous with problems faced by non-English-speaking children in US schools. They resolved to address the issue by recognizing AAL, under the label **"Black English"** or **"Ebonics,"** as a legitimate language variety (Woo & Curtius 1996) and allowing teachers in the district to utilize practices and strategies developed for bilingual education. This approach involves recognizing the students' home language as legitimate and then providing instruction on the differences between their home language and the English of school. There is good evidence that such an approach might be more successful than pedagogies that treated students' language as "broken" or "bad." In spite of that evidence – and well-reasoned advocacy by respected linguists including John Baugh and John Rickford, then at Berkeley and Stanford, respectively – the resolution generated nationwide backlash and ultimately failed to be implemented (see Baugh 2000 and Rickford 1999 for discussion).

---

[7] We follow Lanehart et al. (2015) in the use of "African American Language" to encompass varieties of language common in Black communities in the US. This term includes varieties that we have elsewhere been called "African American Vernacular English" (AAVE) or African American English, but it is more inclusive of varieties that are less closely intertwined with Englishes.

[8] We acknowledge that the term "White English" is also problematic, but we use it to emphasize the point we are making here.

The backlash from white communities was telling. Media reports from mainstream news sources reported that the school district had "declared that Black English is a separate language" and that the teaching of it in schools (which, to be clear, was not what the proposal was advocating for in the first place) would be "another tragic chapter in racial self-destruction" (Lippi-Green 2012, p. 312). Politicians, celebrities, and other public figures decried it as a case of teaching unacceptable "slang" in school (Lippi-Green 2012, pp. 312–313) – again, despite the fact that decades of scholarship on this language variety had shown it to be systematic and patterned across all parts of linguistic structure. Much of the public discussion during this time even used elements of "Mock Ebonics" (Ronkin & Karn 1999) in their headlines to denigrate the language variety as a whole. In short, any move to legitimize Black ways of speaking would be viewed as unacceptable, and the only acceptable pathway to success for Black children had to be not just fluency in White English but complete denunciation of AAL as bad, broken, and unacceptable (Lanehart et al. 2015). As noted by Charity Hudley and Mallinson (2018) and echoed by Rosa and Flores (2017), the focus of this criticism, and much similar discourse in the US, has been on the alleged "deficiencies" of racialized speakers rather than on the uncritically discriminatory views of the white community.

More recently, similar stories of aggressive sentiment against a specific language have been documented in the US state of Arizona, a state that borders Mexico and in which the three most commonly spoken languages are English, Spanish, and Navajo.[9] Here, regular flares of anti-Spanish language rhetoric and legislation have coincided with anti-immigrant sentiment. The use of Spanish in Arizona public schools was effectively banned, and attempts have been made to fire English as a Second Language instructors whose English was "Spanish-accented" (Fountain et al. 2010). Ruiz (1994) shows that these aggressive policies are driven by anti-immigrant sentiment rather than an understanding of the role of language in education, policy-making, or public life. The goal of these policies is to force community members, most especially children, to assimilate to white linguistic practices in order to have access to economic, political, or personal power. What is perhaps most interesting about this anti-Spanish sentiment in Arizona, and throughout many Southwestern US states, is that the region has a much longer history of Spanish speaking than it does of English speaking. It was through the Mexican–American War of 1846–1848 that the United States gained control over these territories which had previously belonged to Mexico, whose

---

[9] US Census community reports, 2010

de facto national language is (and was at the time) Spanish. Thus, when the United States took control of these regions – and the people within them – they found communities in which Spanish had already developed a centuries-long history. However, Spanish was far from the first language spoken in this area: Indigenous languages of the American Southwest such as Tohono O'odham, Navajo, Hopi, and Tewa (just to name a few) were present long before the Spanish arrived. These nested layers of linguistic imperialism highlight how unstable any anti-Spanish rhetoric is in these areas.

As any student of the past and/or the present can attest, languages and language ideologies, connected as they can be to sentiments of nationalism and group identity, are often also used as weapons of warfare. A story perhaps familiar for readers who have studied the Hebrew Bible or the Old Testament of the Christian Bible is that of the "shibboleth." The story discusses a battle in which people on either side had different pronunciations of that single word (which may have meant "ear of corn" or perhaps "stream"). Fighters only needed to ask an individual to say that word, and from their pronunciation they would know whether the person was a friend or a foe (McNamara 2020).

In 1937, such a test was put to individuals living near the border between the countries of Haiti and the Dominican Republic, which share an island. Haiti, a former French colony, is a nation in which Haitian Creole is the most common language; the Dominican Republic is a former colony of Spain and thus Spanish is the national language. Until recently, the Dominican Republic followed birthright citizenship policies, meaning anyone born within its borders was automatically granted citizenship in the country. Since the founding of each colony, there have been populations of individuals living on or near the border of each country, and since birth records were rather rare at the time – particularly for those who lived in poor or rural areas – there were many people for whom their "exact" citizenship may have been difficult to determine.

This presented a problem for Rafael Leonias Trujillo, the dictator of the Dominican Republic who came to power in the early 1930s. Trujillo generally regarded Haitians as an inferior people whose presence in the country was preventing the Dominican Republic from advancing as a nation. In an attempt to control and discourage Haitian migration into the Dominican Republic, Trujillo sent Dominican soldiers in late September and early October of 1937 to the border region with orders to kill all Haitians living on or near the countries' border (Paulino & García 2013). But how to tell who was "truly" Haitian, and who was Dominican? One popular myth that emerged in the aftermath of this genocidal massacre was that Dominican soldiers would hold up a sprig of parsley – in Spanish, perejil – and ask the residents of the border region to name the herb. Since Haitian Creole, and the French from which it is derived, pronounced the "r" differently than Spanish-speakers,[10] the story went that soldiers used this shibboleth to determine whether someone would live or die. Contemporary historians have called into question the extent to which such a linguistic test was actually used in this incident (Derby 2020), but the belief that language could be such a crucial element in this setting was so pervasive that it led to the naming of the event: the Parsley Massacre.

Language tests of this sort continue to occur through the current day. In 2019, for example, two US citizens from Texas were detained by US Customs and Border Patrol because they were speaking Spanish in a convenience store in Havre, Montana (Chappell 2019). The use of Spanish was interpreted as evidence that they were, or might be, "foreigners" who might be in the US illegally – at a time when the US administration was controlled by politicians who saw immigration as a form of "invasion."

A linguist in the community might reasonably be interested in the connections between peoples' language behavior and their political or social affiliations, particularly in times of intergroup conflict. Looking at how we use and understand each other's language behavior as an index of group membership, national affiliation, and the like is an important thread of research in the study of language and social issues.

12.1.3 Language as an Instrument of War: Propaganda

Another way in which language can be used as an instrument of violence and war is in the propagation of **disinformation** and **propaganda**. Propaganda is defined as the systemic dissemination of misleading information in order to promote a political cause or point of view (OED Online 2021), and language communities often use particular kinds of linguistic structures or practices in the production of propaganda. For example, in US and British English during the First World War, racial **epithets** describing German and Austrian people were deployed along with visual references such as are depicted in the US propaganda poster "Hun or Home?" from 1917–1919 (US National Archives and Records Administration) (Figure 12.3).

Propaganda and disinformation campaigns often use linguistic tools like epithets, **smears**, or **hate speech**, but they can also use more subtle linguistic devices intended to fool or mislead people. Framing statements as questions, for example, can both shield the speaker from accusations that they are being

---

[10] Haitian Creole and French speakers would likely pronounce the "r" in this word as uvular approximant or voiced velar fricative, whereas Spanish would likely pronounce it as an alveolar tap.

Figure 12.3 "Hun or Home?," 1917–1919.

Figure 12.4 "Vote Leave, take back control."

malicious and also introduce unstated assertions that set the stage for a biased, hateful, or misleading discussion.

Take as an example the type of graphic in Figure 12.4 promoted in 2018 in the UK as part of the pro-Brexit effort (as adapted by your authors).

The graphic emphasizes the location of Turkey as a neighbor of Syria and Iraq and asks the question, "What does the EU 'tourist deal' mean?" It seems to have been designed to warn residents of the UK that there may be large influxes of people from Turkey, Syria, and Iraq if the UK stayed a part of the European Union based on a false claim that Turkey was poised to join the EU. Turkey was not an EU state at the time, and it is not one at the time of writing. The likelihood of Turkey becoming an EU member state by 2030 was negligible at the time that this campaign was underway (Ker-Lindsay 2018).

Nowhere in the graphic is that false underlying claim made explicit, though. Instead, the designers of the graphic asked a question: "What does the EU 'tourist deal' mean?" This question was framed so that the following unstated claims could be presumed to be true:

- There is a "tourist deal" under consideration or already adopted by the EU, and
- It would include people living in Turkey (on the grounds that Turkey would soon join the EU), and
- That the "tourist deal" would have a meaning relevant to the British public.

The pro-Brexit campaign was criticized for promoting misinformation based on materials like this one. In 2019, the BBC reported (Morris 2019) that Prime Minister Boris Johnson, who had advocated for Brexit, claimed that he "didn't say anything about Turkey" joining the EU. Whether he did or not in other messages, we can see how he can claim that messages such as those suggested by Figure 12.4 provide plausible deniability for a speaker who might wish to engage in propaganda production but retain a public persona that can be distanced from the propaganda message.

12.2 Languages Make Peace

Just as we see language behavior and linguistic identity playing a significant role in warfare and conflict, we also find many examples of these resources being put to the cause of peace and mutual understanding. Some people have imagined that warfare could actually be eliminated by the establishment of a universal shared human language. This viewpoint seems to be undermined by human histories of civil wars, which often involve antagonists who share a language but which are nevertheless at least as common (and vicious) as wars between different language communities. Nevertheless, people have tried, and their efforts are worth reflecting on.

12.2.1 A "Universal" Language of Peace? The Failed Experiment of Esperanto

Since language has been the cause of so much conflict, what are humans to do? One possible strategy is to adopt or create languages that are not associated with the cultural "baggage" that contemporary languages have. The ideal would be a politically and culturally neutral language selected or constructed specifically to allow people around the world to communicate with each other peacefully.

Some people have proposed languages such as English, Latin, or Chinese for this universal language (though obviously no real language can be described as politically or culturally neutral), and more have been created with the intention of divorcing language and culture altogether, such as Esperanto.[11] The problem? Naturally occurring languages retain their associations with power and prestige, while **invented languages** (or **constructed languages**) just haven't quite caught on. (The invented languages we discuss here also happen to be overwhelmingly influenced by Western European languages. By now, you can probably see that this is a big problem!)

Esperanto is the most popular of the invented "universal" languages, with somewhere between a hundred thousand and fifteen million speakers worldwide (Edwards 2010), and is perhaps the most successful invented language in human history. Some children are even raised with Esperanto as one of their home languages! But if a universal language has been a goal for so long and Esperanto is relatively successful, why aren't we all speaking Esperanto?

Esperanto was created by Lazaro Ludovic Zamenhof (Figure 12.5),[12] a Russian Jew born in Białystok, Russia in 1859. Zamenhof was a polyglot,[13] a speaker of many, many languages, which likely influenced Esperanto's makeup. The first grammar of Esperanto was published in Russian in 1887 and subsequently in Polish, French, German, English, and Swedish by 1889. These books were originally written under a pseudonym, Dr. Esperanto, and through common reference, "the language of Dr. Esperanto" eventually was shortened to "the language Esperanto" (Kiselman 2008).

Zamenhof's goal behind creating and promoting Esperanto was to have a culturally and religiously neutral language, as he viewed that people speaking many different languages and practicing many different religions is one of the factors that led to the persecution of Jews in nineteenth-century Russia (Gobbo 2017). Thus, he wanted to create a language that could be comfortably adopted and spoken by large populations, no matter their cultural

---

[11] and Volapük, a language we will not discuss in depth in this chapter.
[12] In the sources we have read, his name has also been documented as Lazaro Ludoviko Zamenhof, Lazar Ludwik Zamenhof, and a few other spellings.
[13] He may have spoken up to a whopping fourteen languages! These languages included his native Yiddish and Russian; he also grew up with German, Polish, and Hebrew; and later, he learned French, English, Latin, Greek, Aramaic, Italian, Lithuanian, Volapük, and, of course, Esperanto.

Figure 12.5 Portrait of Zamenhof, by Universala Esperanto-Asocio. Public Domain, https://commons.wikimedia.org/w/index.php?curid=3181910.

background, nationality, or beliefs. Since the grammar and lexicon of Esperanto was based on Zamenhof's own polyglot experience, its makeup is up to 75 percent Western European in terms of its origin languages (Bergen 2001), which has raised some metaphorical eyebrows about its universality.

Because of this goal of neutrality, Esperanto was intended to be an additional or auxiliary language rather than their primary language of communication for a given community. It could be spoken in addition to the language(s) that you spoke and which contributed to your cultural identity (Kimura 2003). However, in its usage today, that does not seem to be the case. Esperanto speakers are multilingual and use their home language in addition to Esperanto, but a different kind of culture has sprung up around Esperanto speakers: a **community of practice** that identifies as a social group concerned with Esperanto, its history, and linguistic practices (Gobbo 2017). That is, a member of the community who speaks Esperanto may also feel particularly connected to its history and the mission of its founder, while those who do not speak Esperanto do not have the same connection to it. You can attend conferences led by fellow Esperanto speakers, be a member of Esperanto societies, and even work in companies that use Esperanto as their main language of communication (Fiedler & Brosch 2018).

Despite the relative success of Esperanto – the only other constructed language that has caught on with similar fervor is the language Klingon from the TV series Star Trek, which was constructed by Marc Okrand – it has still not achieved Zamenhof's hope of it being a widely used neutral language of diplomacy and peace. One of the largest criticisms from people outside the Esperanto-speaking community is precisely why those in the community tend to believe it is an ideal lingua franca: there are few, if any, native speakers[14] and therefore no ultimate authority on the "correct" way to use Esperanto (Fiedler 2012).

The perceived lack of "native speaker authority" feeds back into some of the other perceptions of Esperanto that cause it to be less popular than one might think. With few native speakers and its status as an artificial language, Esperanto may be seen as less "legitimate" or "real," which then leads fewer people to be inclined to learn to speak it, and thus the cycle perpetuates. The idea of the "legitimacy" of a language as well as its associations with particular groups of people are both things that affect how language is used, as you have read throughout this chapter. There are also interactions with socioeconomic class and gender when it comes to membership in Esperanto societies, as well as the appeal of Esperanto as a common language (as opposed to English). While researchers have found that people of lower socioeconomic status are enthusiastic about using Esperanto as a common language, the membership in Esperanto societies skews more heavily toward men and toward higher socioeconomic status populations (Edwards 2010). This may be in part due to issues of access: the more socioeconomically privileged you are, the more time and resources you are likely to have to devote to the study of a language like Esperanto. Still though, more work should be done to better understand the social factors shaping engagement with Esperanto.

In the end, Esperanto does not seem to be the panacea for society that it was intended to be for a variety of reasons. If a language designed especially for the idea of promoting and maintaining peace is not popular enough to be adopted, are we destined for a future of war and violence?

12.2.2 One Language for One World?

The Esperanto example came from a belief that a single, global language could potentially advance the cause of world peace. That experiment has not succeeded, so perhaps we might consider a different response – propose that one natural language could become a lingua franca for the whole world.

---

[14] There are some, but not many, native speakers of Esperanto – estimates are in the hundreds.

Unsurprisingly, as we discuss this idea with colleagues and students in our own context, the language that is most often suggested for this role is English. Current estimates are that, if we count both first and second language speakers, English has the largest speaker population on earth today, and it is spoken in more countries than any other natural human language (Ethnologue 2023).

As English has become a more globally dominant force through colonization as well as through commercial and political routes, it does not appear that the world has necessarily become more peaceful. Instead, Englishes have arisen and are developing around the world into mutually unintelligible varieties. Nigerian English, Chinese English, Singapore English, and many more local varieties are gaining notoriety for their distinctive grammars, while "standard" English – the British-born varieties associated with wealthy white people and used in diplomacy, science, and international trade – have not functioned to resolve the conflicts that lead to war. In fact, they are increasingly seen as detrimental to the advancement of science (Blasi et al. 2022; Ramírez-Castañeda 2020). We think that you might have many insights about why the idea of monolingualism as a source of peace is misguided, and we invite you to think more about this topic.

12.2.3 Peaceful Coexistence: The Power of Linguistic Diversity

The example of Esperanto shows us that linguistic uniformity is not likely to be a useful strategy for ensuring peaceful coexistence among people. We can also find many examples of war and violence that occur among people who speak the same language (the US Civil War, for example, was one of the bloodiest and most violent conflicts on record, and it was almost exclusively fought by people who shared a common language). Are there ways in which a linguist in the community can study connections between language and peace among different kinds of people?

One approach that is part of a reconciliation process in Canada at the time of writing is based on a vision of healthy multilingualism between Indigenous populations and speakers of English, French, and other colonizing languages. The Truth and Reconciliation Commission of Canada,[15] a group that focuses on addressing the harms of the Boarding School era in particular, describe/discuss the UN declaration of rights of Indigenous peoples:[16]

---

[15] Currently available here: www.rcaanc-cirnac.gc.ca/eng/1450124405592/1529106060525
[16] Currently available here: www.un.org/development/desa/indigenouspeoples/declaration-on-the-rights-of-indigenous-peoples.html

> Indigenous peoples have the right to revitalize, use, develop and transmit to future generations their histories, languages, oral traditions, philosophies, writing systems and literatures, and to designate and retain their own names for communities, places and persons. (United Nations 2007)

As linguists in the community, we can rely on evidence from a variety of domains to confirm that multilingualism and **multidialectalism** hold tremendous promise in the creation and maintenance of a peaceful and just society. These approaches recognize both the right to free expression and to our ability to affirm our social and cultural identities without fear of harm. They also recognize the fact that human communities have always been, and will probably always be, linguistically diverse. Claims that multilingualism, or multidialectalism, are harmful or divisive are easily dismissed based on a quick review of the available facts and disproven by the important scholarship of linguists who work in the area of linguistic rights and justice (see, e.g., Baugh 2000; Charity Hudley et al. 2020; DeGraff 2020; Flores & Rosa 2015; Leonard 2018; Wyman et al. 2013; and many others).

Human history shows that neither monolingual nor multilingual societies are immune from hatred and warfare, but linguists understand that hostility and aggression toward language is always really hostility and aggression toward humans. It might be that accepting and valuing linguistic diversity is necessary but not sufficient for there to be peace and justice in a community.

12.2.4 Finding Peace after War: It's Not Too Late

We end this discussion with a story of hope. As we have discussed earlier in this chapter, the Indigenous peoples of Central and North America represented something like 750 distinct language communities in the era before European contact, and perhaps 500 in South America (Silver & Miller 1994). These communities experienced decimation from disease and warfare upon the arrival of Europeans, and many of the languages survived only a generation or two after contact. One community that experienced very early language shift was the Wampanoag (Wôpanâak), an Algonquian group whose traditional territory overlapped with that of the Plymouth colony – one of the first European settlements in North America. In spite of now-often-repeated fables about how the Wampanoag helped those early settlers beginning with a purported feast in 1621,[17] the Wôpanâak were harassed, murdered, and displaced by European settlers (Hedgpeth 2021). The

---

[17] This is the origin story of the US holiday called "Thanksgiving"; there's no evidence that there was any good faith sharing of a "feast" between the Plymouth colony and the Wampanoag.

Wôpanâak language, which had been studied and described by Thomas Jefferson, and which – more importantly – had been used in written form in a large number of both legal and personal documents by Wôpanâak people for many years, went silent.

In spite of this, and like so many other Indigenous communities, the Wampanoag people survived. Although there was a nearly four-hundred-year disruption of intergenerational transmission and concomitant difficulties surrounding federal recognition, the Wôpanâak language is in use again today thanks to those survivors' efforts to recover and reconstruct it and then breathe life back into it. The Mashpee Wampanoag language reclamation efforts began with a single individual, jessie little doe baird,[18] who describes a dream in which the language began to return to her. She has devoted many years to this effort, in which she has worked to reconstruct the language while learning to speak it and to use it in her home (little doe baird 2016). She used her skills and training in history and linguistics (even an advanced linguistics degree from MIT, where she studied with Ken Hale) in order to solve the puzzles created by the surviving documentation of the language in its context among information about neighboring related languages. As a result, jessie's family and her community now boast fluent speakers of the language – including youngsters who have had the benefit of using the language in the home as they have grown. There is every reason to believe that Wôpanâak will survive and thrive in the future. It does, and will, coexist with a variety of other languages and linguistic varieties in a multilingual and multidialectal community in which the Wôpanâak people can speak and listen to the language of their choice.

Jessie little doe baird's work with Wôpanâak shows that a more accurate description of a language that has been lost would be "sleeping" or "dormant," not "dead." When there are still social uses for a language, even if there are no speakers, it can be revived and used by new generations. In fact, the Wôpanâak story is neither the first nor the most prominent such example – interested readers might wish to learn more about how and why Hebrew is a vibrant and commonly spoken contemporary language shared by communities around the world today, for example.

This sort of framing aligns nicely with a perspective taken by sociolinguist Adam Hodges (2013), whose research on discourses of war allowed him to theorize on discourses of peace as well. Hodges wrote that "instead of the inert absence of the action-filled undertaking of war, peace must be turned into an activity in its own right. To reimagine peace begins by viewing it as a

---

[18] Jessie does not use upper-case letters in the spelling of her name; we follow her preferences here.

practice [of justice]... To practice peace involves promoting education, democracy, and equality. It involves fostering cross-cultural connections that emphasize our common humanity. Whereas to wage war involves increasing social distance and decreasing compassion, to wage peace involves decreasing social distance and increasing compassion" (p. 16). Although some may feel that these calls go beyond the work of linguistics, as practitioners of a human-centered social science, we believe our work has some of its greatest value when put toward these goals.

12.3 Conclusion

In this chapter we've touched on a variety of principles and examples of the interactions we can observe between language behavior, linguistic identity, and very large-scale social and historical events. We have looked at ways in which communities of people come to view particular languages as key components of a nationalist identity, and how minoritized, Indigenous, and stigmatized languages can become the targets of violence against their speakers. We have seen that there are patterns of language use that can be deployed as weapons of disinformation or as ways of swaying national opinions or constructing some languages as dangerous. But we've also seen that languages can be instruments of peace – perhaps not by becoming more uniform, but by retaining and even cultivating their differences. Our discussion has not been exhaustive, but we hope that it is sufficient to inspire you to investigate these phenomena in your own communities.

Linguist in the Community

- Wherever you are in the world, see if you can find out the linguistic history of that place. Have there been languages that were commonly spoken in your area in the past that aren't spoken so often now? If so, what factors have been involved in this shift, and are there people who are working to reclaim languages in your community?
- Look around your community for evidence of language use that you think might fit the definitions of "propaganda" or "disinformation" from this chapter. Pick an example, and see if you can decode the underlying messages. What, if any, claims are asserted to be true, even though they're not explicitly said? What evidence do you find in the message itself that there is an intent to fool, trick, or mislead the receiver? Explain the strategies you find, and share your work with others.

- Make an inventory of communities with whom your own community has engaged in hostilities against – this might include enemies in wars and/or marginalized groups in the context of forced assimilation or other types of group violence. For each community, note the language(s) that are associated with them, and note how those languages are discussed or described in your community. Are they the same as your own languages, or are they different? If they're different, are you allowed to learn them in school? Are there venues where they're not allowed, or places where they're demeaned or treated as dangerous? Describe how these patterns seem to relate to the patterns of hostilities in your inventory.

Linguist in the Classroom

- In small groups, work with peers to collect a set of rules for academic writing that you have been given by your instructors over the years (for example, we've heard students say that they've been told to avoid contractions or informal constructions). Then sort the list into (at least) two categories: advice that's really just about writing (e.g., how to punctuate sentences), and advice that's about language (e.g., don't use informal language). Then review the second list and see if you can find out whether any of those rules reflects bias against language styles associated with a marginalized group. Share your lists with the class, and discuss the ways in which academic language rules might be recapitulating language wars.
- Hold a language conference in class! Assign some students to participate as representatives of various language communities that have been treated as enemies in the past, or today, and others as language policy advisors. Working together, sketch out a set of needs (from the language communities) and responses (from the policy advisors) that your peers think might help your community work toward peace and away from warfare.
- As a class, discuss the role of multilingualism in your community. Ask students to write down a sentence or two about their feelings and experiences in this regard but not sign their contributions. You may want to share your own personal feelings and experiences around the use of languages that you don't understand when that usage happens in your school, in your workplace, or elsewhere in your community; and you may want to share experiences around your use of "enemy" or "stigmatized" language varieties around majority or prestige speakers in your community. Collect all the contributions, and redistribute them to the class. Use these contributions to guide your discussion and reflection.

Glossary

African American Language (AAL) A set of linguistic varieties that are associated with African American identity in North America, and that are sometimes analyzed as varieties of English, and sometimes analyzed as originating with an English-based creole.

Anglo-Saxon A term used to refer to the varieties of West Germanic languages that were spoken by invaders of the British Isles during the fourth and fifth centuries of the common era. Prominent subgroups were Angles, Saxons, and Jutes. More commonly referred to as Old English.

bias A pattern of stigmatizing, penalizing, or ignoring some languages, varieties, or groups in comparison to others.

Black English See African American Language.

Celtic A linguistic group within the Indo-European language family that had expanded into and settled on the British Isles long before the fourth century of the common era. Contemporary Celtic languages include Irish Gaelic, Scots Gaelic, Welsh, Cornish, Breton, and a number of others.

community of practice A group of people who, in engaging in shared activities, cocreate a set of linguistic and other norms that distinguish them from others, and that signal both the individual's own identities and that of the group.

constructed language See invented language; may also be called "conlang."

cultural genocide An attempt to eliminate the cultural practices and distinctness of a community; this may or may not include full-scale genocidal murder. Forced assimilation is a common tool in cultural genocides.

discrimination Acting in ways that are driven by and perpetuate bias.

disinformation False information that is deliberately shared in order to mislead or deceive.

Ebonics See African American Language.

epithets Bad names, usually for groups of people.

Germanic A linguistic group within the Indo-European language family that includes German, Norse, Dutch, and many others, including the several subgroups who colonized the British Isles in the fourth and fifth centuries – the Angles, the Saxons, the Jutes, and others.

hate speech Language use that weaponizes bias with violent intent.

ideologies of nationalism Beliefs that all of the "true" citizens of a nation-state constitute a homogenous group, often conceived of as superior to others, and always in contrast to groups that are stereotypically associated with, or culturally connected to, other nation-states.

invented language A language that is consciously created by one or more individuals.

language shift When a language community adopts a new language in place of, rather than in addition to, their heritage language. Language shift can lead to language loss.

lexicography The practice of writing, compiling, and/or editing dictionaries.

lingua franca A shared language that community members can use with each other as a second language, often across different first language communities. Lingua francas are often used to facilitate trade or other trans-community political or economic interaction.

multidialectalism A system in which community members can comfortably use more than one dialect or language variety; a multidialectal community is one in which multiple dialects can be used successfully in many contexts. A multidialectal person is one who can communicate comfortably in more than one dialect.

multilingualism A system in which community members can comfortably use more than one language; a multilingual community is one in which multiple languages can be used successfully in many contexts. A multilingual person is one who can communicate comfortably in more than one language.

national language A language that is associated with national identity.

official language The formally designated primary language of a particular government or organization, used to conduct official business.

Old English The varieties of Western Germanic that were spoken by Germanic settlers who arrived in the British Isles in the fourth and fifth centuries of the common era.

orthographies Writing systems.

propaganda The systemic dissemination of misleading information in order to promote a political cause or point of view.

smears Insults.

Recommended Readings

After reading this chapter, you're well on your way to becoming an expert in all the ways that language variation can shape the world. The impacts of this power are far-reaching, and we hope what we have discussed here inspires you to learn more. Below you'll find a list of some of our favorite readings that will help you explore these topics in greater detail. As always, a local college or university library can help you access anything here, or in the full reference list at the end of the book.

Baugh, J. (2000). *Beyond Ebonics: Linguistic Pride and Racial Prejudice*. Oxford University Press on Demand.

Charity Hudley, A. H., & Mallinson, C. (2018). Dismantling "the master's tools": Moving students' rights to their own language from theory to practice. *American Speech: A Quarterly of Linguistic Usage, 93*(3–4), 513–537. https://doi.org/10/d5n2

Lanehart, S., Bloomquist, J., & Malik, A. (2015). Language use in African American communities: An introduction. In S. Lanehart (Ed.), *The Oxford Handbook of African American Language* (pp. 1–20). Oxford University Press.

Leonard, W. Y. (2008). When is an "extinct language" not extinct? Miami, a formally sleeping language. In K. A. King, N. Schilling-Estes, L. Fogle, J. J. Lou, & B. Soukup (Eds.), *Sustaining Linguistic Diversity: Endangered and Minority Languages and Language Varieties* (pp. 23–33). Georgetown University Press.

Lippi-Green, R. (2012). *English with an Accent: Language, Ideology and Discrimination in the United States* (2nd ed.). Routledge.

little doe baird, j. (2016). Wopanaak language reclamation program: Bringing the language home. *Journal of Global Indigeneity, 2*(2). www.journalofglobalindigeneity.com/article/33216-wopanaak-language-reclamation-program-bringing-the-language-home

Rosa, J., & Flores, N. (2017). Unsettling race and language: Toward a raciolinguistic perspective. *Language in Society, 46*(5), 621–647. https://doi.org/10/gg2bvm

van Gelderen, E. (2014). *A History of the English Language* (Revised ed.). John Benjamins Publishing Company.

Wyman, L. T., McCarty, T. L., & Nicholas, S. E. (2013). *Indigenous Youth and Multilingualism: Language Identity, Ideology, and Practice in Dynamic Cultural Worlds*. Taylor & Francis Group.

References

Ackerman, L. (2019). Syntactic and cognitive issues in investigating gendered coreference. *Glossa: A Journal of General Linguistics, 4*(1), 117. https://doi.org/10/ggjtbh

Adair, J. K., Colegrove, K. S.-S., & McManus, M. E. (2017). How the word gap argument negatively impacts young children of Latinx immigrants' conceptualizations of learning. *Harvard Educational Review, 87*(3), 309–334. https://doi.org/10/gmh2bq

Adger, D. (2016). Language variability in syntactic theory. In L. Egurin, O. Fernández-Soriano, & A. Mendikoetxea (Eds.), *Rethinking Parameters* (pp. 49–63). Oxford University Press.

Adger, D., & Smith, J. (2010). Variation in agreement: A lexical feature-based approach. *Lingua, 120*(5), 1109–1134. https://doi.org/10/cjj3wk

Ahearn, L. M. (2012). Language and gender. In *Living Language: An Introduction to Linguistic Anthropology* (pp. 187–213). Wiley-Blackwell.

Aikio-Puoskari, U. (2018). Revitalization of Sámi languages in three Nordic countries: Finland, Norway, and Sweden. In *The Routledge Handbook of Language Revitalization* (pp. 355–363). Routledge.

Akinwotu, E. (2023, March 22). Uganda to jail people who identify as LGBTQ in one of world's most anti-gay laws. *NPR*. www.npr.org/2023/03/22/1165317598/uganda-lgbtq-law

Akros, Inc., Wilson Preservation, & Coffman Studios (2007). Tucson post World War II residential subdivision development 1945–1973: Report to the city of Tucson, AZ. *City of Tucson*. www.tucsonaz.gov/files/sharedassets/public/v/1/city-services/planning-development-services/historic-preservation/documents/text_-_tucson_post_wwii_residential_subdivision_development.pdf

Alalou, A. (2006). Language and ideology in the Maghreb: Francophonie and other languages. *The French Review, 80*(2), 408–421. http://doi.org/10.2307/25480661

Alim, H. S. (2007). Critical hip-hop language pedagogies: Combat, consciousness, and the cultural politics of communication. *Journal of Language, Identity, and Education, 6*(2), 161–176. http://doi.org/10.1080/15348450701341378

Alim, H. S., Rickford, J. R., & Ball, A. F. (2016). *Raciolinguistics: How Language Shapes Our Ideas about Race*. Oxford University Press.

Allen, K. (2012, May 10). Diné worker fired for speaking Navajo. *Navajo Times*. https://navajotimes.com/news/2012/0512/051012fir.php

Ambridge, B., Kidd, E., Rowland, C. F., & Theakston, A. L. (2015). The ubiquity of frequency effects in first language acquisition. *Journal of Child Language, 42*(2), 239–273. https://doi.org/10.1017/S030500091400049X

American Institutes for Research and WestEd (2006). Effects of the implementation of Proposition 227 on the education of English learners, K-12. Report submitted to the California Department of Education. *Air.* https://files.eric.ed.gov/fulltext/ED491617.pdf

Angermeyer, P. S. (2015). *Speak English or What?: Codeswitching and Interpreter Use in New York City Courts.* Oxford University Press.

Annamma, S., Morrison, D., & Jackson, D. (2014). Disproportionality fills in the gaps: Connections between achievement, discipline and special education in the school-to-prison pipeline. *Berkeley Review of Education, 5*(1), 53–87. https://doi.org/10.5070/B85110003

Antaki, C., Richardson, E., Stokoe, E., & Willott, S. (2015). Police interviews with vulnerable people alleging sexual assault: Probing inconsistency and questioning conduct. *Journal of Sociolinguistics, 19*(3), 328–350. https://doi.org/10.1111/josl.12124

Austin, J. L. (1975). *How to Do Things with Words* (Vol. 88). Oxford University Press.

Babel, M., & Russell, J. (2015). Expectations and speech intelligibility. *The Journal of the Acoustical Society of America, 137*(5), 2823–2833. https://doi.org/10/f7c68x

Baese-Berk, M. M., Drake, S., Foster, K., Lee, D.-Y., Staggs, C., & Wright, J. M. (2021). Lexical diversity, lexical sophistication, and predictability for speech in multiple listening conditions. *Frontiers in Psychology: Language Science, 12*, 2328. https://doi.org/10.3389/fpsyg.2021.661415

Baker-Bell, A. (2020). *Linguistic Justice: Black Language, Literacy, Identity, and Pedagogy.* Routledge.

Barahona, M. (2015). *English Language Teacher Education in Chile: A Cultural Historical Activity Theory Perspective.* Routledge.

Barkwell, L. (2017, November). Michif language background paper: An overview of the last 35 years. Prepared for the Metis National Council, *Gabriel Dumont Institute and Louis Riel Institute.* www.academia.edu/38926972/Michif_Language_Background

Baron, D. (1990). *The English-Only Question: An Official Language for Americans?* Yale University Press.

Barrett, R. (2006). Language ideology and racial inequality: Competing functions of Spanish in an Anglo-owned Mexican restaurant. *Language in Society, 35*(2), 163–204. https://doi.org/10.1017/S0047404506060088

Barrett, R. (2017). *From Drag Queens to Leathermen: Language, Gender, and Gay Male Subcultures.* Oxford University Press.

Basiliere, J. (2019). Staging dissents: Drag kings, resistance, and feminist masculinities. *Signs: Journal of Women in Culture and Society, 44*(4), 979–1001. https://doi.org/10.1086/702034

Baugh, J. (2000). *Beyond Ebonics: Linguistic Pride and Racial Prejudice.* Oxford University Press on Demand.

Baugh, J. (2003). Linguistic profiling. In S. Makoni, G. Smitherman, A. F. Ball, & A. K. Spears (Eds.), *Black Linguistics: Language, Society and Politics in Africa and the Americas* (pp. 155–168). Routledge.

Baugh, J. (2018). *Linguistics in Pursuit of Justice.* Cambridge University Press.

Becker, K., & Zimman, L. (2022). Beyond binary gender: Creaky voice, gender, and the variationist enterprise. *Language Variation and Change, 34*(2), 215–238. https://doi.org/10.1017/S0954394522000138

Bell, E. A. (2018). *Perception and Production of Welsh Vowels by Welsh-Spanish Bilinguals.* [Doctoral Dissertation, The University of Arizona]. https://repository.arizona.edu/handle/10150/630174

Bender, E. M. (2011). On achieving and evaluating language-independence in NLP. *Linguistic Issues in Language Technology, 6*(3), 1–26. https://doi.org/10.33011/lilt.v6i.1239

Bender, E. M. (2019). The #BenderRule: On naming the languages we study and why it matters. *The Gradient.* https://thegradient.pub/the-benderrule-on-naming-the-languages-we-study-and-why-it-matters/

Bender, E. M., & Friedman, B. (2018). Data statements for natural language processing: Toward mitigating system bias and enabling better science. *Transactions of the Association for Computational Linguistics, 6*, 587–604. https://doi.org/10/gft5d7

Bender, E. M., Gebru, T., McMillan-Major, A., & Shmitchell, S. (2021). On the dangers of stochastic parrots: Can language models be too big?. *Proceedings of the 2021 ACM Conference on Fairness, Accountability, and Transparency,* 610–623. https://doi.org/10.1145/3442188.3445922

Benedict, H. (1979). Early lexical development: Comprehension and production. *Journal of Child Language, 6*(2), 183–200. https://doi.org/10/dv85xn

Berez-Kroeker, A. L., Andreassen, H. N., Gawne, L., Holton, G., Smythe Kung, S., Pulsifer, P., Collister, L. B., The Data Citation and Attribution in Linguistics Group, & The Linguistics Data Interest Group (2018). The Austin Principles of data citation in linguistics. Version 1.0. *Linguistics Data Citation.* https://site.uit.no/linguisticsdatacitation/austinprinciples/

Bergen, B. K. (2001). Nativization processes in L1 Esperanto. *Journal of Child Language, 28*(3), 575–595. https://doi.org/10/c6gnzz

Berlin, B., & Kay, P. (1969). *Basic Color Terms: Their Universality and Evolution.* University of California Press.

Berman, E. (2014). Negotiating age: Direct speech and the sociolinguistic production of childhood in the Marshall Islands. *Journal of Linguistic Anthropology, 24*(2), 109–132. https://doi.org/10.1111/jola.12044

Bertrand, M., & Mullainathan, S. (2004). Are Emily and Greg more employable than Lakisha and Jamal? A field experiment on labor market discrimination. *The American Economic Review, 94*(4), 133. https://doi.org/10.1257/0002828042002561

Besky, S. (2014). *The Darjeeling Distinction: Labor and Justice on Fair-Trade Tea Plantations in India*. University of California Press.

Besnier, N. (2001). Literacy. In A. Duranti (Ed.), *Key Terms in Language and Culture* (pp. 136–138). Blackwell Publishing.

Blasi, D. E., Henrich, J., Adamou, E., Kemmerer, D., & Majid, A. (2022). Over-reliance on English hinders cognitive science. *Trends in Cognitive Sciences, 26*(12), 1153–1170. https://doi.org/10.1016/j.tics.2022.09.015

Bliss, H. A. (2017). Dependencies in syntax and discourse: Obviation in Blackfoot and beyond. *Working Papers of the Linguistics Circle of the University of Victoria, 27*(1), 1–26. https://journals.uvic.ca/index.php/WPLC/article/view/16689

Blommaert, J. (2012). Lookalike language. *English Today, 28*(2), 62–64. https://doi.org/10.1017/S0266078412000193

Bloom, L. (2014). *Suspicion Nation: The Inside Story of the Trayvon Martin Injustice and Why We Continue to Repeat It*. Counterpoint.

Blum, S. D. (2017). Unseen WEIRD assumptions: The so-called language gap discourse and ideologies of language, childhood, and learning. *International Multilingual Research Journal, 11*(1), 23–38. https://doi.org/10/gjm2gq

Borer, H., & Wexler, K. (1987). The maturation of syntax. In T. Roeper & E. Williams (Eds.), *Parameter Setting* (pp. 123–172). Springer Netherlands.

Bourdieu, P. (2003). *Language and Symbolic Power*. Harvard University Press.

Bradley, D. (1977). Modernization and diglcossia in Burmese. *Occasional Papers in Linguistics, 3*, 1–12.

Brannan, K. J. (2011). *The Perception and Production of Interdental Fricatives in Second Language Acquisition*. [Doctoral Dissertation, McGill University].

Braut, K. T. (2010). *To Speak or Not to Speak: Because They Tell Me to Speak Sámi at Daycare*. [Master's Thesis, University of Tromsø]. https://munin.uit.no/bitstream/handle/10037/2965/thesis.pdf?sequence=1&isAllowed=y

Brentari, D. (2019). *Sign Language Phonology*. Cambridge University Press.

Brown, A. (2022). About 5% of young adults in the U.S. say their gender is different from their sex assigned at birth. *Pew Research Center*. https://www.pewresearch.org/fact-tank/2022/06/07/about-5-of-young-adults-in-the-u-s-say-their-gender-is-different-from-their-sex-assigned-at-birth/

Brown, P., & Levinson, S. (1987). *Politeness: Some Universals in Language Usage*. Cambridge University Press.

Bucholtz, M. (2000). The politics of transcription. *Journal of Pragmatics, 32*, 1439–1465. https://doi.org/10.1016/S0378-2166(99)00094-6

Cai, J. (2020, December). The condition of Native American students: This significant minority student group continues to struggle. *American School Board Journal*, 1.

Calder, J. (2019). The fierceness of fronted /s/: Linguistic rhematization through visual transformation. *Language in Society, 48*(1), 31–64. https://doi.org/10.1017/S004740451800115X

Cameron, D. (1997). Performing gender identity: Young men's talk and the construction of heterosexual masculinity. In S. Johnson & U. Meinhof (Eds.), *Language and Masculinity* (pp. 8–26). Blackwell.

Camp, M. (2009). *Japanese Lesbian Speech: Sexuality, Gender Identity, and Language*. [Doctoral Dissertation, The University of Arizona]. https://repository.arizona.edu/handle/10150/195371

Caron, C. (2017, September 17). Sign language interpreter warned of "pizza" and "bear monster" at Irma briefing. *The New York Times*. https://www.nytimes.com/2017/09/17/us/sign-language-interpreter-irma.html

Carpenter, K. A., Katyal, S. K., & Riley, A. R. (2010). Clarifying cultural property. *International Journal of Cultural Property, 17*(3), 581–598. https://doi.org/10.1017/S0940739110000317

Carpusor, A. G., & Loges, W. E. (2006). Rental discrimination and ethnicity in names. *Journal of Applied Social Psychology, 36*(4), 934–952. https://doi.org/10.1111/j.0021-9029.2006.00050.x

Carroll, L. (1871). *Through the Looking-Glass*. Macmillan.

Castilla-Earls, A., Bedore, L., Rojas, R., Fabiano-Smith, L., Pruitt-Lord, S., Restrepo, M. A., & Peña, E. (2020). Beyond scores: Using converging evidence to determine speech and language services eligibility for dual language learners. *American Journal of Speech-Language Pathology, 29*(3), 1116–1132. https://doi.org/10.1044/2020_AJSLP-19-00179

Cavanaugh, J. R. (2016). Talk as work: Economic sociability in Northern Italian heritage food production. *Language and Communication, 48*, 41–52. https://doi.org/10.1016/j.langcom.2016.02.001

Chappell, B. (2019, February 15). Americans who were detained after speaking Spanish in Montana sue U.S. border agency. *NPR*. www.npr.org/2019/02/15/695184555/americans-who-were-detained-after-speaking-spanish-in-montana-sue-u-s-border-pat

Charity Hudley, A. H., & Mallinson, C. (2011). *Understanding English Language Variation in U.S. Schools*. Teachers College Press.

Charity Hudley, A. H., & Mallinson, C. (2018). Dismantling "the master's tools": Moving students' rights to their own language from theory to practice. *American Speech, 93*(3–4), 513–537. https://doi.org/10/d5n2

Charity Hudley, A. H., Mallinson, C., & Bucholtz, M. (2020). Toward racial justice in linguistics: Interdisciplinary insights into theorizing race in the discipline and diversifying the profession. *Language*, *96*(4), e200–e235. https://doi.org/10.1353/lan.2020.0074

Chen, D., & Manning, C. D. (2014). A fast and accurate dependency parser using neural networks. In A. Moschitti, B. Pang, & W. Daelemans (Eds.), *Proceedings of the 2014 Conference on Empirical Methods in Natural Language Processing (EMNLP)* (pp. 740–750). Association for Computational Linguistics.

Chen, M. K. (2013). The effect of language on economic behavior: Evidence from savings rates, health behaviors, and retirement assets. *American Economic Review*, *103*(2), 690–731. https://doi.org/10.1257/aer.103.2.690

Chen, S., Cronqvist, H., Ni, S., & Zhang, F. (2017). Languages and corporate savings behavior. *Journal of Corporate Finance*, *46*, 320–341. https://doi.org/10.1016/j.jcorpfin.2017.07.009

Chin, M. (2020, June 29). Wearable-tech glove translates sign language into speech in real time. *UCLA Newsroom*. https://newsroom.ucla.edu/releases/glove-translates-sign-language-to-speech

Chomsky, N. (1957). *Syntactic Structures*. Mouton de Gruyter.

Chomsky, N. (1965). *Aspects of the Theory of Syntax*. MIT Press.

Chowdhery, A., Narang, S., Devlin, J., Bosma, M., Mishra, G., Roberts, A., Barham, P., et al. (2022). PaLM: Scaling language modeling with pathways. ArXiv:2204.02311 [Cs]. http://arxiv.org/abs/2204.02311

Coates, J. (2013). The discursive production of everyday heterosexualities. *Discourse & Society*, *24*(5), 536–552. https://doi.org/10.1177/0957926513486070

Coats, S. (2024). Naturalistic double modals in North America. *American Speech*, *99*(1), 47–77. https://doi.org/10.1215/00031283-9766889

Comrie, B. (1988). Linguistic typology. *Annual Review of Anthropology*, *17*, 145–159. https://doi.org/10/fb448m

Conley, J. M., & O'Barr, W. (2005). *Just Words: Language and Power*. University of Chicago Press.

Conrod, K. (2020). Pronouns and gender in language. In K. Hall & R. Barrett (Eds.), *The Oxford Handbook of Language and Sexuality* (online ed.). Oxford University Press. https://doi.org/10.1093/oxfordhb/9780190212926.013.63

Cooc, N., & Kiru, E. W. (2018). Disproportionality in special education: A synthesis of international research and trends. *The Journal of Special Education*, *52*(3), 163–173. https://doi.org/10.1177/0022466918772300

Corbett, G. G. (2013). Sex-based and non-sex-based gender systems (v2020.3). In M. S. Dryer & M. Haspelmath (Eds.), *The World Atlas of Language Structures Online*. Zenodo.

Coto-Solano, R. (2022). Computational sociophonetics using automatic speech recognition. *Language and Linguistics Compass, 16*(9), e12474. https://doi.org/10.1111/lnc3.12474

Cotter, W. M., & Valentinsson, M.-C. (2018). Bivalent class indexing in the sociolinguistics of specialty coffee talk. *Journal of Sociolinguistics, 22*(5), 489–515. https://doi.org/10.1111/josl.12305

Counts, J., Katsiyannis, A., & Whitford, D. K. (2018). Culturally and linguistically diverse learners in special education: English learners. *NASSP Bulletin, 102*(1), 5–21. https://doi.org/10.1177/0192636518755945

Courtney, E. H., & Saville-Troike, M. (2002). Learning to construct verbs in Navajo and Quechua. *Journal of Child Language, 29*(3), 623–654. https://doi.org/10.1017/s0305000902005160

Davidson, L. (2017, March 29). Talking while female: The science & censure of women's voices. In NYU Linguistics, *Linguistic Prejudice, Linguistic Privilege: Public Forum (Lisa Davidson)* [YouTube video]. www.youtube.com/watch?v=MmX_p0bpoxs

Davies, D. (2017, August 22). FBI profiler says linguistic work was pivotal in capture of Unabomber. *NPR.* www.npr.org/2017/08/22/545122205/fbi-profiler-says-linguistic-work-was-pivotal-in-capture-of-unabomber

Davies, E. E., & Bentahila, A. (2012). Language attitudes in the Maghreb countries of Northwest Africa. In H. Giles & B. M. Watson (Eds.), *The Social Meanings of Language, Dialect and Accent: International Perspectives on Speech Style* (pp. 84–104). Peter Lang.

Davies, M. (2008–). *The Corpus of Contemporary American English (COCA)* [Data set]. www.english-corpora.org/coca/

Day-Vines, N. L., & Day-Hairston, B. O. (2005). Culturally congruent strategies for addressing the behavioral needs of urban, African American male adolescents. *Professional School Counseling, 8*(3), 236–243. www.jstor.org/stable/42732464

De León, L. (1998). The emergent participant: Interactive patterns in the socialization of Tzotzil (Mayan) infants. *Journal of Linguistic Anthropology, 8*(2), 131–161. https://doi.org/10.1525/jlin.1998.8.2.131

de Saussure, F. (2011). *Course in General Linguistics* (W. Baskin, Trans., P. Meisel & H. Saussy, Eds.). Columbia University Press.

de Waal, F. (2016). *Are We Smart Enough to Know How Smart Animals Are?*. WW Norton and Company.

DeCasper, A. J., & Spence, M. J. (1986). Prenatal maternal speech influences newborns' perception of speech sounds. *Infant Behavior and Development, 9*(2), 133–150. https://doi.org/10/bknzjx

DeGraff, M. (2020). Toward racial justice in linguistics: The case of Creole studies (Response to Charity Hudley et al.). *Language, 96*(4), e292–e306.

Derby, L. (2020). An oral history of a massacre: Interview with Isil Nicolas Cour, Dosmon, Ouanaminthe, Haiti, 1988, conducted with Richard Turits. In L. Dubois, K. L., Glover, N., Ménard, M., Polyné, & C. F. Verna (Eds.), *The Haiti Reader* (pp. 267–276). Duke University Press.

Dewalt, K. M., Dewalt, B. R., & Wayland, C. B. (1998). Participant observation. In H. R. Bernard (Ed.), *Handbook of Methods in Cultural Anthropology* (pp. 259–299). Altamira Press.

Dryer, M. S., & Haspelmath, M. (Eds.) (2013). WALS online. *Max Planck Institute for Evolutionary Anthropology*. http://wals.info/

Dubost, K. (2008, May 6). Utf-8 growth on the web. *W3C Blog*. www.w3.org/blog/2008/05/utf8-web-growth/

Eckert, P. (1996). Vowels and nail polish: The emergence of linguistic style in the pre-adolescent heterosexual marketplace. In N. Warner, J. Ahlers, L. Bilmes, M. Oliver, S. Wertheim, & M. Chen (Eds.), *Gender and Belief Systems: Proceedings of the Fourth Berkeley Women and Language Conference* (pp. 183–190). Berkeley Women and Language Group.

Eckert, P. (2011). Language and power in the preadolescent heterosexual market. *American Speech*, *86*(1), 85–97. https://doi.org/10.1215/00031283-1277528

Eckert, P., & McConnell-Ginet, S. (2013). *Language and Gender* (1st ed.). Cambridge University Press.

Edwards, J. (2010). *Minority Languages and Group Identity: Cases and Categories*. John Benjamins.

EEOC v. RD's Drive In/Exxon | Civil Rights Litigation Clearinghouse, CIV 02 1911 PCT LOA (US District Court for the District of Arizona August 22, 2007). www.clearinghouse.net/detail.php?id=9064

Engber, C. A. (1995). The relationship of lexical proficiency to the quality of ESL compositions. *Journal of Second Language Writing*, *4*(2), 139–155. https://doi.org/10.1016/1060-3743(95)90004-7

Erbaugh, M. S. (2009). Southern Chinese dialects as a medium for reconciliation within Greater China. *Language in Society*, *24*(1), 79–94. https://doi.org/10.1017/s0047404500018418

Eswaran, H., Lowery, C. L., Wilson, J. D., Murphy, P., & Preissl, H. (2004). Functional development of the visual system in human fetus using magnetoencephalography. *Experimental Neurology*, *190*(Suppl 1), S52–58. https://doi.org/10.1016/j.expneurol.2004.04.007

Ethnologue (2023). What is the most spoken language? *Ethinogue*. www.ethnologue.com/insights/most-spoken-language/

European Union (2019). EU languages. *European Union*. https://europa.eu/european-union/about-eu/eu-languages_en

Evidence Data and Knowledge, & Ministry of Education (2021, February). Annual ECE census 2020: Fact sheets. *Education Counts*. www.educationcounts

.govt.nz/publications/ECE/annual-early-childhood-education-census/annual-ece-census-2020-fact-sheets

Farrington, C., & Kendall, T. (2021). The Corpus of Regional African American Language [Data set]. https://doi.org/10.7264/1ad5-6t35

Farrington, C., King, S., & Kohn, M. (2021). Sources of variation in the speech of African Americans: Perspectives from sociophonetics. *Wiley Interdisciplinary Reviews: Cognitive Science, 12*(3), e1550. https://doi.org/10.1002/wcs.1550

Fenson, L., Dale, P. S., Reznick, J. S., & Bates, E. (1994). Variability in early communicative development. *Monographs of the Society for Research in Child Development, 59*(5), i–185. https://doi.org/10/d5btfv

Fernald, A., & Kuhl, P. (1987). Acoustic determinants of infant preference for motherese speech. *Infant Behavior and Development, 10*(3), 279–293. https://doi.org/10/bhpqpc

Ferreira, F., Christianson, K., & Hollingworth, A. (2001). Misinterpretations of garden-path sentences: Implications for models of sentence processing and reanalysis. *Journal of Psycholinguistic Research, 30*(1), 3–20. https://doi.org/10.1023/A:1005290706460

Fiedler, S. (2012). The Esperanto denaskulo: The status of the native speaker of Esperanto within and beyond the planned language community. *Language Problems and Language Planning, 36*(1), 69–84. https://doi.org/10/gj5mhk

Fiedler, S., & Brosch, C. (2018). Esperanto – a lingua franca in use: A case study on an educational NGO. *Language Problems and Language Planning, 42*(2), 220–245. https://doi.org/10/ggxmqt

Figueroa, M. (2024a). Decolonizing (psycho) linguistics means dropping the "language gap" rhetoric. In A. H. Charity Hudley, C. Mallinson, & M. Bucholtz (Eds.), *Decolonizing Linguistics* (pp. 157–172). Oxford University Press.

Figueroa, M. (2024b). Language development, linguistic input, and linguistic racism. *WIREs Cognitive Science, 15*(3), e1673. https://doi.org/10.1002/wcs.1673

Figueroa, M. (2018). *"Who Breaked the Rule?": Rethinking English Past Tense Overregularizations.* [Doctoral Dissertation, The University of Arizona]. http://hdl.handle.net/10150/628007

Figueroa, M., & Gerken, L. (2019). Experience with morphosyntactic paradigms allows toddlers to tacitly anticipate overregularized verb forms months before they produce them. *Cognition, 191*, 103977. https://doi.org/10.1016/j.cognition.2019.05.014

Fischer, H. (2002, September 30). Lawsuit tackles Navajo language ban in workplace. *Arizona Daily Sun.* https://azdailysun.com/lawsuit-tackles-navajo-language-ban-in-workplace/article_2e5f6d1a-f380-53e1-b6b3-26362cafa9ee.html

Fisher, J., Hochgesang, J., & Tamminga, M. (n.d.). Philly Signs [Data set]. *Philly Signs.* https://pennds.org/phillysigns

Fishman, P. M. (1978). Interaction: The work women do. *Social Problems, 25*(4), 397–406. https://doi.org/10.2307/800492

Flannery, R. (1946). Men's and women's speech in Gros Ventre. *International Journal of American Linguistics, 12*(3), 133–135. https://doi.org/10.1086/463902

Flores, N., & Rosa, J. (2015). Undoing appropriateness: Raciolinguistic ideologies and language diversity in education. *Harvard Educational Review, 85*(2), 149–171. https://doi.org/10/ghwgmq

Fodor, J. D., & Inoue, A. (2000). Garden path repair: Diagnosis and triage. *Language and Speech, 43*(3), 261–271. https://doi.org/10.1177/00238309000430030201

Ford, D. Y. (2012). Culturally different students in special education: Looking backward to move forward. *Exceptional Children, 78*(4), 391–405. https://doi.org/10.1177/001440291207800401

Forshay, L., Winter, K., & Bender, E. (2016, May 23). Open letter to the office of news & information, University of Washington. *University of Washington.* http://faculty.washington.edu/ebender/papers/SignAloudOpenLetter.pdf

Fought, C. (2002). *Chicano English in Context.* Springer.

Fountain, A., Bever, T., & Hammond, M. (2010, July 13). Barring teachers with "accents" from teaching English is misguided. *Arizona Daily Star.* https://tucson.com/news/opinion/barring-teachers-with-accents-from-teaching-english-is-misguided/article_bfb4230b-43b0-5e92-975a-580456386279.html

Fraser, H. (2014, April 10). What did Oscar Pistorius really say? *Forensic Transcription Australia.* https://forensictranscription.net.au/what-is-oscar-pistorius-saying/

Fraser, H. (2018a). "Assisting" listeners to hear words that aren't there: Dangers in using police transcripts of indistinct covert recordings. *Australian Journal of Forensic Sciences, 50*(2), 129–139. https://doi.org/10/gnh2s2

Fraser, H. (2018b). Forensic transcription: How confident false beliefs about language and speech threaten the right to a fair trial in Australia. *Australian Journal of Linguistics, 38*(4), 586–606. https://doi.org/10/gd87q9

Fridland, V., & Kendall, T. (2022). Managing sociophonetic data in a study of regional variation. In A. L. Berez-Kroeker, B. McDonnell, E. Koller, & L. B. Collister (Eds.), *The Open Handbook of Linguistic Data Management* (pp. 237–248). The MIT Press.

Fried, D., Surdeanu, M., Kobourov, S., Hingle, M., & Herongrove, G. (2014). Analyzing the language of food on social media. In *2014 IEEE International Conference on Big Data (Big Data)* (pp. 778–783). IEEE Xplore.

Fuentes, A. (2022, May 11). Biological science rejects the sex binary, and that's good for humanity. *SAPIENS.* www.sapiens.org/biology/biological-science-rejects-the-sex-binary-and-thats-good-for-humanity/

Garcés-Conejos Blitvich, P. (2022). Moral emotions, good moral panics, social regulation, and online public shaming. *Language & Communication, 84,* 61–75. https://doi.org/10.1016/j.langcom.2022.02.002

García, O., & Otheguy, R. (2017). Interrogating the language gap of young bilingual and bidialectal students. *International Multilingual Research Journal*, *11*(1), 52-65. https://doi.org/10/gh2ddf

García, O., Flores, N., Seltzer, K., Wei, L., Otheguy, R., & Rosa, J. (2021). Rejecting abyssal thinking in the language and education of racialized bilinguals: A manifesto. *Critical Inquiry in Language Studies*, *18*(3), 203-228. https://doi.org/10.1080/15427587.2021.1935957

Gardner, R. A., & Gardner, B. T. (1969). Teaching sign language to a chimpanzee. *Science*, *165*(3894), 664-672. https://doi.org/10/cphcsj

Garrard, P., Maloney, L. M., Hodges, J. R., & Patterson, K. (2005). The effects of very early Alzheimer's disease on the characteristics of writing by a renowned author. *Brain*, *128*(2), 250-260. https://doi.org/10/dc7w3m

Gawne, L., & McCulloch, G. (2019). Emoji as digital gestures. *Language@Internet*, *17*(2). https://scholarworks.iu.edu/journals/index.php/li/article/view/37786

Gaytan, M. S. (2014). *¡Tequila!: Distilling the Spirit of Mexico*. Stanford University Press.

Gee, J. P. (2014). *An Introduction to Discourse Analysis: Theory and Method* (4th ed.). Routledge.

Gillon, C., & Rosen, N. (2018). *Nominal Contact in Michif*. Oxford University Press.

Gleason, J. B. (1975). Fathers and other strangers: Men's speech to young children. *Developmental Psycholinguistics: Theory and Applications*, *1*, 289-297.

Gleason, J. B. (1987). Sex differences in parent-child interaction. In S. U. Philips, S. Steele, & C. Tanz (Eds.), *Language, Gender, and Sex in Comparative Perspective* (pp. 189-199). Cambridge University Press.

Gleitman, L. (1990). The structural sources of verb meanings. *Language Acquisition*, *1*(1), 3-55. https://doi.org/10/djrxh8

Gobbo, F. (2017). Beyond the nation-state? The ideology of the Esperanto movement between neutralism and multilingualism. *Social Inclusion*, *5*(4), 38-47. https://doi.org/10/gmzd4k

Godley, A. J., Reaser, J., & Moore, K. G. (2015). Pre-service English language arts teachers' development of critical language awareness for teaching. *Linguistics and Education*, *32*, 41-54. https://doi.org/10.1016/j.linged.2015.03.015

Goffman, E. (1981). *Forms of Talk*. University of Pennsylvania Press.

Goldberg, B. (2010, August 5). New Jersey couple loses custody of son named Adolf Hitler. *ABC News*. https://abcnews.go.com/US/parents-cannot-regain-custody-children-nazi-inspired/story?id=11334970

Goldstein, M. H., & Schwade, J. A. (2008). Social feedback to infants' babbling facilitates rapid phonological learning. *Psychological Science*, *19*(5), 515-523. https://doi.org/10/d5gngj

Goldstein, M. H., & West, M. J. (1999). Consistent responses of human mothers to prelinguistic infants: The effect of prelinguistic repertoire size. *Journal of Comparative Psychology, 113*(1), 52–58. https://doi.org/10/dn4xg4

Goldstein, M. H., King, A. P., & West, M. J. (2003). Social interaction shapes babbling: Testing parallels between birdsong and speech. *Proceedings of the National Academy of Sciences, 100*(13), 8030–8035. https://doi.org/10/cjc9ch

Golinkoff, R. M., Hoff, E., Rowe, M. L., Tamis-LeMonda, C. S., & Hirsh-Pasek, K. (2019). Language matters: Denying the existence of the 30-million-word gap has serious consequences. *Child Development, 90*(3), 985–992. https://doi.org/10/gd843v

Goodwin, C. (2004). A competent speaker who can't speak: The social life of aphasia. *Journal of Linguistic Anthropology, 14*(2), 151–170. https://doi.org/10/dwxtp3

Goodwin, M. H. (2006). *The Hidden Life of Girls: Games of Stance, Status, and Exclusion*. Blackwell.

Gordon, P., & Chafetz, J. (1990). Verb-based versus class-based accounts of actionality effects in children's comprehension of passives. *Cognition, 36*(3), 227–254. https://doi.org/10/c77wg7

GPT-3 (2020, September 8). A robot wrote this entire article. Are you scared yet, human? *The Guardian*. www.theguardian.com/commentisfree/2020/sep/08/robot-wrote-this-article-gpt-3

Green, L. J. (2002). *African American English: A Linguistic Introduction*. Cambridge University Press.

Grice, H. P. (1975). Logic and conversation. In P. Cole & J. L. Morgan (Eds.), *Speech Acts* (pp. 41–58). Brill.

Grimes, B. F. (1985). Language attitudes: Identity, distinctiveness, survival in the Vaupes. *Journal of Multilingual & Multicultural Development, 6*(5), 389–401. https://doi.org/10.1080/01434632.1985.9994213

Guo, J. (2016, January 13). The totes amazesh way millennials are changing the English language. *Washington Post*. www.washingtonpost.com/news/wonk/wp/2016/01/13/the-totes-amazesh-way-millennials-are-changing-the-english-language/

Haas, M. R. (1944). Men's and women's speech in Koasati. *Language, 20*(3), 142–149.

Hachimi, A. (2013). The Maghreb-Mashreq language ideology and the politics of identity in a globalized Arab world. *Journal of Sociolinguistics, 17*(3), 269–296. https://doi.org/10.1111/josl.12037

Hall, K. (1995). Lip service on the fantasy lines. In K. Hall & M. Bucholtz (Eds.), *Gender Articulated: Language and the Socially Constructed Self* (pp. 183–216). Routledge.

Hanson, A., & Hawley, Z. (2011). Do landlords discriminate in the rental housing market? Evidence from an internet field experiment in US cities. *Journal of Urban Economics, 70*(2), 99–114. https://doi.org/10/bv9fb5

Hanulíková, A. (2018). The effect of perceived ethnicity on spoken text comprehension under clear and adverse listening conditions. *Linguistics Vanguard*, *4*(1), 20170029. https://doi.org/10/gft5d9

Hardach, S. (2018, February 6). Speaking more than one language can boost economic growth. *World Economic Forum*. www.weforum.org/agenda/2018/02/speaking-more-languages-boost-economic-growth/

Harju-Luukkainen, H., Berg, K., & Kolberg, A. (2022). "I sámifize it…" Preschool in the centre of South Sámi language and culture learning in Norway. *International Research in Early Childhood Education*, *11*(2), 65–79. https://doi.org/10.26180/19130828.V1

Harley, H., & Noyer, R. (1999). Distributed morphology. *Glot International*, *4*(4), 3–9.

Harley, H., & Stone, M. S. (2013). The "no agent idioms" hypothesis. In R. R. Folli, C. Sevdali, & R. Truswell (Eds.), *Syntax and Its Limits* (pp. 283–311). Oxford University Press.

Harrington, J., Gubian, M., Stevens, M., & Schiel, F. (2019). Phonetic change in an Antarctic winter. *Journal of the Acoustical Society of America*, *146*(5), 3327–3332. https://doi.org/10.1121/1.5130709

Harris-Perry, M. V. (2011). *Sister Citizen: Shame, Stereotypes, and Black Women in America*. Yale University Press.

Hart, B., & Risley, T. R. (1995). *Meaningful Differences in the Everyday Experience of Young American Children*. Paul H. Brookes Publishing.

Hart, B., & Risley, T. R. (2003). The early catastrophe: The 30 million word gap by age 3. *American Educator*, *27*(1), 4–9.

Hart Blundon, P. (2016). Nonstandard dialect and educational achievement: Potential implications for first nations students. *Canadian Journal of Speech-Language Pathology and Audiology*, *40*(3), 218–231. https://cjslpa.ca/files/2016_CJSLPA_Vol_40/No_03/CJSLPA_2016_Vol_40_No_3_Blundon_218-231.pdf

Hazenberg, E. (2020). Can you tell someone's sexuality from the way they speak? In L. Bauer & A. S. Calude (Eds.), *Questions About Language* (pp. 108–121). Routledge.

Heath, S. B. (1981). English in our language heritage. In C. A. Ferguson & S. B. Heath (Eds.), *Language in the USA* (pp. 6–20). Cambridge University Press.

Heath, S. B. (1982). What no bedtime story means: Narrative skills at home and school. *Language in Society*, *11*(1), 49–76. https://doi.org/10.1017/S0047404500009039

Heath, S. B. (1983). *Ways with Words: Language, Life, and Work in Communities and Classrooms*. Cambridge University Press.

Heath, S. B. (2012). *Words at Work and Play: Three Decades in Family and Community Life*. Cambridge University Press.

Heaven, W. D. (2021, July 30). Hundreds of AI tools have been built to catch covid: None of them helped. *MIT Technology Review*. www.technologyreview.com/

2021/07/30/1030329/machine-learning-ai-failed-covid-hospital-diagnosis-pandemic/

Hedgpeth, D. (2021, November 4). Thanksgiving anniversary: Wampanoag Indians regret helping Pilgrims 400 years ago. *Washington Post*. www.washingtonpost.com/history/2021/11/04/thanksgiving-anniversary-wampanoag-indians-pilgrims/

Heller, M., Pujolar, J., & Duchêne, A. (2014). Linguistic commodification in tourism. *Journal of Sociolinguistics*, *18*(4), 539–566. https://doi.org/10.1111/josl.12082

Herdt, G. (2020). *Third Sex, Third Gender: Beyond Sexual Dimorphism in Culture and History*. Princeton University Press.

Herongrove, G., Laparra, E., Kousik, A., Ishihara, T., Surdeanu, M., & Kobourov, S. (2018). Detecting diabetes risk from social media activity. In A. Lavelli, A.-L. Minard, & F. Rinaldi (Eds.), *Proceedings of the Ninth International Workshop on Health Text Mining and Information Analysis* (pp. 1–11). Association for Computational Linguistics.

Hicks, J., & Lawler, R. (2022, January 31). Crisis Text Line stops sharing conversation data with AI company. *The Verge*. www.theverge.com/2022/1/31/22906979/crisis-text-line-loris-ai-epic-privacy-mental-health

Hildebrand-Edgar, N., & Ehrlich, S. (2017). "She was quite capable of asserting herself": Powerful speech styles and assessments of credibility in a sexual assault trial. *Language and Law/Linguagem e Direito*, *4*(2), 89–107. https://ojs.letras.up.pt/index.php/LLLD/article/view/3285

Hill, J. H. (1993). Hasta la vista, baby: Anglo Spanish in the American Southwest. *Critique of Anthropology*, *13*(2), 145–176. https://doi.org/10.1177/0308275X9301300203

Hill, J. H. (1998). Language, race, and white public space. *American Anthropologist*, *100*(3), 680–689. https://doi.org/10.1525/aa.1998.100.3.680

Hill, J. H. (2008). *The Everyday Language of White Racism*. Wiley-Blackwell.

Hillard, G. (2019, April 4). Conservatives shouldn't use transgender pronouns. *National Review*. www.nationalreview.com/2019/04/transgender-pronouns-conservatives-should-not-use/

Hockett, C. F. (1960). The origin of speech. *Scientific American*, *203*(3), 88–96. https://doi.org/10/ftqv2r

Hodges, A. (Ed.) (2013). *Discourses of War and Peace*. Oxford University Press.

Holliday, N., Bishop, J., and Kuo, G. (2020). Prosody and political style: The case of Barack Obama and the L+H* pitch accent. In N. Minematsu (Ed.), *Proceedings of the 10th International Conference on Speech Prosody* (pp. 670–674). Speech Prosody.

i-to-I Teaching & Education Experts (2021). What is a native English speaker? *i-to-i*. www.i-to-i.com/tefl-faq/what-is-a-native-english-speaker

International Phonetic Association (2018). IPA Chart. *International Phonetic Association*. www.internationalphoneticassociation.org/content/ipa-chart

Janofsky, M. (2002, December 20). Ban on speaking Navajo leads cafe staff to sue. *The New York Times*. www.nytimes.com/2002/12/20/us/ban-on-speaking-navajo-leads-cafe-staff-to-sue.html

Jefferson, G. (2004). Glossary of transcript symbols with an introduction. In G. H. Lerner (Ed.), *Conversation Analysis* (pp. 13-31). John Benjamins Publishing Company.

Johnson, R., & Liddell, S. (2011). A Segmental framework for representing signs phonetically. *Sign Language Studies, 11*(3), 408-463. https://doi.org/10.1353/sls.2011.0002

Jones, T., Kalbfeld, J. R., Hancock, R., & Clark, R. (2019). Testifying while Black: An experimental study of court reporter accuracy in transcription of African American English. *Language, 95*(2), e216-e252. https://doi.org/10.1353/lan.2019.0042

Jusczyk, P. W., & Aslin, R. N. (1995). Infants' detection of the sound patterns of words in fluent speech. *Cognitive Psychology, 29*(1), 1-23. https://doi.org/10/bbkvzn

Jusczyk, P. W., Cutler, A., & Redanz, N. J. (1993). Infants' preference for the predominant stress patterns of English words. *Child Development, 64*(3), 675-687. https://doi.org/10.1111/j.1467-8624.1993.tb02935.x

Jusczyk, P. W., Friederici, A. D., Wessels, J. M. I., Svenkerud, V. Y., & Jusczyk, A. M. (1993). Infants' sensitivity to the sound patterns of native language words. *Journal of Memory and Language, 32*(3), 402-420. https://doi.org/10/b465sw

Kang, O., & Rubin, D. L. (2009). Reverse linguistic stereotyping: Measuring the effect of listener expectations on speech evaluation. *Journal of Language and Social Psychology, 28*(4), 441-456. https://doi.org/10.1177/0261927X09341950

Kaplan, M. (2007). Fijian water in Fiji and New York: Local politics and a global commodity. *Cultural Anthropology, 22*, 685-706. https://doi.org/10.1525/can.2007.22.4.685

Keating, J. (2017, October 27). Kazakhstan (or is it Qazaqstan?) switches to Latin alphabet. *Slate*. https://slate.com/technology/2017/10/kazakhstan-or-is-it-qazaqstan-switches-to-latin-alphabet.html

Keenan, E. (1974). Norm-makers, Norm-breakers: Uses of speech by men and women in a Malagasy community. In R. Bauman & J. Sherzer (Eds.), *Explorations in the Ethnography of Speaking* (pp. 125-143). Cambridge University Press.

Kellogg, W. N., & Kellogg, L. A. (1933). *The Ape and the Child: A Study of Environmental Influence upon Early Behavior*. Whittlesey House.

Kendi, I. X. (2016, October 20). Why the academic achievement gap is a racist idea. *African American Intellectual History Society, Black Perspectives*. www.aaihs.org/why-the-academic-achievement-gap-is-a-racist-idea/

Kennedy, R. (2018, December 10). On pronoun typology and economic measures. *Language Log.* https://languagelog.ldc.upenn.edu/nll/?p=40957

Ker-Lindsay, J. (2017). Turkey's EU accession as a factor in the 2016 Brexit referendum. *Turkish Studies, 19*(1), 1–22. https://doi.org/10.1080/14683849.2017.1366860

Kiesling, S. F. (1998). Men's identities and sociolinguistic variation: The case of fraternity men. *Journal of Sociolinguistics, 2*(1), 69–99. https://doi.org/10.1111/1467-9481.00031

Kiesling, S. F. (2002). Playing the straight man: Displaying and maintaining male heterosexuality in discourse. In K. Campbell-Kibler, R. J. Podesva, S. J. Roberts, & A. Wong (Eds.), *Language and Sexuality: Contesting Meaning in Theory and Practice* (pp. 249–266). Center for the Study of Language and Information.

Kimura, G. C. (2003). The metacommunicative ideology of Esperanto: Evidence from Japan and Korea. *Language Problems and Language Planning, 27*(1), 71–83. https://doi.org/10/bdf3jp

King, J. (2001). Te Kōhanga Reo: Māori language revitalization. In L. Hinton & K. Hale (Eds.), *The Green Book of Language Revitalization in Practice* (pp. 119–128). Academic Press.

Kirby, J. P. (2011). Vietnamese (Hanoi Vietnamese). *Journal of the International Phonetic Association, 41*(3), 381–392. https://doi.org/10/fb4qr9

Kirkland, D. E. (2015). Black masculine language. In J. Bloomquist, L. J. Green, & S. L. Lanehart (Eds.), *The Oxford Handbook of African American Language* (pp. 834–849). Oxford University Press.

Kiselman, C. (2008). Esperanto: Its origins and early history. In A. Pelczar (Ed.), *Prace Komisji Spraw Europejskich PAU* (Vol. 2, pp. 39–56). Polska Akademia Umiejętności.

Kitzinger, C. (2005). "Speaking as a heterosexual": (How) does sexuality matter for talk-in-interaction? *Research on Language and Social Interaction, 38*(3), 221–265. https://doi.org/10.1207/s15327973rlsi3803_2

Kloss, H. (1968). Notes concerning a language-nation typology. In J. A. Fishman, C. A. Ferguson, and J. D. Gupta (Eds.), *Language Problems of Developing Nations* (pp. 69–85). Wiley.

Kolirin, L. (2018, December 18). Couple who named baby after Hitler jailed for membership of neo-Nazi group. *CNN.* www.cnn.com/2018/12/18/uk/parents-jailed-scli-gbr-intl/index.html

Konnelly, L. (2020). Brutoglossia: Democracy, authenticity, and the enregisterment of connoisseurship in "craft beer talk". *Language and Communication, 75,* 69–82. https://doi.org/10.1016/j.langcom.2020.09.001

Kowal, J. (2006, July 30). In a bid for higher ground, a low-lying Indian tribe raises the stakes. *The New York Times.* www.nytimes.com/2006/07/30/us/30beach.html

Kramsch, C., & Widdowson, H. G. (1998). *Language and Culture*. Oxford University Press.

Kuhl, P. K. (2007). Is speech learning "gated" by the social brain? *Developmental Science*, *10*(1), 110–120. https://doi.org/10/cz3hgh

Kuhl, P. K., & Meltzoff, A. N. (1996). Infant vocalizations in response to speech: Vocal imitation and developmental change. *The Journal of the Acoustical Society of America*, *100*(4), 2425–2438. https://doi.org/10/fd72z4

Kuhl, P. K., Tsao, F.-M., & Liu, H.-M. (2003). Foreign-language experience in infancy: Effects of short-term exposure and social interaction on phonetic learning. *Proceedings of the National Academy of Sciences*, *100*(15), 9096–9101. https://doi.org/10/fdh92p

Kutlu, E. (2020). Now you see me, now you mishear me: Raciolinguistic accounts of speech perception in different English varieties. *Journal of Multilingual and Multicultural Development*, *44*(6), 511–525. https://doi.org/10/ghwsrq

Labov, W. (1966). The effect of social mobility on linguistic behavior. *Sociological Inquiry*, *36*(2), 186–203. https://doi.org/10/fbqf5g

Labov, W. (1970). Finding out about children's language. In D. Steinberg (Ed.), *Working Papers in Communication* (pp. 1–29). Pacific Speech Association.

Labov, W. (1972). *Sociolinguistic Patterns*. University of Pennsylvania Press.

Labov, W. (1981). Field methods of the project on linguistic change and variation. *Sociolinguistic Working Paper*, (81). https://files.eric.ed.gov/fulltext/ED250938.pdf

Labov, W. (1990). The intersection of sex and social class in the course of linguistic change. *Language Variation and Change*, *2*(2), 205–254. https://doi.org/10.1017/S0954394500000338

Labov, W. (2006). *The Social Stratification of English in New York City* (2nd ed.). Cambridge University Press.

Labov, W., Ash, S., & Boberg, C. (2006). *The Atlas of North American English Phonetics, Phonology, and Sound Change: A Multimedia Reference Tool*. Mouton de Gruyter.

Laihi, T.-M. (2017). *Skolt Sámi Language and Cultural Revitalization: A Case Study of a Skolt Sámi Language Nest*. [Master's Thesis, University of Helsinki].

Laitinen, L. (2006). Zero person in Finnish: A grammatical resource for construing human reference. In M.-L. Helasvuo & L. Campbell (Eds.), *Grammar from the Human Perspective: Case, Space and Person in Finnish* (pp. 209–232). John Benjamins.

Lakoff, R. (1973). Language and woman's place. *Language in Society*, *2*(1), 45–80. https://doi.org/10.1017/S0047404500000051

Lakoff, R. (1975). *Language and Woman's Place*. Harper & Row.

Lan, S. (2021). Between privileges and precariousness: Remaking whiteness in China's teaching English as a second language industry. *American Anthropologist*, *124*(1), 118–129. https://doi.org/10.1111/aman.13657

Landau, B., & Gleitman, L. R. (1985). *Language and Experience: Evidence from the Blind Child*. Harvard University Press.

Lane, P., & Makihara, M. (2017). Indigenous peoples and their languages. In O. García, N. Flores, & M. Spotti (Eds.), *The Oxford Handbook of Language and Society* (Vol. 1, pp. 299–319). Oxford University Press.

Lanehart, S. (2002). *Sista, Speak! Black Women Kinfolk Talk about Language and Literacy*. University of Arizona Press.

Lanehart, S., Bloomquist, J., & Malik, A. (2015). Language use in African American communities: An introduction. In S. Lanehart (Ed.), *The Oxford Handbook of African American Language* (pp. 1–20). Oxford University Press.

Lapiak, J. (1996). Entries for "apple" and "onion." *Handspeak*. www.handspeak.com/

Lareau, A. (2011). *Unequal Childhoods: Class, Race, and Family Life* (2nd ed.). University of California Press.

Larson, S. (2020, August 31). "Nice White Parents," "Fiasco," and America's Public-School Problem. *The New Yorker*. www.newyorker.com/magazine/2020/09/07/nice-white-parents-fiasco-and-americas-public-school-problem

Laufer, B., & Nation, P. (1995). Vocabulary size and use: Lexical richness in L2 written production. *Applied Linguistics*, *16*(3), 307–322. https://doi.org/10.1093/applin/16.3.307

Lawson, R. (2020). Language and masculinities: History, development, and future. *Annual Review of Linguistics*, *6*(1), 409–434. https://doi.org/10.1146/annurev-linguistics-011718-011650

Leap, W. L. (1993). *American Indian English*. University of Utah Press.

Leap, W. L. (2019, May). This month in linguistics history: Lavender language/linguistics. *Linguistic Society of America*. www.lsadc.org/Files/This%20Time%20in%20History/This%20Month%20in%20Linguistics%20History_%20Lavender%20Language_Linguistics.pdf

Lee, D.-Y., & Baese-Berk, M. M. (2020). The maintenance of clear speech in naturalistic conversations. *The Journal of the Acoustical Society of America*, *147*(5), 3702. https://doi.org/10/ghtkm4

Leeman, J., & Modan, G. (2009). Commodified language in Chinatown: A contextualized approach to linguistic landscape. *Journal of Sociolinguistics*, *13*(3), 332–362. https://doi.org/10.1111/j.1467-9841.2009.00409.x

Leggett, T. (2019, October 25). Integral to the culture, Sámi languages stay vibrant in Finland. *ThisisFINLAND*. https://finland.fi/life-society/integral-to-the-culture-sami-languages-stay-vibrant-in-finland/

Lehrer, A. (2009). *Wine and Conversation*. Oxford University Press.

Leonard, W. Y. (2008). When is an "extinct language" not extinct? Miami, a formally sleeping language. In K. A. King, N. Schilling-Estes, L. Fogle, J. J. Lou, & B. Soukup (Eds.), *Sustaining Linguistic Diversity: Endangered and Minority Languages and Language Varieties* (pp. 23–33). Georgetown University Press.

Leonard, W. Y. (2018). Reflections on (de)colonialism in language documentation. In B. McDonnell, A. L. Berez-Kroeker, & G. Holton (Eds.), *Reflections on Language Documentation 20 Years after Himmelmann 1998* (pp. 55–65). University of Hawai'i Press.

Lepic, R. (2019). A usage-based alternative to "lexicalization" in sign language linguistics. *Glossa*, *4*(1), 1–30. https://doi.org/10.5334/gjgl.840

Liberman, M. (2020, March 5). Fancy diacritics. *Language Log*. https://languagelog.ldc.upenn.edu/nll/?p=46372

Lieven, E. (2010). Input and first language acquisition: Evaluating the role of frequency. *Lingua*, *120*(11), 2546–2556. https://doi.org/10.1016/j.lingua.2010.06.005

Lillo-Martin, D., & Henner, J. (2021). Acquisition of sign languages. *Annual Review of Linguistics*, *7*, 395–419. https://doi.org/10/gjrnzk

Lindberg, R., & Trofimovich, P. (2020). Second language learners' attitudes toward French varieties: The roles of learning experience and social networks. *The Modern Language Journal*, *104*(4), 822–841. https://doi.org/10/gjhb59

Lippi-Green, R. (2012). *English with an Accent: Language, Ideology, and Discrimination in the United States* (2nd ed.). Routledge.

Litovsky, R. (2015). Development of the auditory system. In M. J. Aminoff, F. Boller, & D. F. Swaab (Eds.), *Handbook of Clinical Neurology*, (Vol. 129, pp. 55–72). Elsevier.

little doe baird, j. (2016). Wopanaak language reclamation program: Bringing the language home. *Journal of Global Indigeneity*, *2*(2). www.journalofglobalindigeneity.com/article/33216-wopanaak-language-reclamation-program-bringing-the-language-home

Lucas, C. (2014). *The Sociolinguistics of the Deaf Community*. Elsevier.

Lush, E. (2015, February 20). Phonetic analysis of Albanian. *Erica Lush*. http://web.archive.org/web/20160817194723/ericalush.wordpress.com/2015/02/20/phonetic-analysis-of-albanian/

Maddieson, I. (2007). Peter Ladefoged. *Language*, *83*(1), 181–188. https://doi.org/10.1353/lan.2007.0030

Maltz, D. N., & Borker, R. A. (1982). A cultural approach to male-female miscommunication. In J. J. Gumperz (Ed.), *Language and Social Identity* (pp. 196–216). Cambridge University Press.

Mampe, B., Friederici, A. D., Christophe, A., & Wermke, K. (2009). Newborns' cry melody is shaped by their native language. *Current Biology*, *19*(23), 1994–1997. https://doi.org/10.1016/j.cub.2009.09.064

Mann, C. C. (2006). *1491: New Revelations of the Americas Before Columbus*. Vintage.

Mapes, G. (2021). *Elite Authenticity: Remaking Distinction in Food Discourse*. Oxford University Press.

Martínez-Celdrán, E., Fernández-Planas, A. M., & Carrera-Sabaté, J. (2003). Castilian Spanish. *Journal of the International Phonetic Association*, *33*(2), 255–259. https://doi.org/10.1017/S0025100303001373

Massey, D. S., & Lundy, G. (2001). Use of Black English and racial discrimination in urban housing markets: New methods and findings. *Urban Affairs Review*, *36*(4), 452–469. https://doi.org/10/fgs75v

McCarthy, C. (2011). The northern cities shift in Chicago. *Journal of English Linguistics*, *39*(2), 166–187. https://doi.org/10/bffxdz

McCarty, T. L., & Nicholas, S. E. (2014). Reclaiming Indigenous languages: A reconsideration of the roles and responsibilities of schools. *Review of Research in Education*, *38*(1), 106–136. https://doi.org/10/f34k

McCulloch, A. M., & Wilkins, D. E. (1995). "Constructing" nations within states: The quest for federal recognition by the Catawba and Lumbee Tribes. *American Indian Quarterly*, *19*(3), 361–388.

McDonough, J. (2016). Determining morphological relations: The Navajo verbal complex -1. *The Paris Lectures*.

McEnnery, T., & Hardie, A. (2012). Support website for corpus linguistics: Method, theory and practice. *Lancaster University*. http://corpora.lancs.ac.uk/clmtp

McGowan, K. B. (2015). Social expectation improves speech perception in noise. *Language and Speech*, *58*(4), 502–521. https://doi.org/10/f75wbq

McGuire, S. Y. (2015). *Teach Students How to Learn: Strategies You Can Incorporate into Any Course to Improve Student Metacognition, Study Skills, and Motivation*. Stylus Publishing, LLC.

McKinley, E., & Hoskins, T. K. (2011). Māori education and achievement. In T. McIntosh & M. Mulholland (Eds.), *Māori and Social Issues* (Vol. 1, pp. 49–65). Huia Publishers.

McNamara, T. (2020). The anti-shibboleth: The traumatic character of the shibboleth as silence. *Applied Linguistics*, *41*(3), 334–351. https://doi.org/10.1093/applin/amaa007

Meek, B. A. (2010). *We Are Our Language*. University of Arizona Press.

Meek, B. A. (2019). Language endangerment in childhood. *Annual Review of Anthropology*, *48*(1), 95–115. https://doi.org/10.1146/annurev-anthro-102317-050041

Mehl, M. R., Vazire, S., Ramírez-Esparza, N., Slatcher, R. B., & Pennebaker, J. W. (2007). Are women really more talkative than men? *Science*, *317*(5834), 82. https://doi.org/10.1126/science.1139940

Mendoza-Denton, N. (2008). *Homegirls: Language and Cultural Practice Among Latina Youth Gangs*. Blackwell Publishing.

Mendoza-Denton, N. (2011). The semiotic hitchhiker's guide to creaky voice: Circulation and gendered hardcore in a Chicana/o gang persona. *Journal of*

Linguistic Anthropology, *21*(2), 261–280. https://doi.org/10.1111/j.1548-1395.2011.01110.x

Merriam-Webster (n.d.). Noah Webster's spelling wins and fails. *Mirriam-Webster*. www.merriam-webster.com/words-at-play/noah-websters-spelling-wins-and-fails

Messenger, K., Branigan, H. P., & McLean, J. F. (2012). Is children's acquisition of the passive a staged process? Evidence from six- and nine-year-olds' production of passives. *Journal of Child Language, 39*(5), 991–1016. https://doi.org/10/dmh4k7

Metcalf, A. A. (1974). The study of California Chicano English. *International Journal of the Sociology of Language, 1974*(2), 53–58. https://doi.org/10.1515/ijsl.1974.2.53

Meyerhoff, M., & Strycharz, A. (2013). Communities of practice. In J. K. Chambers & N. Schilling (Eds.), *The Handbook of Language Variation and Change* (pp. 428–447). John Wiley & Sons, Ltd.

Michel, J.-B., Shen, Y. K., Aiden, A. P., Veres, A., Gray, M. K., The Google Books Team, Pickett, J. P., et al. (2011). Quantitative analysis of culture using millions of digitized books. *Science, 331*(6014), 176–182. https://doi.org/10/akd

Ministry of Social Development (n.d.). The social report 2016 – Te pūrongo oranga tangata: Māori language speakers. *Ministry of Social Development*. https://socialreport.msd.govt.nz/cultural-identity/maori-language-speakers.html

Mithun, M. (2001). *The Languages of Native North America*. Cambridge University Press.

Morgan, M. (2015). African American women's language: Mother tongues untied. In S. Lanehart (Ed.), *The Oxford Handbook of African American Language* (pp. 817–833). Oxford University Press.

Morris, C. (2019). Brexit: Did Boris Johnson talk Turkey during referendum campaign? *BBC Online*. https://www.bbc.com/news/uk-politics-46926119

Motschenbacher, H. (2020). Greece, the Netherlands, and (the) Ukraine: A corpus-based study of definite article use with country names. *A Journal of Onomastics, 68*(1), 1–16. https://doi.org/10.1080/00277738.2020.1731241

Mulac, A., Bradac, J. J., & Gibbons, P. (2001). Empirical support for the gender-as-culture hypothesis: An intercultural analysis of male/female language differences. *Human Communication Research, 27*(1), 121–152. https://doi.org/10.1111/j.1468-2958.2001.tb00778.x

Munson, B. (2007). The acoustic correlates of perceived masculinity, perceived femininity, and perceived sexual orientation. *Language and Speech, 50*(1), 125–142. https://doi.org/10/d7kjxr

Myers-Scotton, C. (1993). Common and uncommon ground: Social and structural factors in codeswitching. *Language in Society, 22*(4), 475–503. https://doi.org/10.1017/S0047404500017449

Naigles, L. (1990). Children use syntax to learn verb meanings. *Journal of Child Language, 17*(2), 357–374. https://doi.org/10/dz7pc3

Nakata, S. (2017). Language suppression, revitalization, and native Hawaiian identity. *Diversity and Social Justice Forum, 2*, 14–27.

Nathan, J. (2012, August 2). The scoop on ice cream's Jewish history, from Häagen-Dazs to Ben & Jerry's. *Tablet Magazine*. www.tabletmag.com/sections/food/articles/ice-creams-jewish-innovators

Natives4Linguistics (2021, June 29). Statement from Indigenous linguists and language scholars on boarding and residential Schools. *Indian Country Today*. https://ictnews.org/the-press-pool/statement-from-indigenous-linguists-and-language-scholars-on-boarding-and-residential-schools/

Nazzi, T., Bertoncini, J., & Mehler, J. (1998). Language discrimination by newborns: Toward an understanding of the role of rhythm. *Journal of Experimental Psychology: Human Perception and Performance, 24*(3), 756–766. https://doi.org/10/bqw3kc

Nazzi, T., Jusczyk, P. W., & Johnson, E. K. (2000). Language discrimination by English-learning 5-month-olds: Effects of rhythm and familiarity. *Journal of Memory and Language, 43*(1), 1–19. https://doi.org/10/d9ft83

Netter, S. (2010, August 23). Wanted: Ebonics translator for federal DEA job. *ABC News*. https://abcnews.go.com/US/wanted-ebonics-translator-federal-dea-job/story?id=11462206

Newland, B. (2022). *Federal Indian Boarding School Initiative Investigative Report* (Vol. 1, pp. 1–106). United States Department of the Interior.

Newport, E. L. (1990). Maturational constraints on language learning. *Cognitive Science, 14*, 11–28. https://doi.org/10.1207/s15516709cog1401_2

Nicholas, S. A. (2018). Language contexts: Te Reo Māori o te Pae Tonga o te Kuki Airani also known as Southern Cook Islands Māori. *Language Documentation and Description, 15*, 36–64. https://doi.org/10.25894/ldd138

Nick, I. M. (2017). Names, grades, and metamorphosis: A small-scale socio-onomastic investigation into the effects of ethnicity and gender-marked personal names on the pedagogical assessments of a grade school essay. *Names, 65*(3), 129–142. https://doi.org/10.1080/00277738.2017.1304100

Nicoladis, E., & Genesee, F. (1997). Language development in preschool bilingual children. *Journal of Speech-Language Pathology and Audiology, 21*(4), 258–270. https://doi.org/10.7939/R3348GW0N

Nilsson, I. (2014). *Analysis of Sápmi: Regional SWOT analysis prepared for the 2014–2020 Rural Development Programme and Maritime & Fisheries Fund* (L. C. Q. Holmström, Trans.). Sametinget.

Noble, S. U. (2018). *Algorithms of Oppression: How Search Engines Reinforce Racism*. New York University Press.

NPR (2018, August 8). Talk American [Audio podcast episode]. In *Code Switch*. www.npr.org/2018/08/08/636442508/talk-american

O'Barr, W., & Atkins, B. K. (1980). "Women's language" or "powerless language"? In S. McConnell-Ginet, R. Borker, & N. Furman (Eds.), *Women in Language and Society* (pp. 93–109). Praeger.

O'Neil, C. (2016). *Weapons of Math Destruction: How Big Data Increases Inequality and Threatens Democracy*. Crown.

Ochs, E., & Schieffelin, B. B. (1994). Language acquisition and socialization: Three developmental stories. In B. G. Blount (Ed.), *Language, Culture, and Society: A Book of Readings* (2nd ed., pp. 470–512). Waveland Press.

Ochs, E., & Schieffelin, B. B. (2017). Language socialization: An historical overview. In P. A. Duff & S. May (Eds.), *Language Socialization* (pp. 1–14). Springer International Publishing.

OED Online (2020). Ask, v. *Oxford English Dictionary*. www.oed.com/view/Entry/11507

OED Online (2021). Propaganda, n. *Oxford English Dictionary*. www.oed.com/view/Entry/152605

Oller, D. K., & Eilers, R. E. (1988). The role of audition in infant babbling. *Child Development, 59*(2), 441–449. https://doi.org/10/cfzzww

Onyeka-Crawford, A., Patrick, K., & Chaudhry, N. (2017). *Let Her Learn: Stopping School Pushout for Girls of Color*. National Women's Law Center.

Ostermann, A. C. (2003). Communities of practice at work: Gender, facework, and the power of habitus at an all-female police station and a feminist crisis intervention center in Brazil. *Discourse & Society, 14*(4), 473–505. https://doi.org/10.1177/0957926503014004004

Ostermann, A. C., & Comunello da Costa, C. (2012). Gender and professional identity in three institutional settings in Brazil: The case of responses to assessment turns. *Pragmatics, 22*(2), 203–230. https://doi.org/10.1075/prag.22.2.02ost

Otsuji, E., & Pennycook, A. (2018). The translingual advantage: Metrolingual student repertoires. In J. Choi & S. Ollerhead (Eds.), *Plurilingualism in Teaching and Learning* (pp. 70–88). Routledge.

Otto Santa Ana, A. (1993). Chicano English and the nature of the Chicano language setting. *Hispanic Journal of Behavioral Sciences, 15*(1), 3–35. https://doi.org/10.1177/07399863930151001

Oxford University Press (2021). *The Oxford English Dictionary (Online)*. www.oed.com

Park, J. S. (2019). Digital media communication, intellectual property, and the commodification of language: The discursive construction of fansub work. *Language, Culture and Society, 1*(2), 244–266. https://doi.org/10.1075/lcs.19001.par?locatt=mode:legacy

Parsons, C. (2012). "Sofa King Low" advert for furniture store banned eight years after first sparking police complaints. *Mail Online*. www.dailymail.co.uk/news/article-2108085/Sofa-King-advert-banned-8-years-sparking-police-complaints.html

Pasanen, A. (2018). "This work is not for pessimists": Revitalization of Inari Sámi language. In L. Hinton, L. Huss, & G. Roche (Eds.), *The Routledge Handbook of Language Revitalization* (pp. 364–372). Routledge.

Pascual, A., Guéguen, N., Vallée, B., Lourel, M., & Cosnefroy, O. (2015). First name popularity as predictor of employability. *Names*, *63*(1), 30–36. https://doi.org/10.1179/0027773814Z.00000000091

Patterson, F. G. (1978). The gestures of a gorilla: Language acquisition in another pongid. *Brain and Language*, *5*(1), 72–97. https://doi.org/10/cjvt6n

Paulino, E., & García, S. (2013). Bearing witness to genocide: The 1937 Haitian massacre and the border of lights. *Afro-Hispanic Review*, *32*(2), 111–118.

Paxson, H. (2012). *The Life of Cheese: Crafting Food and Value in America*. University of California Press.

Pepinsky, T. B. (2022). On Whorfian socioeconomics. *Language*, *98*(1), e44–e79. https://doi.org/10.1353/lan.2021.0093

Pepperberg, I. M. (1981). Functional vocalizations by an African Grey Parrot (Psittacus erithacus). *Zeitschrift Für Tierpsychologie*, *55*(2), 139–160. https://doi.org/10/c56vjx

Pepperberg, I. M. (2017). Animal language studies: What happened? *Psychonomic Bulletin & Review*, *24*(1), 181–185. https://doi.org/10.3758/s13423-016-1101-y

Peterson, P. (1996). *The World's Biggest Baby*. Modern Curriculum Press.

Petitto, L. A., & Marentette, P. F. (1991). Babbling in the manual mode: Evidence for the ontogeny of language. *Science*, *251*(5000), 1493–1496. https://doi.org/10/dm5qb6

Petitto, L. A., & Seidenberg, M. S. (1979). On the evidence for linguistic abilities in signing apes. *Brain and Language*, *8*(2), 162–183. https://doi.org/10.1016/0093-934X(79)90047-6

Petitto, L. A., Holowka, S., Sergio, L. E., & Ostry, D. (2001). Language rhythms in baby hand movements. *Nature*, *413*(6851), 35–36. https://doi.org/10/cmh99d

Philips, S. U. (1982). *The Invisible Culture: Communication in Classroom and Community on the Warm Springs Indian Reservation*. Longman, Inc.

Poplack, S. (1980). Sometimes I'll start a sentence in Spanish y termino en Español: Toward a typology of code-switching. *Linguistics*, *18*, 581–618. https://doi.org/10.1515/ling.1980.18.7-8.581

Poplack, S. (1988). Contrasting patterns of code-switching in two communities. In M. Heller (Ed.), *Codeswitching: Anthropological and Sociolinguistic Perspectives* (pp. 215–244). De Gruyter Mouton.

Porto, M. (2014). Intercultural citizenship education in an EFL online project in Argentina. *Language and Intercultural Communication, 14*(2), 245–261. https://doi.org/10.1080/14708477.2014.890625

Price, T. (2010). What is Spanglish? The phenomenon of code-switching and its impact amongst US Latinos. *Début, 1*(1), 25–33.

Pullum, G. (2010, November 9). Pronouncing it by the book. *Language Log.* https://languagelog.ldc.upenn.edu/nll/?p=2762

Purnell, T., Idsardi, W., & Baugh, J. (1999). Perceptual and phonetic experiments on American English dialect identification. *Journal of Language and Social Psychology, 18*(1), 10–30. https://doi.org/10/c7rb4f

Pyers, J., & Senghas, A. (2020). Lexical iconicity is differentially favored under transmission in a new sign language: The effect of type of iconicity. *Sign Language & Linguistics, 23*(1–2), 73–95. https://doi.org/10.1075/sll.00044.pye

Qi, P., Dozat, T., Zhang, Y., & Manning, C. D. (2018). Universal dependency parsing from scratch. In D. Zeman & J. Hajič (Eds.), *Proceedings of the CoNLL 2018 Shared Task: Multilingual Parsing from Raw Text to Universal Dependencies* (pp. 160–170). Association for Computational Linguistics.

Quillian, L., & Midtbøen, A. H. (2021). Comparative perspectives on racial discrimination in hiring: The rise of field experiments. *Annual Review of Sociology, 47,* 391–415. https://doi.org/10.1146/annurev-soc-090420-035144

Quine, W. V. O. (1960). *Word and Object.* MIT Press.

Ramírez-Castañeda, V. (2020). Disadvantages in preparing and publishing scientific papers caused by the dominance of the English language in science: The case of Colombian researchers in biological sciences. *PloS One, 15*(9), e0238372. https://doi.org/10.1371/journal.pone.0238372

Ramjattan, V. A. (2019a). Racist nativist microaggressions and the professional resistance of racialized English language teachers in Toronto. *Race Ethnicity and Education, 22*(3), 374–390. https://doi.org/10.1080/13613324.2017.1377171

Ramjattan, V. A. (2019b). The white native speaker and inequality regimes in the private English language school. *Intercultural Education, 30*(2), 126–140. https://doi.org/10.1080/14675986.2018.1538043

Rampton, B., & Charalambous, C. (2012). Crossing. In M. Martin-Jones, A. Blackledge, & A. Creese (Eds.), *The Routledge Handbook of Multilingualism* (pp. 482–498). Routledge.

Rice, K. (2011). Documentary linguistics and community relations. *Language Documentation & Conservation, 5,* 187–207. https://hdl.handle.net/10125/4498

Rickford, J. R. (1999). The Ebonics controversy in my backyard: A sociolinguist's experiences and reflections. *Journal of Sociolinguistics, 3*(2), 267–266.

Rickford, J. R., & King, S. (2016). Language and linguistics on trial: Hearing Rachel Jeantel (and other vernacular speakers) in the courtroom and beyond. *Language, 92*(4), 948–988. https://doi.org/10.1353/lan.2016.0078

Ritschel, C. (2018, January 13). Princess Charlotte is already bilingual at age two. *The Independent.* www.independent.co.uk/life-style/princess-charlotte-bilingual-spanish-speaking-age-two-a8156511.html

Roche, G. & Suzuki, H. (2018). Tibet's minority languages: Diversity and endangerment. *Modern Asian Studies, 52*(4), 1227–1278. https://doi.org/10.1017/S0026749X1600072X

Ronkin, M. & Karn, H. E. (1999). Mock Ebonics: Linguistic racism and parodies of Ebonics on the internet. *Journal of Sociolinguistics, 3*(3), 360–380. https://doi.org/10.1111/1467-9481.00083

Rosa, J. (2016). From mock Spanish to inverted Spanglish: Language ideologies in the racialization of Puerto Rican youth in the United States. In H. S. Alim, J. R. Rickford, & A. F. Ball (Eds.), *Raciolinguistics: How Language Shapes Our Ideas about Race* (pp. 65–80). Oxford University Press.

Rosa, J., & Flores, N. (2017). Unsettling race and language: Toward a raciolinguistic perspective. *Language in Society, 46*(5), 621–647. https://doi.org/10/gg2bvm

Roscoe, W. (1987). Bibliography of berdache and alternative gender roles among North American Indians. *Journal of Homosexuality, 14*(3–4), 81–172. https://doi.org/10.1300/J082v14n03_06

Roseberry, W. (1996). The rise of yuppie coffees and the reimagination of class in the United States. *American Anthropologist, 98,* 762–775. https://doi.org/10.1525/aa.1996.98.4.02a00070

Rubin, D. L. (1992). Nonlanguage factors affecting undergraduates' judgments of nonnative English-speaking teaching assistants. *Research in Higher Education, 33*(4), 511–531. https://doi.org/10.1007/BF00973770

Ruecker, T., & Ives, L. (2015). White native English speakers needed: The rhetorical construction of privilege in online teacher recruitment spaces. *TESOL Quarterly, 49*(4), 733–756. https://doi.org/10.1002/tesq.195

Ruiz, R. (1994). Language policy and planning in the United States. *Annual Review of Applied Linguistics, 14,* 111–125. https://doi.org/10/b25q77

Sa'ar, A. (2007). Masculine talk: On the subconscious use of masculine linguistic forms among Hebrew-and Arabic-speaking women in Israel. *Signs: Journal of Women in Culture and Society, 32*(2), 405–429. https://doi.org/10.1086/508501

Sachs, J., Lieberman, P., & Erickson, D. (1973). Anatomical and cultural determinants of male and female speech. In R. W. Shuy & R. W. Fasold (Eds.), *Language Attitudes: Current Trends and Prospects* (pp. 74–84). Georgetown University Press.

Sacks, H., Schegloff, E. A., & Jefferson, G. (1978). A simplest systematics for the organization of turn taking for conversation. In J. Schenkein (Ed.), *Studies in the Organization of Conversational Interaction* (pp. 7–55). Elsevier.

Safadi, H., Johnson, S. L., & Faraj, S. (2020). Who contributes knowledge? Core-periphery tension in online innovation communities. *Organization Science, 32*(3), 752–775. https://doi.org/10.1287/orsc.2020.1364

Säily, T. (2011). Variation in morphological productivity in the BNC: Sociolinguistic and methodological considerations. *Corpus Linguistics and Linguistic Theory*, *7*(1), 119–141. https://doi.org/10/fknbmf

Savage-Rumbaugh, E. S. (1986). *Ape Language: From Conditioned Response to Symbol*. Columbia University Press.

Schembri, A. (2003). Rethinking "classifiers" in signed languages. In K. Emmorey (Ed.), *Perspectives on Classifier Constructions in Sign Languages* (pp. 3–34). Erlbaum.

Senghas, A., & Coppola, M. (2001). Children creating language: How Nicaraguan sign language acquired a spatial grammar. *Psychological Science*, *12*(4), 323–328. https://doi.org/10/dj37mn

Senghas, A., Kita, S., & Özyürek, A. (2004). Children creating core properties of language: Evidence from an emerging sign language in Nicaragua. *Science*, *305*(5691), 1779–1782. https://doi.org/10.1126/science.1100199

Senghas, R. J., Senghas, A., & Pyers, J. E. (2005). The emergence of Nicaraguan sign language: Questions of development, acquisition, and evolution. In S. Taylor Parker, J. Langer, & C. Milbrath (Eds.), *Biology and Knowledge Revisited: From Neurogenesis to Psychogenesis*. Routledge.

Shahidullah, S., & Hepper, P. G. (1994). Frequency discrimination by the fetus. *Early Human Development*, *36*(1), 13–26. https://doi.org/10/fn8v6c

Shane, J. (2020, January 31). AI recipes are bad (and a proposal for making them worse). *AI Weirdness*. www.aiweirdness.com/ai-recipes-are-bad-and-a-proposal-20-01-31/

Shane, J. (2021, March 22). GPT-3 tries pickup lines. *AI Weirdness*. www.aiweirdness.com/gpt-3-tries-pickup-lines/

Shane, J. (2022, January 28). New AI paint colors. *AI Weirdness*. www.aiweirdness.com/new-ai-paint-colors/

Shapiro, L., & Long, H. (2018, August 20). Analysis: Where do you fit in the global income spectrum?. *Washington Post*. www.washingtonpost.com/graphics/2018/business/global-income-calculator/

Sheppard, B. E., Elliott, N. C., & Baese-Berk, M. M. (2017). Comprehensibility and intelligibility of international student speech: Comparing perceptions of university EAP instructors and content faculty. *Journal of English for Academic Purposes*, *26*, 42–51. https://doi.org/10/ghd6kd

Sherouse, P. (2015). Russian presence in Georgian film dubbing: Scales of inferiority. *Journal of Linguistic Anthropology*, *25*(2), 105–237. https://doi.org/10.1111/jola.12090

Siegel, R., & Labov, W. (2006, February 16). American accent undergoing great vowel shift. *NPR*. www.npr.org/2006/02/16/5220090/american-accent-undergoing-great-vowel-shift

Silva, W. D. L. (2020). Multilingual interactions and code-mixing in Northwest Amazonia. *International Journal of American Linguistics, 86*(1), 133–154. https://doi.org/10.1086/705756

Silver, S., & Miller, W. (1994). *American Indian Languages: Cultural and Social Contexts*. University of Arizona Press.

Silver, S., & Miller, W. R. (1998). *American Indian Languages: Cultural and Social Contexts*. University of Arizona Press.

Silverstein, M. (2003). Indexical order and the dialects of sociolinguistic life. *Language and Communication, 23*(3-4), 193–229. https://doi.org/10.1016/S0271-5309(03)00013-2

Silverstein, M. (2006). Old wine, new ethnographic lexicography. *Annual Review of Anthropology, 35*, 481–496. https://doi.org/10.1146/annurev.anthro.35.081705.123327

Skattum, I. (2009). French or national languages as means of instruction? Reflections on French domination and possible future changes. In B. Brock-Utne & G. Garbo (Eds.), *Language and Power: The Implications of Language for Peace and Development* (pp. 172–181). Mkuki na Nyota Publishers.

Slobe, T. (2018). Style, stance, and social meaning in mock white girl. *Language in Society, 47*(4), 541–567. https://doi.org/10.1017/S004740451800060X

Smitherman-Donaldson, G. (1987). Toward a national public policy on language. *College English, 49*(1), 29–36. https://doi.org/10.2307/377787

Socolovsky, J. (2022, January 25). Kyiv or Kiev? Why people disagree about how to pronounce the Ukrainian capital's name. *NPR*. www.npr.org/2022/01/25/1075357281/how-do-you-pronounce-kyiv

Soja, N. N., Carey, S., & Spelke, E. S. (1991). Ontological categories guide young children's inductions of word meaning: Object terms and substance terms. *Cognition, 38*(2), 179–211. https://doi.org/10/bmj2k5

Sorensen, A. P., Jr. (1967). Multilingualism in the Northwest Amazon. *American Anthropologist, 69*(6), 670–684. https://doi.org/10.1525/aa.1967.69.6.02a00030

Special Committee on Indian Education (1969). Indian education: A National tragedy – a national challenge. (US Senate Special Report No. 91-501). Committee on Labor and Public Welfare, United States Senate. https://narf.org/nill/resources/education/reports/kennedy/toc.html

Sperry, D. E., Sperry, L. L., & Miller, P. J. (2019). Reexamining the verbal environments of children from different socioeconomic backgrounds. *Child Development, 90*(4), 1303–1318. https://doi.org/10/gddn24

Spradlin, L. (2016). OMG the word-final alveopalatals are cray-cray prev(alent): The morphophonology of totes constructions in English. *University of Pennsylvania Working Papers in Linguistics, 22*, 275–284. https://repository.upenn.edu/handle/20.500.14332/45098

Stahlberg, D., Sczesny, S., & Braun, F. (2001). Name your favorite musician: Effects of masculine generics and of their alternatives in German. *Journal of Language and Social Psychology, 20*(4), 464–469. https://doi.org/10.1177/0261927X01020004004

Starbird, K., Dailey, D., Mohamed, O., Lee, G., & Spiro, E. S. (2018). Engage early, correct more: How journalists participate in false rumors online during crisis events. *Proceedings of the 2018 CHI Conference on Human Factors in Computing Systems*, (105), 1–12. https://doi.org/10.1145/3173574.3173679

Starbird, K., Maddock, J., Orand, M., Achterman, P., & Mason, R. M. (2014). Rumors, false flags, and digital vigilantes: Misinformation on Twitter after the 2013 Boston Marathon bombing. *iConference 2014 Proceedings*. https://doi.org/10.9776/14308

Statista (2022, November). Global top websites by monthly visits 2022. *Statista*. www.statista.com/statistics/1201880/most-visited-websites-worldwide/

Steinfjell, R. B. (2014). *"Taking our language back home": Motivation and Challenges in the South Sami Area* [Master's Thesis, University of Tromsø]. https://hdl.handle.net/10037/7087

Stenzel, K. (2005). Multilingualism in the Northwest Amazon, revisited. In *Memorias Del Congreso de Idiomas Indigenas de Latinoamérica-II* (pp. 1–28). University of Texas.

Suire, A., Tognetti, A., Durand, V., Raymond, M., & Barkat-Defradas, M. (2020). Speech acoustic features: A comparison of gay men, heterosexual men, and heterosexual women. *Archives of Sexual Behavior, 49*(7), 2575–2583. https://doi.org/10.1007/s10508-020-01665-3

Sullivan, B. (2022, November 18). Why Qatar is a controversial host for the World Cup. *NPR*. www.npr.org/2022/11/18/1137204271/qatar-world-cup-controversies

Taboada Barber, A., Cartwright, K. B., Hancock, G. R., & Klauda, S. L. (2021). Beyond the simple view of reading: The role of executive functions in emergent bilinguals' and English monolinguals' reading comprehension. *Reading Research Quarterly, 56*(S1), S45–S64. https://doi.org/10.1002/rrq.385

Tauber, J. (2021, March 14). Tokenizing *The Hobbit*. *Digital Tolkien Project*. https://digitaltolkien.com/2021/03/14/tokenizing-the-hobbit.html

Tauber, J., Palladino, C., O'Rear, P., Mambrini, F., Mueller-Harder, E., Trudel Cedeño, E., & Truffelli, U. (2022). *Digital Tolkien Project*. https://digitaltolkien.com/

Taylor, A. (2013). Why Ukraine isn't "The Ukraine," and why that matters now. *Business Insider*. www.businessinsider.com/why-ukraine-isnt-the-ukraine-and-why-that-matters-now-2013-12

Taylor, A. R. (1982). "Male" and "female" speech in Gros Ventre. *Anthropological Linguistics, 24*(3), 301–307.

Tebaldi, C. & Rereza, R. (2024). Ethnographic empathy and research ethics as methodological whiteness. In *The ethics of researching the far right*. Manchester University Press. https://doi.org/10.7765/9781526173898.00016.

Templin, M. C. (1957). *Certain Language Skills in Children: Their Development and Interrelationships*. University of Minnesota Press.

Terrace, H. S. (1979). How Nim Chimpsky changed my mind. *Psychology Today, 13*(6), 65.

Thomson, R. I. (2012). Accent reduction. In C. A. Chapelle (Ed.), *The Encyclopedia of Applied Linguistics* (pp. 8–11). John Wiley & Sons.

Tocker, K. (2015). The origins of Kura Kaupapa Māori. *New Zealand Journal of Educational Studies, 50*(1), 23–38. https://doi.org/10.1007/s40841-015-0006-z

Toribio, A. J. (2002). Spanish-English code-switching among US Latinos. *International Journal of the Sociology of Language, 2002*(158), 89–119. https://doi.org/10.1515/ijsl.2002.053

Townsend, L., & Wallace, C. (2017). The ethics of using social media data in research: A new framework. In K. Woodfield (Ed.), *The Ethics of Online Research* (Vol. 2, pp. 189–207). Emerald Publishing Limited.

Truth and Reconciliation Commission of Canada (2015). *Honouring the truth, reconciling for the future: Summary of the final report of the Truth and Reconciliation Commission of Canada*. Truth and Reconciliation Commission of Canada.

UNESCO (2019). I'd blush if I could: Closing gender divides in digital skills through education. *UNESCO*. https://en.unesco.org/Id-blush-if-I-could

United Nations (2007). United Nations declaration on the rights of Indigenous peoples. *United Nations*. www.un.org/development/desa/indigenouspeoples/declaration-on-the-rights-of-indigenous-peoples.html

US Bureau of Labor Statistics (2022, September 8). Occupational Outlook Handbook: Interpreters and Translators. *U.S. Bureau of Labor Statistics*. www.bls.gov/ooh/media-and-communication/interpreters-and-translators.htm

US Census Bureau (2018). Language Other Than English Spoken at Home in the United States. *US Census Bureau*. https://data.census.gov/cedsci/all?q-language&g=&hidepreview=false&table=s1601&tid=acsst1y2018.s1601&lastdisplayedrow=14

Valentinsson, M.-C. (2018). Stance and the construction of authentic celebrity persona. *Language in Society, 47*(5), 715–740. https://doi.org/10.1017/S0047404518001100

Valentinsson, M.-C. (2020). English and bivalent class indexicality in Buenos Aires, Argentina. In S. Brunn & R. Kehrein (Eds.), *Handbook on the Changing World Language Map* (pp. 1–18). Springer.

Valentinsson, M.-C. (2022). Semiotic disruption and negotiations of authenticity among Argentine fans of Anglophone media. *Journal of Linguistic Anthropology, 32*(2), 345–363. https://doi.org/10.1111/jola.12355

Valenzuela-Escárcega, M. A., Babur, Ö., Hahn-Powell, G., Herongove, G., Hicks, T., Noriega-Atala, E., Wang, X., Surdeanu, M., Demir, E., & Morrison, C. T. (2018). Large-scale automated machine reading discovers new cancer-driving mechanisms. *Database*, 2018, 1–14. https://doi.org/10.1093/database/bay098

van Gelderen, E. (2014). *A History of the English Language* (Revised ed.). John Benjamins Publishing Company.

van Velzen, M., & Garrard, P. (2008). From hindsight to insight: Retrospective analysis of language written by a renowned Alzheimer's patient. *Interdisciplinary Science Reviews*, *33*(4), 278–286. https://doi.org/10/dvkn43

Vaswani, A., Shazeer, N., Parmar, N., Uszkoreit, J., Jones, L., Gomez, A. N., Kaiser, Ł., & Polosukhin, I. (2017). Attention is all you need. *Advances in Neural Information Processing Systems*, *30*, 5999–6009. https://proceedings.neurips.cc/paper_files/paper/2017/hash/3f5ee243547dee91fbd053c1c4a845aa-Abstract.html

Villarreal, D., Clark, L., Hay, J., & Watson, K. (2020). From categories to gradience: Auto-coding sociophonetic variation with random forests. *Laboratory Phonology*, *11*(1), 6. https://doi.org/10.5334/labphon.216

W3Techs (n.d.). Usage statistics of content languages for websites. *W3Techs*. https://w3techs.com/technologies/overview/content_language

Walker, A. G. (1990). Language at work in the law. In J. N. Levi & A. G. Walker (Eds.), *Language in the Judicial Process* (pp. 203–244). Springer US.

Warner, S. L. N. (2001). The movement to revitalize Hawaiian language and culture. In L. Hinton & K. Hale (Eds.), *The Green Book of Language Revitalization in Practice* (pp. 133–144). Academic Press.

Wassink, A. B. (2015). Sociolinguistic patterns in Seattle English. *Language Variation and Change*, *27*, 31–58. https://doi.org/10.1017/S0954394514000234

Weikum, W. M., Vouloumanos, A., Navarra, J., Soto-Faraco, S., Sebastián-Gallés, N., & Werker, J. F. (2007). Visual language discrimination in infancy. *Science*, *316*(5828), 1159–1159. https://doi.org/10.1126/science.1137686

Werker, J. F., & Tees, R. C. (1984). Cross-language speech perception: Evidence for perceptual reorganization during the first year of life. *Infant Behavior and Development*, *7*(1), 49–63. https://doi.org/10/cg29bj

Whalen, D. H., Moss, M., & Baldwin, D. (2016). Healing through language: Positive physical health effects of indigenous language use. *F1000Research*, *5*, 852. https://doi.org/10.12688/f1000research.8656.1

Willie, M. (1991). *Navajo Pronouns and Obviation*. [Doctoral Dissertation, The University of Arizona]. http://hdl.handle.net/10150/185691

Wilson, W. H., & Kamanā, K. (2001). "Mai Loko Mai O Ka 'I'ini: Proceeding from a dream" – The'Aha Pūnana Leo connection in Hawaiian language revitalization. In L. Hinton & K. Hale (Eds.), *The Green Book of Language Revitalization in Practice* (pp. 147–176). Academic Press.

Wolff, J. (2016). New constitutions and the transformation of democracy in Bolivia and Ecuador. In A. Schilling-Vacaflor (Ed.), *New Constitutionalism in Latin America: Promises and Practices* (pp. 183–202). Routledge.

Woo, E., & Curtius, M. (1996, December 20). Oakland School District recognizes Black English. *The Los Angeles Times*. www.latimes.com/archives/la-xpm-1996-12-20-mn-11042-story.html

Woods, T., & Hanson, D. (2016, October 18). Over half of children of immigrants are bilingual. *Urban Institute*. www.urban.org/urban-wire/over-half-children-immigrants-are-bilingual

World Bank (2023). GDP per capita (current US$) | Data. *World Bank Group*. https://data.worldbank.org/indicator/NY.GDP.PCAP.CD?most_recent_value_desc=true

World Medical Association General Assembly (1964). Declaration of Helsinki: Ethical principles for medical research involving human subjects. *World Medical Association*. www.wma.net/policies-post/wma-declaration-of-helsinki-ethical-principles-for-medical-research-involving-human-subjects/

Wright, K. E. (2019). *Experiments on Linguistic Profiling of Three American Dialects*. [Master's Thesis, University of Michigan].

Wright, K. E. (2021a, August 27). Race & language: Considering black linguistic experiences. Department of Linguistics Colloquium Series, University of Arizona. https://youtu.be/np46elWCaKc?si=YwiZMr8zQTCtSbi8

Wright, K. E. (2021b, September 17). "You have to be better": Confronting linguistic inequities with experimental sociolinguistics. [Invited talk]. https://youtu.be/U2EK28radIg

Wright, K. E. (2022). *Black Professionalism: Perception and Metalinguistic Assessment of Black American Speakers' Sociolinguistic Labor*. [Doctoral Dissertation, University of Michigan]. https://doi.org/10.7302/6091

Wyman, L. T., McCarty, T. L., & Nicholas, S. E. (2013). *Indigenous Youth and Multilingualism: Language Identity, Ideology, and Practice in Dynamic Cultural Worlds*. Taylor & Francis Group.

Zaleska Onyshkevych, L. M. L., & Rewakowicz, M. G. (2014) *Contemporary Ukraine on the Cultural Map of Europe*. Routledge.

Zanuttini, R., Wood, J., Zentz, J., & Horn, L. (2018). The Yale Grammatical Diversity Project: Morphosyntactic variation in North American English. *Linguistics Vanguard*, *4*(1), 20160070. https://doi.org/10.1515/lingvan-2016-0070

Zepeda, O., & Hill, J. (1998). Collaborative sociolinguistic research among the Tohono O'odham. *Oral Tradition*, *13*(1), 130–156.

Zhang, L.-T., & Zhao, S. (2020). Diaspora micro-influencers and COVID-19 communication on social media: The case of Chinese-speaking YouTube vloggers. *Multilingua*, *39*(5), 553–563. https://doi.org/10.1515/multi-2020-0099

Zhang, Q. (2005). A Chinese yuppie in Beijing: Phonological variation and the construction of a new professional identity. *Language in Society, 34*(3), 431–466. https://doi.org/10.1017/S0047404505050153

Zhang, Q. (2008). Rhotacization and the "Beijing Smooth Operator": The social meaning of a linguistic variable. *Journal of Sociolinguistics, 12*(2), 201–222. https://doi.org/10/d4rn38

Zhang, Q. (2018). *Language and Social Change in China: Undoing Commonness through Cosmopolitan Mandarin*. Routledge.

Zhou, Z., Chen, K., Li, X., Zhang, S., Wu, Y., Zhou, Y., Meng, K., et al. (2020). Sign-to-speech translation using machine-learning-assisted stretchable sensor arrays. *Nature Electronics, 3*(9), 571–578. https://doi.org/10.1038/s41928-020-0428-6

Zimman, L. (2018). Transgender voices: Insights on identity, embodiment, and the gender of the voice. *Language and Linguistics Compass, 12*(8), e12284. https://doi.org/10.1111/lnc3.12284

Countries Index

Algeria, 130
Aotearoa, 161, 233–234, 238–241
Argentina, 125, 236
Australia, 136–137, 139, 143, 160, 225, 233–234, 238, 317–318

Bermuda, 287
Botswana, 233
Brazil, 130, 132, 147, 311
Burma. *See* Myanmar

Canada, 84, 126–127, 136–137, 139, 143, 226, 230, 232–234, 236, 318, 334, 338, 348
China, 234–235, 333
Colombia, 130, 132

Dominican Republic, 341

England. *See* United Kingdom, Britain, England

Finland, 32, 238, 242–243
France, 123, 127, 236, 279

Germany, 123
Guyana, 233

Haiti, 341
Hawai'i, Kingdom of, 238, 240–241
Hong Kong, 233

India, 233–234
Ireland, 233–234, 236, 287, 331–332

Jamaica, 233
Japan, 234, 297

Korea, 232, 234

Libya, 130
Liechtenstein, 287
Luxembourg, 287

Madagascar, 258
Malta, Republic of, 126, 233
Marshall Islands, Republic of the, 164–165, 169
Mauritania, 130
Mexico, 79, 163, 169, 256, 296, 340
Monaco, 287
Morocco, 130
Myanmar, 124

New Zealand. *See* Aotearoa
Nicaragua, 236
Norway, 238, 242

Oman, 232

Papua New Guinea, 160, 164, 169, 261
Philippines, The, 233–234

Russia, 242, 333–334, 345

Samoa, 162, 164, 169
Scotland. *See* United Kingdom, Scotland
South Africa, 233–234
South Korea. *See* Korea
Spain, 232, 236
Sweden, 238, 242
Switzerland, 123

Taiwan, 234
Thailand, 234
Tibet, 333
Tunisia, 130

Ukraine, 333–334
United Kingdom, 68, 76, 85, 119, 125, 232–234, 277, 279, 318, 323–324, 331–332, 343
    Britain, 13, 191, 282, 323
    England, 8, 310, 330–331
    Scotland, 236, 331–332
    Wales, 125, 236, 310, 331–332

United States, 3, 5, 9, 13, 35, 39, 43, 49, 59, 66, 74, 76, 79, 85, 98, 102, 110–111, 124, 126, 130, 133–137, 139, 143, 159, 168–170, 173, 188, 193–194, 196, 205, 210, 216, 221–231, 233–234, 236, 240, 246, 248, 250, 253–254, 256–257, 264–265, 267, 270, 272, 275, 278–281, 285–288, 291, 296, 302, 304–308, 318, 320, 323–325, 329–335, 337–340, 342, 349

Wales. *See* United Kingdom, Wales
Western Sahara territory, 130

Languages Index

AAE. *See* English, African American
AAVE. *See* English, African American Vernacular
African American Language, 69, 326, 338–339, 353
  Ebonics, 326, 339, 353
African American Women's Language (AAWL), 256
Albanian, 26
American Sign Language, 13, 18–19, 21, 26, 31–32, 76, 78, 285, 308, 320, 323–324
Anglish, 331
Angloromani, 332
Arabic, 17, 126–127, 131, 193, 195, 202, 205, 266, 282
  Egyptian, 131
  Lebanese, 131
  Maghrebi, 131
  Mashreqi, 131
  Modern Standard, 131
Arapaho, 130

Basque, 13, 18, 130, 236
Bengali, 282
Berber. *See* Tamazight
Bermudian English, 287
Black English. *See* English, Black
Breton, 122, 236, 353
British Sign Language, 13, 323, 332
Burmese, 124

Canadian French, 27
Cantonese. *See* Chinese, Cantonese
Catalan, 130
Cheyenne, 130
Chinese, 193, 195, 202, 345
  Cantonese, 12
  Mandarin, 12–13, 18, 71, 130
Cook Islands Māori, 238
Cornish, 353
Cree, 127–128
  Plains, 127
Croatian, 333

Desano, 132
Diné Bizaad, 13, 18, 32, 130, 152–153, 253, 319, 340–341
Dutch, 150, 238, 353

Ebonics. *See* African American Language, Ebonics
English, 230
  African American, 36, 286, 295, 305–306, 309, 315, 326, 339
  African American Vernacular, 339
  American, 32, 53, 58, 69, 116, 136, 143, 170, 254, 305, 309
    White, 248
  American, historical, 85
  Black, 225–227, 304, 326, 339, 353
  British, 33, 76, 189, 287, 330, 342
    White, 248
  Chicano/Chicana, 230, 262, 304–305
  Chinese, 348
  Native American, 230
  Nigerian, 348
  North American, 73, 256
  Scottish, 36
  Singapore, 348
  standard, 305, 348
  US, 2–3, 5–9, 13–14, 18, 28, 57, 65, 68–69, 80, 110, 213, 230, 265–266, 303–304, 330
    mainstream, 305–306
    written, 2
  White, 28, 73, 116, 230, 286
  Mainstream, 176, 226
Esperanto, 344–347
Estonian, 242

Finnish, 32–33, 242
Flemish, 122
Frankish, 331
French, 26–27, 37, 121–123, 126–128, 131, 194, 202, 224, 241, 250, 277, 283, 287, 297, 304, 330–333, 341–342, 345, 348
  Norman, 114, 331–332

Gaelic, 236
　Gaeilge, 274
　Irish, 331–332, 353
　Scots, 331–332, 353
German, 122, 135, 202, 250–252, 287, 331, 342, 345, 353
Gothic, 331
Gros Ventre, 257

Haitian Creole, 129, 308, 341–342
Hawaiian, 236, 238, 240–242
Hawaiian Pidgin, 129
Hebrew, 330, 333, 341, 345
Hindi, 250, 282
Hungarian, 202, 242

Idioma de Señas Nicaragüense. *See* Nicaraguan Sign Language
Irish Sign Language, 332
Italian, 127, 202, 287, 296, 345
　Sicilian, 126

Japanese, 150

Kaluli, 161
Klingon, 347
Koasati, 257

Lahnda, 282
Latin, 122, 332, 345
Ligurian, 287
Luxembourgish, 287

Malagasy, 258
Maltese, 127
Mandarin. *See* Chinese, Mandarin
Manx, 331
Māori, 236, 240
Marshallese, 167
Michif, 128
Mohawk, 236

Nakoda, 127
Navajo. *See* Diné Bizaad
Nicaraguan Sign Language, 236–237
Northern Ireland Sign Language, 332

Ojibway, Plains (Nakawēmowin), 127

Polish, 345

Quechua, 32, 152–153
Quileute, 111

Russian, 32, 34–35, 189, 250, 333, 345

Sámi, 236, 244
　Inari, 242
　Kildin, 242
　Lule, 242
　Northern, 242
　Skolt, 242
　Southern, 242
Samoan, 161–163
Saxon, 331
Scots, 332
　Ulster, 287
Serbian, 333
Spanish, 33, 72, 124–125, 130, 134, 136, 164, 194, 202, 224, 230, 246, 250–251, 263, 275, 296–297, 319–320, 340–342
　Castilian, 23
Swedish, 242, 251, 331, 345

Tahitian, 238
Tamazight, 131
Tohono O'odham, 79, 130, 256–257, 276, 341
Turkish, 32–33
Tzotzil, 163–164

Ukranian, 33
Urdu, 282

Vietnamese, 24, 27, 32, 65, 121
Volapük, 345

Wampanoag. *See* Wôpanâak
Wanano, 132
Welsh, 125, 130, 236, 331–332, 353
Wôpanâak, 349–350

Yana, 257
Yiddish, 130, 345
Yuruti, 132

Main Index

accent, 5, 12, 25, 27, 29, 135–136, 142, 221
   foreign, 135, 142
accent hallucination, 135, 142, 230
accent reduction, 279
acceptability, 65, 93
accomplishment of natural growth, 159
acoustic phonetics, 23–24, 56
acoustics, 191, 207
adjacency pair, 49–50, 56–57, 60
African American Language, 69, 281, 338–339, 353
agglutinative, 33, 56
algorithm, 186, 204–206, 214, 216
alignment, 53, 78, 190, 311, 326
American Standard Code for Information Exchange. *See* ASCII
amplitude, 22, 25, 56, 61, 321, 327
Anglo-Saxon, 331–332, 353
animacy, 252–253, 274
animator, 52, 56
anonymity, 99–100, 102–103, 118–119
antinomy, 56
Antiracist Black Language Pedagogy, 227–228, 246
articulatory phonetics, 23, 56, 290
   filter, 23, 57
   source, 23, 60
artificial intelligence, 110, 181, 184, 207, 214–215, 218, 280
ASCII, 193–196, 205
augmented intelligence, 181, 215
authenticity, 295
   elite, 295–296, 299
author, 52, 56

babbling, 150–151, 178
bag of words models, 197, 199, 215, 217–218
Baker-Bell, April, 176, 226
bald on-record utterance, 47, 56
Baugh, John, 99, 109, 305, 339
beat gesture, 190, 215
Bender Rule, 116, 118, 172

bias, 33, 103, 119, 212, 224, 279–280, 318, 326, 330, 352–353
bigram model, 198–199, 215
bilingual education, 135, 246
bivalent class indexicality, 293, 299
blended languages/varieties, 125–126, 142
brutoglossia, 294–295, 299

caret, 7, 13
case marker, 32, 56
Celtic, 122, 331, 353
Charity-Hudley, Anne, 340
Chomsky, Noam, 152
coda, 288–289, 299
codeswitching, 123–126, 128, 131, 142–143
   intersentential, 142
   intrasentential, 142
collection (conversation analysis), 69–70, 93
collocation, 88, 93
commodification, 296, 299
community of practice, 107, 262, 274, 346, 353
community-based research, 102–103, 119, 209
computational linguistics, 181, 184, 215
computer, 181, 193–195, 199, 202, 204, 205, 215–216, 280
concerted cultivation, 159, 178
concordance, 69, 93
confidentiality, 100, 102–103, 118–119
confirmation bias, 326
consonant, 24, 73, 91, 189, 290, 299
constituent order, basic, 35
constructed language, 345, 347, 353
context, pragmatic, 41–45, 47, 54, 56
continuer, 313, 326
contrast (phonological), 25–26, 30, 56, 64, 150–151
conversation, 13, 17, 52–54, 56, 64, 67, 78, 81, 91, 114–115, 123, 158–159, 162, 191, 207, 223, 239, 252, 259–260, 265, 274, 312, 326–327

conversation analysis, 47–48, 52, 69, 82, 93, 312
conversational shitwork, 259, 274
cooperative principle, 43, 56
corpus, corpora, 65, 68–70, 85–86, 88–90, 93, 106, 110, 122, 142
co-speech gesture, 190, 215
creaky voice, 261, 263, 274, 276
creole, 128–129, 142, 286, 326, 353
critical language pedagogy (CLP), 221, 227, 246
crossing, 264, 274
cultural genocide, 337, 353
Cyrillic, 333

de facto, 134, 142, 226, 246, 332, 341
de jure, 226, 246
deficit-based (pedagogy, messages), 227–228, 246
dialect, 5–6, 13, 36, 53, 55, 70–71, 124, 127, 133, 135, 142–143, 170, 177, 221, 244, 290, 300, 305–306, 309, 316, 324–325, 354
  regional, 5, 14, 26, 73, 124, 264
diglossia, 123, 131, 142
directive, 42, 185, 320, 326
disalignment, 190, 311, 326
discourse, 9, 13, 51–53, 189, 264, 293, 295, 330, 340, 350
discourse analysis, 47–48, 51–52, 82, 325
discrimination, 3, 103, 133, 138, 172, 212, 221, 247, 254, 262, 275, 279, 302, 309, 318, 320, 323–324, 353
  economic, 280
  employment, 279, 304
  housing, 304–306
  linguistic, 133, 136, 138, 212, 224–225, 230–231, 245, 302, 322
  raciolinguistic, 222
disinformation, 99, 119, 342, 351, 353
dispreferred (response), 50, 57
dispreferred (segments), 50
disproportionality, 223–224, 246
double consciousness, 227, 246

Ebonics, 326, 339, *See* African American Language
Ebonics (mock), 340
Eckert, Penny, 265, 270, 275
electropalatography, 25, 57
elicitation, 64–65, 71, 93

emblem, 190
emblem gestures, 215
encoding, 194–195, 205, 218
English
  African American, 36, 286, 305–306, 309, 315, 326, 339
  Black, 225–226, 326, 339–340, 353
  Chicano/Chicana, 230, 262, 305
  Chinese, 348
  language, 13
  Middle, 73, 252, 332
  Nigerian, 348
  Old, 252, 331, 353–354
  Scottish, 36
  Singapore, 348
  US, 2–3, 5–9, 13–14, 18, 28, 57, 65, 68–69, 80, 110, 213, 230, 265–266, 303–306, 330
  White American, 28, 116
English-only movements, 134
engma, 8, 13
entailment, 40, 57
epithet, 254, 322, 342, 353
ethics board, 96–98, 102, 117, 119
etymology, 122, 142, 334

face, 45–46, 57, 311–312, 327
  face-threatening act (FTA), 45, 47, 57, 311
  facework, 45–46, 57, 311, 327
  negative, 45–47, 59
  negative face-threatening act, 47
  positive, 45–47, 59
felicity condition, 41–43, 45, 57
femininity, 256, 263–264, 266, 268, 275
fieldnotes, 71, 92–93
fieldwork, 71, 94, 163–164, 227
Figueroa, Megan, 223
first language, 27, 61, 141–142, 145, 149, 152, 157, 159, 167–168, 178–179, 229, 233, 282, 308
floor (conversational), 2, 13, 18, 49, 56
foreigner talk, 321, 327
forensic linguistics, 98, 119
formant, 22, 57
Fraser, Helen, 317
frequency, 87
  acoustic, 22, 24–25, 57, 59, 261
  statistical, 85–86, 88–90, 93–94, 106, 151, 196, 218
  raw, 86, 94

fronted, 28, 57, 270
fusional, 33, 57

gender
  conceptual, 251–253, 255
  grammatical, 38, 250–252, 254, 275
  social, 3–5, 24, 29, 36, 38, 89, 139, 191, 249–275, 299, 305–308, 312, 325, 347
generalized, pretrained, transformer (GPT), 110, 181, 188, 208, 215
Germanic, 122, 283, 297, 331, 353–354
gestational age, 149, 179
Goffman, Erving, 52
GPT-2, 187, 216, 218
GPT-3, 216
grammar, 6, 19, 61, 126, 129, 155, 209, 252–253, 287, 321, 346, 348
  grammatical, 9, 30, 32, 34–36, 65, 94, 99, 126–127, 154, 200, 248, 253, 287–288
  grammaticality, 64–66
Grice, H. P., 43
gross domestic product (GDP), 282, 299

harmonics, 25, 57
hate speech, 99, 119, 353
Heath, Shirley Brice, 134, 158, 173
hedging device, 307, 327
heritage language, 102, 137, 142–143, 354
heterosexual marketplace, 270–271, 275
heterosexuality, 270–271
Hill, Jane, 136, 144, 256, 296
Hockett, Charles, 20–21
homesign, 236, 246
homophobia, 269
homophony, 38, 57
homosexuality, 269–270, 272
human subjects, 96–98, 103, 118–119, 273
Human Subjects Protections Program, 96, 98, 117, 119
hypernymy, 39, 58
hyponymy, 39, 58

identity, 3, 6, 53, 72, 125, 143, 220–221, 249–250, 262, 264–265, 270–271, 273, 275–277, 279, 293–295, 305, 319, 329, 344, 346, 351
  gender, 139, 251, 267–269, 272–275
  national, 329–333, 354
ideologies of nationalism, 332, 353

ideology of monolingualism, 221, 247
idiolect, 5, 13
image processing, 186, 195, 205, 216
immersion programs, 236, 241, 247
implicature, 45, 58
index, 53, 58, 224, 256, 258, 261–263, 265–266, 268, 270, 272, 275, 288, 297
indexicality, 53, 58, 265
infant-directed speech, 157, 179
inflection, 30, 58, 93
informed consent, 97, 100–101, 103, 111, 118–119
interlocutor, 2, 4–5, 9, 12–13, 47–48, 51–52, 56, 59–60, 83, 207, 259, 271, 313, 321, 326–327
International Phonetic Alphabet, 13
interpretation, 284–286, 299, 308, 324
interruption, 10, 18, 46, 49, 58, 83, 226
intersectionality, 221, 247, 256, 275
intonation, 12, 17, 58, 75, 124, 142, 150, 225, 270, 307
invented language, 345, 353–354
Inverted Spanglish, 125, 142
IPA. *See* International Phonetic Alphabet
isolating language, 33, 58

Jeantel, Rachel, 286, 309, 314–315, 320, 322
Jefferson, Gail, 82

King, Sharese, 309
Koko, a lowland gorilla, 19

labeling, 69, 195, 200–201, 216
Labov, William, 29, 66, 222–223, 288
Lanehart Rule, 116, 118, 172
language, 13, 18
  acquisition, 135, 148, 156–157, 167, 172, 177, 179
  community, 58, 91, 94, 136, 143, 247, 284, 354
  gap. *See* word gap
  loss, 137, 143, 354
  model, 191, 197, 202, 206, 216
    large language model (LLM), 181, 188, 216
  nest, 236–239, 242–243, 247
  shift, 137, 143, 243, 332, 337, 349, 354
  socialization, 145–147, 151, 156–160, 163–164, 167, 169, 173, 176–177, 179

Latin alphabet, 92, 193, 333
lemmatization, 195, 200–201, 216
lexical diversity, 90, 94
lexical sophistication, 90, 94
lexical variation, 33, 58
lexicography, 330, 354
Limited English Proficiency, 134, 143
lingua franca, 333, 347, 354
linguicide, 138, 143
linguist, 13
linguistic capital, 277–279, 281–283, 300
linguistic exogamy, 132, 143
linguistic landscape, 297, 300
linguistic marketplace, 277–279, 281, 283–284, 300
linguistic profiling, 305, 327
linguistic repertoire, 2, 12–13, 125, 235, 244, 246, 271, 290, 298
linguogenesis, 236–237, 247
literacy, 146, 157, 167, 172–176, 179, 245

machine, 216
machine language, 193, 216
machine learning, 184, 186–188, 204, 212, 215–217, 280
machine-reading, 181, 206
maintenance work, 259, 274–275
majority language, 111, 226, 240, 247
manner of articulation, 24, 58
markedness, 186, 216
Martin, Trayvon, 309, 319, 322
masculinity, 264, 268, 271, 275–276
maxim
   conversational, 43, 54, 56, 58–59, 61
   flouting, 43–45, 50, 55, 57
   of manner, 44, 58
   of quality, 43, 55, 58
   of quantity, 43–45, 55, 58
   of relevance, 44, 58
   violation, 43, 45, 61
McConnell-Ginet, Sally, 265
medium, 1–3, 7, 10, 13
Meek, Barbra, 84
Mendoza-Denton, Norma, 67, 262
message, 13
metadata, 89, 94
Metalinguistic Method of Sociolinguistic Interview, 281, 300
minority language, 141, 247
monodialectal, 123, 143

monolingual, 123, 133, 137–138, 140, 143, 147, 149, 224, 229, 241, 244, 282, 303, 308, 321, 349
morpheme, 30–33, 37, 39, 56–58, 60
   derivational, 30, 57
morphology, 17, 20, 31–32, 58, 78
multidialectalism, 123, 128, 143, 305, 349–350, 354
multilingual education, 221, 247
multilingualism, 123–125, 128–130, 132–134, 137–138, 140–141, 143, 147, 149, 155–156, 213, 224, 282–284, 296, 308, 324, 329, 331–333, 337, 346, 348–350, 352, 354
mutual exclusivity, 154, 179

named-entity recognition, 200, 202, 217
national language, 233, 246, 330–333, 341, 354
native language, 130, 145, 149–150, 163, 167, 179
natural language processing (NLP), 85, 184, 202, 210, 216–217, 280
neoliberalism, 295, 300
neopronouns, 251, 275
neural net, 200, 217
ngram model, 199, 217
nonbinarity, 275
NORM (non-mobile, older, rural male), 275
Northern Cities Chain Shift, 28–29, 59, 261

observer's paradox, 66, 81, 94
obstruent, 24, 59
Ochs, Elinor, 157
oenophile, 300
official English
   English-only movements, 134
official language, 130–131, 134–135, 142–143, 239–240, 285, 330, 332–333, 354
oinoglossia, 294, 300
optical character recognition (OCR), 204–205, 216–217
opt-out, 59
oralist, 236, 247
orthography, 81, 84, 92, 115, 124, 152, 194–195, 205, 217, 315, 317, 333, 354
other-selection, 49, 59
overlap, 49, 51–52, 58–59, 83, 315

pantomime gestures, 190, 217
parser, 69, 94, 201
participant observation, 70, 92, 94, 118, 164
participant roles, 52, 59
participants, 119
parts of speech, 36, 59, 201
peer review, 105, 117, 119
performative, 41–43, 45, 49, 57, 59
phonemic inventory, 27, 59
phonetic transcription, 7, 14, 71–73, 81
phonetics, 8, 13, 17, 22–23, 25, 59, 68, 115, 259
phonological rule, 27, 29, 31, 59
phonological word, 31, 59
phonology, 17, 22, 25, 28–29, 55, 59, 115, 118
phonotactics, 27, 59
phrase, 5, 8–10, 14, 30–31, 33–34, 36–37, 45, 53, 60, 64, 71, 89, 92–94, 98, 118, 120, 128, 152, 197, 203, 224, 233–234, 238, 289, 297, 317, 327
pidgin, 128–129, 142–143
pitch, 17, 22, 24, 59–60, 149, 157, 161, 255, 258, 260–261, 265, 268, 270
place of articulation, 24, 27, 59
plagiarism, 103–104, 120
politeness
  negative, 47, 59
  positive, 46, 59
pragmatics, 17, 41, 45, 47, 51–52, 59, 205–206, 225
prenatal development, 149, 179
prestige, 283, 290, 352
prestige variety, 76, 94, 247
presupposition, 40, 60
principal, 52, 60
Principle of Contrast, 154
privacy, 11, 45, 96, 99–103, 118, 120
professionalism, 280–281, 300
propaganda, 342, 344, 351, 354
protected characteristics, 304, 324, 327
pumpkin
  gourd, 2
  term of endearment, 2

racial slur, 99, 120
raciolinguistics, 221, 247
reference
  bibliographic, 94, 104–106, 108–109
  lexical semantic, 37–38, 41, 60

register, 6, 14, 132, 157, 179, 294, 299–300, 321
regular expression, 86, 94
repair
  other-initiated, 50, 59
  self-initiated, 50, 60
  sequence, 50
Respectability Language Pedagogies, 227, 247
response, preferred, 49–51, 60
rhotacization, 71
Rickford, John, 309, 339

Schieffelin, Bambi, 157
schwa, 7, 14
second language, 106, 129, 149, 178–179, 319, 331, 348
  English as a second language, 13, 229, 232, 248, 340
segment, 18, 21–22, 25–31, 48, 50, 60, 64–65
  preferred, 50
self-selection, 60
semantics, 17, 37, 41, 60
  compositional, 37, 39–40, 56
  lexical, 37–39, 58
  vector, 203–204, 218
semiotics, 291, 294, 299
  cue, 300
Senghas, Ann, 237
sense, 37–38, 41, 60
sequence of speakers, 49, 60
sex, 254, 260, 267, 275
sexuality, 249–250, 253–254, 269–273, 276
signed languages, 2, 10, 13–14, 20–22, 26, 69, 72, 76–77, 91, 123, 140, 147, 151–152, 168, 173, 177–178, 202, 209, 224–225, 236 237, 247, 258, 284–285, 299, 314, 323–324
significance testing, 88, 94
Silverstein, Michael, 294
smears, 342, 354
social meaning, 53, 60, 82, 223
socioeconomic class, 277, 287, 298, 300, 347
sociolinguistic interview, 66–67, 94, 281
sociophonetics, 68, 94
sociopragmatics, 155, 166–167, 179
Spanglish, 124, 143
speaker selection, 49–50, 60

spectrogram, 25, 60
speech act, 41–42, 45–46, 60
  direct, 42, 57
  indirect, 42, 58
speech community, 3, 6, 9, 14, 28, 129, 133, 151, 156–157, 177, 265, 271
speech style, 14. *See* register
speech-to-text, 191–192, 207, 217
spoken languages, 2–3, 14, 17, 20, 22–23, 72–73, 77, 91, 123, 140, 152, 168, 173, 177, 224–225, 236, 281, 285, 314, 323
stance, 52–53
stance-taking, 52, 60
standard language, 222, 224, 248
stigmatized (language, variety), 98, 120, 155, 223, 225, 230, 247, 264, 279, 304, 309, 315, 351–352
Swadesh List, 64
synonymy, 38, 60
syntactic bootstrapping, 154, 179
syntax, 17, 20, 34–36, 54, 60, 70, 118, 154–155, 237, 321
synthetic (language), 33, 60

taboo, 46, 166, 177
tag question, 327
TEFL/TESL, 232, 235, 248
terms of service (TOS) agreements, 101, 120, 191, 206
text-to-speech (TTS), 191–192, 206, 217
token, 74, 87–88, 93–94, 195–197
tokenization, 195–196, 217
tone, 24, 60, 149
topic-change response, 327
topic-related response, 327
transcription, 8, 10, 14, 71, 76–78, 84, 115, 314–315, 327
  conversation analytic, 82
  courtroom, 286, 325
  forensic, 315, 317
  Jeffersonian, 82–83, 91
  multi-line, 81
  phonetic, 80, 91
transformer, 188, 208, 214–215, 218
transition relevance place (TPR), 312, 327

translanguaging, 125–126, 143
translation, 10, 78–80, 127, 141, 213, 284–286, 297, 300, 321, 324, 333
  machine, 141, 190, 207–208, 213
truncation, 189, 218
Turing Test, 207
turn-taking, 10, 48, 60, 70, 151, 158
type, 88, 93–94, 195, 197
type/token ratio, 88, 90, 94, 196–197, 218

un- or under-documented language, 34, 61
ungrammaticality, 34, 36, 41, 227, 255, 296
unicode, 194, 205, 218
unigram, 198, 218
utterance, 2, 18–20, 22, 31, 40–42, 44, 47, 49–50, 52, 56–61, 65, 78, 88, 142, 191, 207, 261, 265, 289, 300, 307, 314

variety, 5–6, 14, 78, 84, 122, 128–129, 290, 317, 320, 330, 339–340
Vincent, a rabbit, 223
virilocal, 132, 143
vocal folds, 23, 61, 261, 274, 276
vocal fry, 255, 261, 276
vocal tract, 23–25, 56, 59–61
vowel, 7, 13–14, 24, 28–29, 53, 61, 73–74, 91, 125, 261
vulnerable population, 102, 120

Wassink, Alicia, 67
waveform, 25, 61
WEIRD (western, educated, industrialized, rich, democratized), 170, 179
White Mainstream English, 176, 226
white public space, 136, 144
whole object assumption, 154, 180
word gap, 146, 156, 167–168, 170–172, 178, 180
Wright, Kelly, 281, 305–306

yuppie, 290, 293–294, 300

Zepeda, Ofelia, 256
Zhang, Qing, 290

For EU product safety concerns, contact us at Calle de José Abascal, 56–1°, 28003 Madrid, Spain or eugpsr@cambridge.org.